To Sheelagh,
I think your Mum's
family played a part
in this book!!
Enjoy!
Love from Di & Jim
x
2011

TEA

By the same author

Non-fiction

Afghanistan
Afghanistan: A History of Conflict
Afghanistan: Key to a Continent
Fathercare: A Handbook for Single Fathers
Flashpoint Afghanistan: A Guide for Sixth Formers
Hostage: The History, Facts and Reasoning behind Hostage-taking
Modern Iceland
Nimbus: Technology Serving the Arts
The Science of Winning Squash
The Third Man: A Biography of William Murdoch
Three Tomorrows: A Comparative Study of Russian,
American and British Science Fiction

Fiction

The Survivors
The Queen of Spades

TEA

The Drink That
Changed the World

John Griffiths

André Deutsch

A tribute to "PJ" and Michael, and to Liz, who kept
the cups coming at all hours.

First published in Great Britain in 2007 by

André Deutsch
an imprint of the
Carlton Publishing Group
20 Mortimer Street
London W1T 3JW

2 4 6 8 10 9 7 5 3 1

A catalogue record for this book is available from
the British Library

ISBN 978-0-233-00212-5

Typeset by E-Type, Liverpool
Printed and bound in Great Britain by Mackays

Contents

Other Men's Leaves

"There are a thousand and ten thousand teas," Lu Yu

"What," I wondered half aloud, "do we do now?" Our Land-Rover had crossed two-thirds of yet another glacial river in Iceland's central desert (see my book *Modern Iceland*), but was now confronted by a final stretch that looked as if it might be more hazardous. Although we had come to rest on a dry spit of shingle above river level, the water hissed and bubbled ominously over the ever-shifting dull grey gravel ahead. My wife and two sons, aged 10 and 11, looked expectantly, if a little apprehensively, in my direction. There was nothing for it, I supposed, but to take off my shoes and socks, roll up my trousers, grab my stick and cautiously probe the crossing on foot. In two seconds I had changed my mind. The rivers that flow off the Vatnajökull glacier are as near freezing as you can get short of actually turning solid. My wife eyed me a little less confidently and enquired, "Well, what *do* we do now?" Then inspiration struck. "We have a nice cup of tea," I replied firmly. So we got out kettle and gas stove, teapot and tea leaves, brewed up, drank up and with renewed, if slightly euphoric, courage drove unhesitatingly across the remaining fork of the river.

Safely on the far bank, I marvelled yet again that a simple cup of tea had cleared the mind and braced the heart so that what had seemed intractable became more manageable. What pharmacological cocktail could have that effect and how did people know that it would? How could the simple infusion of a few dry brown leaves in boiling water have become the world's most common drink after water itself? Why and how had tea drinking come to play so significant a role in the religious rituals and meditative techniques of the East? How did tea then become such an important – but purely secular – drink in the daily life of the West?

My Icelandic adventure took place almost 40 years ago and the same questions have occurred to me many times since. But are there any definitive answers?

Though I have been enthused – and infused – with tea all my life I have no practical experience of growing, processing or selling it. I have listened times without number to my father, "PJ", adviser to the Indian Tea Association and author of *The History of the Indian Tea Industry*, and enjoyed the various packets of tea he sent me until he died, pen in hand, at the age of 93. As a youngster I heard with equal awe my tea-planter older brother's jungle adventures and watched with amazement, tinged with radical disapproval, his patriarchal style of management on his farm at Chota Nagpur in Bihar. I fear some bias toward the tea of India is inevitable in one so immersed in the tea lore of the subcontinent. In any case a source which dominated world markets for a century, until the emergence of Ceylon – as I shall call Sri Lanka throughout this book to avoid confusion – and later East Africa, is entitled to some prominence.

So this is inevitably an eclectic work, a gathering of other men's leaves. Only when I embarked upon it did I realize in what an extensive garden these leaves have been grown. The British Library index alone has almost two thousand entries with the word "tea" in the title, and there were many others I could not find there. These publications ranged from highly abstruse treatises on the cultivation and chemistry of tea to slim volumes of verse, from planters' tales to social anthropologists' theses, from teapots to tea-leaf reading, from the mundane to the bizarre – my favourite among the latter being *Killer Tea Cosies and How to Make Them*. Reading the accounts of soldiers and statesmen, tea planters and government officials in nineteenth-century India and Ceylon, when Britain was at the height of its imperial power, inclines me to look a little less censoriously on the arrogance and outrages of the contemporary

American imperium. I hope, as the radical son of a much-admired and enlightened imperialist, I shall be able to give a balanced account of the political, economic and social complexities surrounding this most influential of plants.

However, of all the numerous books, articles and papers I had read, few in recent times tried to treat tea as a global phenomenon that changed people's lives rather than just as a commodity or a vehicle for personal anecdote. Most were also limited in scope or geography, or both. So I thought that I would try to tackle the daunting, and perhaps impossible, task of trying to write an all-embracing *tour d'horizon* of a drink I have drunk in Afghan *chai khanas* and surrounded by Persian bandits, with Sandhurst-smart officers of the Waziristan Scouts on the North-West Frontier and with English tramps, stuck in the middle of an Icelandic glacial river, and as a cure when sunstruck in the desert – and almost dumbstruck on addressing the formidable ladies of the Fawcett Society. It is a drink that has saved my life, fuelled my midnight studies and lifted my spirits on numerous occasions.

On the night of 10–11 May 1941 the Luftwaffe managed to destroy much of Mincing Lane, the historical heart of the world tea business, and consequently half the industry's original records. Thus a twenty-first-century writer is heavily dependent on those who made use of primary material before then, or on rare caches of original texts, such as may be found in the James Insch bequest to the Linnean Society or the library of Lawrie Plantation Services. I am deeply indebted to the librarians and staff of both. I am also most grateful to the other experts in various fields who have commented and advised on the pertinent passages in this book, chief among them Francesca Altman, Edward Bramah, Ian Davidson, Andrew Davis, Patricia Graham, Richard Gregson, Christopher Griffiths, Richard Griffiths sen., Peter Leggatt, Tom Nutt, Babise Paasman, Nico van Horn, Clive Roberson and especially Derick Mirfin and my editor, Richard Dawes.

I shall not write about the estimable maté, *Ilex paraguayensis*, which is a holly, nor of rooibos, redbush (*Aspalathus linearis*), of the pea family, nor of any of the flowery infusions from camomile to hibiscus which have usurped the name of tea. I shall confine myself to *Camellia sinensis* var. *sinensis*, the true tea, and its two principal variants, *Camellia sinensis* var. *assamica* and *Camellia sinensis* var. *cambodiensis* and their innumerable subspecies. These offer challenge enough, for there are more kinds of tea in China alone than there are wines in France. Indeed, as the first great writer about tea, the Chinese philosopher Lu Yu, observed, "There are a thousand and ten thousand teas."

CHAPTER ONE

Whose Cup of Tea?

Jan van Linschotten waited until he heard the last of the Indian servants retire to their own compound before slipping barefoot into the corridor. Pausing for a moment outside the archbishop's room, he eased aside the beads that hung before its door with one finger and listened to the old man's pious snores. He had plied Vicente de Fonseca with an extra glass or two of Madeira at supper to ensure just such a peaceful repose as he now observed. Smiling, he took a last glance up at the motionless canvas sheet on its bamboo frame that told him that the punkah-wallah in the basement below was as fast asleep as his reverend master. All clear.

Jan lifted one of the softly burning oil lamps from its bracket in the corridor and strode confidently across the courtyard, like a man on authorized business, to the door that led down to the crypt of the mission church on the opposite side of the square. The *chowkidar* supposedly guarding the entrance barely opened one sleepy eye before reaching up to hand Jan the key without even being asked. He and his fellow watchmen had grown used to the young Dutchman's nocturnal visits, lamp in hand and gunny-sack of writing materials over his shoulder. They presumed these wanderings to be in order since he had also come openly in daylight with the archbishop. Besides, he was a European, and not to be gainsaid.

Once Jan had settled himself at the long teak table in the centre of the crypt, he carefully set out parchment, quills and ink before crossing to the wine-rack-like pigeon-holes along the far wall and extracting a rolled-up chart from its slot. From under the table he lifted half a dozen fist-sized stones and weighed the coarse paper down flat. Peering closely at the finely drawn lines by the dim light of his lamp, he resumed the meticulous copying he had begun several nights before. "Let this be the last time," he muttered to himself with a mixture of regret and relief. No more excited anticipation, but no more fear of discovery. Two years it had taken him to make Fonseca so dependent on him that his trust was absolute, and two more years to copy every one of the dozens of charts and navigational notes that had given the ever-greedier Portuguese almost exclusive access to the riches of the East. His work done, he returned the final chart to its pigeon-hole exactly as it had lain before, so that no one would know it had been disturbed. For the last time he repacked his writing things and his copy, locked the crypt door, dropped the key into the lap of the still-sleeping *chowkidar* and climbed serenely back up to his bed. In minutes he was fast asleep and dreaming of the fame and fortune that would await him when he spread his pirated charts before the merchants and ship's captains of his native Holland.

Although a fanciful reconstruction, this account of Jan's adventure is, in essence, true. The Portuguese, who enjoyed a monopoly of the maritime trade with the Far East in the sixteenth century, hugged the secrets of how to get there very close to their chests. Charts were kept in secure buildings under lock and key, and issued only sparingly. It took the guile and bravery of Jan Huygen van Linschotten (1563–1611) to extract them. Linschotten was the James Bond of his day: traveller, merchant, adventurer, spy, thief and obviously a very persuasive talker. At the Spanish court in 1583 he wangled himself a recommendation to the post of secretary to Vicente de Fonseca, Archbishop of Goa, Portugal's pivotal trading entrepôt on the west coast of India. There he so ingratiated himself with the archbishop that he was trusted with access to the jealously restricted maritime archives. In the best traditions of espionage, he not only abused that trust to make careful copies of all the charted sea routes to the East, which were known only to the Portuguese, but took careful note of the tides and currents, winds and shoals, harbours and hazards that a navigator might encounter. No less importantly, he highlighted the straits and narrows in which the formidable Portuguese warships might pounce on any other European vessel daring to intrude upon their lucrative trade. When the archbishop died in 1587, Linschotten returned to Holland, though not without surviving shipwreck, from which he rescued his precious maps, and a two-year enforced stay in the Azores. After he finally got home he published his findings in 1595 as an account of *Portuguese Navigation in the Orient*.

The Dutch, along with Britain and Portugal one of the three main European maritime powers of the age, capitalized on their newly gifted knowledge rapidly to open up a trade with the Far East that matched and then eclipsed that of their unwitting Portuguese benefactors. The British, tired of having to pay such high prices for the spices of the Orient, were soon hot on the heels of the Dutch. The *Edward*, sole surviving vessel of a fleet of three merchant ships licensed by Elizabeth I to sail to the East, reached Malaya in 1591, and returned laden with spices. A large part of its cargo had been plundered from Portuguese ships. Ever alert to means of replenishing her empty treasury, Elizabeth foresaw the vast wealth to be won from regular trade with the East and licensed "The Governor and Company of Merchants of London trading into the East Indies", a group of merchants under the leadership of London's mayor, Sir John Smythe.

It was Linschotten's next book, his picaresque *Itinerario*, published in English in 1598 as *Discours of Voyages into ye East & West Indies*, that first alerted the educated Briton generally to the existence of a drink that was to become so ingrained into the daily life of the population that drinking it at all hours and on every occasion would become synonymous with being British.

Other Europeans had already gradually become aware of the existence of tea during the latter part of the fifteenth and early sixteenth centuries – surprisingly late in view of Western contacts with China over the previous three hundred years. Marco Polo makes no mention of tea in his travels at the end of the thirteenth century (though I wonder if his references to "The Dry Tree" could have been to a tea tree) nor do the early European travellers to India.

The habit of tea drinking appears to have spread outwards initially overland from China to the neighbouring territories of

Tibet and Mongolia, but for some reason no further north-west than Ladakh. The Mongols, who dominated Russia under Genghis Khan (d. 1227) and his successors, probably took tea with them, though the first factual record is of a Cossack diplomat bringing tea back from Mongolia in 1616. Two years later it was one of the gifts of a Chinese embassy to the Tsar, and was drunk frequently by the end of the century at the court of Peter the Great (1682–1725). However, it did not become Russia's most popular hot drink until the nineteenth century. Likewise – and surprisingly, in the light of Persia's regular commercial intercourse with China – tea did not become the most common hot beverage there until that time, though it was drunk by the better-off. An intrepid British officer, Captain Mignan, took his wife and two small children overland to India via Russia and Persia in 1829 and was entertained by Prince Mirza, the heir apparent. Mignan "was much surprised at having tea handed round to us in place of that universal beverage of the East, coffee". Adam Olearius, on a Holstein embassy to Persia in the 1630s, reported that the Persians liked to drink Chinese green tea with sugar. Another member of the same embassy travelled adventurously on to India and wrote in 1638 that "at our ordinary meetings every day, we took only The, which is commonly used all over the Indies, not only amongst those of the country, but also among the Dutch and English", who no doubt talked about this novel drink when they returned home.

Tea's diaspora by sea began slowly sometime in the sixteenth century, perhaps when Captain Diego Lopes de Sequiera commented in 1509 on the porcelain drinking cups used by the merchants with whom he traded. He makes no mention of what they contained, but it must surely have been tea. Perhaps he just politely swallowed the rather bitter contents and tried to forget about it.

By 1559 the armchair traveller Gianbattista Ramusio – the Hakluyt of Venice – was regaling his readers in the second volume of his *Navigatione et Viaggi* with an account of Haji Mohammed, a Persian who had been telling him about *chai Catai*, infused by the inhabitants of Sichuan and taken medicinally "for gout and stomach-ache". Similarly, Giovanni Botero's *On the Causes of Magnificence and Greatness of Cities* (1590) referred to a Chinese herb "out of which they press a delicate juice, which serves them for a drink instead of wine, it also preserves their health ...". However, oriental tea drinking still baffled Occidentals. When a group of Japanese Christian converts visited Rome in 1585, the onlookers mistook their tea brewing for the pointless drinking of hot water.

The diaries (1583 to 1610) of the learned mathematician and Jesuit missionary to Peking, Matteo Ricci, give him a claim to be the first serious Western sinologist and in them he refers specifically to tea as having a "peculiar mild bitterness not disagreeable to the taste". In his *Itinerario* Linschotten had described at some length the tea and tea drinking he observed on a visit he made to Japan from his base in Goa:

> After their meat they [the Japanese] use a certaine drinke, which is a pot with hote water, which they drink as hot as ever they may endure ... the aforesaid warme water is made with the powder of a certaine herbe called Chaa. ... When they will entertain any of their friends, they give him some of that warme water to drink; for the pots wherein they sieth [boil] it, and wherein the herbe is kept, with the earthen cups which they drinke it in, they esteeme of them as much as we doe of Diamants, Rubies and other precious stones, and they are not esteemed for their newness, but for their oldness, and for that they are made by a good workman.

Quite possibly it was from Japan rather than China that the first samples of tea were taken to Holland at this time.

Reading about tea was all very well, but when did Europeans first taste it at home? One Victorian scholar claimed that the Portuguese were trading tea by the late 1570s and this is quite possible given its subsequent popularity in the seventeenth century at the Portuguese court. After all, when Catherine of Braganza came to England in 1662 to marry Charles II, she not only brought Bombay in her dowry but tea and the fashion for drinking it. However, I have found no hard evidence of significant imports of tea to Portugal in the 1570s, and tea was certainly the last, and most expensive, of the three alkaloid drinks (chocolate and coffee being the others) to reach Europe.

We do know that by 1596 the Dutch had established a trading post at Banten (modern Bantam, now distant from the sea because of silting up) in Java and were importing tea there from China by 1606 – presumably for onward shipment to Holland. The Dutch most often paid for their early supplies of tea with sage, of which the Chinese were inordinately fond, at the rate of 1lb of sage for 4lb of tea. Tea was certainly being imported to Holland in 1610, though a price equivalent to about £60 for 1lb of leaf confined its use at that time to the very rich. Dutch imports had been established on a substantial and much more regular basis by 1637, if we are to judge from a letter of the Directors of the Dutch East India Company in that year instructing the governor general in Batavia to send "some jars of Chinese, as well as Japanese tea with each ship". Tea, they observed, "begins to come into general use with some people". At this time, because quantities were still relatively small, tea was packed in sealed earthenware jars to prevent it going mouldy on the voyage to Holland and was sold in 1oz packets in apothecaries' shops for medicinal use. However, by 1650 tea was also on sale in the grocery stores of the day, the colonial warehouses. By 1675 tea was in general use in Holland at all levels of society.

Elsewhere in Europe, a German doctor fulminated about its use in 1635, and a French one, Dr Paton, described it as "the impertinent novelty of the age" in 1648. Nine years later another French physician, Dr Jouquet, reported that the Chinese "l'appelait une herbe divine et la comparait à l'ambroise". Paris took to tea with passion. Cardinal Mazarin, Racine and Madame de Maintenon were all keen tea drinkers on medicinal grounds and from Madame de Sévigné's letters in the second half of the century we learn that she took it with milk, perhaps the first to do so in Europe. But, before the end of the century, the French abandoned tea almost entirely and with a zeal equal to the fervour with which they had originally embraced the fashion. Although Voltaire's household accounts in the second half of the eighteenth century have eight entries for tea, there are three times as many for the much cheaper chocolate. The French author J.-G. Houssaye, in his treatise *Du Thé* (1843), urged his compatriots to build up a direct tea trade with China and Indo-China rather than rely on Britain and

America. He speculated that tea had previously become popular in France largely as a result of the influence of French Jesuit missionaries in China. Therefore, when they were turned out so was the fashion for tea. This seems plausible, since the drinking of wine in France, which is sometimes suggested as the reason for the disappearance of tea, did not become commonplace until the nineteenth century. In any case, coffee from Turkey and from France's own colonies soon became more easily and cheaply available.

After the Revolution there was no coming back for tea in France precisely because of its identification with a wealthy aristocratic elite. Whereas the café was the place where intellectuals, artists and workmen with pretensions to culture and philosophy gathered to argue, the salon, even the *salon de thé*, was seen as the wateringhole of the effete to exchange vapid inanities. As Roland Jaccard put it, they were "tepid, draught-proof homes for old people".

The British were again a little behind the game, though in 1615 a Mr Wickham, the new East India Company's agent on the Japanese island of Hirado, scrawled a note to his colleague in Macao asking him to send a jar of "the best sort of chaw". Since the *Treatise on Warm Beer* of 1641, a compendium of all hot drinks then known in England, makes no reference to tea, we may reasonably assume that it was not drunk in Britain at that time.

The first concrete evidence of British tea drinking on a commercial basis comes from the account books of Thomas Garway in 1657 referring to his dealings in tea. These show that tea was being sold for between 16 and 60 shillings for 1lb (for comparative-value table, see p.377). They also refer to "its former scarceness and dearness" and imply that it was used only on special occasions by the great and the wealthy. Garway was to become celebrated not for what he did or achieved, but for the wonderful hyperbole of his advertisement in 1660 of tea as a universal panacea that could be bought from his coffee-house in Exchange Alley in London. He claimed that tea was able to cure everything from consumption to colic, from lassitude to lipitude, from ague to scurvy. His claims are all "supported" by an account of tea's growing, gathering and processing, and by the commendations of obscure classical authors. He also claimed in the same broadsheet that he had been the first to sell tea "in leaf and drink, made according to the directions of the most knowing merchants and travellers into eastern countries". "Tea, or rather Tcha or Tay alias Tee" had been first advertised for sale two years earlier, in the last week of September 1658 in *Mercurius Politicus*, as a medicinal drink "by all physitians approved" and available at the Sultan's Head coffee-house.

The rate at which tea drinking then developed in Britain was truly phenomenal. During the eighteenth century the population of Britain nearly doubled from just under seven million to well over 13 million. During that time annual consumption of sugar from the West Indian colonies rose from 4lb a head in the 1690s to 24lb in the 1790s. Slavery provided the free labour that fuelled this growth, most of it on the back of tea drinking. Tea was taken without milk, so usually sugar was added to offset the bitter taste from leaves that had been processed many months before and were often ill-packed for their long sea voyage from China.

The even more astonishing growth of tea drinking could equally be said to have ridden on the back of sugar. Without this sweetener, the cup for which Mr Pepys is so often quoted as having "sent out" in 1660 would not only have been tepid by the time it reached him but probably intolerably bitter. In that year only a few hundred pounds of tea were imported to Britain, courtesy of the Dutch East India Company, which had been founded in 1602 in imitation of its London rival. Even the 4,713lb shipped to London in 1678 was commented on as being a remarkably large amount. By then the (British) East India Company had secured its stranglehold on tea imports: no tea was supposed to be brought from Holland after 1669. William III briefly slackened this hold by allowing imports from any country where tea was not actually grown, but the Company soon re-established its grip. Tea in England was a luxury commodity that had been deemed sufficiently exotic and rare for the East India Company to present the tea-drinking monarch Charles II in 1666 with 22¾lb of it at 50 shillings per pound. By 1700 tea imports still stood at only 20,000lb, scarcely surprising when even six years later, at Thomas Twining's Golden Lion in the Strand, a small cup – Chinese porcelain, presumably – cost a shilling. Tea could also be bought there "in the leaf".

Because of the Scottish connections of several Canton tea traders, and the proximity to the capital of the port of Leith, tea drinking became a habit with the better-off in Edinburgh (and Glasgow) almost as soon as it did in London. As so often where luxuries were concerned, Wales and Ireland lagged behind, though the Irish were to become in the twentieth century the world's foremost drinkers of tea. Between 1721 and 1790 British official annual tea imports climbed from one million pounds to 16 million and more than doubled again by 1816 to 36 million (to these figures must be added a large volume of smuggled tea, which is considered in Chapter 15). By 1721 tea drinking had begun to spread to all classes and, a century later, the 36 million pounds of 1816 meant that an average of just under 3lb of legal leaf was being consumed by every man, woman and child in the UK. And every pound of it had to be imported from China.

While the leaf itself had become relatively familiar early in the eighteenth century, it was another 60 years before much was known about the Chinese tea bush – *Camellia sinensis* var. *sinensis* – itself. In 1668 John Nieuhof published an account of his adventures and observations during an embassy to the Emperor of China and throughout his extensive travels in Japan and much of the Far East. In his *Legata Batavia* there is a drawing of a tea plant in flower – located, it must be presumed from the figures of Chinese farmers in the background, in China. It is labelled "Thee or Cha". Jakob Breyne's *Plantarum Exoticarium*, published a decade later, relied solely on second-hand reports but has an appendix of several pages on "Fructice Thee". The engraving of the plant is thought to be by another Dutchman, Willem Ten Rhijn, a physician who had spent many years in Japan.

But the first tea plant to reach Europe alive was quite probably that brought from the island of Chusan by the English doctor James Cunningham in 1702 or 1703, when an account of it was published by an apothecary who had seen it. A number of other attempts were made to transplant and grow tea bushes in England later in the eighteenth century. One at Kew, *Thea bohea* in *Hortus Kewensis*, is listed as having been planted by John Ellis in 1768, but the Duke of Northumberland may have had one growing successfully at Syon

House at Brentford, near London, a little earlier, to judge from the drawing of a bush already in flower published by Act of Parliament in 1771. The same Act refers to bushes in Kent and in the Physic Garden at Chelsea.

The most persistent in his attempts to grow a tea bush in Europe was the famous Swedish taxonomist Carl Linnaeus (1707–78), who is reported to have tried 20 times. Like Breyne, Linnaeus was an armchair and laboratory botanist as far as any exotic species were concerned. Specimens and reports of these were brought to him by pupils and travellers from all over the world. It was on the basis of these and his own observations that he devised the first systematic and comprehensive method of naming and identifying plants unambiguously. The most unlucky of his students was Per Osbek, whose misadventures were almost tragicomic. One plant he had collected and brought safely as far as the Cape of Good Hope was blown overboard by an unexpected whirlwind. Another suffered the same fate from the blast of his ship's guns, fired in salute on leaving harbour. His successor, one Lagerstroem, suffered an even more farcical outcome. Having safely brought back a plant to Uppsala, he nurtured it for two years only to find it was an altogether different *Camellia*. Other young tea plants were eaten by ship's mice on the voyage or by rats once they had arrived. It was only when Captain Ekeburg managed to get two plants into Linnaeus's hands in October 1763, after all the others had perished on the way, that the famous Swede was able to grow them successfully in his botanical garden. And it was not until 3 May 2005, on Lady Falmouth's Tregothnan estate overlooking the banks of the River Fal in Cornwall, that the head gardener, Jonathon Jones, supervised the plucking of Europe's first commercial tea crop. Until the third decade of the nineteenth century even attempts to grow tea in more suitable conditions, such as a Dutch trial of Japanese tea plants in Java back in 1684, were unsuccessful. Until that time if you wanted to trade in tea you had to get it from China, which could be almost as difficult as growing it.

Two men in particular have left a fascinating record of their time as tea traders based in China: Samuel Ball, who was the East India Company's Inspector of Teas in Canton from 1804 to 1826; and

William Melrose, who traded independently on his father's behalf from that city from 1845 to 1855. When Ball took up his post only a handful of traders (and missionaries) were based in China. He did not write his account of the trade he supervised until 22 years after returning to England, and then only in response to what he saw as misconceptions in the parliamentary papers published in 1839 to broaden the discussion about developing a tea industry in India. Ball's *An Account of the Cultivation and Manufacture of Tea in China*, first published in 1848, is the first detailed and comprehensive account generally available in England of how tea was grown and processed in China. It covers everything from the early history and mythology of tea in China to nomenclature and the different methods of manufacture for black and green tea, so helping to dispel the erroneous assumption that they came from different species of tea bush.

When Ball arrived in Canton the East India Company had been trading with China from the port for well over a century. At first these commercial exchanges on the Chinese side had been conducted by a rather amorphous, but single-minded, collection of merchants, a Co-Hong (*hong* being the Chinese word for merchant). The power of this monopoly had made transactions very one-sided in favour of the Chinese, particularly as trade with foreigners was, for much of the time, confined to the ports of Canton and neighbouring Whampoa. In 1771 the Co-Hong had been replaced by a baker's dozen of Chinese merchants who formed a commercial oligarchy, but each of them was permitted also to deal separately with the barbarians. Their number never exceeded 13 and trade was always referred to as "tribute" to sustain the belief of the Chinese in their racial and cultural superiority. As Ball put it: "This important and beneficial change having been effected in the conduct of the trade, sufficient competition and rivalry were now created among the Hong merchants to secure to the foreigner something like fair dealing."

The East India Company's monopoly of the tea market had made life both simple and profitable for London wholesalers as the capital was the only British port through which tea might legally enter the country. The Company ensured a regular supply of a wide range of teas and ironed out fluctuations in supply and demand so as to give relatively stable prices. The broker tasted the teas and advised the wholesaler on what to buy for the peculiarities of his particular markets. Thus the shock was considerable when the end of the monopoly came into force on 22 April 1833 and the scramble of Free Trade began. Moreover, four more ports were designated through which tea could enter Britain and be traded: Liverpool, Leith, Glasgow and Bristol, though trade at the latter three never really took off after an initial burst of enthusiasm. It soon became apparent that survival as a tea wholesaler, whether in London or the provinces, would now depend on luck as well as judgement. Nor were the benefits of either likely to be derived without a representative in Canton, particularly as Jardine Matheson (still flourishing today) was rapidly establishing a stranglehold on exports that amounted almost to a monopoly. The grip this trading company had on a large part of the tea trade was a cause for much complaint by other dealers, for it often bought up much of the best Conjou and scented Orange Pekoe that were vital to a balanced and profitable shipment.

In the seventeenth century foreign traders had been prevented from trading directly with Chinese suppliers by difficulties of language. Not only was Chinese hard to learn for all but the most diligent and gifted of Europeans, who were few and far between, but any Chinaman caught teaching any Chinese language to a barbarian could be summarily executed. Western merchants had to rely on the services of an interpreter in their dealings with the Hongs. These "interpreters" often had a less than perfect command of English or any of the other European languages in use in Canton. It was out of this linguistic confusion that "pidgin English" came into being as virtually the only means of direct dialogue between occidental and oriental traders and their servants. In may be imagined that in such a situation sharp dealing and outright fraud and extortion were rife, even before the Westerners paid the numerous official duties and taxes, which were calculated in the main on the size of the ship and the value of its cargo. There was also a type of compulsory insurance against the very unlikely event of a Hong going bust. These levies were exacted – and often augmented to their own advantage – by officials of the Emperor. On top of these burdens lay the profit margins, usually of the order of 25–30 per cent, of the Hongs, who became extraordinarily wealthy. Shopping in China was not cheap.

Ball explains how "the tea plant, though spread over the 'hills of note', was first discovered, or first attracted attention in the Th-ye, or Bohea district (as Europeans have corrupted the name) in the province of Fo-kien". He goes on to explain that, because of Portuguese hostility, the British were obliged to trade out of Amoy in Fukien province, where the word for tea was "*te*" (pronounced "tay" at first in England), rather than basing themselves in Canton, where tea was called "*cha*" – hence, via India, the subsequent army slang "char". Even after the British were established in Canton, countries whose supplies arrived by sea still called it tea, whereas those where tea arrived overland, such as Russia, Persia and Mongolia, called it "*cha*".

Ball is interesting, too, on the origin of other nineteenth-century tea-trade terms. He notes in a Chinese work of 1693, which by then he was able to read for himself, that "The hill or mountain where tea is produced is called Singlo mountain. A Bonze of the sect of Fo taught a Kiang Nan man, named Ko Ty, the art of making tea; and thus it was called Singlo tea. ... That which is called Yuen or garden tea is the Singlo tea planted in gardens. ... In the reign of Cang Hee (1661–1722) a man used for his Chao Pay (firm or sign) the two characters Hee Chun, or Hyson. Shortly after all garden tea was called Hee Chun, or Hyson."

A company man to his fingertips, Ball had little time for the independent traders who went to Canton in the wake of the East India Company's loss of its monopoly:

Although far from meaning to advocate monopoly in any form, yet justice compels me to say that, had the privilege of trading to Foo-chew-foo been obtained during the existence of the East India Company's charter, from the unity of action and energy which a corporate body possesses over individual traders pursuing their separate interests, the greater part of the black teas would have been shipped from this port in less than four years. The usual

contracts would have been made with the tea-men at Canton …
can it be doubted that these people would gladly have hailed a
change which ceased to inflict on them the penalty of a tedious and
harassing journey, as well as a long and painful separation from
their homes and families?

Ball is full of praise of Sir Henry Pottinger for threatening to
renew the hostilities of the First Opium War (1839–42; see Chapter
5) in order to secure the opening to the British of the more conveniently situated port of Foochow. Scathingly he adds: "It is to be
hoped that advantages thus obtained by arms, may not be cast to
the winds and rendered nugatory, through the supineness and want
of enterprise on the part of the British merchants established at
Canton." However, Foochow was soon closed again to all
foreigners and by the time William Melrose had established the tea-
trading arm of his father's business in Canton in 1842, trading
conditions were again much as they had been in Ball's day.

The ideal agent to have in Canton was a man who had been a
broker in London and so developed the skill to taste the tea to be
exported and who could "pay great attention to the imports and
consumption, etc., for more depends on that than being a judge of
tea". William Melrose was just such a man. When in October 1842,
at the age of 25, he arrived in Canton, his father's company,
Andrew Melrose and Sons of Edinburgh, had already claimed to
have shipped the very first consignment of genuine post-monopoly
tea, which it had ordered through Jardine Matheson, its supplier
for another 10 years. This cargo of tea was dispatched from Canton
on 28 November 1833. In fact, another ship, the *Georgiana*, had
already arrived in Liverpool in the first week in November, having
set out from Canton just three days after the Act ending the
Company's monopoly came into force. Likewise tea from the
Camden was auctioned in Glasgow on 24 November. All three
shipments were almost certainly part of the last East India
Company tea to leave China.

Young Melrose would have found himself in a situation in
Canton not only completely different from anything in his experience while he had been learning the trade in Scotland but one which

was hot, unhealthy, uncomfortable and at times dangerous. As he wrote to his father: "You can form no idea in England what a luxury a glass of iced soda water or fine pale beer is; you want the thermometer at 90 before you can appreciate it." To start with he would have had to rely on the "interpreters" to carry out his transactions with the Chinese merchants. He would also have been almost entirely reliant on his own judgement as to how much of what to buy and when, and what he could afford to pay for it, and still make a profit when the tea was eventually sold in Scotland.

It could take between 52 and 56 days for a letter to go from Hong Kong to Edinburgh by the small steam-driven mail packets, which carried letters and passengers but otherwise only samples and a few small parcels of the very best and most expensive tea. The first steam-packet service was between Holyhead and Dublin in 1821 and when Melrose was first in Canton the last of the paddle-steamers was just giving way to the first of the steamships driven by screw propeller. These almost halved the journey time between Canton and London. Even so, four months could easily elapse between the issue of an instruction from Edinburgh and the receipt of its execution in a delivery back in Scotland. Similarly the orders based on intelligence from China could also be four months or more out of date by the time they were executed. The more successful traders were those who left most to their man on the spot in Canton. On one occasion Melrose, criticized by his father's manager for having exactly carried out an order which turned out to be unprofitable rather than exercising his own judgement, justifiably riposted that "instructions are of no avail unless they are to be obeyed, and better send none unless such is the understanding". Nor would this time-lag problem lessen until the opening of the Suez Canal in December 1869.

A motley collection of foreigners, consisting of some two hundred Dutch, Portuguese, French, Swiss, Germans, Moors, Arabs, and Parsees as well as Englishmen, or rather mostly Scots, were confined to their factories (where they factored) in an area in Canton not much larger than a London square. The British, at least, could enjoy a walk in the celebrated English garden, virtually the only safe open-air exercise open to them other than rowing in the harbour. It was there that the annual regatta became the major expatriate event of the year.

The Chinese regarded the foreign merchants as "barbarians", racially inferior subject peoples, who were allowed to trade on sufferance and under the strictest rules. The foreigners regarded the Chinese as ignorant and God-forsaken and likely to be rapacious in their dealings. Seldom can two ethnically different groups of people have so thoroughly misunderstood and underestimated each other. Even William Melrose, for all his linguistic skill and his honourable and positive approach to the Hong merchants with whom he dealt, would go so far as to observe: "the Chinamen have so little of those feelings [affection and love] and put so little value on them that it must take a long time to make them understand the principal feature in our religion: Our Saviour making a voluntary sacrifice of himself for love. I think a 'nigger' a much more hopeful subject for conversion. ... but the Chinaman is very apathetic to anything like fine feeling, and you must give him a new heart before you can make much of him, I think."

Not surprisingly, violence broke out from time to time between the local Chinese and the foreigners. Sometimes this was provoked by the latter – one English merchant, Charles Compton, was notorious for giving any Chinaman with whom he fell out "a good thrashing" – and sometimes it was orchestrated by the Chinese authorities to let the "barbarians" know just how precarious their position was. A couple of months after he arrived Melrose witnessed the burning of the Dutch, Greek and English factories; and four years later, in response to one of Compton's outbursts, the mob tried to burn down his Hong merchant's factory with the pair of them inside and to "kill the foreign devils".

Outside the cantonment the greatest danger was from pirates, both locally and on the voyage home. In October 1852 Melrose wrote to his father that a shooting party of four young British men

> were boarded by thirty pirates when at anchor and at dinner. As soon as the cry of pirates was raised, young Anderson seized a gun and looked out, saw a pirate lighting a fire pot to throw at them and shot him dead on the spot. The row then commenced; fire pots

were thrown in numbers, spears and so on. But the four foreigners stood firm with their double barrels and shot coolly the most conspicuous in the row. The pirates were not to be intimidated; they stood firm throwing their spears and making rushes forward until no less than eight of them were shot dead and lastly their leader, when they went away swearing they would soon be back again. The four had a lucky escape.

It was no doubt part of the necessary British phlegm that a dangerous encounter should be described as no more than a "row".

Earlier in the same year Melrose had reported a more serious case of piracy. With a nice mixture of humane compassion and commercial glee he comments: "The *Herald* for Leith will not be much opposition to you; the poor captain and officers were murdered by the crew, principally Manila men; after that they scuttled the vessel and she is, of course, totally lost. I will send you the newspaper account of it. Were it not for the loss of life, we might be glad of it rather than otherwise and, I suppose, so might the shippers as, if they are well insured, they have gone to a good market. I did not know the captain; his poor wife must have suffered dreadfully. I hope they will hang all those Manila men, cold-blooded rascals they must be." (Some of the mutineers were put to death in May.)

Melrose's first task when tea was offered for sale would have been to taste, or "character", it. This term derives from putting a character or symbol on all the containers of a "chop" of tea. (A chop was the personal mark put by a merchant on a uniform batch of tea and could refer to a quantity ranging from a few packets to hundreds of chests provided they were all of the same quality.) The sensitive nose and palate of the taster had to detect and evaluate the smallest nuances of flavour in as many as a couple of hundred teas in a day in order to provide the wholesaler with exactly the right combination of teas for the blends he would require to cater profitably for his customers' varied tastes.

Having identified the teas he wanted, Melrose would then have had to negotiate quantities and price with the appropriate member of the Hong in competition with other would-be purchasers. Once a deal had been negotiated there were broadly three methods of paying for it: in cash using Spanish and Mexican silver dollars (the Chinese themselves had only small-denomination copper coins suitable solely for minor domestic transactions); by letters of credit or bills of exchange; or in cotton or opium.

The First Opium War had been over only a couple of months when William arrived in Canton, and Jardine Matheson was already ruthlessly exploiting the opening that victory had enlarged, either by direct barter or by selling opium for silver with which to buy tea. Somewhat speciously, the company argued that by so doing it had "enormously extended the export of tea and silk ... and enabled these articles to be supplied ... at a lower price than could otherwise have been the case". In other words, drug trafficking was subsidizing the British tea drinker. William paid only in paper and his profit, and that of the other traders who had rejected paying in opium, depended in part on his ability to negotiate a good rate on his bills of exchange or on the difference between what was paid for silver coin and the price obtained when the tea was sold.

One early result of the freeing of the trade in tea was that the market was flooded with excessive amounts, much of it of undrinkable quality. These bad chops of tea were usually voluntarily withdrawn from sale by the British brokers themselves, who thus upheld their previous reputation for competence and integrity in judging and pricing tea. Withdrawn tea was then sold for as little as a farthing a pound, though no one seems to have enquired too closely what became of it subsequently. Melrose's own straight dealing with the Chinese also worked to his advantage. On one occasion when he bought an unsatisfactory chop the Chinese merchant who had supplied the tea took it back at his own cost without question. It is noteworthy that, in an era of much shady business practice, in the tea industry at least a man's word really was his bond, whatever the cost to his pocket.

At the onset of a new Chinese tea season (in April or May) there was a frenzy of activity as the captains of the incoming merchant vessels tried to judge their passage from Europe and America so as to minimize their time in harbour, where the dues were heavy, and to depart in time to catch the last of the favourable wind home before the south-west monsoon confronted them with a headwind as they sailed through the South China Sea. Most important for the merchants was catching the mail steam-packet, which by the mid-1840s could convey their letters of intelligence and instruction and their samples to London more speedily than any sailing ship:

> Everything has to be done just in a few days before the mail leaves: the bills to be sold first, tea to be weighed, shipped, and tonnage to be engaged in some vessel that is to go directly after the mail. However, they are all off now and I wish we may make something out of them and think we will. I must say I have been very lucky in getting them all shipped in splendid vessels, and all of them sailed almost as soon as the tea was on board. In fact the *Dauntless* sailed two or three days before the steamer and the other two were off as soon as her or a day or so after. They are all first class ships and fast sailers especially the *Hugh Walker* and *Marian* and should make good passages.

Catching the right vessel to get your tea to the right part of the British market at the right time was crucial to profitability. Tastes (and water) varied from one part of Britain to another and what might go down well in Liverpool would not do at all in Leith or Glasgow. Usually small quantities of the very best, and most expensive, tea were sent as soon and as swiftly as possible, for demand for them was limited and the loss if they were unsold the greater. For the more ordinary teas, freight charges and market conditions anticipated at home were the determining factor. Freight costs could vary from 2½ per cent to 7½ per cent of gross sale receipts. For example, in 1849 William paid £4 10s for 50 cubic feet of space, but in 1852 only £2 15s. On one occasion he gloats at rivals who paid much over the odds for freight on the *Oriental* only to find her cargo of second-class teas arriving in Britain long after the other ships. However, his letters reveal that in 1852 he found himself in a similar bind on account of the cumbersomely named *Auguste and Bertha*, which he dubbed a "regular clumbungie", when he learned from his father's letter of 22 March 1852 that she had not yet arrived. In response to a letter dated 21 April he writes on 19 June:

"what a clipper that *Auguste and Bertha* must be. However, I don't think she will have done us much harm by staying out so long, provided she does not damage her cargo." On 20 July he writes: "I have yours of 21 May and am glad to see ... that the *Auguste and Bertha* is in at last. People here are laughing and saying she has made the best passage of the season, meaning that she has arrived at the best time." On 27 September he reflects: "Her long passage was a fortunate one, though: she would have lost if she had made a quick passage." Such were the vagaries and happenstance of trading in tea from China in the middle of the nineteenth century.

Toward the end of Melrose's time in Canton the political climate became even more turbulent as the Taiping rebellion gathered momentum. He sent his father a perceptive comment on the looming crisis:

These are strange times what with the rebels here and the duty coming off at home; there is no saying what may take place. There seems little doubt now but the rebels or patriots are a formidable body, and Chinamen who laughed at them as fools before now appear to think they are very dangerous. I suppose you know that many years ago the Chinese were conquered by the Tartars; and the very tail they wear, and of which now they are so tenacious, is a badge of victory on the part of the Tartars and a mark of degradation to the Chinamen, the Tartars having insisted on their wearing a tail and shaving their heads after their conquest. Since then their rulers have been Tartars. Now they are trying to upset the Tartar rule and put a real Chinaman on the throne, and they are gaining ground.

Andrew Melrose and Sons made surprisingly modest profits from their China trade, but, unlike many others in the next few years, they survived. Although a particular consignment might make a good return, others had to be sold at a loss. As William Melrose pointed out: "In good years everything pays, in bad years everything loses; and those who make money in the China trade [are those] who do nothing at all as soon as they see bad times coming on." Four years after expressing this view he "broke his tasting cups" and returned home to marry, only to die soon after, his health probably undermined by the diseases and debilitations suffered during his sojourn in China.

When William Melrose left Canton in 1855, China still supplied 99 per cent of the world's tea. But its days of dominance were already numbered. It was not the hardship nor the shenanigans of tea trading in Canton, nor even the political, social and military upheavals throughout China, that caused the decline of the China tea trade. A much more gradual change was taking place fifteen hundred miles away.

CHAPTER TWO

Just Another Camellia

"It is," pronounced Dr Nathaniel Wallich, "just another camellia." The verdict in 1824 of the botanist in charge of the Horticultural Society's botanic gardens in Calcutta delayed the commercial growing of tea in India by a decade and also deprived Major Robert Bruce of recognition as the first European to realize that tea was indigenous to India. (Wallich, formerly Nathan Wolff, came to Bengal as a surgeon with the Danish East India Company in 1806. Hooker regretted that the Calcutta Botanic Garden "had fallen into the hands of a learned botanist but a rather poor landscape gardener". Wallich also produced two marvellous florilegia of subcontinental plants illustrated by paintings and drawings by Indian artists. The camellia was named after George Josef Kamel, a Moravian missionary who collected plants in the Philippines in 1639.)

Many writers on tea have expressed surprise that Dr Wallich failed to identify *Camellia sinensis* var. *assamica* as being a true tea plant, but his reluctance so to pronounce is really not surprising. Although the number of named camellias at the beginning of the nineteenth century was fewer than a hundred rather than the 55,000 known today, the leaves of the Chinese and the Assam tea bush are very different and that was all Wallich had to go on. He would have had in his mind's eye an image of the accepted tea plant of the time, *Camellia sinensis* var. *sinensis*. He also thought the leaf specimen sent to him by David Scott might have been *Camellia oleifera*. His decision is understandable since even the great taxonomist Carl Linnaeus was confused as to whether or not there was more than one distinct tea plant and it took professional botanists another 180 years to settle on a definitive conclusion, and even then they continued to argue about its subdivisions.

The trouble really started in 1753 when John Hill was categoric, in his *Treatise on Tea*, in naming two separate plants for black and green tea. In the first edition of *Species Plantorum*, published in the same year, Linnaeus had opted for a single description: *Thea sinensis*. However, since the first edition he must have read both Hill and the much-travelled German scholar Engelbert Kaempfer, who wrote on Japanese tea in the second edition (1762) of his *Amoenitates Exoticae* (Exotic Pleasures) and in his monograph of 1765 *Potus Thea*. Linnaeus follows their practice and lists two separate species: *Thea viridis* (green tea), the flower of which had nine petals, and *Thea bohea* (black tea), which had six. Professional botanists did not finally correct this error until Sir George Watt did so in 1898. This is surprising as those on the ground as early as Dr Abel in 1818 and Ball, Bruce and Fortune, among others in the next 30 years, were quite clear that the difference between green and black tea was solely due to the way the leaves were processed, regardless of which bush they came from.

Until the Botanical Conference in Amsterdam in 1933, which settled on our current clumsy name *Camellia sinensis (L) O. Kuntze*, the term *"thea"*, or at least *"theifera"*, as in *Camellia theifera*, appeared in virtually every description of tea. Now "Theaceae" has a continuing life only in the family name to which the genus *Camellia* belongs, which has largely replaced the older Ternstroemiaceae family.

The China bush, of which there are numerous sub-varieties in that country and Japan, has many stems and stands naturally a little under three metres high. These are hardy bushes, able to withstand temperatures from 38°C to –20°C. They produce the teas with the most distinctive flavours over a useful lifespan of 90–100 years, though many remain fruitful for much longer. China bushes are usually grown at altitudes over 900 metres in Darjeeling, the central highlands of Ceylon, northern China and Caucasia. In their natural state the Assam jats (from the Hindi word for "caste"), or types, are trees varying in height from six to eighteen metres. The bushes cultivated in tea gardens stand at convenient plucking height of about 1.5 metres as a result of a strict regime of pruning. Assam jats are much more prolific than the China variety and produce a "good liquoring" tea – dark and strong. Usually they only have a useful lifespan of 40–50 years and are susceptible to early frost and strong early sun. However, their general superiority means that they are ousting, or have ousted, China plants in many parts of the world and are the variety of choice for initial planting in most places. As the Bible – or at least the Old Testament – of tea, Harler's *Tea Growing*, points out: "Experience in India has shown that the inherent characteristics of the individual bush or the general characteristics of the jat outweigh any other factor, be it climatic, soil or, even to a large extent, fineness of plucking, in their influence on the quality or the flavour of the tea."

If anyone can be assigned the credit for discovering and utilizing *Camellia sinensis* var. *assamica* in north-east India it is the Singpho (Chaw Paw) Kochin tribesmen on the border with Upper Burma. It was there that their chief, Beesgaum, gave Major Robert Bruce a drink of native tea sometime in 1823. "The Singphos have known and drank the Tea for many years, but they make it in a very different way from what the Chinese do. They pluck the young and tender leaves and dry them in the sun ... ." Bruce, who had been trading illegally in this remote area for some time, passed the information, together with some raw leaves, to his brother Charles, who then was in command of a flotilla of gunboats on the Brahmaputra river. There had also been rumours that Chinese soldiers, returning from Nepal after General Ochterlony's 1814–18 campaign there, had been brewing tea from a local leaf, having given away their own in exchange for tobacco; and the Resident of the East India Company in Kathmandu had reported it growing in a private garden there in 1816. The aroma of tea was in the air.

To my mind, Charles Alexander Bruce is both the most significant and one of the most underrated figures in the early development of commercial tea cultivation in India. (He was one of seven members of the family adventuring in India in the early nineteenth century. When Bruce is referred to below by the initials C.A. or without a forename, Charles Alexander is meant.) Before becoming involved in tea, this intrepid character had joined the Navy as a midshipman in 1809 before, in his own words, he was "twice captured by the French on my way out, after two hard fought actions; was marched across the Isle of France [Mauritius] at the end of the bayonet and kept prisoner on board of a ship until that island was taken by the British; thus I suffered much and twice lost all my possessions, and was not remunerated in any way. I afterwards went as an officer of a troop ship against Java, and was at the taking of that place." In 1823, at the outbreak of the first war with Burma, he volunteered and was given command of that flotilla of gunboats. Bruce passed both his brother Robert's information and the leaves (which eventually finished up in the herbarium of the Linnean Society, and I am assured by the conservator that they are definitely tea) to his senior officer, David Scott, who had just been appointed the first Commissioner and Agent to the Governor General for the North-East Frontier province. Scott in turn, in 1824, passed the by now rather dilapidated leaves to Wallich – with the result we know. The same off-hand dismissal was to greet the equally sorry-looking leaves sent direct to Calcutta by Lieutenant K. Charlton in 1831.

By 1823 the idea that tea might be cultivated in India was by no means new. The ubiquitous Sir Joseph Banks had already suggested in 1788 that certain areas of Bengal, which subsequently became major tea-growing districts, might be suitable for such cultivation – though, of course, it was the China bush he had in mind. Spencer Percival – a British Prime Minister (1809–12) otherwise distinguished only for being shot dead by a disgruntled bankrupt in the lobby of the House of Commons – also advocated the growing of tea in the British colonies. He was followed in a desultory and theoretical way by a number of others, of whom the only one of importance was "a very intelligent gentleman called Walker". Important because it was his letter on the subject that stimulated the interest, shortly after he took office in 1828, of one of the most dynamic men to exercise the role of Governor General in India: Lord William Bentinck.

John Walker pointed out that the use of tea "was so intermingled with our habits and customs, that it would not easily be dispensed with". However, the Chinese could at any time cut off its supply and had done so in the past. It was "therefore of considerable national importance, that some better guarantee should be provided for the continued supply of this article than that at present furnished by the mere tolerance of the Chinese government". The solution he proposed was to grow tea in India, "where the camellia and other plants of a character similar to the tea plant are indigenous". By this means it would "be easy for us to destroy the Chinese monopoly". "We can scarcely doubt," he added, "that, when the skill and science of the Europeans, aided by thermometers &c. shall once be applied to the cultivation and preparation of tea in favourable situations the Chinese tea will soon be excelled in quality and flavour." Bentinck agreed and the only difficulty that occurred to him was "the impossibility of having access to the tea countries and thus of having personal and local knowledge of all particulars relating to the culture and manufacture". So he sent Captain Francis Jenkins to Sadiya in 1832 to find out and on 1 February 1834 Bentinck set up the Committee on Tea Culture, consisting of seven civil servants of the East India Company; Wallich as botanist; George Gordon, his Lordship's nominee as Secretary; two Indians; and a Dr Lumqua, a respected Chinaman living in Calcutta. The Committee was to look into the subject carefully and urgently and seems to have been remarkable among such committees in that it actually carried out its brief. Not everyone was enthusiastic about the remit. One correspondent to the *Calcutta Courier*, a week after the Committee's birth, argued that tea "thrives as ... mere vegetation ... but nowhere except in China has any successful effort been made to render it a profitable product of industry ... this arises from causes that will be found a bar to the profitable cultivation of the plant in India".

As far as the tea Committee was concerned, there were now three issues to be resolved. Was tea indigenous to India, and if so of what species was the plant that had been discovered? If it were indigenous, would it or the well-established China plant be the more suitable for commercial exploitation in India? Where in India could the most suitable conditions for its cultivation be found? The members did not realize it at the time but the latter problem consequently raised the crucial question of what species was to be planted.

Not long after it was set up the Committee pre-empted the answer to the second question by dispatching its Secretary, George Gordon, to China to collect tea plants, seeds and skilled cultivators and manufacturers. Wallich took over his role as Committee Secretary. Poor Gordon was not only shuttled to and fro between Calcutta and China as the Committee changed its mind but was so naive that he was duped by his Chinese contacts into accepting poor-quality seeds and plants on hearsay that they were from the prime tea-growing areas when in fact they were any old rubbish that could be quickly and cheaply gathered from the tea gardens nearest to Canton. On top of this he perpetuated the notion that black and green tea came from different species of tea bush.

In March 1834 the Committee circulated widely throughout India a request for information about tea plants and got a prompt reply from Lieutenant Charlton via his superior officer, Captain Francis Jenkins. On 17 May Charlton wrote: "I have little doubt but that that found near Beesa is a species of tea; and though it may be spurious or even a Camellia, as Dr. Wallich suggests, its growing there indigenous and in great abundance affords good grounds for supposing that the introduction of the Chinese plant into Upper Assam would be attended with success. ... I have written to Sadiya for a specimen of the tea prepared in this manner and for plants and seeds." Charlton wrote again on 8 November: "I am sorry that the unsettled state I have been in for the past three months [he had been suppressing a rebellion] prevented me sending them as soon as I intended. The leaves you have had before, but I was anxious to make them into something like tea, the best test that this is not a camellia as Dr. Wallich suggests." How well he understood the bureaucratic mind.

Jenkins hastily passed on his dispatch on 22 November: "I have only time to send this and to say, I have sent a jar of tea-leaves and a box of tea seeds to go by today's Dak" – the relay of government native postal runners. Again the leaves passed through a number of hands before reaching Calcutta, but this time they were dispatched through official channels with rather more urgency and persistence as to what they were.

Jenkins was an officer of rare energy and perception (he later became a general) and also an experienced amateur botanist, so his observations carried weight with the Tea Committee, to which he had already written on 7 May 1834. "I am so fully impressed with the belief of the fitness of the mountainous region which divides Cachar from Assam for the growth of tea, that I beg to call the attention of the Committee to that region in the most favourable manner I can. ... I would beg to recommend the expediency of some well qualified person being at once sent up for identification of the plants beyond any objection, for the examination of the soil in which it grows, as reported, and for an inspection of the tract of mountains between Cachar and Assam."

Dr Wallich was man enough to change his mind and accepted that, this time at least, the leaves were definitely from a tea plant. So the Committee was finally able to report to the Governor General on 24 December: "It is with feelings of the highest possible satisfaction that we are enabled to announce to his Lordship in Council, that the tea shrub is beyond all doubt indigenous in Upper Assam ... ." There was a passing nod to the specimens dispatched so much earlier by David Scott from Manipur in 1824, but the Committee had "no hesitation in declaring this discovery, which is due to the indefatigable researches of Capt. JENKINS and Lieut. CHARLTON, to be by far the most important and valuable that has ever been made in matters connected with the agricultural or commercial resources of this empire. We are perfectly confident that the tea plant which has been brought to light, will be found capable, under proper management, of being cultivated with complete success for commercial purposes, and that consequently the object of our labors may be before long fully realised."

The Committee also took up Jenkins's suggestion and recommended the immediate dispatch of a scientific investigation team to the areas from which the tea specimens had been sent. Accordingly, on 29 August 1835, a three-man team, consisting of Wallich himself, the medical man and distinguished botanist William Griffith and another doctor and highly competent amateur geologist, John McClelland, was sent on its travels up that "uninteresting river, the Burampooter [Brahmaputra]". In January 1836 they arrived in

Sadiya, where they were taken under the wing of Bruce, who had recently taken over as superintendent of the Government's experimental tea plantations in the place of the unfortunate Charlton, who had no sooner been appointed than he was wounded storming a barricade in one of the innumerable skirmishes with local tribesmen and invalided home.

Wallich had already written on 8 February 1835 to recall Gordon, "whose continuance in China ... is therefore useless and unnecessary". No sooner had the poor man got back to Calcutta than the Committee decided that, though it might not now want China seed (a decision it would reverse yet again in a year's time), it did need experienced Chinese cultivators and manufacturers, so packed him off back to Canton. Gordon was no more successful at recruiting skilled manipulators, as they were then called because of the entirely manual nature of tea manufacture, than he had been in securing quality seed. Skilled workers were deterred from leaving the country by harsh imperial edict, for the Celestial Empire was determined to hang on to its monopoly of assuaging an ever-growing British thirst for tea. The families of defectors were tortured and deprived of all their possessions. Inevitably in these circumstances, the Chinese Gordon did recruit were urban ne'er-do-wells with little or no idea how to process tea.

The scientific expedition soon found itself beset by dangers and difficulties in what was still one of the most turbulent and unstable parts of India, as Charlton had found to his cost. Wallich wanted to turn back, but the others, under the protection of Jenkins and Bruce, insisted that they all press on. The team sent back its first report from Cherrapunjee, which holds the world's annual rainfall record at 901 inches.

In the summer of 1836 Wallich, Griffith and McClelland wrote separate sections of their report to the Tea Committee and from these it emerges that there was a degree of professional, and probably personal, hostility between the two botanists. Griffith, in his *Report on the Tea Plant of Upper Assam*, published in 1838, takes a side-swipe at Wallich's earlier failure to recognize the tea-plant. "Now, although reasons certainly existed why the alleged Tea might have proved, as the Tea Committee suggested, nothing but a Camellia yet the very fact of a Camellia being reported to exist, should at once have pointed out the immediate necessity of a proper examination of the plant on the spot."

Wallich defended himself in a note attached to the Committee's own triumphant report to the Governor General. "There is no danger of mistaking any plant for the tea except the Camellia. Both are very closely allied to each other in general appearance, in the form of their leaves and the structure of the flowers. It is by the character of the fruit alone that they can be satisfactorily distinguished for practical purposes." And the fruit, in the shape of Charlton's made tea, had not long been provided.

Nor was this the only matter the two men disagreed about, though Griffith, aware that the views he expressed might be resented in some quarters, "hoped his observations would be taken in the proper light, that they will not be received as originating in a spirit of scepticism, but as a strong wish to protect the interests of the Government he had the honour to serve". Thus with weasel words he excused his disagreements with Wallich. One was about where tea could best be grown. Griffith argued that it should only be planted in locations as closely akin as possible to those where it grew best in China – which as far as I can ascertain he had never visited. Wallich did not, as Griffith implies, say that tea could not be grown in the plains, only that it would be poorer than tea grown high up, and in this, in terms of flavour at least, he was right. Another spat arose from Griffith's scornfully dismissing Wallich's and Jenkins's strictures on the unhealthiness of the Assam climate: "the extreme insalubrity of Upper Assam is totally unfounded, at least so far as Europeans are concerned, and has originated from persons of timid habits in whose eyes blades of grass are death-bearing toorais".

They also had sharp differences over the suitability of Bruce to be in charge of the Government's experimental tea plantations, to which he had been appointed superintendent in May 1836 on the strength of high praise from Wallich. Quite possibly Bruce, in practical charge of the expedition, at some time in their arduous journey had been obliged to give the tetchy Welshman a piece of his mind. Behind damning faint praise Griffith reciprocated: "It will be evident that certain qualifications are necessary [botanical knowledge and tea-planting experience] in the person who has the general superintendence of the whole plan ... to do Mr. Bruce justice, I believe he does not pretend to possess either one or the other. As a zealous, hard-working person, Mr. Bruce cannot be well exceeded; and to these good qualities, he adds those of a *tolerable acquaintance* with the natives of Upper Assam, and of the Assamese language so far as *colloquial intercourse with the lower orders*, and the possession of strong physical powers [italics added]." Then, having suggested Bruce be sacked, he adds that he "would beg to urge ... the placing of the scheme under Captain Jenkins, the Head Authority in Assam, who in addition to his well-known zeal for the welfare of the Province under his charge, adds a degree of scientific knowledge which few possess".

Jenkins, a well-trained Army officer, would perhaps have been more deferential in his dealings with Griffith than the self-made Bruce. But it was Bruce, the eminently practical Navy man, who not only successfully cultivated the first tea from Assamese stock but produced from it, in 1836, the first drinkable tea. "Five boxes were made of tea prepared from leaves gathered out of season, dressed according to the process used for black tea, and with a very imperfect apparatus." These were sent to Calcutta, where they passed professional muster and a cup brewed from them was sipped with approbation by the Governor General. On 6 May 1838 the first Indian tea was sent to England, where it was auctioned on 10 January 1839 and pronounced "not inferior to ordinary tea from China".

Griffith cannot resist winding up his contribution to the report with one last dig at Wallich: "I cannot conclude this part of my report without adverting to the extremely desultory manner in which the question of tea cultivation in India has been treated by every other author who has written on the subject with the exception of Mr. McClelland."

John McClelland must have been something of a peacemaker, for no one has a bad word to say about him, perhaps precisely because he did *not* share a scientific discipline with Griffith and Wallich. His report, published separately in 1837, is both balanced and objective. He begins by examining the possibility that the tea bushes, which they found only in the alluvial basin, were not indigenous: "May not these colonies of wild tea plants have been cultivated gardens into which the plant was introduced artificially? A doubt would thus be cast at once upon the indigenous nature of the tea plant, and though it may have propagated and grown spontaneously for ages, yet the chances against its successful cultivation for commercial purposes would perhaps in consequence be increased." Another possibility is that "a single seed may have fallen from a Chinese caravan, near the source of one of those fluvatile ramifications which converge to the valley on every side ... where it may have been deposited under circumstances favourable to its growth and propagation". From this he sees a colony spreading out to form other colonies. Having dismissed these two rather far-fetched hypotheses, he concludes that "the tea plant of Assam grows spontaneously under slightly distinct circumstances ...".

The geologist goes on to commend further research based on Bruce's nurseries: "Little is to be expected from any attempts that can at present be made to manufacture tea from the uncultivated plant: but still as there is a small establishment on the spot for the purpose consisting partly of Chinese, they might be employed in constant trials upon the leaves ... ." His caution about preserving the native stock uncontaminated in order to supply the nurseries is equally prudent: "The importance therefore of abstaining from offi-cious interference with the original colonies must be evident. None of them are very great in extent, and it is possible to conceive that as they are all in retired forests some attempts may he directed to the transplantation of the trees in a more convenient but less appro-priate situation (as is almost sure to happen on such occasions if *convenience* be at all allowed to enter into our views) and thus exhaust, if not totally destroy the means of conducting more judi-cious experiments." Reading the reports of the three men, I get the impression that the geologist often talked more botanical sense than the two botanists, for he observes that from zoology and the "sister sciences" we "are taught to look upon the tea plant in Assam, thus associated with the natural productions of Eastern Asia, not as an alien estranged from its own climate, but as an indigenous plant, neglected it is true by man, but in the full enjoyment from nature of all those peculiar conditions on which its properties will be found under proper management to depend."

Although all three scientists eventually agreed that the tea bushes they had seen were indigenous, Wallich's reservations about commercial development with China, rather than Assam, stock were swept aside by the high-handed Griffith, who prefaced his argument for the China jat with a typically scornful comment: "The discovery of the Tea within the British Dominions in India has excited more speculation among scientific men on the Continent, than in England itself." And he quotes Alphonse de Candolle's reference to the Burmese using Assam tea as a pickle rather than drinking it to reinforce his case for the China jat. "Le Thé sauvage pourrait bien donner une saveur plus forte, plus acre, et un parfum peu délicat. Cette considération cependant ne diminue pas, à nos yeux, l'intérêt de la découverte des Anglais." From this Griffith concludes: "I think most persons will agree with me, that the importation of even the inferior kinds [of Chinese seed and plants] would be more likely to lead to the produce of a marketable article than the cultivation of wild or, to use to our Indian notions a more expressive term, Jungly tea."

Unfortunately most persons did agree with him and "inferior kinds" was exactly what they got, particularly from those plants and seeds Gordon had brought back. It is a nice irony that Griffith, the ruthlessly logical advocate of China stock, would turn out to be wrong and the apparently panic-prone Wallich right.

Bruce also made his bid to be recognized in 1838, writing his own report with a lengthy title ("An Account of the Manufacture of the Black Tea as now practised at Suddeya in Upper Assam, by the Chinamen sent thither for that purpose, with some observations on the culture of the plant in China, and its growth in Assam") that did justice to its even lengthier contents. In a moving and authentic claim for priority, he wrote from Jaipur on 10 June 1839:

In looking forward to the unbounded benefit the discovery of this plant will produce to England, to India, – to Millions, I cannot but thank God for so great a blessing to our country. When I first discovered it, some 14 years ago, I little thought that I should have been spared long enough to see it become likely eventually to rival that of China, and that I should have to take a prominent part in bringing it to so successful an issue. Should what I have written on this new and interesting subject be of any benefit to the country, and the community at large, and help a little to impel the Tea forward to enrich our own dominions, and pull down the haughty pride of China, I shall feel myself richly repaid for all the perils and dangers and fatigues, that I have undergone in the cause of British India Tea.

The bulk of his report, however, is a detailed practical treatise on the natural habitat of Assam tea and how it could best be cultivated and manufactured. In one passage he describes how some Assamese villagers took the tea plant to be so much jungle, and therefore cut nearly all of it down close to the ground, set fire to the whole and then planted paddy (rice) on the spot. "The crop of paddy had just been cut and brought in when we saw the plants, the shoots were coming up from the roots and old stumps thick and numerous. ... I afterwards converted this piece of ground into a tea garden on account of the Government, and now it is one of the finest I have." He also tried to propagate his plants by taking cuttings and growing them in shade – no easy matter since most Assam bushes are self-sterile and have to be propagated from seed. Nor was his strict adherence to the ruthless total plucking method of his Chinese coolies (the Chinese word for the labourer who worked on tea gardens and a much more convenient term, which I shall use throughout to avoid confusion, and which did not have its present derogatory sense) calculated to get the best from his bushes. Even so he went about things in an experimental way with a high degree of scientific discipline despite being no scientist.

Sadly for Bruce, his legitimate bid for fame was ignored and not long afterwards he transferred his allegiance from the Government to a leading commercial tea company to exploit the potential for growing *Camellia assamica* in Assam itself. The establishment, ever ready to promote the reputation of its own at the expense of the original and uncomfortable outsider, ascribed the honour of being the discoverer of tea to Lieutenant Charlton and for bringing it to official notice to Captain Jenkins by awarding them gold medals of the Agricultural and Horticultural Society of India. Bruce's contribution to the Indian tea industry was well summed up by an 1839 article in the *Asiatic Journal*:

Mr. Bruce, a gentleman who by long residence in the province had become habituated to the climate and well acquainted with the country and inhabitants, was appointed Superintendent of Tea Culture. His attention has previously been given to other pursuits, and he does not seem to have possessed any knowledge of botany or horticulture, or indeed any special qualifications for the post, but his intelligence and activity supplied every deficiency, and enabled him to render very valuable service. He discovered that the tea plant, instead of being confined to a few isolated spots, was over a great extent of country and though his researches were at first viewed with great jealousy by the native chiefs, he not only succeeded in removing their prejudices but persuaded them to contribute their hearty assistance to his labours.

Even after the discovery of the indigenous tea plant in Assam, the emphasis on the attempts of nearly all the early pioneers of tea growing in India was to try to replicate as nearly as possible the lucrative tea trade from China. This they did not only by importing and planting seed from China but by bringing in Chinese technicians and techniques as well. Only the very occasional far-sighted objector argued the case for the native Assam variety. Only when the drawbacks and failures using China seed hit home financially were the gardens of north-east and south-west India, and indeed of Java, converted to the superior merits, in their particular conditions, of the Assam jat, or at least its hybrids with China jat.

Dr William Jameson, a Government-appointed botanist in charge in 1843 of various experimental gardens in India, thought he knew how to make tea growing pay and although his arithmetic did not always quite add up and his assumptions were optimistic, he demonstrated that he could make good tea from the China bushes he had grown. So good was his leaf that it fetched 7s. 1d. a pound in the local market at Almora, 180 miles north-west of Delhi. Jameson's report persuaded the Government of India to send Robert Fortune to China, where he arrived in August 1848. Fortune was chosen because he had already undergone a series of hair-raising adventures in China a few years earlier when plant-hunting there for the Royal Horticultural Society. Now, once again, he would sport his pigtail, don Chinese clothes and, using his good knowledge of the language, penetrate into the very heart of the tea-growing districts. Daring and tenacious, he was also a canny Scot. Where Gordon had been deceived into thinking that the tea seed brought to him was the genuine article when it came in fact from the nearest convenient garden, Fortune devised a trick to ensure that his collectors brought him only the best. From his previous journey he knew that *Berberis japonica* grew only in the prime tea districts, so he told his collectors that, unless they brought samples of that plant along with their tea seeds, he would not buy from them: no berberis, no cash. (*Cash* is the Mandarin word for money and crept thence into English.)

In view of the contemporary obsession with China in matters horticultural, it was only natural for Fortune to push hard for the use of Chinese tea stock, rather than Assamese. He went to great lengths to see that it reached Calcutta in a usable state; but it was not until after several failures that he hit on a way to utilize the long sea voyage to bring the seeds to the point of germination on arrival. These early seeds on their journey to the coast from the hinterland "were carefully packed with their roots in damp moss, and the whole package was then covered with oil-paper. The latter precaution was taken to screen them from the sun, and also from the prying eyes of the Chinese, who, although they did not seem to show any great jealousy on the point, yet might have annoyed us with impertinent questions." He goes on:

In the autumn of 1848 I sent large quantities of tea-seeds to India. Some were packed in loose canvas bags, others were mixed with dry earth and put into boxes, and others again were put up in very small packages, in order to be quickly forwarded by post; but none of these methods were attended with much success. Tea ... seeds retain their vitality for a very short period if they are out of the ground. ... In 1849, however, I succeeded in finding a sure and certain method of transporting tea-seeds to foreign countries in full life; it is simply to sow the seeds in Ward's cases [rather like miniature greenhouses] soon after they are gathered.

My first experiment was tried in the following manner. Having procured some fine mulberry-plants from the district where the best Chinese silk is produced, I planted them in a Ward's case in the usual way, and watered them well. In two or three days, when the soil was sufficiently dry, a large quantity of tea-seeds were scattered over its surface, and covered with earth about half an inch deep. The whole was now sprinkled with water, and fastened down with a few cross-bars to keep the earth in its place. The case was then screwed down in the usual way, and made as tight as possible.

When the case reached Calcutta the mulberry plants were found to be in good condition, and the tea seeds had germinated during the voyage and were now covering the surface of the soil. A Dr Falconer, writing to Fortune upon receipt of this case, said, "The young tea-plants were sprouting around the mulberries as thick as they could come up."

Quite possibly Fortune learned not a little about the best way to transport tea seeds successfully from one of his principal suppliers, A Ching, whom he quizzed about how he sent his seeds to foreigners:

"I want to see your method of packing seeds for foreigners. Take me to your seed-room and show me the whole process from beginning to end." The old man led me up to the middle of his garden, where he had an ornamental shed or seed-room. It was nicely fitted up with shelves, on which were arranged a great number of small porcelain bottles, such as I had often seen in London with seeds from China. "Sit down," said he, "and I will explain the business to you. I first gather the seeds from the plants. I then put each kind, separately, into one of these small bottles, and then pack the whole into a little box, ready for being shipped to Europe or America." "I understand that part of the business," said I; "but what is the substance which you put into the bottles along with the seeds?" This was a white ashy-looking matter, which we supposed in England might be burnt bones, and some conjectured that it was mixed with the seeds for the purpose of manure. "Burnt lice," said A Ching. "Burnt what?" I asked, with a smile which I could not conceal … . It was burnt rice, or the husks of rice reduced to ashes, that he meant. I then asked him the reason why he used this substance in packing seeds, and he replied, in Canton English, "S'pose my no mixie this seed, worms makie chow-chow he."

As a result of his diligence and curiosity Fortune could write with ample justification: "The important objects of my mission have been brought to a successful termination. Upwards of twenty thousand tea plants, eight first rate manufacturers and a large supply of implements were procured from the finest tea districts of China and conveyed in safety to the Himalayas."

Apart from his preference for China seed, Fortune was often right in his prescriptions for the best way to cultivate tea in India. He urged that gardens be grouped close together and preferably near rivers as he foresaw the critical role water transport would have to play in getting tea to market. He warned against employing any but the most skilled and experienced Chinese manufacturers "as it is a great pity to teach the natives an inferior method of manipulation".

Perhaps Robert Fortune's most far-sighted piece of advice concerned the development of an internal market for tea, a market that today takes up over 80 per cent of India's enormous tea production:

> The people of India are not unlike the Chinese in many of their habits. The poor of both countries eat sparingly of animal food, and rice with other grains and vegetables form the staple articles on which they live; this being the case, it is not at all unlikely the Indian will soon acquire a habit which is universal in China. But in order to enable him to drink tea, it must be produced at a cheap rate; he cannot afford to pay at the rate of four or six shillings a pound. It must be furnished to him at four *pence* or six *pence* instead, and this can easily be done, but only on his own hills. If this is accomplished, and I see no reason why it should not be, a boon will have been conferred upon the people of India of no common kind, and one ... which an enlightened and liberal Government may well be proud of conferring upon its subjects.

Jealousy and petty professional quarrels seem to have been endemic to the early tea industry in India. William Jameson disagreed quite pointedly on several issues in his report submitted three weeks later. Fortune had considered that the development of tea in India ought to be in the hands of a Government organization rather than in those of private interests such as the Assam Company. In view of the state of the latter's management and cultivation at the time, he had a point. Jameson, the civil servant, unexpectedly disagreed and proposed that development should be left in private hands: a view that coincided with that of the Government of India. Jameson was none too polite in expressing his disagreement. He dismissed Fortune's report as showing the explorer in a poor light and claimed that many of its proposals had been put forward earlier by himself and, what was more, "translated into a number of local languages for the guidance of native planters". "Mr Fortune might," Jameson suggested, "make himself thoroughly acquainted with all the processes (particularly the proportion of coarse leaf in black tea) [which] was one of my chief reasons for recommending his second deputation [i.e. original trip to China in 1848]."

Fortune had seen the prospect of a considerable native tea business developing, particularly in the hands of the zemindars, the local small-scale landowners, but, as is often the case, the civil servant had the last word when reporting to the Commissioner for Kumaon in February the following year. Jameson considered that "The manufacture of tea, must in my opinion, remain in the hands of Europeans for many years." And for insulting good measure, he added: "It is difficult to conceive any European settler with energy to embark capital and expend time on a tea plantation who had not the intelligence of a native with six rupees per mensem." He was wrong and Fortune right.

With hindsight, it is easy to condemn the Tea Committee and the Government of India for their initial headlong pursuit of the China jat that would so quickly become "the curse of India" except in the highlands of Darjeeling and the Nilgiris in southern India. But it must be remembered that before tea cultivation began in India the China jat *was* tea as far as all but a few far-sighted men, such as Bruce, were concerned and that the British were by then importing almost 50 million pounds of it annually, all of which had to be expensively purchased from a capricious and uncertain China. It soon became apparent that the native plant was better suited not only to Indian conditions but to the developing British taste. As William Roberts, a plantation supervisor, wrote in 1867: "The Assam variety has been greatly injured by close contact with the

China, the stems presenting a bare lanky appearance and the branches covered with moss and lichen. Should the Assam kind throw out vigorous shoots, the China plants may then be eradicated; in some places, where the Assam plants are in better condition, the China kind is to be removed at once."

In the Nilgiris another medical man, by name Christian, ordered some plants with which to try growing tea locally. He died before the plants arrived. Eventually it was a French botanist, M. Perrottet, who planted the seeds supplied by the Government of Madras in 1835. In Ceylon, too, there is early evidence of attempts to grow tea. An army officer of the 80th Regiment of Foot stationed in Ceylon claimed to have seen tea growing there wild in 1814, but the idea that it might be grown commercially was first mooted by a missionary, the Reverend Ringeltaube, to a new colleague in 1816. "In the garden of Mr Cripp, Master Attendant at Colombo, I am told grows the TEA PLANT. Were you to offer that you would introduce the culture of this most valuable PLANT in Ceylon ... perhaps the offer would take." Nothing came of the proposal until, in 1839 and 1840, Dr Wallich sent some of the Assam seeds he now espoused to the botanic gardens at Peradeniya, near Kandy, as it was thought that tea might be a "new and profitable speculation" and "a valuable source of Revenue". By 1842 small batches of Assam plants were being cultivated on a trial basis on one or two coffee plantations and one planter, Maurice Worms, had brought seeds back to Ceylon from a trip to China.

The highly successful coffee planters of Ceylon, who by mid-century were second in the world after Brazil in terms of amount grown, sent Arthur Morice to the tea districts of India in 1866 to investigate the potential for tea growing. Until the coffee blight of 1869 struck there had never been more than a few hundred acres under tea in Ceylon. Morice's report contained two recommendations that have been the partial salvation of today's Ceylon tea business: that Assam seed should be used and that Ceylon should concentrate on quality tea grown at altitude. The report also reflected the warning to Morice from another planter who had made the same trip 15 years earlier: "in his inquiries as to the profits to be derived from this scheme, let him be careful to distinguish between the money that has been made in Assam by Estate jobbing and by bonafide tea planting". Perhaps in this spirit of cynicism about the tea business, the prosperous coffee planters, little imagining the disaster that awaited them, dismissed almost *en passant* Morice's report and his belief that there was "every possibility of tea being grown successfully in Ceylon". "Among subjects of *less* importance the Committee have to notice the publication, in the course of the year, of the report of the Tea Districts of India by the Commissioner of the Association, Mr Arthur Morice." Morice would shortly have the last laugh and for a time in the twentieth century Ceylon would become the world's largest exporter of tea.

For all these British-inspired developments on the Indian subcontinent, it is on the Dutch that the accolade must be bestowed for the first successful commercial tea cultivation outside the Chinese and Japanese empires. Tea seeds from Japan were planted at Buitenzorg in Java in 1824 on an experimental garden set up by the Dutch government, but they did not take. Slightly better results were obtained in 1826 from a small batch of China seed, but it was the impact of one man that changed the fortunes of tea cultivation in this Dutch colony. J.I.L.L. Jacobson, an Amsterdam tea merchant and taster, was sent by his government to Java in 1827 and there became the first, and one of the greatest, of the European cultivators of tea well before Bruce and other Britons began to grow it systematically in India. Jacobson made several trips in disguise to China to undertake the perilous role of tea spy and find out for himself exactly how the Chinese grew and processed tea. By 1832 his garden was growing and processing good China seed and using a number of skilled Chinese workers. As he wrote in his seminal and often quoted handbook of 1843: "The cultivation of tea in Java is carried on in the same spirit, and the manufacture every way the same as in China; but the manufacturing with more order and cleanliness."

Over the next 15 years Jacobson refined and developed tea cultivation in Java. In the light of his experience he produced a logically structured, meticulously detailed and entirely lucid manual on every aspect of tea production. Not only was he ahead of his rivals in the British Empire but much of what he wrote has stood the test of time. His misfortune was to be dependent on China seed, workmen and methods. Although he exploited these to the limit, he would have

been amazed at the revolution in output and quality that the replacement of China bushes in Java by those from Assam would effect by
the end of the nineteenth century.

Perhaps as a result of his observation of oolong manufacture in
China and Formosa Jacobson always left his leaf spread out in the
sun for 15–20 minutes before sending it to the leaf shed for
processing. This would have slowed the process of fermentation. Java
tea's good reputation for flavour may have been in part due to this.
Jacobson, who already knew that the difference between black and
green tea lay in the manufacture, also thought that the quality of the
soil was a determinant of flavour and his method of checking it could
certainly be described as down to earth: "it is not easy to taste the
earth itself; but notwithstanding, in first touching it with the tongue,
the taste is easily distinguished".

Java tea was mostly planted at heights above 3,500 feet, "where
the air is so cool Fahrenheit's thermometer at sunrise indicates 58
degrees in the morning and 74 degrees at two o'clock in the afternoon. On still higher elevations, even 5,000 feet and more, the tea
will be highly flavoured: but in lower districts the flavour deteriorates
in proportion as the situation is low."

There is one notable omission in Jacobson's handbook compared
with those written subsequently by planters in India and Ceylon:
there is no section on the habits and management of native labour.
Indeed there is hardly a mention of the subject anywhere in the narra-
tive. The few references to it are all positive, with none of the
animadversions of his British counterparts. "It is not advisable to
exercise too strict a superintendence over the people and come upon
them suddenly and by surprise, it does not answer in work of this
nature." That this may have been due to the different basis of native
employment will be examined further in Chapter Seven.

On the attractions of tea planting from the European manager's
point of view Jacobson was more expansive:

> For the planter as well as the people the cultivation of tea is an agree-
> able, and at the same time neat and clean work. With order,
> judgment, and good directions as well as proper use of the labor on
> hand, the plucking at proper time, and the paying of wages by

"tyams," not too greedy for a day's work. The work of the women and children should be encouraged by pay and not too cheap a price be given for the produce; all this together duly observed will make it an easy and profitable thing and the work will prove favorable. ... Above all the most favorable result will be felt a few years hence when Java tea, which is not like many of the China kinds mixed with flowers, herbs or injurious mineral colors, shall find everywhere a sale; when shipping and trade will still more flourish by it, and the enterprising capitalist, who yearly exports 30 to 40 millions of pounds of this produce, will meet his reward by hundred millions of florins.

And profitable it quickly was. The use of seed from Jacobson's nurseries had increased the 16,000lb grown in 1835 on one major garden alone to 200,000lb by 1841 and two million by 1859. By 1851 Dutch tea production was consistently, and sometimes hugely, profitable. The Dutch East Indies – modern Indonesia – was to prove a potent competitor to the British Empire in the tea markets of the world for the next 90 years.

CHAPTER THREE

The Chambers of Death

"When you drink tea," admonished the great preacher and scholar John Wesley (1703–91), "it has brought you near the chambers of death." This extravagant warning in *A Letter to a Friend Concerning Tea* (1748) arose from a disconcerting experience Wesley had as a pupil of Charterhouse School in 1719. There he "was a little surprised at some Symptoms of a Paralytick Disorder. I could not imagine, what should occasion that shaking of my Hand; till I observed it was always worst after Breakfast, and that if I intermitted drinking Tea for two or three Days, it did not shake at all." Although he had identified the apparent cause of the tremors and confirmed his diagnosis from the experience of others, Wesley continued to drink tea for another 27 years until, when working among the poor of London, he observed that an "abundance of the People ... laboured under the same, and many other Paralytick Disorders, and that in a much higher Degree; insomuch that some of their Nerves were quite unstrung; their bodily Strength was quite decay'd, and they could not go through their Daily Labour". Having established that they were not drinkers of alcohol (or said they were not) but drank only tea, he "immediately remembered my own Case; and after weighing the Matter thoroughly, easily gathered from many concurring Circumstances, that it was the same Case with them. I considered, What an Advantage would it be, to these poor enfeebled People, if they would leave off what so manifestly impairs their Health, and thereby hurts their Business also?" It might have been even more to their "advantage" if they had had more to eat! At Charterhouse Wesley had become convinced that the safest drink was "small", or weak, beer and now promoted its supposed virtues as a beneficial substitute for tea.

One consequence of his concern for the economic and social effects of tea drinking among the working class was that on 6 July 1748 he exhorted the members of his London Society, of whom there were about a hundred, to give up tea and devote the money saved to the relief of the poor. It is some measure of the scale of tea drinking among even temperate and abstemious people that, I calculate, within a year they had raised £1,000 by this self-denial. Nor was Wesley's motivation entirely based on personal experience; it may also have been in protest against the slavery by which tea's accompanying sugar was obtained. His own abrupt cessation of tea drinking resulted in a severe three-day bout of the withdrawal symptoms we shall consider later.

Like many another opponent of tea drinking, Wesley recommended its substitution by an infusion of herbs, though he had the sense not to be specific. A dozen years later, on the advice of his physician, he resumed tea drinking in moderation and his return to the fold was marked by Josiah Wedgwood's presenting him with the largest teapot in England at the time, which held a gallon of tea. No doubt he dispensed the reinstated brew to his reconverted ministers before they went out to preach. But in his advocacy of total abstention from alcohol he did not urge working people to drink tea in its place, possibly because he feared that it would make too big a hole in their meagre budgets. Massive tea-drinking sessions, involving many hundreds, sometimes thousands, would later become a feature of the temperance movement. Perhaps Wesley's physician had been influenced by the first attempt at an objective and scientific investigation into the effects of tea.

Early assessments of such effects, from Lu Yu to the beginning of the eighteenth century, tended to be hyperbolic and panegyric, though some of what appear to be their wilder claims have recently turned out to be true. By the time Lu Yu wrote his book, in the eighth century BC, tea was already well recognized by the Chinese as a treatment for many ailments. He commends it: "If one is generally moderate but is feeling hot or warm, given to melancholia, suffering from aching of the brain, smarting of the eyes, troubled in the four limbs or afflicted in the hundred joints, he may take tea four or five times. Its liquor is like the sweetest dew of heaven." Hyperactive children were to be given a mixture of tea and onion beards. If you are thirsty, Lu Yu suggests, then drink rice water; if melancholy or angry, take wine – surely unwise advice? "But if one would dispel an evening's unproductive lassitude, the meaning of 'drink' is tea." I am a little more doubtful about the cure for chronic skin ulcers: "Mix bitter tea and centipedes together. Roast them until there is a sweet odor and continue to cook until they disintegrate. Then pound and strain them and boil into a soup mixed with sweet herbs. Then wash the sores and apply the decoction." Gu Yuanching, author of *The Classification of Tea* (1541), claims that "tea helps quench the thirst, aids digestion, checks phlegm, wards off drowsiness, stimulates renal activity, improves eyesight and mental prowess, dispels boredom, and dissolves greasy foods".

In China, as tea became more widely and more cheaply available, its pleasurable and restorative role gradually became more important than its pharmacology. But it was its medicinal value that first commended it to the West, where it was for many years sold through apothecaries. Haji Mohammed told Ramusio in 1559 that the Chinese "take of that herb, whether dry or fresh, and boil it well in water. One or two cups of this decoction taken on an empty stomach removes fever, headache, stomach ache, pain in the sides or in the joints, and it should be taken as hot as you can bear it. He said, besides, that it was good for no end of other ailments which he could not remember but gout was one of them."

The eccentric Sir Kenelm Digby, in his *Book of Receipts* (1669), recommends a couple of egg yolks beaten up in a pint of tea if you "come home very hungry after attending business abroad and do not feel like eating a competent [substantial] meal". This concoction not only "satisfied all rawness of the stomach" but "flew all over the body and into the veins". Thirty years later John Ovington, chaplain to William III, told Queen Mary that tea "cures everything under the sun, from gravel [to] vertigo and corrects nauseous humours that offend the stomach, throwing off abundances of those crudities created in the body through excess". "This admirable drink," he adds – in what is surely the most erudite claim for a hangover cure – "reconciles men to sobriety, and may be deemed an anti-Circe, counter charming the enchanted cup, and changing the beast into a man."

Ovington may have been guided by the most influential book about tea of the next hundred years or so, Pechelin's *Theophilus bibaculus sive' de potus Theae dialogus* (1684). Joannes Pechelin, physician to the King of Denmark, argues that "tea abounds with a brisk, volatile salt which is very agreeable to our northern constitutions whose blood is naturally very heavy and sluggish". And Pechelin features again in Nahum Tate's "A Poem Upon Tea" (1702), where Queen Anne's Poet Laureate repeats the doctor's claim that tea "sweetens the Blood, revives the Heart, refreshes the Spirits, relieves the Brain, quickens Apprehension, strengthens Memory and preserves the just Temperament of Body and Mind". An even more minor poet, Adam Fergusson, attributed even greater miraculous powers to Anne's favourite tipple:

> *Celestial tea—a fountain that can cure*
> *The ills of passion, and can free from frowns,*
> *And sobs, and sighs, the disappointed fair.*

Yet a generation that suggests "a nice cup of tea" as the cure for every ill should not be too critical.

In the first half of the eighteenth century, with Wesley among the earliest protagonists, there was an outbreak of attacks on the pernicious effects of the rise of tea drinking among the "lower orders". This was, in part, an example of the tendency of the upper and middle classes to deplore the spread to the working classes of expensive habits which they had come to regard as marks of their social superiority but it was also prompted by a number of experiments which, albeit inspired by the new spirit of empirical scientific enquiry, might not have quite satisfied the rigours of modern methodology.

Jonas Hanway was something of an old curmudgeon. In 1756 he wrote one of the best-known attacks on tea, *Considered as Pernicious to Health, obstructing Industry and impoverishing the Nation*, in a 25-letter addendum to an exceedingly tedious account of a journey from Southampton to Kingston-upon-Thames. It is worth considering Hanway's diatribe at some length because he was no ignorant ranter but an adventurous and widely travelled man who was justly commemorated in Westminster Abbey for his many acts of philanthropy and charity. His main concern was for the children of the poor, foundlings, orphans and those sent up the narrow, soot-laden chimneys of London. (He also walked the city's streets for many years protected from rain by the first recorded umbrella and ignoring the jibes of passers-by who within 50 years would have adopted his practice.) Yet it was not for his many benefactions that he wished to be remembered, but for his opposition to tea. Long before it was needed he even devised his own epitaph: "*To* the remembrance of *the fair guardian spirits* of BRITAIN, Whose influence and example abolished the use of a *Chinese* drug called TEA; the infusion of which had been for many years drank in these realms and dominions, injuring the health, obstructing the industry, wasting the fortunes, and exporting the riches, of his *majesty's* liege subjects &c. &c."

Although Hanway undoubtedly had a very loud bee in his bonnet, the bonnet covered a considerable brain. Samuel Johnson, himself "a hardened and shameless tea drinker", considered him a serious enough opponent to indulge in a rare (Boswell says unique) personal riposte to another's publication. Hanway's argument is three-pronged: tea damages both mental and physical health, subverts both morals and national morale, and undermines the economy. The origin of his antipathy lay in personal experience: he suffered a severe stomach ache after drinking tea. In all probability Hanway's colic was caused by an excess of the slightly poisonous Prussian blue (ferric ferrocyanide), which the Chinese added to their tea to generate the colour that appealed to English consumers.

Like the German physician who thought the Chinese had wrinkled skins because they drank tea, Hanway confuses the effects of the tannin in tea with the very different tannin which was used to tan leather. He relied for his medical evidence on two sources: the celebrated if not medically very successful physician Dr Hales; and Dr Pauli, a German doctor whom he quotes, though not without a touch of the xenophobia that marks the whole discourse: "It is dessicative [sic], or in plain English, that it is of a very drying quality, and therefore ought by no means to be used after the fortieth year of life." He clearly enjoys regaling his lady correspondents with an account of Dr Hales's experiment in which he immersed the tail of a sucking pig in water at just under 46°C, after which the skin peeled away. From this he infers that, since tea is drunk at the same temperature, it must have the same effect on the human intestine. "You have seen how the hands of a washerwoman are shriveled by hot water … [so] after all do you imagine nature requires our drinking liquids even warmer than our blood?" With evangelical zeal to equal Wesley's, he asks why we need to drink anything except when we are thirsty. He concludes this part of his argument with some wit: "it is absolutely poisonous and if doctors spend too long debating its effects, you may depend on it the patient will be dead before the consultation breaks up, and I shall be entitled to a diploma."

Hanway concedes that tea may cure scurvy, but uses the concession as the bridge to a denunciation of the impact of such "hot liquors" on the nervous system which "occasions instantaneous trembling of the hands as well as cholics and low spirits; and how must it disorder the finer parts of the frame, when there is such visible effect [as] languishing, lassitude and sleeplessness?" He even bemoans the fact that it has made chambermaids less pretty. Although his comparison of the addictive effects of tea with those of opium and tobacco we now know to be ridiculous, he had a point when he described the contemporary tea drinker as "partly ignorant of the injury it does, and partly consenting to be injured" and added that thus "we become the slaves of custom". This concern about slavish devotion to tea was one that William Cobbett would take up 74 years later in his *Advice to Young Men*, but by then the anti-tea argument would have been lost.

In helping the poor, Hanway had seen for himself the terrible effect of the flood of cheap gin on women and children, so graphically satirized by Hogarth. So it seems odd that he should equate the modest stimulus of tea with this scourge. He goes further and denounces the combination of the two as worse. He believed that tea led to a higher incidence of suicide among its drinkers, and because the nurse had her attention focused on her bohea "the poor infant left neglected expires while she is sipping her tea". He deplores the fact that "servants down to the very beggars consider it their Magna Carta and will die by the sword or famine rather than *not* follow the example of their mistresses". But tea is permissible, he concedes, "for those choice spirits who soar above common mortals" – of whom Johnson presumably considered himself to be one. Hanway admits that "Tea, in a doctor's hands, may sometimes be used to more advantage than many drugs which load the shelves of apothecaries." However, some of the herbal remedies (ground ivy, for one) he recommends in place of tea would have given him more than stomach ache had he actually tried them. Hanway thought tea drinking had become such an epidemic that it could only be defeated by the example of "the better sort" in giving it up. It is a good illustration of how habits may undergo complete social reversal that gin, once drunk by the poor, is now the drink of the affluent middle class; and that tea, once confined to the salons and withdrawing rooms of the wealthy, is now the comforting drink of the poor as well.

Men do not escape Hanway's strictures, especially soldiers and sailors. Were the victors of Crécy and Agincourt, or the heroes who dyed the Danube with Gallic blood, the sons of sippers of tea? he scornfully demands. He goes on to attack those who argue that the great tonnage of shipping required to bring tea from India and the sugar to sweeten it from the West Indies will serve to train up seamen for time of war. He calculates that the saving by giving up tea could build and fit out a 74-gun ship of the line, though that calculation hardly squares with his main economic argument. For with spurious exactitude and at great length, Hanway calculates that the loss to the national economy is £2,691,665 and £3,041,666 if loss of labour is also calculated. He goes on to argue that tea consumption will make us lose the war against France by weakening our economy. Though he writes a deal of nonsense on the subject, he does once more put his finger on a real problem when he calculates, however incorrectly, that tea trading leads to a bullion drain of £300,000 a year. It would be this very problem that led in due course to the Opium Wars in the nineteenth century. To replace the revenue lost by abandoning tea drinking, Hanway also advocated a series of taxes to delight the wildest radical: on women's jewels, on coaches, gold and silver, on servants, periwigs and playing cards. Having stated his case, he concludes that it would be a "national reproach if we should suffer such evils, for so silly, so ridiculous gratification as the drinking of tea".

This was too much for the patience of the "Great Cham". As Boswell wrote, "Johnson's defence of tea against Mr. Jonas Hanway's violent attack upon that elegant and popular beverage, shows how very well a man of genius can write upon the slightest subject, when he writes as the Italians say, *con amore*: I suppose no person ever enjoyed with more relish the infusion of that fragrant leaf than Johnson." Johnson's review of Hanway's essay in the *Literary Magazine* is flagged as a humorous demolition job by his early warning that no justice can be expected from such an inveterate tea drinker. He suggests that Hanway finds chambermaids less easy on the eye because he is past the age when they might have an eye for him. He suggests that nervous disorders are not caused by tea drinking but by tea drinkers' habit of staying up all night playing cards and spending most of the day in bed and that the problem is not the "tea but the tea-table". Having had his fun, Johnson effectively concedes all Hanway's main points. Tea is not suitable for the working class because – though he can see no sign of it keeping them from their labour – it contains no food value and is a waste of their wages. It is a drain on bullion. It leads to smuggling. In short, if it does these things, "let us at once resolve to prohibit it for ever". Hanway, a man whose writings show him to have no sense of humour, is not mollified by Johnson's concession to his argument, but, furious at being mocked, writes an angry letter to the *Literary Magazine* which provokes Johnson into what Boswell regards as his only instance of personal riposte.

The debate about the effects of drinking tea conducted in this polemical and rumbustious way seems totally to have ignored the first serious attempt, in 1753, to examine the case scientifically. Dr Thomas Short first published his *Dissertation Upon Tea* in 1730, but it was the second edition of 1753 that attracted more attention, the subject being then more contentious. Short was provoked by the excessive praise of tea in the early eighteenth century, which he attributes to the cynical desire of merchants to "enhance their importations. ... Nor, as far as I can remember, have these authors proportioned its strength, quantities and use, to any distinct or designed purposes ... [I] wonder that out of so much as has been writ upon tea, we should find so little to the purpose." He was particularly incensed by Willem Ten Rhijn's "Japanick observations", which claim for tea the cure of some 20 ailments from "Acrimony of the Humours" to promoting "Kind Correspondence between both Sexes". Short complains that he "attempts not to give any rational Account *why* we may expect such extraordinary benefits from it, or what constitutions and Countries 'tis most agreeable to...". On the one hand there were those who speak of tea "as if t'was able to eradicate or prevent the spring of all diseases; and extol it to a degree that renders their panegyrics too near to satyr". Dr Waldsmich of Marburg dubs it "the universal panacea" and "leaves no chronical distemper unplucked up by the roots". On the other hand there are those who "impute the most pernicious consequences to it; accounting it no better than a slow, but efficacious poison, and a seminary of diseases".

Short then demands "due enquiry" in the spirit of the age. To appreciate how radical was the approach of Short and other empiricists of the Enlightenment, it is necessary to realize just how atrophied medical knowledge had become at that time. Until late in the eighteenth century medical theory was still based on the system of Hippocrates (460–377 BC) and Galen (born c. AD 130). Against this background Short carried out a very detailed series of experiments within the resources of his day in order to determine the composition of tea in terms of its constituent parts of "Air, Phlegm, Salt, Oil and Earth". (In this system, Air means the scent plants breathe; Phlegm means water; Oil is "soft and unctuous, its parts being entangled with one another cement and keep together the other principles; Salt gives solidity to bodies yet is dissolvable in water; Earth is the residual element that cannot be destroyed by fire or water"). He also examines the history and processing of tea, pointing out that the Chinese consider it "the balsam of life to the human machine" and that "Cannibal Tartars" use it as an aid to digestion after "a delicate dish of raw horse flesh". As for the fact that "The subtle Chinese have several ways to falsify tea", he does not see "what harm this cheat can do, except to such as have too elastic solids, and then the daily use must tend to stiffen the fibres, or contract the vessels more, or to them whose lungs are obstructed, or loaded with too much matter; wherein the person's life depends on the expectoration, and in these cases it may do much harm, first by crisping up the obstructed vessels, which should be relaxed; and secondly, by stopping the spitting, and loading the bronchial vessels."

Moreover, unlike most contemporary medical polemicists, Short does not neglect to take account of the role tea played in the British economy and urges his readers to consider well "what a superior figure this humble shrub makes in commerce, what an important article it is in the Traffick of the East India Companies, what a great revenue the duty upon the little crumbled leaf returns to the Crown of England whereby the general taxes are so much lessened to the Poor".

It is in this kind of balanced approach that Short foreshadows the analytic methods that would be applied to the subject in the second half of the twentieth century. There had been previous attempts at scientific enquiry, surprisingly by the French during their brief flirtation with tea. Louis XIV had ordered Nicolas de Blegny to investigate the medical effects of tea, which he did in *Le bon usage du thé du caffé et du chocolat pour la préservation & pour la guérison des maladies*, published in Paris in 1687 with lovely engravings. Again at the King's behest, in 1688 Philippe Dufour published his *Traités nouveaux et curieux du café, du thé et du chocolat*, which he modestly claims is "A work equally necessary for doctors and for all those who care for their health".

As we shall see, some of Short's conclusions were shrewdly prescient. One example is his acknowledgement that green tea can alleviate the symptoms of migraine:

... doubtless 'tis of special Service in Disorders of the Head, proceeding from cold and sluggish Causes, which so alter the mass of Blood, Lymph and Spirits, that they have not a free Course thro' the vessels of the Brain ... the Water thins, its Salts separate the sluggish Mass, they stimulate and invigorate the Vessels, increase the Celerity of the Blood's Motion, its Earth and Oil draw up and contract the relaxed inelastick Tubes, and dispose the slimy adhesive *Mucus* to be thrown back into the circulating mass and thereby widen the narrow, and open the obstructed vessels of the Brain. The

Fluids being thus disposed for Motion, and the vessels for action the different Cohesions of the first will be broken and expelled by proper Outlets: The Blood being thus thinned, 'tis fitter to pass all the Meanders, Windings and Circumvolutions of the Brain.

Two hundred and fifty years later researchers would establish that, by dilating the blood vessels, tea does indeed improve the flow of blood to the brain, lack of which causes migraine.

The processing of tea, Short rightly thought, altered its characteristics and effects. He deduced that green tea might cause "trembling and convulsive motion of the nerves" but once it is processed into bohea the leaves lose the ability to cause this "in the drying and rolling which expresses the clammy, yellowish, corrosive juice that causes these tremors; yea so corrosive sometimes is this juice that it excoriates the hands of the Roasters and Rollers". However, in this he was wrong, for processing increases the tremor-causing caffeine content.

Not all Thomas Short's successors were so precise. John Coakley Lettsom (1744–1815) was another in the long tradition of Quaker philanthropist-physicians whose science was sometimes coloured by their views on the virtues of abstinence and self-denial. If some of his conclusions about tea seem laughable today, he was in other respects an admirable man. When Lettsom was quite young his father died, leaving him well off. At once he returned to the sugar plantation in the British Virgin Islands where he had been born, to free all its slaves before returning to London, where he was already a celebrated and influential physician. In 1773 he would found the Medical Association of London, the first body in Britain to bring together members all three branches of medicine: physicians, surgeons and apothecaries (pharmacists); and he was involved in setting up the Royal Humane Society and other charitable ventures. He had obtained his MD in 1769 with a thesis entitled "The Natural History of the Tea Tree", which became influential when published in 1772 as a book. The attack on tea it encapsulated was a considerable act of altruism, for any reduction in tea drinking would lead to a reduction in the import of the sugar to put in it on which his own wealth was based.

Lettsom drew his conclusions from a series of experiments in which he injected the stomachs of frogs and dogs with varying doses of green and black tea of differing strengths. The frogs were paralysed by the black tea but not the green. No wonder Samuel Johnson called such experimenters as Lettsom and Hanway's favourite, Dr Hales, "doctors who extend the art of torture". In another experiment Lettsom immersed two identical pieces of beef, one in water and one in weak tea. When the former turned putrid well before the latter he inferred that tea was antiseptic. In this he was right, for tea can indeed be used for this purpose on mild abrasions and sore eyes.

Sensibly, he observed that "as the constitutions of mankind are various, the effects of this infusion must be different also, which is the reason so many opinions have prevailed upon the subject ... it requires no small share of sagacity to fix the limits of good and harm in the present case". After further experimentation he concludes from general observation that the strong and healthy are unaffected but the "less hardy and robust" after a tea breakfast "find themselves rather fluttered". Others have the same trembling effect in the afternoon and yet others are made sick and have stomach ache after a single sup. He also deduces that tea's negative effects are most evident in those of nervous disposition – though he conspicuously fails to test whether tea or nerves are the cause of the symptoms he observes. On the positive side, he thinks tea produces watchfulness "when drunk substantially" in the evening and that it "enlivens, refreshes and exhilarates". While proposing that it should not be given to children and young persons, he recommends it "after violent exercise or great fatigue". The action of tea, which "contains an active penetrating principle speedily exciting the action of the nerves", therefore depends on the constitution of the imbiber and the "fineness" of the tea. This reaction is diminished "by the addition of milk and sugar".

Lettsom also believed that the "pernicious habit [of drinking spirits] is often owing to the weakness and debility of the system brought on by the daily habit of drinking tea". On the basis of his work he advises that "It ought by no means to be the common diet of boarding-schools; if it be allowed sometimes as a treat, they should be at the same time informed that the constant use of it would be injurious to their health, strength, and constitution." While this is a little far-fetched, it is not actually risible. However, the cases he cites to illustrate his belief that breathing tea dust will cause spitting of blood are ludicrous and can only have been based on hearsay and gossip. In one he reports that a tea broker called Marsh, having breathed in the aroma of a greater than usual number of chests of tea, was afflicted with "giddiness, headache, universal spasms and loss of speech and memory" and, despite a brief remission, died from "effluvia of tea". Another broker, he claimed, died from the same cause despite bleeding and electric-shock treatment, though he is honest enough to admit it might have been the shocks that killed him.

Finally, he turns to the Chinese to illustrate his thesis, claiming that they are "pusillanimous, cunning, extremely libidinous, effem-inate, vengeful and dishonest" because of generations of tea drinking. He adds as an afterthought that "it would be unjust to ascribe all these qualities to their manner of living".

Lettsom was lampooned in a popular limerick of the day which is often attributed to the victim of it himself – in which case he had a better sense of humour than Hanway:

> When any sick to me apply
> I physics, bleeds and sweats 'em,
> If after that they chose to die,
> What's that to me I Lettsom.

From time to time during the nineteenth century further occa-sional but less frenzied criticisms of tea re-emerged. William Cobbett, in *The Cottage Economy* (1822), thought tea would "render the frame feeble, and unfit to encounter hard labour or severe weather". *The Tea Cyclopaedia* (1881) warned: "It is not an uncommon practice with ardent students, when pushing their studies far into the night, to resist the claims of nature for repose, and keep themselves awake by the frequent use of tea. That it answers the purpose at the time cannot be denied, but the object is often attained at a fearful price, the destruction of health and vigour both of mind and body being the penalty." Such criticisms, however, were by now nearly always made in a more balanced context which recognized the multiple influences that might be the cause of nervous disorders hitherto attributed to tea. The same publication pointed out: "It would perhaps be more just to attribute the increase of such complaints to the more complicated state of our social relations, arising from an augmented population, and an advance in luxury, with the more frequent infringement of the natural laws, particularly turning night into day, and not seldom day into night ... ." The argument had already been won by tea's advocates, even if they were not certain why. As a contributor to the *Edinburgh Review* in 1890 put it, "though very palatable to those who [first] had the courage to taste it; resisted as it encroached; abused as its popularity seemed to spread; and establishing its triumph at last, in cheering the whole land from the palace to the cottage, only by the slow and restless efforts of time and its own virtues".

It was the setting up of scientific research stations by the tea industry itself early in the twentieth century that initiated the next major advance in understanding the medical effects of tea drinking and precisely what its virtues were. Although these institutions were primarily intended to apply a rigorous scientific analysis to the problems of growing tea, during their analysis of the constituents of the tea leaf more also came to light about the probable consequences of drinking the infusion. From the latter part of the twentieth century to the present day there has been a great expansion of research into the medical effects of tea drinking and related subjects. This growth has been driven both by the growth in scientific research generally, with large numbers of postgraduate students and new PhDs needing research subjects, and by the Western obsession in an age of the diseases of prosperity with personal health, particularly as it relates to diet. So, with the caveat that future scientific advances may make our conclusions as unsound as we now know some of those of earlier investigations to have been, let us try to summarize what we know about tea drinking today. Like Dr Thomas Short, we must start with the plant itself.

A tea leaf contains some four hundred chemical elements. Of these the three most important to the tea drinker are the polyphenols, or flavonids (which give its curative powers and astringency); caffeine, also known in the context of tea as theine (which gives its "kick"); and the essential oils which provide the distinctive smell and flavour. Freshly plucked tea also contains a dozen or so vitamins, of which the most significant are B2 (Riboflavin), C and E. Vitamin C has an important role in the relief of stress and vitamin E in slowing down the natural process of ageing. It is the degree of fermentation that is allowed to take place during the manufacture of raw tea into leaves that determines the respective concentrations of caffeine, polyphenols and vitamin C in the teacup. Fermentation trebles the concentration of caffeine in black tea but greatly reduces the concentration of polyphenols and vitamin C which are greater in the less stimulating green tea. Citric juice in black tea will make up for its loss of vitamin C.

The most prevalent inorganic elements in tea are potassium, calcium, phosphorus, magnesium and iron, though they are present in only tiny quantities. Drinking very strong black tea can actually cause potassium loss, which is why the Uzbeks, who like their tea very black indeed, eat with it dried fruit, which is rich in potassium. Among the other inorganic constituents there are minute quantities of zinc and copper. The latter plays a key role in the enzyme oxidization of the polyphenols. It is the enzymes and the polyphenols in the untreated leaf, and the extent to which they are retained in processing, that largely determine the quality of the tea in the cup. A tea leaf is about 25 per cent solids (mostly wood fibre and cellulose) and 75 per cent water (in which the polyphenols and caffeine are in solution). It is the latter two with which we are chiefly concerned.

We now know that caffeine, thought even late in the nineteenth century to be present in only three or four plants, is present in over 60. Several of these plants, besides tea, are widely used in infusions. Until fairly recently research into the medical effects of tea was often defensive and focused mainly on the possible deleterious effects of caffeine. The 1970s and 1980s saw the indictment of caffeine on numerous charges. It stood accused of causing "hypertension, infantile hyperactivity, osteoporosis, kidney and bladder stone formation, impairment of fertility, insomnia, diabetes mellitus, cardiovascular related illness and breast cancer". It was also labelled an addictive drug. Research papers on the subject of caffeine alone were appearing at a rate of some two hundred a year.

In 1989 the United States Research Council acquitted caffeine on all counts, finding that "tea drinking has not been associated with an increase in the risk of any chronic disease". The verdict, nevertheless, came with the stern rider that caffeine must not be taken in excessive amounts if it was to retain its innocence. The problem is to define what is an excessive amount. The numerous papers studied give an acceptable daily dose ranging from 300mg to 500mg. The normally beneficial range is probably between 300mg and 400mg daily, 370mg being the level at which the Institute for the Study of Drug Dependency noted withdrawal symptoms when intake was abruptly stopped. It is clear from the research in question that an individual's position on the acceptable intake scale is also governed by such factors as body mass, metabolism, circulatory health, age, gender and any tendency to stress and hypertension.

Infused tea contains between 32mg and 42mg of caffeine per 150ml (a politely filled teacup or half a brickie's mugful), depending on the leaf used and the length of time it is infused. There is a paradox here in that, although a longer infusion releases more caffeine, it also increases the levels of polyphenols that balance caffeine's effect. As a consequence of this balance, while the initial impact of a cup of tea will be stimulating, this will be followed by a calming effect, which does not happen with coffee. Caffeine also speeds up the heart rate and metabolism, stimulates large muscles and the central nervous system, aids peristalsis and can lower body temperature by dilating blood vessels. (I can vouch for the latter effect. When I was struck down by heat exhaustion on the edge of the Great Salt Desert in Persia, as it then was, local villagers revived me by making me drink endless glasses of hot, sweet, black tea while bathing the back of my neck with cold water.)

It is also important to distinguish between the effect of the caffeine in a cup of tea and that in a cup of coffee. Although on average 1lb of leaf tea contains twice as much caffeine as 1lb of coffee beans, because of the way drinks made from them are prepared a cup of coffee will contain roughly twice as much caffeine as a similarly sized cup of tea. Moreover, coffee releases its caffeine in a sudden short burst whereas in tea the release is more gradual and prolonged. To draw an analogy, it is the difference between giving a horse a crack on the hindquarters with the whip to make him bound briefly ahead and delivering a series of sharp taps with the heels to keep him going steadily forward. It is for this reason that pharmaceutical companies have recently been coming up with slow-release synthetic-caffeine drugs for people doing jobs that require lengthy periods of sustained alertness and vigilance, both of which are greatly improved by caffeine. Many traffic and other accidents, for example those involving machinery, are the result of tiredness, which as a cause of such accidents comes second only to alcohol, so it is better when taking a break on a long drive to have two or three cups of tea than the traditional cup of black coffee. The British worker's much-derided tea break actually contributes both to improved performance and to greater safety.

The consequence of taking more caffeine than can be comfortably tolerated may be extremely unpleasant and in a few cases even dangerous. The symptoms of caffeine overdose are increased anxiety, nervousness, irritability, insomnia and poor concentration. Oddly, these symptoms, together with tremors, nausea and vomiting, are also symptoms of sudden caffeine deprivation, as John Wesley discovered when he wrote that his head ached for three days and he was continually half-asleep. By Wednesday of the third afternoon of abstinence from his usual copious intake of tea, his memory had failed completely and he sought a remedy in prayer. The next day all his symptoms vanished. He was a cured man and a classic example of the fallacy of *post hoc ergo propter hoc*.

However, while caffeine is the most widely used drug that affects behaviour, as psychologists define behaviour, it should not be confused with addictive drugs in general. There is an important difference between dependence and addiction. "Caffeine does not share with the common drugs of abuse the ability to stimulate functional activity and dopamine release in the shell of the nucleus accumbens, the anatomical substrate of addiction." Or, in lay language, you are unlikely to get "hooked", although it may be briefly unpleasant to give up caffeine, whether in tea, coffee, cola or any other caffeine-containing drink taken regularly. Depending on the individual, a sensible daily intake of tea is no more than 8–10 teacups, or four or five mugfuls. An empirical approach is the only sensible one: drink as much as makes you feel good in particular circumstances and no more. This approach isn't recommended with coffee, however, as drinking a lot can energize you at the time but the jitters and insomnia may well follow.

Far less controversial is another medically significant constituent of tea, the polyphenols, of which tea accounts for more than half of the average Briton's intake. Green tea is one of the best sources of polyphenols, though they are also present in lesser quantities in black tea. There is increasing evidence that, by their antioxidant ability to counter the appearance of free radicals in the blood, polyphenols contribute considerably to protection against a wide variety of cardiovascular diseases and cancers. Free radicals are blood platelets that damage and destroy cells and enzymes and can even alter DNA. The antioxidant property of polyphenols enables them in turn to destroy free radicals and also, to some extent, to repair damaged cells; and by raising the white blood-cell count they also improve the body's ability to counter infection. Polyphenols are found in various vegetables and fruits – notably onions, lettuce, oranges, apples and grapes – and in red wine as well as in tea.

Among the many ills that flesh is heir to, heart disease and cancer are the two most fatal in the Western world and tea has a prophylactic role to play in both. Less destructive, but still debilitating, ailments in which the role of tea is significant are obesity and digestive problems, respiratory illness, dental health and fatigue. In recent years a substantial body of research has demonstrated that both green and black tea, in different measure in different circumstances, have a considerable contribution to make in combating all of these. There is a growing body of evidence that black tea in particular reduces the risk of blood clotting, high blood pressure and blood cholesterol, all of which can lead to heart attack and stroke. *A Systematic Review of the Effects of Black Tea* carried out by King's College London explains that, by preventing oxidation of LDL ("bad") cholesterol, regular consumption of tea appears to reduce the risk of heart attack by 11 per cent. Moreover, the high potassium level of green tea and its low sodium level make it a beneficial drink for sufferers from hypertension, though these same patients are also vulnerable to excessively high levels of caffeine.

Cancer-causing cell mutations can be blocked by the anti-mutagenic polyphenols in tea. There is substantial evidence from Japan to show that a high regular intake of green tea has reduced the incidence of stomach cancer in the population studied and Australian research indicates that in regular drinkers of both black and green tea the onset of papillomas and skin cancer is deferred. There is also evidence that black tea can reduce the incidence of lung and breast cancer in those on high-fat diets. On the downside, there have been claims that drinking very hot tea might lead to cancer of the oesophagus. However, if tea has been properly infused for long enough its temperature will have fallen well below any possible danger level: a warning, perhaps, to the "mash the tea bag in boiling water for 15 seconds" school of tea makers.

The psychological satisfaction derived from caffeine has been well established. Early morning, tea-in-bed drinkers from Boswell to Tony Benn have experienced the special "lift" that the first cup gives. This is why so called "breakfast tea" is blended to contain more caffeine than most others. This "lift" is due to caffeine's ability to release dopamine in part of the brain, which could account for the lower suicide rate in one group of women studied and the lower incidence of Parkinson's in another. As one researcher demonstrated, "Habitual caffeine consumption can clearly improve mood and not worsen depressive disorder." We have also already noted the anti-hypnotic effect of the caffeine in tea. Sleepiness is caused by the accumulation of adenosine in the brain, and tea prolongs wakefulness because its caffeine occupies the adenosine receptors. Nor, as far as can be ascertained, does caffeine consumption during the day adversely effect normal sleep quality.

There are a number of other areas in which tea has a useful role to play in maintaining good health. There are, for example, minute amounts in tea of theophylline, a drug used in the treatment of asthma as it opens up the bronchioles, the constriction of which can cause breathlessness. Too much theophylline, on the other hand, can lead to stomach ache and nausea.

Fluoride keeps teeth healthy and combats osteoporosis, but few households even in Britain have fluorided water and in any case black tea contains at least three times and green tea six times more fluoride than is in treated water. Some people even use a mouthwash of green tea as an effective antidote to bad breath.

Tea can be a useful aid to those trying to lose weight, for an ordinary cup of tea has only four calories, though if sugar and milk are added it will have much more. There also seems to be some evidence that tea emulsifies fats in the digestive tract and so helps to burn off the yellow fat that contributes to weight gain. The polyphenols in tea also assist digestion and can be used to treat diarrhoea, though an excess of tea can cause constipation.

Moderate tea drinking is a valuable part of a healthy lifestyle. I would recommend dividing tea consumption roughly equally between green and black tea to get the optimum health benefit; but claims for its efficacy as a cure-all must be tempered by the reality of medical research. In our irrational age are we simply looking to tea for yet another miracle cure? Or have we largely proved, by rigorous scientific analysis, that much of what the enthusiasts of the seventeenth and eighteenth centuries claimed on the basis of instinct and general observation is indeed true? In our present state of knowledge it is reasonable to state that drinking tea, green or black according to the appropriateness of each, contributes significantly to human health. Modern research has shown that tea plays a positive role in protecting those who drink it from several cardiovascular diseases, a range of cancers, some neurological diseases such as epilepsy, Parkinson's disease and possibly Alzheimer's; that it combats obesity and hypertension, strengthens teeth and bones, and is mildly antiseptic. Because of its dual caffeine and polyphenol action it both reinforces long-term alertness and wakefulness and has a simultaneous calming effect. In short, tea was and is good for us. Whether, until recent times at least, it was good for the peoples of the Far East, India, Ceylon and East Africa whom we compelled to supply it to us is another question.

CHAPTER FOUR

The Rights of Englishmen

It is curious that the 50 or 60 young men at the "Boston Tea Party" of December 1773 should have chosen to dress up as Red Indians to protest against what they saw as an act of tyranny and oppression. After all, their fellow countrymen, as they spread westward, were busy oppressing and butchering those very same despised native Americans with little protest from any quarter, British or Colonial. The motive could not have been to prevent identification of those taking part, for the war paint and feathers and burnt cork were but perfunctorily applied and many a participant in the aftermath would proudly "remember, with advantages, what deeds he did that day". Bostonians, royalist and republican alike, knew not only who had carried out the sabotage but who had incited them to it. There is one possible ironic explanation: the party-goers had no other way to set themselves apart as Americans rather than British colonists.

It is a mistake to think of the America of the 1760s as a united nation. The frontiersmen of the West despised the "civilized" Easterners; Episcopalians and dissenters scorned each other's beliefs; the enfranchised, fewer than 10 per cent of the colonists, were resented by the disenfranchised; an anglicized aristocracy looked down on would-be democrats; the provinces, themselves usually at loggerheads over many issues, were run by a small plutocracy of planters, landowners and merchants at the expense of small farmers and labourers and a growing urban underclass; republicans and royalists differed on the proper relationship of their colonies to the mother country. Most divisive of all was the inevitable isolation of one province from another as a result of distance, topography and poor communications.

They had been briefly united in opposition to the Stamp Tax on newspapers and legal documents imposed in 1765 in what the British Parliament saw as a reasonable measure to finance a mere third of the cost of administering the colonies and defending their frontiers from Spanish and French threats and native attacks. In similar vein, the Mutiny Act had earlier given the authorities the right to levy supplies and quarter troops on the civilian population whenever and wherever they needed to do so, and though this was subsequently modified to exempt private citizens, it remained a source of indignation. Nevertheless, the great majority of influential colonists were relieved when a combination of Benjamin Franklin's charm and eloquence and Lord Rockingham's common sense resulted in the repeal of the Stamp Act in 1766. On to this temporary resolution of the tension between Americans' material interests and their loyalty to the Crown there had been deliberately tacked a Declaratory Act which asserted the right of Parliament to tax the colonies. "Parliament assembled, had, hath, and of right ought to have, full power and authority to make laws and statutes of sufficient force and validity to bind the colonies and all the people of America ... in all cases whatsoever." At the time it suited both parties to play down the implication. While the previous impositions had been widely resented they had affected directly only a relatively small part of the colonial population.

Tea was quite a different matter.

It is difficult to say when tea was first drunk in significant quantities in America. Because the East India Company could sell its tea only through London merchants, and because the records of many of these are now lost, those early shipments to North America cannot be individually traced. However, it seems highly likely that tea was among the earliest commodities shipped by the Dutch in the first half of the seventeenth century to their settlement at New Amsterdam. Certainly, not long after that city became the British colony of New York in 1674, it was a fashionable drink in tea gardens modelled on those in London, and the habit of tea drinking had spread throughout the wealthier classes of America before the end of the century. By the late 1750s the use of tea, along with coffee, was widespread among all but the poorest colonists. It was particularly appreciated as a light, compact, refreshing stimulant by those pushing out new frontiers while trekking across little explored America. Lettsom, in his *A Natural History of the Tea Tree* (1799), quotes a contemporary professor thus: "Where the water is unfit for use ... in such cases it is very pleasant when boiled and tea is drank with it; and I cannot sufficiently describe the fine taste it has in such circumstances ... on such journeys tea is found to be almost as necessary as victuals."

To avoid the high British import duty passed on to the American consumer by the London merchant, most of the tea drunk in America was smuggled in from Holland. Light, high value, undistinguishable once in pot and caddy from "legal" tea – and in any case easily provenanced by forged customs documents bought for a modest bribe from venal customs officers – tea was an ideal candidate for smuggling. No accurate measure can be made of the amount of contraband involved, but estimates in America itself put the proportion at between 75 and 96 per cent of the total. A reasonable guess based on official import figures is that a million to a million and a quarter pounds were drunk annually in America in the 1750s, of which less than a quarter was legally imported. By the 1760s the proportion of smuggled tea had declined, partly because of a steady fall in prices on the London market, and partly because the stricter enforcement of the "Acts of Trade", designed to confine the trade of the colonies to merchant ships of the mother country, greatly reduced the presence of continental vessels, smugglers among them, in colonial ports.

Then, in January 1767, Charles Townshend, Chancellor of the Exchequer in the administration of Pitt the Elder, finding himself in charge in the absence of his sick and gouty leader, introduced three simultaneous measures that would light the fuse of revolution. First, to save money, he cut the size of the British Army in America and withdrew much of the remainder to the more economic but less pertinent safety of the East Coast. This not only further alarmed pioneers and settlers confronted with savage Indian resistance to their incursions but weakened the capacity of the British government to impose its will throughout the colony. Secondly, by suspending the New York Colonial Assembly until it should recognize the supremacy of the Westminster Parliament, Townshend made it clear that the authority of such assemblies must in all things be subordinate to a Parliament which could close them at will. Thirdly, to replace the £130,000 a year lost by the repeal of the Stamp Act, he imposed excise duties on glass, paper, lead and painters' colours and – most onerously – on tea. The revenue thus raised was intended to defray in part the cost of civil and military administration in the colony. In reality, once the expense of collecting the tax had been deducted, there was practically nothing left in the kitty.

The Townshend tax prompted a widespread boycott of British merchandise throughout the colony. Imports were either put into store unsold or, in a few instances, shipped straight back across the Atlantic by patriotic Americans. Tea could not be dealt with in this way. Held in store, it would go mouldy and useless after a few months. Once it was taken out of the customs shed, the duty would have to be paid by the consignee. The option of returning it to Britain was not then open since it would have been confiscated on arrival and the original consignee held liable to the East India Company for its value. In practice, little or no glass or paper was shipped from Britain owing to the fragility of the one and the susceptibility to damp of the other. As cargo, lead was heavy and painters' colours of marginal importance, so both were equally unattractive as freight. In any case the colonists were perfectly capable of producing all of these for themselves. Tea they could not. This addictive commodity could only be obtained by breaking the law through smuggling or by paying over the odds resentfully because it was taxed. Tea came to be so equated with injustice that the rule of law was weakened in a country where military and civil resources were now quite inadequate to impose it without the willing consent of the people.

Townshend was no fool, so it is likely that he was quite willing, even eager, to provoke the anger of the despised colonists in order to win the plaudits of his wealthy and aristocratic friends in England. For appearance's sake and to win over the House of Commons, he argued that these were all external taxes and therefore compatible with the premise that Franklin had defined when urging the repeal of the Stamp Act, namely that Parliament might levy dues on items entering the country but not raise taxes within the country without the concurrence of the colonial Assemblies. That the new taxes were levied in America on Americans to pay for a colonial administration of Americans in which they had no say not unreasonably inclined the colonists to see them in a different light. Having lit the fuse to this particular charge (the Bill was enacted on 13 May 1767), Townshend, conveniently perhaps for such an egotist, died on 4 September, before he could see the mess the explosion made.

Only two months after Townshend's threepenny tax on a pound of tea became operative, Parliament also passed an Indemnity Act whereby the East India Company, and thus the London tea merchants, would be reimbursed the import duty paid on any tea re-exported to the colonies. The price of tea dropped 25 per cent to 2s. 1d. a pound, the smugglers were undercut and the amount of "legal" tea imported to America rose to around half a million pounds in weight in 1767 and to 869,000lb in 1768. Probably a quarter to a third as much again continued to be smuggled.

This growth in tea imports came about despite an enthusiastic campaign against the use of "foreign" tea, by which the campaigners meant British rather than the identically sourced Dutch. The idea of a boycott was probably put forward in late 1767 on the initiative of William Johnson, Connecticut's man in London, and was eagerly taken up in America and sustained by a multitude of rallies, petitions and printed exhortations of every kind from quasi-learned articles to the most dreadful doggerel. The campaign was two-pronged. Like their anti-tea exemplars in eighteenth-century England, the American opponents of tea fulminated against its toxic properties. Tea was bad for the nerves, bad for the stomach and bad for the (political) constitution. The second prong of the fork was to urge the patriotic virtue of abstaining from tea drinking by replacing it with such locally derived concoctions as Hyperion or Liberty Tea, Yaupon and Labradore. Society leaders, mainly women, would sign and publish petitions in the press declaring that they would no longer "conform to the pernicious habit of drinking tea until such time as all Acts that tend to enslave our native country shall be repealed".

That the campaign had relatively little initial success was due to a number of factors. First and foremost was the mildly addictive nature of tea itself. As we saw in the previous chapter, there are unpleasant, if not medically serious, withdrawal symptoms on suddenly ceasing to drink tea. Abstinence was not easy. As one commentator observed in 1769, "as to our people giving up tea, it is really a joke. It would be full as reasonable to imagine they will cease to drink New England Rum or Cyder." His analogy with another addictive substance, alcohol, was perhaps more pertinent than he realized.

Secondly, the alternative infusions suggested are truly disgusting to all but the greenest palate. Hyperion, brewed from dried raspberry-vine leaves, smells of old, damp dish cloths and has an insipid taste which modern herbalists have to pep up with ginger and apple. Yaupon (*Ilex vomitoria*) has unfortunate emetic and purgative effects; and the famed Labradore (*Ledum latifolium*) is so astringent it is used by the Russians for tanning leather. Labradore is, in fact, an *Erica* whose leaves are slightly poisonous to animals and although some find it spicy its bitter taste puts me in mind of an infusion of old socks. You had to be stout-hearted indeed willingly to swallow these particular patriotic medicines. Moreover, because none of them contained caffeine, these infusions lacked the stimulating effect of a good cup of tea. The objectors would have been better off drinking hot water or, as many of them did who could afford it, coffee. (All these observations are based on personal experiment and though I detected no anti-somnific effect from them, one analysis suggests raspberry leaves may contain minute amounts of caffeine.)

Thirdly, in many areas it was still possible to obtain smuggled Dutch, Swedish or French shipped tea and here it was possible for Americans "*not* to have their tea and drink it". As Thomas Hutchinson, merchant son of the Governor of Boston, put it in an indignant letter to the Secretary for the Colonies in England, "tea from Holland may lawfully be sold. It is a high crime to sell any from England." Finally, while many considered the Townshend taxes "an infringement of our common rights as *Englishmen*" (italics added), there remained a significant minority who grumbled but, as subjects still loyal to the Crown, paid up and reluctantly conceded Parliament's right to tax them if it wished.

Numerous American merchants, who would have suffered from a fully effective boycott, were able to continue to trade profitably while pleading reluctant obligation to the British Crown. Richard Clarke, a leading Boston merchant, pointed out that dutied tea had been imported for several years and that this "small branch of the Revenue" was negligible compared with the duty levied on wine, sugar and molasses, which also went to pay for the civil and military administration. His views were not uncommon. A supporting letter from a local shopkeeper in the *Boston Newsletter* pointed out that a well-known "patriot" had just bought a pound of Bohea at the not inconsiderable price of 4s. 6d. The same grocer vowed to keep on selling taxed tea and even offered to provide the next town-protest meeting with a list of the "patriotic gentlemen and ladies" who continued to buy it. As another merchant succinctly put it, "tea is as necessary in our business as any one thing".

March 1770 was a momentous month on two counts in the affair of tea and America. By now the implication of the Townshend duties had percolated even to the most remote corners of the colonies and the general boycott of British imports that had come into effect in April 1769 was beginning to hurt the merchants of the home country. By the end of that year it had already hit the East India Company in the pocket. If the trade in the other Townshend items was relatively small and its effect spread widely among British business interests, the impact on legitimate tea trading was deep and focused on a single, highly influential concern. By 1769 the volume of taxed tea landed in New York had dropped from the previous year's 350,000lb to 17,000lb and by 1770 to 147lb. In Philadelphia the story was the same; 1769's 112,000lb became a mere 65lb in 1770.

Not surprisingly, the matter came up for debate again in Parliament with the suggestion that all the Townshend duties be repealed. Grafton's Ministry had succeeded Chatham's in October 1768 and it was not long before its more enlightened members realized that the conflict with the colonists over the Townshend tax was both absurd and commercially damaging for "so petty a sum in the eyes of a financier, so insignificant an article as tea in the eyes of a philosopher".

Grafton himself was in favour of repealing all the duties, but in Lord North he had a Chancellor of the Exchequer as stubborn and anti-colonist as Townshend had been vain and anti-colonist. North conceded the minor items but insisted on the more stringent application of the tax on tea in the light of the illegal and riotous response to it in America. He claimed that, while he had once been in favour of its repeal, now, when Parliament's right to tax was being repudiated, was "the properest time to exert our right of taxation. The properest time for making resistance is when we are attacked". As Thomas Pownall, an experienced colonial administrator in America (at the time MP for Tregony, in Cornwall, and author in 1764 of the influential treatise *The Administration of the Colonies*), pointed out in the debate, there were Americans who wanted the tax to remain because by encouraging substitution it would further encourage independence. Moreover, it was clear that the tea boycott at least was now highly effective and unless the duty on it were removed the entire trade would be lost to the Dutch. Repeal of the duties would restore British commerce without yielding anything in principle since the right to tax had been clearly set forth in the Declaratory Act and exercised by the levying of the tax on sugar, molasses and other goods. North was not convinced.

It was a Mexican stand-off, with even those willing to repeal the Townshend duty unable to win the argument while the colonists continued to defy Parliament, and with the American colonists too far committed to the boycott to back off until the duty was repealed. Even so, the retention of the tea tax was passed by only a single vote in a cabinet meeting, so closely divided was opinion on the proper relationship of England with its turbulent colony.

With the repeal of all but one of the duties, the American patriots, as they styled themselves, were in a quandary. Should they proclaim the boycott a success or continue to fight on for total victory? The matter was largely taken out of their hands by the willingness of a majority of American merchants, hard pressed by the losses incurred in sustaining the exclusion, to resume importing the wide range of British goods on which their prosperity still largely depended. By mid-October 1770 the boycott was virtually over, though in those places that still had access to tea smuggled from Holland British tea was bought in only small quantities. In 1771 legal tea imports rose substantially once more. Even in loud-mouthed Boston they increased sixfold in that year. Right across the board something very like normal trade was resumed between Britain and America over the next two years.

The renewal of imports exacerbated the differences and divisions among the colonists, but poor intelligence left London-based polit-icians largely unaware of the situation. The irony is that, had the tea tax been repealed after the lapse of sufficient time for Parliament to make its point, much of the force would have been taken out of the incipient rebellion. As Dr Samuel Cooper wrote to Benjamin Franklin in January 1771: "Should Government be so temperate and just as to place us on the old ground on which we stood before the Stamp Act, there is no danger of us rising in our demands." However, it was decided to try to enforce the collection of the tea tax more rigorously; and this, coupled with the corruption of many customs officers and the alternative supply of smuggled tea, led to attacks on George III's officials, and the burning and destruction of his vessels and buildings. This growth of mob rule, of which we shall see more later, was trans-formed into resistance against tyranny by the rhetoric of revolutionary leaders, such as Sam Adams: the arch rabble-rouser who tousled his hair and donned worn-out clothes to make the common folk of the mobs he incited more readily identify with him.

On 5 March 1770, three thousand miles away from the heated but bloodless exchanges in Parliament, occurred a relatively minor incident that would serve Adams and his fellow radicals as a well-managed pretext for a gradual change in mood among Americans. As in so many international crises, the germ of this one lay in a rela-tively trivial incident. A lone sentry guarding the Boston Custom House was mocked, abused and pelted by a jeering crowd. Panicking as the crowd grew larger, he called out the guard. In the confusion, by accident or design – no one knows by which side – a musket was loosed off. Incensed, the mob charged the soldiers, who no less incontinently fired upon it, killing five people, one of them a black man. One of the mortally wounded was reputed to have declared on his deathbed that "he had seen mobs in Ireland, but never knew troops bear so much without firing as these had done".

The colonists of Boston in particular were skilfully played upon with masterly rhetoric by Adams. "A colonist cannot make a button, a horseshoe, nor a hobnail but some sooty ironmonger or respectable button-maker of Britain shall bawl and squall that his honour's worship is most egregiously maltreated, injured, cheated and robbed by the rascally American Republicans." The alliteration, the qualifying adjectives, the mounting string of insult, the sarcasm – tricks of the inflammatory orator of any age – Adams employed to utmost effect. He was, in fact, a man of perfectly respectable, middle-class origins whose cousin, John Adams, a far more moderate and balanced person, would also become an iconic figure of the American struggle for independence. No less significantly, Sam had a genius for political organization. Recognizing that the imperial power could best rule by dividing, he saw that the lack of links between the provinces, and thus of any common purpose, was the greatest obstacle to revolution. He had overcome the obstacle by using the brief unity of opposition to the Stamp Act and the Mutiny Act to initiate the Committees of Correspondence that were to be as critical to the success of the struggle for independence as the sense of grievance. Through these Committees an embryonic system of organization and communication was established throughout the American colonies that was to become in due course the nerve-system for coordinated rebellion.

Order was soon restored. The soldiers involved – whose defence, with a nice touch of irony, was conducted by John Adams – were tried and acquitted of the grounds that they had acted in self-defence. This was a verdict with which most Americans concurred. Such niceties were of little concern to Sam Adams, and the unscrupulous demagogue made sure that under the apparent calm a growing anger festered. Had it not been for what, over the following three years, he repeatedly called the "Boston massacre", he might well not have been able to whip up the citizens of that town in December 1773 to be any more intransigent about the East India Company's unwelcome shiploads of tax-liable tea than those at Charleston, where they were allowed to rot on the quay, or at

Philadelphia and New York, where they were turned back to Britain. In this he was amply aided by his enemies.

A series of broadsheets and satirical cartoons tried to keep the March incident in the public eye, but those colonials who were in privileged positions quickly realized that all this rabble-rousing might pose as great a threat to their own influence and affluence as to that of the Crown. They wanted "a stop put to mobbing", for, as the *New York Gazette and Weekly Mercury* pointed out in July 1770, if it were not, "property will soon be very precarious as God knows where it will end". One Virginian was in no doubt where his own advantage lay and hoped that "there are not five men of sense in America who would accept independence if it were offered; we know our circumstances too well; we know that our happiness, our very being depend upon our being connected with our Mother Country."

It is quite possible that, in the light of the considerable residue of loyalty to the Crown and without the initial arrogance and intransigence first of Townshend and then of Lord North, the seeds of rebellion would not have taken root, or at least not at that time. However, toward the end of 1772 the troubles of the East India Company gave new momentum to the conflict.

Tea now served as the catalyst for two highly volatile elements that needed only to be brought into contact by its agency to cause an explosion whose echoes still reverberate round the world today. On the one hand a disgruntled and to a degree justifiably discontented, if hitherto largely loyal, populace; on the other the King and a Parliament most of whose members regarded "colonials" as no better than their domestic servants: bound by birth and duty to keep their proper station and do their master's bidding, however distasteful, on pain of chastisement. The Speaker of the Massachusetts Assembly asserted that "if Parliament could bind the colonies they were all slaves", while the King was equally vehement in declaring that "that distant possession standing upon equality with a superior State is more ruinous than being deprived of such connections".

Even so, had the Crown not been represented by obtuse or timid men, such as General Gage in Massachusetts or Governor Hutchinson in Boston, the situation might still have been contained.

The majority of colonists still saw themselves as Englishmen who happened to be living in America. As our previously quoted Virginian put it, "we claim nothing but the liberty and privileges of Englishmen, in the same degree as if we had continued among our brethren in Great Britain". Much of the animosity of the ordinary colonist was still directed, not toward the Crown, but toward a new, high-living American plutocracy which enjoyed the patronage and protection of the English Parliament.

Had the East India Company been indifferent to the loss of the bulk of its American trade, which only represented 3 per cent of its total tea sales in 1772, the issue of taxed tea in America might not have served as the ultimate catalyst for rebellion. However, in that year the Company found itself in the uncomfortable position of being heavily in debt to the Government, running at a large deficit in India and with 17 million pounds of unsold tea stockpiled in its London warehouses. This rose to over 21 million pounds in 1773. Its dividends were limited by Government until its public debt was cleared, and the stockholders were getting restless. It was at this juncture that one of these, Robert Herries, came up with what looked like a good solution to the Company's difficulties. Why not ask the Government to allow it – after keeping a year's supply of tea in hand in Britain (2,700–3,600 tons) – to export the balance of the surplus directly to Europe, instead of having to sell it on the London market, and to grant the refund of the import duties paid? Herries put forward his idea in December 1772 and a desperate Court of Directors seized on it with ill-considered haste. On 7 January 1773 they agreed to ask Parliament "to enable the Company to export to Foreign Dominions with an allowance of the Drawback of all the Duties of Customs, a part of their Surplus Quantity of Tea...". They added, almost as an afterthought, the suggestion that the Townshend tea tax be lifted as well.

Hope & Co, the Company's principal agent in Amsterdam, and incidentally one of the largest suppliers to Dutch smugglers, was consulted. Its principals scoffed at the notion. They pointed out that the dumping of so much tea so precipitately on the Amsterdam market would depress the price there and increase it in London, thus inviting smugglers simply to return it to England to their profit and the Company's loss. The Hopes suggested instead that the tea be distributed throughout Europe by the usual London merchants and thus lessen the impact on the price. The East India Company's directors were not taken with this alternative, which would have left them little better off, so on 17 February they sought instead permission to send an exploratory shipload of tea to America, whence it could not be smuggled profitably back to Britain. They also pointed out again that, if the Townshend duty were removed, their tea would comfortably undersell the Dutch illicit trade. Although the Tea Act subsequently passed in Parliament with relative ease, the debate which preceded it on 26 April 1773 was a heated one.

William Dowdeswell, MP for Worcester and Townshend's brief predecessor as Chancellor, put his finger on the critical point: "I tell the noble Lord now, if he don't take off the duty they won't take the tea." But Lord North was "unwilling to give up that duty upon America ... I must see a very substantial reason before I part with a fund so applicable to the support of Civil Government." In vain did Dowdeswell sneeringly point out that, for a net gain of £400, a trade of two million pounds of tea was being rejected. North remained unmoved, arguing that there might one day be a more significant American revenue. Dowdeswell saw the flaw in North's argument and suggested that, instead of an import duty in America, the Townsend tax of threepence should be lifted and charged instead as an export duty paid in Britain. It would thus be up to the Company to decide how much, if any, of the duty it wished to recoup by raising its price in a competitive market. Almost all speakers in the debate supported Dowdeswell's suggestion, but North, stubborn to the last, did not yield and on 10 May 1773 the Tea Act became law. Its significance seems to have been entirely lost on the British media of the day, which reported it only in tandem with a Bill "to prevent the murdering or destroying of Bastard Children".

The East India Company remained nervous of the American market solution, so it proposed a number of transparent devices to mollify the colonists but which served only to rouse their indignation further. As Americans were reluctant to see specie go out of the country, it proposed that the tea could be paid for in bills of exchange and the duty need not be paid until the tea had been sold. The Company havered until July and made such a fuss about its intentions that the radicals among the colonists were amply fore-warned. So long did it take to find shippers willing to take the first consignment of tea that not until 18 October did a six-vessel convoy set out across the Atlantic.

By allowing the Company to export tea direct to America and cut out the British middlemen, North in practice enabled tea to be sold at a lower price in America than in London despite his insist-ence on retaining the threepenny tax. The East India directors now had a chance to get their own back on those who had smuggled them out of business, by deciding to supply almost exclusively merchants who had supported the Government. Smugglers, among them Independence hero John Hancock, quickly displayed their new-found American patriotism by denouncing the move as an attempt to establish monopoly: a fear to which colonial merchants were naturally prone. A satirical handbill in October, supposedly from the smugglers of New York, highlighted the absurdity of the objection by complaining that smuggled tea "without paying any duty in America" would give "people here the opportunity of buying good English tea for half the price we expect to extort from them for the trash lodged in [their] hands from Holland".

Another ploy was for preachers to admonish the women of America that they "must not suffer themselves to sip the accursed stuff, for if you do the devil will immediately enter into you and you will instantly become a traitor to your country". Most of the oppo-sition was based, however, on serious objection to the probability of an East India Company monopoly in this trade and to the quan-tity of specie that would flow out of America to pay for it: an argument we shall see deployed in reverse to justify the British opium trade to China 60 years later. In the face of such clamorous opposition, most merchants decided to forgo the honour of selling Company tea rather than imperil their business and their safety.

Not so the Hutchinson brothers nor Richard Clarke, all of Boston. Their stance soon drew down on them the anger of the mob. Clarke's offices were besieged on 2 November 1773 while he and his staff and family barricaded themselves in on the upper floor.

A fortnight later a mob again besieged the family and its employees on their top floor. When one of the Clarkes fired a pistol into the air by way of warning, the rioters went berserk, wrecking the offices and much of the building and hurling missiles at the occupants, several of whom were injured. But the Clarkes were not alone in their stance and were joined by a number of their friends. Together they held the rabble at bay until a peacemaker intervened, suggesting that the crowd disperse in return for a promise from the Clarkes to appear before the town meeting next day. The Clarkes, however, steadfastly refused to be intimidated and declined to do so. Eventually, as is often the case, the mob grew bored and dispersed of it own accord. Ominously, even those in Boston who opposed violence did so half-heartedly because of "the danger of lives being lost which must not be ventured on *except in the last extremity*" (italics added).

Not surprisingly, the Clarkes demanded on 19 November that the Governor and Council restore order and protect them and their property. But by now, despite the family interest, Governor Hutchinson was more concerned for his own safety and already contemplated retreating offshore to Fort William, where the British troops were garrisoned. He felt that any attempt to restore order could only end in bloodshed. Though the Governor's pusillanimity contributed much to the eventual debacle, it is hard not to feel a little sorry for him. The Council which was supposed to help him govern refused to act. As he wrote to his fellow governor in New York on 21 November, "no person who shares any part of the authority of government concurring with me in measures for the support of it". Armed insurrection seemed imminent in his eyes, and the citizens gathered nightly to concoct "unlawful measures and very dark proposals". This last was written on 24 November, probably to Andrew Oliver, his deputy, whose views on the maintenance of order were such as to render him unsympathetic to Hutchinson's plight. Oliver had written in reaction to an earlier failure to enforce the law – in which his brother, a customs officer, had been subjected to attack – that as a result his fellow Americans "were swelled with their own Importance, and had felt so little from British Power, that they now hugged themselves in Security, regardless of what a Power at 3000 Miles distant could do unto them; ... A Law without Penalties, or one with Penalties not exacted, is ... useless to Mankind ... . It is in Government as it is in private Life: a desultory, undetermined Conduct often induces Contempt."

Of the four ships destined for Boston, one, the *William*, ran aground off Cape Cod and its 58 chests of tea were promptly "salvaged" and spirited away into the illicit tea pipeline. When the *Dartmouth*, the first of the remaining three to reach Boston, hove in sight on 28 November Governor Hutchinson told the consignees to order its captain to anchor below Fort William. As this stood on an island in the bay, and was thus not actually *in* Boston harbour, any consignment of tea anchored there would not become legally liable to duty. In this way the *Dartmouth* could keep open the option of turning round and sailing back home without risk of forfeiture of its cargo. Adams was having none of it and instructed Captain Hall to berth his ship in Boston harbour, "at his peril" if he refused. This Hall did on the 30th. Normally, when a ship entered the harbour, the captain had 48 hours in which to enter the cargo with the customs officers. Once he had done so he became liable to pay the duty due within 21 days. If he did not, Customs was entitled to seize the cargo and impound it in the Custom House, where it would have been out of the reach of Adams short of a major criminal act if not open rebellion. This would have put Adams at both a military and a psychological disadvantage in a town as yet far from wholly given over to the cause of the radicals.

The Governor felt time was on his side. Once the period of grace had elapsed he could legitimately use military and naval might to escort the cargo from ship to Custom House and there protect it till the issue was resolved. His earlier order to the mobs to disperse had been hissed and booed, and he had withdrawn to Fort William troops who had proved insufficient in calibre and quantity to keep order on all the streets of Boston. However, concentrated on this one task, they would be more than adequate. It seemed that Hutchinson – no doubt urged on by his sons and their fellow merchants – was at last bracing himself to assert the rule of law. To this end he ordered the navy to blockade the harbour lest the tea ships sail again for Britain without paying duty. But Adams was quicker on his feet than

Hutchinson and set small watches on board the three ships now alongside Griffin's Wharf, ostensibly to protect the cargo but in practice to prevent it being unloaded and, quite possibly, to suborn the crew by explaining the radical case. When the confrontation came it would be on ground of Adams's choosing.

There now intervened a period of relative calm while Adams planned his next move and the Governor waited, somewhat complacently, on his hour. Town meetings were no longer convened because the radicals did not trust the "select men" to be tough enough in their demands in the face of the perfectly correct procedure being followed by the authorities. There were still unofficial rallies of some five thousand people, which must have encouraged the conspirators, but despite a number of inflammatory speeches these passed off peaceably enough. Adams realized that, as the deadline approached when duty would become payable, the Governor's hand would grow stronger. So on the night of 16 December he launched his famous pre-emptive strike.

The controversy surrounding the taxing and importing of tea in America was not itself the cause of revolution, but it did serve to focus minds and hearts on the social and psychological forces driving toward revolution. The authorities appointed by the Crown, mostly themselves Americans, had, by their habitual practice of ignoring a plethora of breaches of the law, made such law-breaking seem a socially acceptable practice – rather as speeding has become among many people today. Such was the spirit of recalcitrance, or independence, depending on your point of view, inculcated by this practice that subsequent attempts to enforce the law were seen, like fines for speeding, as an attack on personal freedom and collective liberty. But, as with speeding, a substantial minority, though inconvenienced, felt the law should be upheld.

The words of Locke's radical and provocative *Treatise on Government* and the wild gestures of John Wilkes, the radical winner of the recent Middlesex by-election, alike resonated on both sides of the Atlantic. The Common Man, and indeed many of his middle-class masters, was growing increasingly restless with the old order and ever more willing to do more than grumble *sotto voce* to bring about a new one. I can think of no other explanation for two of the questions raised by the sequence of events in the unfolding drama of the Boston Tea Party. The first question is: why did the captain of the *Dartmouth* (followed by the captains of the other two ships) give in to Adams's demand that he berth his ship alongside Griffin's Wharf "at his peril" if he refused? What peril? Under the guns of Fort William and in the lee of the Royal Navy ships of Admiral Montagu, Captain Hall was in no danger whatsoever from Adams and his mob. Did the merchant captains, independent and often both of humble origins and quite wealthy in their own right, perhaps sympathize with the Boston radicals? Or were they under pressure from their crews? Or both?

The second question follows on the first. Did the seamen at least, and perhaps their officers as well, assist the raiders in their destructive act or at least acquiesce in it? I draw this conclusion from the events of that December night in 1773. All the accounts and illustrations I have come across, fanciful as some clearly were, show that the chests were hoisted on deck and there broken open and their contents tipped into the "tea pot" of Boston harbour and that this action was all over in a couple of hours. Whole chests of tea at that time weighed 450lb, half chests about 250lb. The former at least were surely too heavy for even a couple of the strongest men to have hoisted up from the hold on to the deck without the aid of block and tackle rigged from a yard or "A" frame, and probably capstan-wound. If the 340 chests which were broken open had been below decks and the 92,586lb of tea shovelled up by the bucketful it would have taken the 50–60 men involved all night to empty it out of the three vessels. No account I have read speaks of hoisting tackle being prepared and taken on board in anticipation by Adams's men. Yet surely such must have been used. I therefore conclude that the sailors, from sympathy with the American cause, either actively helped Adams's "braves" to rig and operate such a hoist, or at least made no attempt to stop them using the ship's own equipment.

Governor Hutchinson's failure either to anticipate or to prevent the raid is puzzling, but more explicable. There is a paralysed-rabbit syndrome that has seized many a colonial official of all nations and at all times when confronted with such crises of revolt against the edicts of the imperial power. "If I intervene and bloodshed ensues

with untold long-term consequences, I shall be blamed and
disgraced and possibly even killed. If I do nothing and sit tight
matters may go gradually from bad to worse as a result, but, while
I shall be blamed, I shall not be disgraced or killed. So I shall do
nothing." It would have been a relatively simple matter to put a
couple of the sections of the troops recently withdrawn from the
streets of Boston on board each vessel, to protect the cargoes until
the due customs date and then to oversee their transfer to the
Custom House to be held in bond until the duty was paid. The ships
would have served as mini-forts almost impossible to take in the
face of determined defence except by a scale of attack that would
have been an open act of rebellion that Boston's citizens did not
then seem ready to take. Perhaps Hutchinson felt that he could not
rely on a determined defence being offered by soldiers who were
among some of the least effective, and possibly least loyal, in the
British Army as a result of the heavy demand for fighting men elsewhere in the Empire. Such a defence would also have required the
cooperation of the captains and crews, and again perhaps this was
not forthcoming. Whatever the explanation, every step taken by all
concerned was a step relentlessly in the direction of a denouement
that defied the authority of the British Government in a way that
could not be ignored.

In January 1774, when news of the Boston outrage reached
London, indignation waxed great. Most concurred with the sentiment that grapeshot should be rammed down American throats if
they did not agree to drink tea "without making damned wry faces".
Only a few voices of reason and restraint were raised. One
condemned the belligerent language used as "monstrously absurd".
Another, Thomas Crowley, a habitual writer of letters to the newspapers, suggested that Americans be given seats in Parliament and be
liable only to the same taxes as the British. But despite these cautions,
the Bill to close the port of Boston until it apologized and compensated the East India Company was passed with ease. Only two
Members of Parliament spoke out on the colonists' behalf. When one
of them, the radical John Sawbridge, tried to argue that Parliament
had no right to tax the colonists, he was drowned out by such a
cacophony of noise that he had to change tack in order to be able to

continue. He pointed out that the attack on the ships had never been authorized by the Boston town council – "the town of Deal may as well be made answerable for a set of smugglers" – and urged North to demand recompense from Boston before instituting coercive measures. This was a course of action which Benjamin Franklin himself earnestly recommended, but an indignant and affronted Parliament brushed Sawbridge aside and passed the Boston Port Bill without further demur. This in effect severed the town from all outside commerce. When hot on the heels of the Port Bill came further legislation for the central authorities to take over the entire government of Massachusetts, not even Franklin's eloquence could assuage colonial anger. The rest, as they say, is history.

It is not the place of this book to follow the momentous events that ensued, but it is reasonable to surmise that the role played by tea in them had both a psychological and a practical consequence in the subsequent dominance of coffee as the American drink of choice at the expense of tea and perhaps in the ambivalence of the love-hate relationship between Britain and the United States ever since. We shall be concerned later with the largely fruitless struggle of the British tea interest for the next two hundred years to recover the lost El Dorado of the American market. John Adams, writing to his wife of an experience when travelling to sign the Declaration of Independence, encapsulated the extent of the transformation in American drinking habits which now took place. When he stopped at an inn he asked the barmaid, "Is it lawful for a weary traveller to refresh himself with a dish of tea, provided it has been honestly smuggled and has paid no duty?" "No, sir!" she replied. "We have renounced tea under this roof. But, if you desire it, I will make you some coffee."

Tea had played a catalytic part in bringing about the demise of British rule and that in turn brought about the virtual demise of tea drinking in America.

CHAPTER FIVE

Empire and Opium

Opium, much used in Europe in the nineteenth century for the legitimate conversion to laudanum, was a valuable addition to the pharmacopoeia as both a painkiller and a soporific in the days before anaesthetics and effective analgesics. Its subsequent use and abuse, while not on the scale experienced in China (where it had been domestically produced since at least the sixteenth century), would become a serious health problem in Europe. Such prominent Englishmen as De Quincey, Coleridge and Clive of India became addicts. In China one official painted a grim picture of a typical opium smoker once he or she had become addicted: "Afterwards they find themselves beyond the possibility of cure. If for one day they omitted smoking, their faces suddenly became shrivelled, their lips opened, their teeth were seen, they lost all vivacity, and seemed ready to die. Another smoke, however, restored them. After three years all such persons die." Just as opium's medical derivative, morphine, was to become a more effective painkiller than laudanum in the twentieth century, so its narcotic offspring, heroin, would become an even greater scourge than opium.

The rulers of China had long recognized the dangers posed by the opium-smoking (and ingesting) habit and its import had been specifically banned by a decree of 1727. The prohibition seems to have been largely effective since 60 years later only two hundred chests, about 2,800lb, was imported according to Chinese figures. (I have used these rather than the lower European figures on the grounds that they were more likely to be accurate than those provided by the smugglers.) But by 1800 highly profitable opium imports had risen tenfold to meet an expanding demand. They doubled again in the next 10 years, and again in the following 10, despite a series of increasingly vehement Imperial prohibitions and increasingly severe punishments, including execution, for those found trading in it. On the eve of the First Opium War in 1839 over forty thousand chests, containing some 5.5 million pounds of opium, were finding their way into China. Successive emperors recognized clearly that opium was a "poison undermining our good customs and morality" and made strenuous efforts to prevent it doing so. So why did these fail? Was failure entirely due to the criminal greed of Western merchants? The answer is, largely but not entirely.

In defence of Britain, which, as the superpower of the nineteenth century, was the lead player in a confederation of European and American interests, it should be pointed out that opium trading took off on a large scale only when all other attempts to trade with standard Western products had been blocked or severely restricted. The Chinese on the whole either despised or had no need for Western merchandise. Most surprisingly, they did not much care for the main export of the British Industrial Revolution: cotton goods.

Britain made two serious, if rather arrogant, attempts to persuade the Chinese to open up their borders to the free trade that had already become for many the watchword of the Western economy. In 1792 Lord Macartney led an embassy to the Chinese court to seek trade concessions and presented the usual courtesy gifts from one monarch to another on behalf of George III. As far as the Emperor was concerned this envoy was just another barbarian bearing tribute from a suppliant vassal. When Macartney refused to kowtow to the Emperor – he thought a slight downward twitch of the knee quite sufficient for an Englishman – he was sent packing empty-handed. In 1816 the second Lord Amherst, who would become Governor General of India in 1823, tried again with even less success: he was not even granted an audience with the Emperor, the contentious issue of the kowtow having been diplomatically explored to the satisfaction of neither party.

As one East India Company representative put it, "at no very distant period and from some apparently accidental event, not only the British Nation but other foreigners might be prohibited from entering the Chinese territories". No entry, no tea. Another anonymous Company servant suggested that the answer was to grow tea elsewhere, in Nepal for example, but at this time such a solution was dismissed as impractical. But the Chinese did covet silver, preferring it even to gold (in which, on aesthetic grounds, I must agree with them). Apart from "*cash*" – small copper coins of little value – they had no acceptable means of conducting business with foreigners. So, if the British and others wanted tea they would have to pay for it in silver bullion, or Mexican or Spanish silver dollars. This was all very well, but the drain on silver was soon hurting the economies of Britain and India. As Linnaeus put it when admitting that his attempts to grow tea in Europe were not just motivated by botanical curiosity, he "looked upon nothing to be of more importance than to shut the gate through which all the silver went out of Europe". However, there was one other thing that shady Chinese merchants were even more anxious to obtain because of its exorbitantly profitable internal market: opium. And for opium they were willing to pay in silver. So began a strange ritual dance on the spot in Canton. As tea and opium could not be bartered directly, opium was sold for silver, which in turn paid for tea. This suited Western merchants very well, for it saved them a long journey in pirate-infested waters with cargoes of silver.

As with all drug-related crime, there would have been no trade if there had not been as many Chinese willing to buy opium for selling on as there were British, other Europeans and Americans willing to provide it. There were two main sources of opium at the time: Turkey and India, of which India was by far the more significant. At the end of the sixteenth century the Mogul emperor Akbar took over the opium production of Bengal and Bihar as a state monopoly, a monopoly which the East India Company in its turn was quite happy to assume. Before long the Company tightened its grip on the trade by cutting out the middlemen by decree and buying the opium direct from the cultivators at a not very generous price that it fixed in advance. The entire operation was conducted by the Company's Opium Department under the direction of the Opium Agent and his subordinates, and with the cooperation of many local British officials. As one of them wrote in 1836: "The great object of the Bengal opium agencies is to furnish an article suitable to the peculiar tastes of the population of China."

Nor were the officials alone. Many planters and other civilians, as well as the military, doled out opium to natives, particularly porters and boatmen on long journeys, both as a reward and because it enabled their ill-nourished bodies to endure hardships to which they would otherwise have succumbed. Such men were convinced that "this country could [not] have been opened up without the opium pipe". Warren Hastings, Governor General from 1777, who was later impeached and acquitted for his dealings in India, believed opium was "a pernicious article of luxury which ought not to be permitted *but for the purpose of foreign commerce only*" (italics added).

But British involvement in this nefarious trade in opium did not pass without protest from those who could see that it inflicted almost as much damage on the country that produced it as on the one that received it. C.A. Bruce in his report on tea plantations in Assam, published in 1839, wrote:

Opium ... that dreadful plague, which has depopulated this beautiful country, turned it into a land of wild beasts, with which it is overrun, and has degenerated the Assamese, from a fair race of people, to the most abject, servile, crafty, and demoralized race in India. This vile drug has kept, and does now keep, down the population; the women have fewer children compared with those of other countries, and the children seldom live to become old men, but in general die at manhood; very few old men being seen in this unfortunate country, in comparison with others. Few but those who have resided long in this unhappy land know the dreadful and immoral effects, which the use of Opium produces on the native. He will steal, sell his property, his children, the mother of his children, and finally even commit murder for it. Would it not be the highest of blessings, if our humane and enlightened Government would stop these evils by a single dash of the pen, and save Assam, and all those who are about to emigrate into it as Tea cultivators, from the dreadful results attendant on the habitual use of Opium?

He goes on to recommend suppressing cultivation and levying a high duty on opium imports. All to no avail. His successor planters 25 years later were still having to make the same plea.

Technically, selling opium directly to the Chinese would have been a breach of the Company's charter. With a fine example of the hypocrisy that typified the whole sordid chain of traffic from start to finish, it ceased to sell direct but instead auctioned off the entire opium crop in Calcutta to British and Persian concerns, known as "country firms", which then smuggled the opium into China. The Company stipulated that the country firms must be paid for the opium in silver, which they in turn would pay over to the Company's agents in Canton to offset their bills of account drawn in London and Calcutta. The agents were then able to buy all the tea they wanted with the necessary silver and indeed to have a good bit left over. In 1810, 983 tons of silver were shipped from Britain to China. In 1840, 366 tons flowed the other way on top of the substantially greater sums that had been paid for tea in Canton. By this stage some 15 per cent of the Government of India's revenue came from this source, and the British Government was collecting £3–4 million in duty levied on imported tea. No wonder the authorities in both countries chose to turn a blind eye.

Chinese officialdom was no better. The Emperor's magistrate in Canton and the magistrate's own officials accepted large bribes from their fellow countrymen who were acting as brokers between the smugglers and the network of criminal domestic opium distributors. Officially, since the importing of opium could not be countenanced, no opium was actually landed in Canton harbour. The island of Lintin conveniently lay in the Kiang delta, which forms Canton's long outlet to the sea, and in its lee were anchored a series of well-armed hulks. Here the country firms would deposit their illicit cargo to await the "centipedes" and "scrambling dragons" (multi-oared galleys) that would collect the opium on behalf of the Chinese brokers.

From time to time a happy charade would be acted out by all involved. The Canton magistrate would issue an edict forbidding foreign vessels to "loiter" in the estuary, ordering them either to come into harbour and be properly (and expensively) processed or sail away. They did neither. The magistrate would then order the "dragons of war", the war junks that constituted the rather inadequate Chinese navy, to seize the delinquent vessels. Naturally he did not issue the order until he was quite sure the smugglers had completed their business. Once the merchantmen raised anchor, the "dragons of war" made a great show of pursuit, firing off numerous salvoes from their ineffectual guns while keeping safely out of range of any retaliation. Some of the more mischievous merchant captains would sometimes suddenly shorten sail and slow down or heave to, thus obliging the Chinese hastily to do the same in a panic lest they come within range of a fearsome broadside and be blown out of the water. Once the merchants had safely sailed away, the junks would loose off a few more salvoes and sail home to report another famous naval victory to the Emperor.

The East India Company and, after its monopoly ceased in 1834, the private companies that took over the trade, chief among them Jardine Matheson and the Indian Parsees led by Heerjeebhoy Rustumjee, were caught in a trap fashioned by their own greed. To oversee their activities and protect their interests Lord Palmerston, as Foreign Secretary, appointed Lord William Napier Chief Superintendent of Trade in Canton in May of that year. Napier had not even been allowed to present his credentials before he was ordered back to Macao by the Chinese authorities. When he refused to go the Chinese blockaded the Canton factories, their favourite means of exerting pressure on the barbarians, and laughingly countered Napier's attempt to lift the siege with two British frigates by opposing a fleet of "dragons of war" so large that he was obliged to flee to Macao with his tail between his legs. He died there a few weeks later in October.

By no means all the foreign merchants supported the opium trade and a number of them declined to have anything further to do with it. The British merchants' house journal, the *Lintin Bulletin and River Bee*, summed up the situation neatly in its issue of October 1838:

1. The Chinese Government wishes to extirpate a vicious trade which ruins the health of its subjects and drains its treasury of precious specie.

2. The English Government admits the immorality of the trade but cannot afford to lose its vast profits.

By putting the onus for its suppression on the Chinese Government, saying piously that one sovereign power may not interfere in the internal affairs of another, Britannia has the best of all worlds: she gets the lucre, yet washes her hands of all moral responsibility. We do not think this can continue.

Nor did it, but the situation was resolved by one of the more shameful episodes in British history, triggered by the Emperor's finally appointing an honest magistrate to "sever the trunk from the roots". Lin Zexu (now a Chinese national hero who even has a street in New York named after him) was only three months into his post as Imperial Commissioner when he ordered the Hongs to hand over the opium from the hulks on pain of confiscation of all their possessions and the execution of a randomly selected number of them. The Europeans, and the Americans who were by now substantial traders, assumed Lin would be as ineffectual as his predecessors, so they surrendered 1,056 cases as a face-saver for the Commissioner. But Lin was not to be fobbed off. He ordered the arrest of the leading foreign opium trader Launcelot Dent, allowed no foreigners to leave Canton and blockaded the factories. The barbarians had by now been joined by the British Superintendent of Trade, Captain Charles Elliott. After they had held out for 47 days, Elliott persuaded them to hand over some twenty thousand chests of opium – 2.8 million pounds, worth some £2 million – on his guarantee that they would be compensated by the British Government.

Lin was taking no chances. He had the chests taken to the Canton foreshore and counted and re-counted to make sure there was no trickery before ordering them to be destroyed. Some accounts say they were burned, others that they were buried in quicklime. One even suggests that they were deposited in that customary receptacle of unwanted British imports: the sea. Lin's subsequent exhortation to Queen Victoria – justly pointing out that China's exports had never harmed anyone, but were so beneficial that the rest of the world could not do without them – implied that, were Britain to continue exporting opium to China, these benefits would be withdrawn. His assessment and his threat were equally misplaced.

Lin's actions gave Palmerston the chance he sought to work off the grudge he had held against the Chinese since the Napier debacle. He promptly sacked Elliott on the grounds that "Throughout the whole course of your proceedings you seem to have considered that my instructions were waste paper, which you might treat with entire disregard, and that you were at full liberty to deal with the interests of your country according to your own fancy." He was replaced by Sir Henry Pottinger, who had strict orders to demand compensation for the destroyed opium, indemnity against future behaviour, free trade, the legalization of opium and the ceding of the island of Hong Kong.

On the advice of the leading opium trader William Jardine, who happened to be in Britain at the time, Palmerston ordered the blockade of all Chinese ports to give weight to his demands. Perversely the Chinese Emperor had sacked Lin, the only man who had stood up to the barbarians and their noxious trade in opium, and replaced him with Ch'i Shan, who agreed at once to Pottinger's demands. Yet again the Emperor changed his mind, sacked Ch'i Shan, gathered what he thought would be an invincible host and dug in his heels.

This was all the excuse Palmerston needed and he called for war. Thomas Macaulay, the celebrated imperial historian and Secretary at War in Melbourne's cabinet, expressed the Government's view and indeed that of the majority of his fellow countrymen, when he declared that Britain was "a country unaccustomed to defeat, to submission or to shame ... a country which had exacted such reparation for the wrongs to her children as had made the ears of all who heard it tingle". In opposition Gladstone thundered, "a war more unjust in its origin, a war more calculated in its progress to cover this country with permanent disgrace I know not of ... The flag is become a pirate flag to protect the infamous traffic." He thundered to no avail. No more effective was the opposition outside Parliament of the great orators and "moral" free-traders Cobden and Bright, who detested Palmerston and opium trading with equal vehemence. The First Opium War was launched.

An invasion fleet carrying four thousand troops was assembled off Macao in June 1840, leaving a derisory handful of troops to defend Canton – such was British confidence in the superiority of their arms – and sailed up the coast of China to the island of Chusan in an attempt to cow the Emperor into giving in. The islanders of Chusan, seeing an unexpected fleet of barbarian ships offshore, thought that they were in for a trade bonanza. They were quickly disabused. Once the Chinese had rejected a demand to surrender, the ships bombarded the town to smithereens and sacked what was left of it. With Canton in British hands and a British army breathing down his neck after heavily defeating Chinese armies in the field en route to Peking, the Emperor was brought up sharply against the reality of the shift in world power. He conceded all that was asked in exchange for peace.

Again the man on the spot exercised his discretion. In the treaty of Nanking, signed on 29 August 1842, Sir Henry Pottinger did *not* insist on the legalization of opium. All the other demands were conceded, including the ceding of Hong Kong. This would make many British fortunes and remain an irritant to the Chinese that would colour their relations with Britain until it was handed back to them in 1997.

The British are blamed exclusively for the act of naked imperialism that the Opium War undoubtedly was. But, while as principals they must bear the lion's share of responsibility, as they did of the spoils, they were enthusiastically supported by the Americans, the Dutch, the Portuguese and the other Europeans and Indians who had been making a commercial killing at the expense of the lives of the Chinese. The Americans, to their credit, now almost all withdrew from the opium trade, but the Frenchman J.-G. Houssaye, writing in the immediate aftermath, best expressed the collective view of Europe:

Thanks to the outcome of the Anglo-Chinese war, the Celestial Empire has become an open market for Europe and America. The triumph of British arms may be seen in the future as a benefit to the country of Confucius, frozen in its time-honoured stasis, which by continual rubbing up against our civilization may be gradually torn away from its prejudices and its mistrust and take up our arts and sciences. It is providential that Great Britain, in pursuing her own egotistical plans for domination with tenacity and indomitable energy, may as a result have unintentionally brought about the progress of civilization.

Whether the French Jesuits who had initiated French involvement in China could be said to have contributed to "civilization" is debatable. What is more certain is that when they were eventually expelled French interest in tea virtually disappeared. Houssaye's plea that France should develop its own tea industry in its colonies in South-East Asia was ignored and wine and coffee reigned supreme.

The rate of increase in the amount of opium sold to the Chinese actually slowed after the treaty of Nanking, but in 1850 it was still a devastating seven million pounds in weight. The amount of opium needed to provide a consciousness-obliterating smoke is about 1/10oz, so the addicts in a population of some three hundred million Chinese were taking 1,120 million smokes a year.

The effect of opium smoking on the Chinese was graphically described by Robert Fortune in his account, published in 1848, of his incognito journeys into the interior of China:

> The effects which the immoderate use of opium had produced upon this man were of the most melancholy kind. His figure was thin and emaciated, his cheeks had a pale and haggard hue, and his skin had that peculiar glassy polish by which an opium-smoker is invariably known. His days were evidently numbered, and yet, strange to tell, this man tried to convince others and himself also that he was smoking medicinally, and that the use of opium was indispensable to his health. As I looked upon him in these moments of excitement I could not help feeling what a piteous object is man, the lord of Creation, and noblest work of God, when sensual pleasures and enjoyments take such a hold upon him.

However, Palmerston was not yet done with the miserable Chinese, 10 million of whom (according to one estimate) were by now addicted to opium. He made his views clear again in 1850: "The time is fast coming when we shall be obliged to strike another blow in China. These half-civilised governments such as those in China, Portugal and Spanish America, all require a dressing every eight or ten years to keep them in order." And in 1856, by which time he was Prime Minister, he decided to seize the opportunity to administer another "dressing" on the flimsiest of excuses.

Smuggling of opium by sea had continued apace and although one of the smuggling vessels, the *Arrow*, was almost certainly flouting Britain's own laws forbidding it, the seizure of the ship by the Chinese gave Palmerston the excuse he needed. He sent an expeditionary force under Lord Elgin to rub in the lesson that "a British subject, in whatever land he may be, shall feel confident that the watchful eye and strong arm of England will protect him against injustice and wrong". Another trouncing of the technologically inferior Chinese yielded another 10 ports to European trade in the Tientsin Treaty of 1858. Travellers and missionaries were to be allowed into all parts of China, there would be a British Resident in Peking to make sure the treaty was observed and opium trading *would* be legalized.

One last attempt by the Chinese to block the implementation of the treaty by force shortly afterwards led to an initial defeat for the Anglo-French forces but this success was short-lived. This time the British went all the way and occupied Peking, burning the Emperor's summer palace to make their philistine point. In 1860 China had to pay an additional indemnity to the £5 million previously imposed, cede Vladivostok and large areas of its hinterland to the Russians, and hand over the peninsula opposite Hong Kong to the British. Significantly for the future, this latter concession was not made in perpetuity, and it was its legitimate return to Chinese sovereignty that, in due course, made further tenure of Hong Kong itself no longer viable. Surprisingly, despite two wars in less than 20 years, the tea trade with China hardly missed a beat, thanks to comfortable buffer stocks in London.

Indian opium, a more valuable commodity by far than tea and which at its height employed a million people, was exported to China until 1911. There was even an Opium Department under the

Indian Civil Service in 1930, though its role was then one of policing and control. Chinese domestic cultivation also grew to the point where opium addiction reached epidemic proportions and famine, as a result of the neglect of traditional agriculture in what should have been a rice-rich land, struck on a number of occasions. More significantly, the Manchu dynasty was fatally weakened and grew incapable of defending its authority internally or externally. Xenophobia became rampant and the Chinese learned the lesson that however many legions you may have they will prove of little avail against a technologically and economically superior enemy.

Before the Opium Wars the Chinese despised foreigners as barbarians whose power could safely be ignored; after them, China realized that while, on the whole, foreign barbarians were still to be despised, their power and the means by which they obtained it were to be discreetly emulated. It may not be too fanciful to see China's isolation from and hostility to the West in the twentieth century as stemming from that traumatic experience. When China is once again the world's greatest power, as it assuredly will be some time in the mid-twenty-first century, it will be interesting to see what its attitude will be to the barbarians who flooded it with narcotics and went to war so that they could continue to enjoy their cup of tea.

The painful blow to national pride inflicted by the Opium and *Arrow* Wars, and the undermining of both secular authority and cultural cohesion begun by the intrusion of Western commerce and the proselytizing of Western missionaries, was completed by the Sino-Japanese Wars of 1894–5 and 1931–45. The first of these was fought ostensibly over the status of Korea, but in reality it was an inevitable conflict between a weak and passive oriental state stuck in the past and an increasingly strong, modernizing one. In the 1931–45 war Japan again invaded mainland China, inflicting numerous defeats and perpetrating many atrocities. They were no less brutal when in 1941–2 they seized the Dutch colonies of Indonesia and turned many of the tea plantations over to the production of coca for the manufacture of the cocaine with which they were attempting to debilitate the population of mainland China. It is perhaps not too fanciful to see the different attitudes of Chinese and Japanese to war and diplomacy in the traditional hedonistic approach to tea drinking of the one and the highly disciplined, impersonal ritual of the other.

In 1942, when the Japanese seized the islands of what is now the Republic of Indonesia, they effectively ended 340 years of Dutch trading and 120 years of tea cultivation on a substantial scale. In response to the founding of the English East India Company on the last day of 1600, the Dutch had formed their own Dutch East India Company two years later. Queen Elizabeth's charter had granted the consortium of English merchants who formed their East India Company a monopoly of trade with the East Indies in an attempt to break the hold of the Dutch, whose exorbitantly high prices for the spices that made palatable the often unwholesome food of Tudor cuisine had become burdensome. Elizabeth's charter "for the honour of the nation, the wealth of the people ... the increase of navigation and the advancement of lawful traffic" also empowered the Company to raise armies, build forts, make treaties, administer justice and coin money wherever it chose to establish itself in the East. The West was specifically precluded.

The Dutch, not to be outdone, did the same in 1602, modelling their Dutch East India Company quite closely on the English enterprise but going one better by describing those in charge not as a Court of Directors (as the East India Company had done) but as Lords, of whom there were 17. The tactics of the Dutch in trying to exact trading concessions from the Chinese by plundering villages and setting fire to ships backfired. They were compelled to trade from Taiwan, which then was not, as it became later, part of the Chinese empire. In 1688 they were driven thence to Java, which became the focus of their trading activity. The Dutch did not begin to trade through Canton until 1728, well after the British (who started in 1689) and the French. By 1610, barred from direct trading at Chinese ports, they had already established a trading post at Banten, on the north-west tip of Java, and it quickly became a regular port of call for Chinese merchant junks. Instructions from the Lords to their agents in Batavia (modern Djakarta) show that by 1637 tea had already become one of the commodities bought from China. "As tea begins to come into use by some of the people, we expect some jars of Chinese as well as Japanese tea with each ship." By the end of seventeenth century the some had become many as tea came into general use in Holland.

By the beginning of the nineteenth century the Dutch, like the British, had become concerned about the balance of trade and the implications of the drain of specie caused by the ever-growing importation of tea from China. Again like the British, they engaged in the opium trade to redress this imbalance, though on a smaller scale, and were firmly behind their British competitor in all its attempts to impose the same on China. They were even quicker to embark on the other solution to the problem: to grow their own tea. The hero of early tea growing in the Dutch East Indies was J.I.L.L. Jacobson. In 1827, at the age of 29, the already experienced Amsterdam tea merchant and taster was given the task by the Lords of trying to establish tea cultivation in Java, where tea that had been planted earlier from Japanese seed had not taken. Like Robert Fortune 20 years later, Jacobson faced the problem of getting the necessary seeds and know-how in the face of Chinese secrecy and the deterrent of the severe punishment meted out to any Chinaman who betrayed it. Jacobson solved the problem by travelling into China in disguise several times between 1827 and 1833 and bringing back both seeds and workmen. We shall see later how he successfully went about converting his daring into large-scale tea cultivation.

Added impetus toward a plantation economy in the Dutch East Indies had been indirectly supplied by the British. During the Napoleonic Wars, when Holland was in the hands of the French, the Dutch had no national base out of which to run either shipping or trade, so the British took over the protection and administration of their ally's colonies in the east. It was under the Java governor-ship of Sir Stamford Raffles (later immortalized as the cricketing gentleman burglar "Raffles" by E.W. Hornung) between 1811 and 1815 that large tracts of land in Java and Sumatra were sold off to Dutch and English entrepreneurs or to combines of the two. P&T, a company still operating today, was fairly typical. In 1815 more than half a million acres were sold to this new Anglo-Dutch consortium for just 100,000 guilders (£8,200). At first the focus was on coffee, sugar, cinchona (the source of quinine), tapioca and rice, but rubber and tea were gradually introduced and assumed ever-increasing importance.

Where the British had shed public and quasi-public ownership of tea gardens as soon as they could, the Dutch retained many in state hands until 1860, and between 1914 and 1919 took back uncultivated land into state ownership. After the First World War the Dutch Government was restrained only with difficulty from renationalizing productive tea gardens as well, the significant element of British ownership being a crucial factor in keeping plantations in private hands. It was in the private era that the Dutch established the world's first formal tea research unit in 1894 in the botanical gardens at Buitenzorg in Java and as an entirely separate operation in 1902. This scientific approach may in part account for the fact that in the post-First World War boom-and-slump cycle, tea planting in the Dutch East Indies expanded three times faster than it did in India and Ceylon. This was achieved largely on the back of the earliest pre-harvest fixed price contracts with the British companies Brooke Bond and Lyons, but also as a result of harsh reductions in wages.

The Dutch were also the first to recognize that price stability was vital and that it could only be achieved by agreement at government level to restrict output to match probable demand. This was briefly achieved from 1933. Faced in their traditional markets in Europe with price competition from India and Ceylon because of the introduction of Britain's Imperial Preference scheme, the tea producers of the Dutch East Indies turned their attention to markets nearer at hand, and in particular in Australia, where the advantages of distance and time would be in their favour. So successful were they that not only did their tea supersede tea from India and Ceylon in these markets but the Australians became so enamoured of it that in 1932 they declined to join the Imperial Preference scheme for tea.

But for the Second World War invasion by Japan in February 1942, tea from Java and Sumatra would have continued to flourish to the present day. This invasion not only provided further evidence of the sadistic nature of Japanese imperialism but set off a chain of events that would send Indonesian tea tumbling down the export league table. In the course of their occupation the Japanese turned many tea gardens over to rice production and, as we have seen, others to coca. Even so, many Indonesians went hungry and the motivation to stay tied to their tea or rubber estates, where there might at least be enough to eat, was very strong. But such security came at a price because the Japanese reimposed the strict labour laws that the Dutch had abandoned well before the war.

Such were the cruelties of the Japanese that many of those who had endured the hardship and inferior status involved in working for Dutch and Anglo-Dutch companies with little active protest now took to the jungle to fight the new Asian enemy. In this they were encouraged and equipped as far as practicable by the British. When the war ended British forces moved in to give the Dutch time to recover from the lengthy German occupation of their homeland and to reorganize colonial garrisons and policing of their own. The British were taken aback to be greeted, not as the liberators they thought themselves, but as yet another oppressor. The retreating Japanese and the guerrillas of the new republican nationalist movement and of the communists destroyed about half the remaining plantations and much of the manufacturing machinery. When Dutch troops did eventually arrive they were opposed by well-disciplined and well-equipped freedom fighters as well as by numerous marauding criminal gangs. European managers and technicians, and indeed Indonesians, working in the tea gardens and other plantations went armed and at the risk of their lives – which were quite often lost. Though many Indonesians welcomed the return of the Dutch in the hope that they would restore stability and prosperity, the trend of the majority was in the opposite direction: toward militant nationalism and independence. Caught between nationalists who wanted to take over everything and communists who wanted to abolish the entire capitalist set-up, the Dutch accepted the inevitable, as the British had done in India, and in 1952 the Independent Republic of Indonesia was created.

By accepting Indonesian independence with fairly good grace, and by accelerating the takeover of most senior posts by Indonesians, the Dutch and their British business partners were usually able to hang on to their plantations. As happened elsewhere in the debilitating wake of the Second World War, unionized labour was able to secure much higher wages. This, together with the neglect of the bushes and the difficulty in securing fertilizers and other necessities, pushed up costs sharply. Output fell by 28 per cent. The reaction of the Indonesian Government in 1958 was to nationalize Dutch tea plantations, along with most other Dutch enterprises. The military coup of 1965 cut the plantation labour force by half, evicted many tea workers from their estate homes and imposed on those who remained draconian laws more severe than any imposed by the Dutch. Nationalist reaction to imperial rule in Java and Sumatra, as elsewhere, left the ordinary tea-garden worker both poorer and less free than he had been in recent years. Tea from Indonesia, a leading element in the international tea market in the days of the Dutch East Indies, ceased to be of great significance in terms of the post-war volume of world trade in tea until recently.

In many ways the most powerful player in the tea market of this immediate post-war period was Ceylon, another former Dutch colony of the seventeenth and eighteenth centuries. The Portuguese were the first Europeans to trade with Ceylon in 1502 and they enjoyed a monopoly of its spices until the Dutch came looking for cinnamon in 1636. Siding first with the King of Kandy against the Portuguese, then vice versa and finally with Kandy once more, the Dutch became the *de facto* colonial power by the middle of the seventeenth century and remained so for 140 years. Their monopoly of the cinnamon trade was so lucrative that smuggling out any of its products, or even damaging a plant, was punishable by death. The British East India Company, eyeing the spice trade with envy from southern India, briefly occupied Trincomalee in 1782 only to lose it to the French and see it restored to the Dutch by the Treaty of Paris in 1784.

As with the Dutch East Indies, the Napoleonic wars put a Dutch colony in the hands of the British, who offered "protection" to the Dutch and did not wait for an answer before seizing Trincomalee again. The British Government, thinking the Company had been dilatory in securing this valuable possession, took over the island and made it a Crown Colony on 1 January 1802. By the time Napoleon was finally defeated in 1815 the British had more or less established control of the whole island.

This background would be marginal to our tale of tea but for two factors: coffee blight and the proximity of a potential garden labour force in the Tamils of southern India. Over the next 125 years the great majority of Ceylon's plantations were owned and run by former British coffee planters and the great majority of the workers on them were these Tamils. When coffee was wiped out in the late 1860s, cinnamon, cinchona and other "spice" crops failed to plug the economic gap, so it was tea that took over. Within three-quarters of a century Ceylon had become the world's largest exporter of tea. When, as Sri Lanka, the country gained its independence from Britain in 1948 there were well over half a million acres under tea and more than half a million Tamils employed on them. The word "Ceylon" had become synonymous with tea, and tea was the new nation's greatest economic asset.

Unwisely, the new Sinhalese government of the United National Party, in the heady euphoria of its new-found power, made two mistakes which seriously damaged the tea industry and the economy: it threatened nationalization of the tea gardens and discriminated against their Tamil workers. The mere mention of nationalization was enough to frighten off many of the mostly British plantation owners, who sold out to indigenous businessmen. Whereas more than two-thirds of tea plantations were in foreign hands at independence, by 1964 fewer than a third were. This panic sale was amply justified in 1975, when all the larger gardens were nationalized with very little compensation to those companies that had stayed on. Incensed at this treatment, their parent concerns ceased to bid in any significant way for Ceylon tea at the Colombo auctions, and both quality and output declined. Nationalization may have been good for national pride, but it was bad for business. A new government in 1984 had the sense to denationalize the industry and, by concentrating on the high-quality tea which could be grown at altitude in the island's central highlands, went some way to restore the standing of Ceylon tea.

A much more damaging crisis arose from the Sinhalese government's treatment of the million Tamils of southern-Indian origin, many of them third- or fourth-generation immigrants, and the smaller indigenous Tamil population that had lived in Ceylon for two thousand years. Under the British, Tamil voting rights had been restricted, but they were sufficient to return several members to the Ceylon Parliament. Now, despite the objections of its large neighbour only 30 miles away across the Palk strait, half a million Tamils were forcibly repatriated to an India most of them had never known. Fewer than 10 per cent of the remainder were enfranchised, their language was marginalized and they were discriminated against in employment and education. The result was the Tamil Tigers and decades of bloody civil war only recently eased by a truce which nevertheless looks likely, as this book goes to press, to be broken by the Colombo government's renewed oppression. With such instability, tea from Ceylon, while still a major element on world markets, has never regained its former dominant position.

Two other nineteenth-century events in the Indian heartland of British imperialism were crucial to the birth of the modern tea industry in the subcontinent: the Anglo-Burmese wars of the 1820s and the Indian Mutiny of 1857.

In 1822 Robert Bruce, a former major in the Bengal Artillery, was taking advantage of the brutal anarchy in the region where India bordered on Burma (now Myanmar) to do a bit of illicit trading (no one at this time was permitted to carry out any commercial activity in India without the express permission of the East India Company) while acting as a mercenary on the side. It was in the course of these adventures that he discovered and forwarded to his brother the specimens of indigenous tea described in Chapter 2.

Major Robert Bruce first took service in 1821 with Purandah Singh, an aspirant to the role of Raja of Assam, against the incumbent, Chandrakant. This attempted coup was defeated and Bruce was taken prisoner. By promising, and later delivering, 300 muskets and 750lb of ammunition, he secured his release. He then entered the service of Chandrakant, leading a number of successful engagements against the Burmese in the following year while at the same time trading. Both the Raja of Assam and the pretender treated their subjects with great cruelty and their minor military successes against the Burmese were transitory.

It is as well to remember that Britain was not the only imperial power on the subcontinent with expansionist ambitions. By 1824 Burma had completely occupied Assam and treated its inhabitants with even more appalling cruelty than its rajas had. Men, women and children fled the country in droves and many that stayed were slaughtered by flaying and boiling alive in oil, disembowelling and slashing with knives or being herded into their prayer houses and burned alive. In this chaotic scene there sprang up many marauding bands who afflicted the peasant population with equal ferocity. One contemporary estimate claimed that at least half the population of Assam had been killed or fled the country.

Had this remained the situation perhaps the cultivation of tea in India might have been delayed by many years. However, the Burmese made the mistake of launching too-frequent predatory incursions into the East India Company's territory of Bengal a little further south at Arakan. The Company's combined naval and land operations in 1824, although so incompetently executed as to have cost some fifteen thousand (mostly Indian) soldiers' lives, resulted in the capture of Rangoon and the complete defeat of the Burmese. By the Treaty of Yandabo in 1826, the Burmese ceded what were to become the prime tea-growing regions of Assam and Cachar and, more troublesomely, the border areas, which the British suddenly found themselves having to defend against the incursions of the adjacent hill tribes. Unusually, therefore, the first experience the Assamese had of the British was as liberators: a positive reputation further enhanced by the abolition of slavery and the freeing of some twelve thousand slaves.

At first the British divided Assam into an area of direct administration and an area under the control of a puppet raja, the same Purandah Singh already mentioned. But when chaos continued under his rule the Company took over the administration of the entire territory in 1838. Robert's brother, the tea pioneer C.A. Bruce, was quite clear about the motive for this annexation. "With respect to what are called the *Singpho* Tea tracts, I am sorry to say we have not been able this year to get a leaf from them, on account of the disturbances that have lately occurred there: nor do I believe we shall get any next year, unless we establish a post at *Ningrew*, which I think is the only effectual way to keep the country quiet, and secure our Tea … . It is therefore important for us to look well to our Eastern frontier, on account of our capability to extend our Tea cultivation in that direction."

Thus did the Forward Policy evolve as much piecemeal on the ground as in the corridors of Parliament in Westminster. Despite occasional setbacks, such as the massacre of the garrison at Sadiya in 1839, a high degree of peace and stability was established in the territory. Many of the refugees returned and the traditional occupations of agriculture were resumed to the extent that there was at least the basis for a local labour force for the new tea gardens, albeit one that had to be heavily supplemented by recruits from Bengal and other parts of India.

By this time, 1833, when the East India Company's monopoly-bestowing charter came up for renewal, legislation of the British Parliament stripped the Company of all its commercial activities bar the trade in salt and opium. Otherwise it was left solely with the governance of the extensive areas of the subcontinent now under its control. A comfortable annual dividend of 10.5 per cent made this a fairly painless deprivation for the shareholders, though paying the £5-million annual burden of the dividend and of administering the country out of the Indian exchequer was resented by all Indians and by many of the British in India. At the same time the Government of India decided that in "such a wild land, long misgoverned and scantily populated" it would be necessary to encourage foreign, by which of course it meant British, entrepreneurial drive and capital. Concessions of land on very generous terms were on offer to any who wished to take them up, including Indians. Without this injection of British drive and the imperial stability enjoyed by the region, tea cultivation could not have established itself in north-east India. It is also noteworthy that in tea's fledgling days relations between managers and tea-garden labourers were generally good and the Europeans who ran them usually mixed well with their local communities. The events of 1857 would change all that.

The Indian Mutiny was not a national uprising, though it became mythologized as such in the rhetoric of the independence movement of the late nineteenth and twentieth centuries. It was almost exclusively confined to the catchment area of the Ganges, and even there the majority of the population was indifferent to it. Nor did the Native Princes anywhere in India join in. It was, by and large, just what it said it was – a mutiny – and even then one in which large sections of the Indian Army not only remained loyal to the Crown but helped to suppress the mutineers. Nevertheless, the butchering of European women and children, and incidents such as the massacre at Cawnpore on the one side and, on the other, the public hanging of many innocent Indians and the sadistic execution of others by binding them over the mouths of cannon and blasting them to pieces, created a demonology of its own. The easy-going relationship that had usually obtained hitherto between British settlers and the local Indian population was replaced by one of mutual suspicion, of contempt and paranoia on the one hand and resentment on the other.

The Government of India Act, which in 1858 followed the Mutiny, not only took away the political power of government from the East India Company, for it to be vested in the Crown, but set forth the high ideals to be observed by those who governed, along with ample rights for the governed. As P.J. Griffiths writes in *The British Impact on India*, "It promised that all British subjects, of whatever race or creed, should be freely admitted to the public services; it recognised Britain's obligation to India; and it declared that 'their prosperity will be our strength, and their contentment our security, and in their gratitude our best reward'. It deeply touched the hearts of educated Indians, and might have been the starting point of a new era in Anglo-British relations." Unfortunately the new attitude of nervous superiority of so many of the British in India meant that theory was seldom turned into practice. The arrival of the memsahibs, the wives and daughters of the businessmen, civil servants and military men, carrying the baggage of their Victorian class attitudes and sense of national superiority, widened the gap still further. The surprise is not the divergence between Briton and Indian that ensued, but that so many transcended its limitations to form genuine interracial friendships and develop mutual respect.

In the current climate of anti-imperial sentiment it should be noted that many of the British who worked in India, and particularly members of the Indian Civil Service, strove to fulfil the ideals of the Government of India Act. The Indian National Congress itself was founded in 1885 by a member of the Indian Civil Service and he did so with the Viceroy's blessing. Its second president, the leading tea trader George Yule, spoke movingly in his presidential address of the hope that India and Britain would be united "not by the hard and brittle bonds of arbitrary rule which may snap in a moment, but by the flexible and more enduring ligaments of common interests promoted, common duties discharged, by means of common service, chosen with some regard to the principles of representative government". Throughout the years European members of national and regional assemblies, regardless of their commercial interests, spoke out against government measures they thought against the interests of the people of India. (My father, for example, when leader of the European group in the Indian Legislative Assembly, threatened to cross the floor and join the Congress if Britain reneged on its promise to give India independence.) Such views, however, remained generally in a minority.

From the mid-century onwards the number of British needed to run the country and of those who came to take advantage of the new freedom to do business in India without Company permission rose substantially. This provided sufficient critical mass to create a much more exclusive expatriate community than had been possible before the Mutiny. During the period of Company rule the sparseness of Europeans on the ground in all but a few centres of commerce and government obliged them to socialize with their upper- and middle-class Indian neighbours. Now, even if it meant a long ride, they could do so with fellow countrymen at the nearest "club", which specifically excluded Indians except as servants. To quote Sir Percival Griffiths again: "It is beyond reasonable doubt that in the quarter of the century after the Mutiny many Englishmen developed an intolerant and arrogant attitude toward educated Indians which would have shocked men of an earlier generation. Their feeling toward the ordinary cultivator was not affected by this change – perhaps because he was neither a rival for power nor yet politically conscious – and it became increasingly common for British officials, at any rate in Bengal, to say: 'I like the peasant, he is a good fellow;

but I do not like the babu.'" ("*Babu*", literally a clerk, was a derogatory term for those literate Indians with some slight element of English education who naturally aspired to greater freedom and to equality with their often less able and less well educated masters.) How this relationship between peasants and patrician managers evolved on the tea plantations of the British and Dutch empires is the subject of the next three chapters.

CHAPTER SIX

Planter Sahibs

Once tea began to be grown outside the Far East, the characteristics of its cultivation changed completely. In China, in particular, tea growing was – and still largely is – carried out by many thousands of peasant farmers on marginal land on which they could not grow more staple crops. Sometimes a number of these smallholders would group together to process the raw leaf into the finished product in a single place, whereas many others would undertake the whole process on the home farm from start to finish. When the Indian tea industry was launched as a large-scale commercial enterprise by the British in the mid-nineteenth century, the approach had to be different from that of the Chinese, on whose expertise it relied at first. However, there was no precedent on which to base the management of a tea garden of hundreds of acres and on which the man in charge did not actually cultivate the tea bushes himself. Elsewhere, outside the Far East, tea had followed, or would follow, in the footsteps of other plantation crops: coffee in Ceylon and southern India, spices and palm oil in the Dutch East Indies. Northern India was hostile, virgin territory.

So the terms on which the Government of India offered leases of potential tea-growing land to anyone who would take them up were correspondingly generous. A quarter of the land was to be rent-free in perpetuity and the remainder for 15 years, which would be followed by a derisorily low annual charge. Leases were for 99 years and could be renewed on favourable terms. The only stipulation, far from onerous and also hard to enforce, was that an eighth of the land should be cleared within five years and half within 20.

It is scarcely surprising that such an inducement should have tempted a variety of rogues and vagabonds as well as many genuinely entrepreneurial adventurers. A mere 20 years after the Assam Company's first foray in 1839, there were 51 privately owned tea gardens in Assam alone. In 1870 Edward Money, a young tea planter and agronomist, wrote in a prize-winning essay: "Tea Planters in those early day were a strange medley of retired or cashiered Army and Navy officers, medical men, engineers, steamer captains, chemists, shopkeepers of all kinds, stable keepers, used up policemen, clerks and goodness knows who besides." Nevertheless, the great majority of the occupations that Money cited with such derision would have given their practitioners a pragmatic and practical approach to problem solving of which they would be in eminent need as tea-garden managers and assistants.

The Assam Company's first superintendent of tea gardens, J.W. Masters, had already complained in the 1840s that "it must be evident to the Directors that a passionate European entirely ignorant of the language and entirely ignorant of every part of his duty can but be worse than useless". Robert Fortune, writing a report to the Government of India in 1856, was equally scathing: "Somehow or other, in India, every man seems to think himself qualified to undertake the management of tea cultivation, without having any knowledge of the subject whatsoever. ... I can only account for this by supposing there is a charm about the name of our national beverage which has a tendency to mislead the judgement of persons who are, in other respects, rational and intelligent."

In 1867 a Commission appointed by the Government of Bengal observed that this wildly rapid expansion (of which more in Chapter 16) "necessarily threw the management of numerous gardens into the hands of inexperienced persons, many of whom were young men fresh from England, who had no knowledge whatever of the business in which they were engaged, of the habits and languages of the people who were under their control, or of the difficulties to be met and overcome. Under these circumstances, it was impossible that mistakes should not occur. Everything had to be learnt, and, as there were few or no competent teachers, each man gained his experience for himself at the expense of repeated failures."

A significant proportion of the early pioneers came from working- or lower-middle-class backgrounds. Typical of such men were Andrew Yule and Charlie Ansell. Yule came from a family of yeoman farmers on the estates of the Earl of Buchan in Scotland. He had already left the land to work as a warehouseman in Manchester before seeking his fortune in India. In 1855 he arrived in Calcutta with nothing but a spinning machine, on the basis of which he built a thriving local business. From this he branched out into tea and built up a financial empire managing gardens which is still flourishing today. Without any shame he could adopt as his company's emblem a single ear of wheat – by implication making 10 grow where only one grew before – and the motto of his erstwhile feudal overlords, the Buchans, "by strength and courage".

Ansell came into the business by chance, or rather mischance, at about the same time. A mechanic on a steamship, he was so badly burned in a boiler explosion that he was put ashore in Calcutta to recover. He used his knack with machines to persuade a tea company to take him on as *Kulwallah* (machine man). Soon he became one of the leading planters in Darjeeling and attained the dizzy social height of colonel of the North Bengal Mounted Rifles, the local European militia. His success as a planter owed no little to what a fellow planter described as his "sailor's free and easy-going ways in his attitude to his fellowmen of all classes and races".

The early tea planters of India were a colourful, varied and totally inexperienced collection of men, who usually had no idea where were the best places to plant tea bushes, let alone how to cultivate them and process their leaves. Often the mere presence of a few bedraggled wild plants in a patch of neighbouring jungle would be sufficient for one of these optimists to start a garden in the most unpropitious and unhealthy places. "New gardens were commenced on impossible sites and by men as managers who not only did not know a tea plant from a cabbage, but who were equally ignorant of the commonest rules of agriculture." None were more ignorant than those who went to northern India. Moreover, the men who tackled this task had to be the hardiest of the tea pioneers, for they had no precedent to follow and were the first Europeans to try to settle in these initially inhospitable areas.

Alexander MacGowan, writing in 1861 of his first encounter with a non-government European trying to establish a home and a tea garden in India, reveals the ambivalence of many early planters in their approach to relations with the native population. A "certain Mr M-k-n" (Makin?) had pitched his tent where he proposed to build on a spot that overlooked the home of a local Brahmin. Since a Brahmin's home must not be overlooked by one of a lower caste – which an Englishman would have been assumed to be – this gave rise to opposition that would have stymied M-k-n's project at the outset. The problem was resolved by moving the Brahmin, but MacGowan observes: "It will be clear from the above instance what obstacles such individuals prove to the progress of civilization." He goes on that the site is soon "a scene [where] the greatest activity prevailed. Close to, a row of huts for the workpeople were being made, while, in different spots, gangs of men were hacking up the soil that, in native hands, had lain so long neglected and barren, but from which English capital and energy were about to reap a golden harvest".

MacGowan dismisses the natural anxiety caused to the local inhabitants by this unprecedented intrusion on the grounds that

with the innate roguery natural to a race of fanatical heathens, they believed [it] must conceal some object injurious to their interests. It is, therefore, not astonishing that at first they were hostile to him. With but a limited knowledge of their language, his was an up-hill struggle; but by perseverance, patience, and kindness, their scruples were overcome, and he at last procured a lease of land. This was the small end of the wedge; and, on the inhabitants finding that money began to flow from the stranger, that numbers of unemployed labourers could easily get work and were fairly dealt with – being regularly paid, and not left to be ground down by native contractors – the popular feeling changed; and, at the time of our visit, it was amusing to observe the respect shown to Mr. M—k—n, and the alacrity with which his wishes were complied with.

MacGowan's attitude was fairly typical during the runaway expansion of tea cultivation in India in the 1860s, and if it seems high-handed to the contemporary eye, such views were even then tempered by the enlightened instincts of many front-line imperialists. For example, the debate, not irrelevant in our own day, as to whether more socially responsible economic benefit would be derived from large corporations or numerous small-scale entrepreneurs was vehemently conducted on both sides. MacGowan comments:

By some, it is thought that to grant to a wealthy company large tracts of country suitable for tea-cultivation, or entire existing plantations, would be the only sure way of extending the manufacture of tea. By others this system is condemned as tending to the monopoly of the tea-country, the profits on which would find their way into the pockets of wealthy absentee capitalists, while a small staff of officials to work the speculation would alone live in the tea districts; whereas by placing a limit on the grants the prize might be shared by persons of moderate means, and a class of settlers thus be formed, who, living on the spot, would improve the condition of the natives of the soil, by spending among them a considerable portion of the competence realized by their labour, thus connecting by ties of interest a people hitherto kept in check by armed force.

This was an enlightened point of view to express only four years after the Indian Mutiny of 1857.

MacGowan saw himself agreeably placed among

Those (and the class is numerous in England) who, possessing but a moderate sum of money, wish, nevertheless, to maintain the position in life to which they have been educated, to whom trade or the professions are obnoxious, who, having no military tastes or nautical tendencies, are still anxious to use that energy and enterprise which are said to belong to the British – to such, tea planting offers peculiar inducements. An employment in itself agreeable, entailing no hard physical labour, but merely sufficient exercise for both body and mind as is essential to their healthy preservation,

and eventually so lucrative as to amply repay the anxieties incidental on the earlier years; with a property safe against the many
ills that other crops are liable to, and withal of such a nature, when
in full bear, as to give ample time for recreation, or even to permit
of a prolonged absence; and, lastly, when it is taken into consideration that the cultivation of tea can only be carried on in those
districts eminently adapted for the European constitution, and that
it does not entail a shortening or deterioration of life, as a residence
in the plains of India (notwithstanding occasional exceptions)
undoubtedly occasions ... an occupation will be supplied by tea
planting, the prospects of which, if equalled by some others, are at
any rate scarcely to be excelled.

Naturally he felt it would have been ill-advised to extend this
opportunity for leisurely enrichment to the lower classes. When the
Government of India considered settling discharged army privates
and junior NCOs in the tea areas in order to provide the nucleus of
a trained local militia, and thus reduce the need for stationing costly
regular regiments in India, the excuse for opposing the idea was the
entirely erroneous belief that "they could not compete with the
teeming native population, for although a native workman cannot
be compared with an English one, still the low rate of wages of the
former allows an employer to make up by numbers the absence of
the individual excellence and physical force so remarkable in the
latter". MacGowan's opposition to encouraging discharged NCOs
and "Other Ranks" was shared by Lord William Hay, who doubted
that such men "of slender means, [and] somewhat addicted to
drinking ... will make successful colonists. As a general rule, they
have a great dislike for the natives of the country, and are imper-
fectly acquainted with their language and habits, and, from having
had everything provided for them during a long course of years,
they are quite at a loss when they have to depend on themselves."
Another area to attract early attention in north-east India was
the Western Dooars, which was annexed from Bhutan to Bengal in
1865. "The district is traversed from north to south by innumerable
rivers and streams which in the rainy season become raging torrents
and perpetually change their courses. In the middle of the last [nine-

teenth] century it was covered with almost impenetrable jungle containing much valuable but unexploited timber, giving shelter to all manner of wild beasts and inhabited only by primitive tribes such as Garos, Mechis, Totos, many of whom lived in trees or crude huts and lived by hunting and fishing." It was, moreover, an area plagued by malaria and blackwater fever. The word "malaria" comes from the Italian *mal aria*, or bad air. In the early twentieth century the disease was still thought to be caused by swamp miasmas, hence the custom in much of Assam of building planters' bungalows on stilts. Then in 1925 Dr Ramsay dissected fifty thousand *anopheles minimus* mosquitoes for the Indian tea industry. He postulated that these were the disease-carrying parasites and proposed shading the drains and swamps where they bred. This was quite extensively done, but to little avail. Further work between the wars, at India's Ross Institute, demonstrated that it was *anopheles fluviatilis*, which bred in gently running water under diffused sunlight, that was the carrier. Once streams and rivers were cleared of obstructions and oiled and their grassy banks cut back the incidence of malaria was greatly reduced and in some areas virtually eradicated. Even a twentieth-century planter described the Western Dooars as "a land only for saints or satans". Nevertheless, the area was climatically ideal for tea growing, and it was here, at Jalpaiguri in 1879, that the first Indian-owned and managed tea garden in Bengal was started by a few lawyers and clerks.

As knowledge and experience accumulated generally, so it became evident what qualities constituted the essential make-up for the successful planter. One of their number, E.F. Bamber, writing in 1866 – only 10 years after Fortune's scathing criticism cited earlier – was confident he knew the prescription: "The cultivation of the tea plant is an occupation which may be carried out profitably by anyone possessing the average amount of intelligence. The characteristic qualification most requisite for its successful prosecution being economy, tact, ability and willingness to devote constant supervision to the work. It is an occupation from which the greatest pleasure may be derived, there being few things so interesting as to watch the operations of nature, as they gradually but steadily unfold themselves to the view." Four years later, as general recognition dawned of the advantages of applying science to the art of tea production, Edward Money added to the list of desiderata knowledge of agriculture, tea cultivation and manufacture. In 1870 the Ceylon Planters' Association asked members to send in soil samples. Most just sent in a chunk of earth and a manuring schedule, but one, John Taylor, whom we shall meet again, went about it more thoroughly. He dug a hole from which he re-created the layers of soil in a sample box, so that they could be seen as such when the side of the box was removed. He also pointed out that tea-bush roots usually occupy only the top 5–8cm of soil: important knowledge for their subsequent care. By the start of the twentieth century the scientific officers appointed by the Indian Tea Association were contributing significantly to the rapid rise in yield per acre. In 1912 the Indian tea industry's official research station was formally established at Tocklai in north-east Assam, and the planters of Ceylon followed suit in 1925. However, the Dutch had yet again beaten the British to the draw by establishing their research station at Buitenzorg in 1893.

By 1887 the *Tea Cyclopaedia* was able confidently to repeat the claim of one anonymous manager that "skilful men have charge of the garden now. Instead of tea being the refuge and last resource for the comparative destitute as it was not many years since, it is now looked upon as a profession of a high order, and into which men of the highest social rank are entering". It is probable that in some cases their "high social rank" and its accompanying public-school ethos may have contributed to the growing gulf between the British and their Indian subjects in the second half of the nineteenth century. Not until 1907, when addressing the Leesh River debating society, could G.E.B. Peacock assert with confidence: "The first thing I consider a necessity is to know the language and be able to speak it fluently; much depends on the amount of tact employed in each individual case." He still felt it necessary to warn against giving some coolies an inch lest "it be looked upon by them as a sign of weakness on the sahib's part".

In Ceylon the managers of the earliest tea gardens – though bene-fiting from the pioneering of the coffee planters, whom they superseded after the coffee blight of 1867 had virtually destroyed that business – had to contend with similarly unpropitious conditions. James Taylor, who was signed on to plant coffee in the 1850s for £100 a year less the cost of his kit and passage, was one of the first to make the transition. His tea garden at Loolecondera, which he began in 1867, was situated at 900 metres above sea level and rose to 1,530 metres. "It would be hard to find a stonier place. On some fields the tea seems to cling to great slabs and boulders of naked rock, like the bones of the earth sticking out. Divine madness of the old planters who fought their way into such limbos – one man alone, as often as not – and then collected labour, marked out the ground, burnt down the jungle, cleared away the wreckage (in itself a work for giants), and set about planting up every square yard where a bush could get a foothold!" In southern India, too, tea took advantage of the inroads of coffee blight. It was "extraordinary courage and determination which enabled the pioneers, here, as in the other tea districts, to cope with the difficulties of opening up jungle land. They had to begin by cutting bridle-paths through dense forests; they had to persuade primitive tribal people to work for them; they had to live in considerable discomfort in crude shacks built by themselves; and they had to act as doctors and surgeons to their labour forces. They succeeded because of their toughness."

It is hard to appreciate just how tough these early tea planters had to be to survive. In the most remote place, today's "intrepid pioneer" almost always knows that – by means of satellite phone and radio, his whereabouts pinpointed by sat-nav – expert help, complete with antibiotics and every other medical aid, can be summoned by helicopter to augment his chances of survival. Not so his nineteenth-century predecessor. Even when those young Englishmen (or, as often as not, Scots) had acquired sufficient knowledge and experience to make good tea-garden managers, the chances were that they would be struck down by disease, most prevalently the still mysterious malaria, of which cause and cure alike were equally unknown. Most planters (and the very occasional European wife who bravely chose to join her husband) had contracted malaria within their first six months in India and often within their first six weeks. Many were so weakened by its recurring bouts that, even if it was not immediately fatal, they might have to be invalided home to Britain after only one or two tours of duty, there to die prematurely. Dysentery, cholera, typhoid, blackwater fever and parasites of every description further undermined the constitutions of Europeans unaccustomed to the heat and humidity in which they had to live and work in all but the high-altitude districts of Darjeeling (originally earmarked only as a recuperative sanatorium for civil servants and the military) or the highland plantations of Ceylon and Java.

The nearest doctor was seldom less than a day's ride away, and usually more. The "doctor babu" (an Indian trained to medical-orderly level to look after plantation workers), or a mission post where basic medical knowledge and medicine might be available if he were lucky, was the best the planter could hope for by way of outside assistance. Usually he had to be his own doctor and dose himself, his assistants and his plantation workers with whatever was to hand and try to keep them healthy by doctoring them with "quinine every morning, castor oil twice a week and calomel at the change of the moon". (My father never had a day's illness in 50 years in India and attributed this to drinking a pint of water every evening, though I suspect it had as much to do with the liberal addition of whisky or gin.) Whether a "strong emetic of tartar and horse leeches, applied to the temples" during recurring bouts of malarial fever was an appropriate remedy is doubtful. Certainly, it cannot much have helped reduce the enlargement of the spleen that is caused by that disease.

Nor were purely physical ailments the planter's only problem. Once the initial overstaffing with Europeans – seldom fewer than three, sometimes as many as 11 on a single tea garden – had been cut back by death and economies, a planter might well be working and living completely on his own, apart from his plantation workers in their own "native lines". On a larger garden he might have one or two European assistants, but this was not necessarily a blessing. Diaries and letters home are full of accounts of fierce, and indeed sometimes violent, clashes between autocratic and bullying managers and their often innocent and ignorant assistants. There were, of course, also many instances where an almost familial bond developed between them, but outbursts of rage and fits of depression were the not unusual, nor surprising, results of such a taxing environment, and both were frequently exacerbated by the heavy consumption of whisky and beer that was often the planter's only escape from boredom and exhaustion.

From time to time these lonely men would make the arduous and lengthy trek to foregather at the bungalow of one of them: usually the most senior. By the end of the nineteenth century the rendezvous, still a distant one, was more usually the district club. These get-togethers were often the excuse for prodigious orgies of boozing and much very rough, and sometimes humiliating, horseplay. F.A. Hetherington, a planter writing in his diaries for the years 1900 to 1902, records one occasion when he and 16 colleagues "drank thirty-six bottles of champagne and a dozen of brandy" at dinner and after a brief sleep had "more champagne and large quantities of stout, Munich beer and pale ale for breakfast". At least such temporary oblivion must have afforded relief from what were usually very primitive living conditions.

The image so often portrayed of the leisured planter lolling on his verandah, beer or whisky in hand, or setting off into the jungle for a spot of sporting "shootin'", is a crude distortion. Of course, many planters did enjoy the danger and the excitement, the sporting challenge, of hunting game, big or small. But as well as a pastime *shikar* was a valuable contribution both to their often very limited cuisine and to the local community. Tigers killing livestock, and sometimes humans; an elephant on *musth* (rutting) rampaging through a village; an angry water buffalo, perhaps the most dangerous animal of all, making it impossible to harvest the paddy; each and all could seriously threaten not only the lives but the precarious livelihoods of the villagers in the neighbourhood of a tea garden, as well as the well-being of the garden itself. Few Indians could afford the wherewithal to hunt such dangerous beasts, and though some of the villagers and tribespeople possessed unparalleled knowledge of the ways of their local fauna, they were only too glad to be able to call on one of the sahibs to tackle the problem. The sahibs themselves were often keen to learn, and a few became not only skilled *shikari* but expert zoologists and naturalists, with a real love of the fauna and flora of their districts, who added to the sum of scientific knowledge. (My brother Michael, who was a well-respected *shikar*, would spend days and nights in the jungle not shooting but observing. His patience was once rewarded with the rare sight of an elephant funeral.)

The planter's role as a defender of his workers against wild beasts or dealing with a snake (thousands still die from snake bite every year in India) had not only practical but psychological consequences. His show of courage or cowardice in the face of a predator could be crucial in determining the degree of respect or disdain in which he was held by his workers. One such assistant manager, summoned by frightened pluckers to deal with a leopard crouching among the tea bushes, realized that although he was inwardly quaking, his future authority depended on his at least appearing to deal with the situation calmly, courageously and effectively. If he did not he knew he would "be known in the lines as a coward and God knows what they will cook up". The leopard dispatched and his prestige enhanced, he was later able to assert with confidence that he did not "accept any nonsense from the men workers". Nevertheless, he admitted that he was still careful to assert his authority on his own ground – on his bungalow verandah, at the pay desk or in the factory – rather than in the field, where, as Piya Chaterjee puts it, "the hoe and the sickle always have the potential to be transformed into lethal weapons". And they quite often were. In the Indian food riots of 1921, for example, a number of Europeans were killed by mobs driven desperate by the fact that the post-war cut in wages had not been met by a corresponding cut in the cost of subsidized food. Deep beneath the warm waters of the adulation, and even genuine affection, for the sahibs, there sometimes flowed a cold current of resentment and anger that could break chillingly to the surface.

Until late in the nineteenth century the "home" of the European garden assistant, and often that of his manager, would have been little more than a large mud hut, roofed with leaves or thatch and divided into living and sleeping areas. If he were lucky he might enjoy what would later become the ubiquitous verandah of the plantation bungalow. (I have never understood why, in copying the bungalow's grosser architectural features, the British suburbanite seldom adopts its saving grace.) Such was the discomfort of his accommodation that one young planter, writing in 1866, preferred to be "out in all weathers from 7.0 am to 5.0 p.m.". Pouring rain or beating sun was nothing compared with what might be endured "at home".

It may be inferred from the description of his "home" by another young planter, Kenneth Warren, that conditions had not much improved 40 years on in 1906:

The ceilings of the rooms were hessian cloth also white-washed. The space between the ceiling cloth and the thatch roof was the home of bats and occasionally snakes. My furniture consisted of my bed, which I had bought in Calcutta, and two chairs bought in the local bazaar, the rest consisted of tea-boxes inverted, with a "Mull-Mull" (coarse muslin) cloth covering, serving as a table, and six tea-boxes standing up sideways, with a strip of Mull-Mull hung in front, used as a chest of drawers or wardrobe and a similar arrangement of inverted boxes for a dressing table. Lighting consisted of a hurricane lamp and candles on the table with beer bottles as candle sticks.

For bathing he had recourse to

a tin hip-bath on a cement floor bathroom under one's bedroom approached by a ladder through a trap door in the bedroom floor. Owing to the number of bats inhabiting most bungalow roofs it was advisable to take an old tennis racquet down with you to the bathroom to keep them from sharing the bath, as they seemed to take a delight in splashing into the water as they flew around your head. After your bath the custom was to upturn the bath on to the cement floor and the water then ran out through a hole in the wall away into an open drain outside. Unfortunately this hole in the wall not only allowed the bath water to get away but also gave access to creatures from outside.

Yet by the time Warren went home to England, after 20 years' service, he also clearly appreciated the benefits of the planter's life, even one on only £33 a month, which was his final pay. He recognized that "the cost of living was very much less in those days as I was able to keep two or three polo ponies and train a further two or three for members of the Tingri Polo Club and also to employ an ex-NCO of the Deccan Horse as 'Riding-Boy' in charge, and a Sikh chauffeur, keep a well run bungalow and entertain, and be a regular attendant at our local club – polo, tennis, etc. – and also manage a certain amount of shooting and fishing and take part in our local race meets. On the whole a very pleasant and enjoyable as well as interesting life at a minimum cost."

A typical planter enjoyed having half a dozen coolies to act as ballboys when he played tennis; and another in the Nilgiris had 16 men take eight days to carry a billiard table the six miles to the club. Tea-garden workers were often employed about the personal business of their managers and assistants in this way. Bridge, billiards and downing innumerable "pegs" – a *chota* (Hindi, "small" or "lesser") peg, or measure, was a small whisky, about a finger's depth in a standard tumbler; a *burra* (Hindi, "large" or "greater") peg, was a large one, at least double the size of a *chota* peg – were the most common indoor pastimes and although there were occasionally amateur concerts and play-acting, usually initiated by the civilizing influence of the women, the evening would probably end with "the usual sing-song and a little wrestling".

Life was rather less enjoyable for "Carver" Marsh and his companions in southern India when

The monsoon proved to be a very continuous and heavy one, and the discomforts endured by all of us living in temporary houses with mud floors and thatched roofs, were very considerable. Every room leaked; there were no doors and windows, the wet and mist soaked into everything in the building, and the only possible way of maintaining any sort of dryness was to keep a large fire burning on the floor in the middle of the room. This was done continually, and frequently the smoke was so heavy that the only place to sit was on the floor, and even then one's eyes were full of it. It was quite a common happening on a Monday morning to wake up and find our whole staff had bolted at daybreak with the shandy coolies, and that we were left to fend for ourselves.

At such times a government surveyor called Loam took over the culinary duties. "A born cook, he practically always did the whole of his own cooking on a series of kerosene oil tins built into the stone work in the form of ovens along the inside edge of his verandah, where he used to sit in a chair attending to the cooking of the day."

Loam's cookbook would make interesting reading since he often had to make do with the remnants of the week's supply of rice, which came up by coolie or pack bullock once a week – if all went well. Sometimes, when it did not, he used the grain brought for the horses, together with whatever vegetables could be scratched from the garden, supplemented occasionally by any game the planters managed to shoot.

Early tea-planting conditions in Ceylon were no better. James Taylor describes one spell of less than 24 hours in which five and a half inches of rain fell during the night and another four in 20 minutes the following morning. In his very basic bungalow "whenever the light went out a flock of rats from the jungle beside us come in looking out for something to eat, and then the wind, of which we have plenty at this time of year, blows a perfect hurricane in the bungalow, sometimes so as to put out the lamp".

Nor were actual hurricanes round the Indian Ocean such a rarity, and they were usually accompanied by torrential rain and rivers and streams that broke their banks, almost while you were watching them. One Assam planter, A.R. Ramsden, described experiencing such a storm early in the twentieth century:

The wind sighed and woofed in the distance, the ominous pink and yellow line on the horizon grew stronger, trees bent and straightened up again as the puffs of wind became gusts changing to blasts ever increasing in fury as the cyclonic centre approached. When the storm was at its height with huge hailstones cascading on the roof it was quite impossible to make oneself heard in the office, so I wrote on a piece of paper, "Let's have a look outside," and handed it to Sailor. I lip-read his reply: "Not bloody likely!" And then he wrote down, "Impossible stand against it." Just then there was a shattering report and a flash of lightning came coiling down an H iron column in the middle of the factory. Wooden rafters splintered, a large part of the roof sagged, the H iron column, eight by twelve inches, was twisted like a piece of barley sugar, and an extra violent gust of wind blew a huge area of the roof clean away, the corrugated iron sheets flying in the wind like bus tickets on a windy day on Blackpool front. For about three minutes there was a howling, roaring tempest that gradually decreased in fury till all became dead still, the sun shone again and the birds sang – but the landscape looked like a stricken battlefield.

It was not just the threat to the planter's personal safety that might be the consequence of such storms. When it was cold enough to turn the rain to hail, the damage to the tea bushes could be severe and long-term, not only stripping off the leaves but so damaging the stock that it had to be rested in order to allow the plant to regenerate.

Most alarming of all must have been the frequent and often severe earthquakes, measuring 4–7 on the Richter scale. (Certainly one of the most nerve-racking experiences I have had was to watch buildings sway precariously out of the vertical and the ground turn to flowing liquid under your feet, or judder to and fro, as if a crazed gardener were frantically sieving the earth beneath you.) Such cataclysms were all too regular in most of the tea-growing countries, but particularly in northern India along the line of the Himalayas. One such struck in 1897 and its death toll of 1,542 was considered slight. Two people were actually swallowed by a crevasse that suddenly opened in the ground where they stood and they vanished for ever. E.C. Dozey, the author of an early history of Darjeeling, describes what I infer to have been the same 1897 earthquake:

His attention was first drawn to a deep, dull rumble in the earth which equalled in volume the sound created by 10 train loads of empty wagons being shunted; the next, thousands of bubbles were seen welling up from the bottom of the tank [small-scale water reservoir], to be followed by the water being churned as in a maelstrom until whirled over the embankment 3 feet high, while the fishes, from midgets to those weighing fully a maund [82lb], leapt clean out of the water on to the land. The birds swept round in circles giving tongue to plaintive notes, the earth heaved, the chimney attached to this press, which was over 50 feet in height, swayed 4 feet on either side out of plumb, while the wall of the main store-house, which is fully 400 feet long, sinuated like a snake and opened out in large fissures through which the light of day shone ... At the foot of the Chitpore bridge the market had collapsed, the walls of many houses *en route* had cracked and fallen, while not 10 *per cent* of the parapets were left standing. The spires of the St. Paul's Cathedral and the Sacred Heart of Jesus, Calcutta, had snapped in twain, while many of the dwellings of the poorer order had ceased to exist. Such was the panic in that city that thousands slept in the open parks and public warehouses for the whole of the week following.

In another earthquake a young planter's wife was killed when she rushed back into her collapsing bungalow to rescue her baby, unaware that its *ayah* (nursemaid) had already done so. On a lighter note a planter's wife, caught in the bath by a 'quake, grabbed a cushion to protect her head from falling debris, but when she ran outside to safety her indignant husband commanded her to "place it elsewhere".

Given such frequent and alarming onslaughts of nature as hurricane, earthquake and deluge, the danger posed by man and beast must have seemed relatively tame. But these also constituted significant, and often more immediate, additional dangers. In 1885 planters in Cachar protested vigorously at a government proposal to withdraw police, as an economy measure, from their outposts in the rainy season. In 1888, when it was suggested that the regiment posted in Shillong be withdrawn, local Europeans pointed out that many of them, and local natives as well, had been killed in raids by savage frontier tribes, and that they would prefer preventing their throats from being cut to official revenge afterwards. The situation was no better four years later. In one incident alone 38 men were murdered and six women abducted. *Dacoities* (highway robberies) took place on the main roads in broad daylight and the police appeared to be "more employed in the impressment of labour than their legitimate business, and the officer in charge too listless or indolent to trouble himself to make any personal enquiries when robberies are reported to him". The response of district commissioners tended to be that, if the planters wanted armed police guards, they should pay for them.

However, by the end of the nineteenth century, it can be inferred from the absence of the previously prominent subjects of crime and police from the annual reports of the Indian Tea Association, that pax Britannica was more or less established in all those parts of the subcontinent under the rule of the Crown, either by more effective policing or by the rather gung-ho self-help of the planters' own mounted militia. In 1967 one planter reminisced about such a punitive foray, in which he had been involved, in much the same terms as he might have described a tiger hunt. Bengali dacoits had raided the armoury at Chittagong, and killed the British sergeant in charge, before invading the local club intent on murder. Luckily there were no Europeans there at the time, but the Surma Valley Light Horse chased the dacoits into the jungle. There the pursuers came under fire. "Fortunately the mob's shooting was so poor that only one man was slightly wounded. Together with armed police, the SVLH had some good target practice, and many of this band of insurgents were killed."

It should be taken into account, when judging Europeans' attitudes, that in their colonies during the nineteenth and much of the twentieth centuries native society itself was essentially violent. Disputes were often settled by blows, and sometimes by worse – as in the case of Bonki, a key native team supervisor on an Assam tea garden, early in the twentieth century. Provoked to fury by his wife's insults, Bonki had hit her on the head with an axe. Her dead body was discovered not long afterwards, so the husband was arrested and locked up in the local police station without his manager knowing. Without Bonki the garden could not be run effectively, so, for rather less than altruistic reasons, when the garden manager learned of Bonki's arrest he intervened on his behalf, but seemed remarkably offhand about the whole affair when he recollected it later:

This was terrible news for me so I at once jumped on my pony and rode off to the Doom Dooma Thana [police station]. There I met the "Police Sergeant in Charge" who told me what had happened. I told him this was a very serious matter as Bonki could not be spared and that owing to his absence the work on the garden was being held up and that I could not agree to the Police holding him under arrest. I demanded his immediate release. After some heated argument the Police Sergeant reluctantly agreed to my demand and Bonki was brought from his cell and handed over to me on my guaranteeing his good behaviour in future. Bonki then came back with me to Hansara, took over his labour chalan [team] and their work then proceeded smoothly as usual. I never heard anything more from the police ... .

The incident is significant, not only in indicating the inferior position of women in Hindu society at the time but in that the probable perpetrator of a serious crime could be exculpated by being declared under the protection of a British planter.

In the nineteenth and early twentieth centuries plantation managers treated their employees on the tea gardens of India, Ceylon and the Dutch East Indies in what we should regard as an unacceptably proprietorial, and often brutal, way. In 1873 a Government of India report somewhat dispassionately observed that "many planters still seemed to regard flogging as the best way of dealing with labourers who regretted having come to the tea districts". The response to almost any misdemeanour or crime – from the trivial to the serious, from idleness and insult to theft and assault, from cheating to cheek – was to administer "a good thrashing". But before we hasten to condemn, we need to take account of context, contemporary culture and the social and economic consequences of the alternatives.

At that time in England, and to a lesser extent in the Netherlands (as Holland became in 1815), it was considered perfectly normal, and indeed necessary, for husbands to beat wives, fathers to beat sons, and even occasionally to give their daughters a good hiding. It was commonplace in the schools of the day for senior boys to beat junior boys, and still was until fairly recently. (At school between 1947 and 1952 the author was in receipt of many such beatings.) European garden assistants' introduction to plantation life at the hands of their managers could be profoundly humiliating and sometimes physically violent. Once broken in they were soon elevated to "prefect" status and entitled to administer punishment themselves. The assistant, in turn, was expected to exercise the necessary physical control over the coolies, not only to maintain good order among them but to ensure a high level of output, and he was often only too eager to cross the divide from bullied to bully to enhance his own standing and security.

John Taylor's first manager in Ceylon in 1867 was, appositely, called Pride. Pride was "a little fellow who in his passions was fearful and who had no control of them – there he stands thumping his foot on the ground and cursing. One day he thumps a coolie for nearly half an hour." Taylor himself was another who would knock a man down on the least provocation, though it was more often incompetence than insolence that provoked his anger. Yet when he died "the Kanganis and the labourers walked behind the coffin. They called him sami dorai ['master who is god']". ("Foreman" is close but does not do full justice to the term "*kangany*". He both recruited and subsequently oversaw a single work gang on a Ceylon tea garden. His nearest equivalent in India was the *maistri*, or recruiting overseer.)

Hetherington, in his endearingly honest diaries of life on an Indian tea garden in the first two years of the twentieth century, reveals the young assistant's dilemma in judging how far to go in physically disciplining his workers. He seems to have been an irascible young man, his ire fuelled perhaps by the drinking described earlier and the death of his wife from malaria only six months after joining him. A series of incidents in which he was involved, if a little extreme, was fairly typical of planters' conduct in general at the time.

> Went round the new lines plucking and nearly caused a riot by clouting three women, one of whom happened to be Moorali Sirdar's [a village headman] wife. They were plucking into kapre, which was strictly forbidden. The punishment was in accordance with Dunlop's ways, but I was too new to inflict it myself ... and Dunlop pitched into me. A few days before he had censured me for

not punishing them, so neither way could I do right. Am getting sick of the place and feel inclined to chuck up the job. I can't hit it off with the coolies.

Dunlop had a row with the Goungusti, headed by the dak wallah [post runner]. Having been sent to the office they arrived looking innocent enough but after Dunlop hit one for calling him a liar, out came sticks previously concealed and the four of them wired in. But after a vain attempt they turned tail and ran and men were sent to head them off the factory.

Then, with the same stroke of the pen, he writes:

Dunlop drove me to polo where Mrs Macrae and Lillifant turned up. We have thoroughly reduced that busti [native village] now that Soma is ruined and the natives may see once more that the sahib can still beat them. Soma is to be allowed to stay on his land but we can turn him out any day. Of course the darogha [police sergeant] expects and gets a little backshish for his part in the business ...

... Trouble in my bungalow which resulted first in Kaddo, then in Nando Lal getting thrashed. The latter broke from me when I hit him about the face with my fists for a while and threw himself over the back verandah railing, falling about eight feet onto his back. He got up, however, and ran off. Dunlop arrived, sent for the chowkidars [watchmen or guards] and found Nando back at his work again. We sent them both to the hospital for the night. Investigated the case at the office and found them only partially guilty, there having been provocation, so my thrashing was considered sufficient punishment and they were restored to the bungalow once more, instead of going to hoe on hard clay. Left at 10.30 a.m. for Borpukri.

Lest we be too hard on Hetherington, it is clear that he also had a softer side to his nature, even if he did not allow it to interfere with productivity. "[When] I arrived in the tea house I saw a crowd round No. 1 paragon. They made room for me and there lay the poor little chap. He had been cleaning out the machine and some one had shut him into a temperature of over 2000. The skin was burnt off his face, knees and feet where he must have touched the trays in his struggle. What an awful death! I was nearer crying than I have been for years. The darogha arrived about 11.30 a.m. and made a lot of useless inquiries about the accident. But every coolie denied having shut the door and we personally don't wish to know, so the matter ended."

This novice planter was not alone in his approach. An Assam tea-garden manager, writing of the years immediately before the Second World War, could offer his offending *ticcadar* (wages clerk) the standard basic choice: "If you do that again, ticcadar, I will either go to the police or give you a damn good hiding on the spot."

Here we have one of the crucial reasons why native garden workers usually put up with this kind of treatment: the economic and social consequences of the more formal, judicial alternative. The threat of police intervention and subsequent trial before a British magistrate had even more unpleasant consequences than a slap, a punch or even "a good thrashing". The magistrate, who was usually regarded as fair and impartial by all parties, or even thought by Europeans to lean toward the native point of view, would have been bound to impose a fine or, even worse, imprisonment. Such punishment would have undermined, or completely destroyed, the coolie's ability to earn his already precarious living and to feed his probably numerous family, though some of these, too, might be working for the same employer. It may have been this same sense of security-in-oppression that accounted for the fact that some of the senior Indian employees also recalled this relationship with blind nostalgia. Wrote one *babu*: "I agree with the sahib and what he did! Why not! But you see in those days, there weren't all these unions and party politics and the sahibs could do anything. I remember in front of my eyes, on the factory verandah, men being beaten. Now things like that can't happen."

Let it not be thought that nineteenth-century British tea planters were alone in their rough treatment of native labour. Conditions on Dutch tea gardens in Java were largely determined by those established for the more economically important cultivation of palm oil and spices. Theoretically the introduction of the Coolie Ordinance of 1880 secured by contract, for plantation workers generally, basic minimum standards of treatment and remuneration. In practice the clauses most often invoked were those penalizing him for "excessive idleness", "wilful disobedience" or "absconding". Fighting, drunkenness or insulting or threatening a manager or supervisor were construed as a punishable breach of the Coolie Ordinance. A coolie could be compelled to make up at the end of his contract for any time lost due to illness, imprisonment or absence, and any absconder had deducted from his meagre wages the cost of recapturing him. For all these offences he could be fined or imprisoned. A third of those sentenced to more than three months in prison died there. One argument put forward in 1925 to justify instant, on-the-spot chastisement was that "instead of locking them [coolies] up in prison, where they died like rats, chastisement on the plantation itself meant that a pack of disorderly and low grade coolies could be disciplined into honest and skilled workers".

By the 1920s the Coolie Ordinances were more honoured in the breach than the observance, and assaults by coolies on white managers and assistants, and, more particularly, their often harsher Asian surrogates, became increasingly frequent. The Dutch authorities chose to attribute these incidents to "estates ... being infiltrated surreptitiously by communist agitators, 'extremist' elements, and nationalist trouble-makers who were allegedly turning the coolies on a radical bent".

In reality they were the desperate response to "cramped and poor housing, widespread disease, high adult and infant mortality, along with verbally and physically abusive disciplinary measures". Workers were often beaten so severely that they died. One of the largest plantation owners in Sumatra had to flee the country secretly to avoid seven charges of murder by flogging. Female workers would be tied to a post outside the manager's house and have their genitals rubbed with finely ground pepper. No one knows how many died from malaria, infected cuts and ulcers, infectious and contagious diseases or simply from overwork and exhaustion, but one authority puts the proportion at one in four. When a coolie finally cracked under the strain of abuse or debility and attacked his manager or foreman, he was classified as "running amok", a supposed congenital defect of the native, and to kill him in self-defence was quite legitimate. It was surprising in what unlikely situations gratuitous violence by planters qualified as self-defence. However, if a planter "flipped" in the same way, it was deemed to be a touch of "tropical madness" and excused. Even if the death or serious injury of a coolie resulted, prosecution was as rare in the colonial era of the Dutch East Indies as it was in India.

It should not be thought that such abuses went unnoticed or un-opposed by many Dutchmen. In 1904 the liberal lawyer Van den Brand protested that "while the mere bringing of a charge against a coolie was sufficient cause for the latter to be given a disproportion-ately severe punishment, the planters who indulged in cruel and horrifying treatment of their workers went scot-free, unlikely to be prosecuted". He went on: "it is a matter of indifference to me whether planters or companies show a greater or lesser degree of philanthropy and show their workers better or worse treatment or care. The only thing that concerns me is that it is contrary to the honour of God; it is contrary to humanity. Truly, the lack of freedom cannot be recom-pensed with a nice hospital and a handful of money."

Under the Dutch system of *heerendienst* any indigenous people living on the plantation were liable to give free service to the owners as and when called upon. Legally they could buy themselves off; in practice none of them could afford to do so. Moreover, under Dutch law the plantation owners were entitled to take a fifth of the native's own produce, though the locals were often cunning enough to conceal the quantity and evade the exaction.

Not all Dutch plantations were run on such ruthless lines. P&T's attitude to those many natives who worked for it was relatively enlightened for the time, but uncompromising. Wise plantation managers recognized the value of keeping these virtual slaves *senang* (content) as a means of ensuring the profitability of their holdings. They were to be worked "with due regard to the interests and comfort of the native population which it is the proprietors desire to promote *as far as practicable*" (italics added). There was, of course, a caveat: "Keeping in view that the proprietors are desirous to give a fair remuneration for the services of those employed by them, the most rigid economy must be observed in the management of these unfortunate estates."

A final Indian example of managerial attitudes is worth recounting in some detail as it well illustrates the various checks and balances still in play, even in the late colonial period. When Jim Glendinning renewed his post as a garden manager in the last days of the Raj he was greeted on arrival with cries of "kill the manager and burn his transport". This was disconcerting, since a previous manager had been beaten up and left for dead. Agitation among an otherwise mainly inert labour force was kept on the boil by a small group of Communists who made themselves conspicuous by wearing red hats. The management, in turn, made a point of finding – or inventing – fault with the work of anyone wearing a red hat and thus provided themselves with an excuse for having tasks redone or docking pay. This rather petty game escalated to a situation where riots were in prospect due to a dispute between the Communists and the Congress Party over whether or not to call a strike.

On being tipped off about this, Glendinning went through the motions of asking the local police sergeant to intervene, knowing full well that, from a combination of disdain for the British and reluctance to become involved, he would decline to do so. This gave the manager the excuse he needed to adopt a high hand. The Communists, under their leader, one Mangroo, had set up an open-air meeting that seemed to combine the attributes of a picnic and a political rally: tables, chairs and umbrellas in profusion, and, in their midst, on a rickety pole, the Communist flag. Glendinning relished the opportunity to drive the company truck straight through the middle of this assembly, at which there was "a fearful crunch of bamboo and umbrellas and a general scattering of people". Order was restored and the coolies returned to their plucking.

Such a loss of face was more than Mangroo could bear, so not long afterwards his Communists chased the workers off another part of the garden and, armed with sticks and stones and a few bows and arrows, incited a riotous mob to march on the office and factory. Alerted to the mob's approach, Glendinning grabbed his loaded shotgun, jumped into his pick-up with his driver, cut off the marchers and ordered them to halt. Let him take up the tale in his own words:

The assailants at the front of this motley gang when they saw the gun shouted back to their brave leaders at the rear, "Look out; the Sahib has a gun". Everything stopped and we all waited. This was their great chance. They, the minority leftwing party, had said since my return to the estate "kill the manager and burn his transport". There it was all waiting for them ... A few stones whistled our way. "Anymore stones and I will fire" I shouted, "now turn round and cross the Chaity bridge and stay there". Very slowly the mob backed off. The driver drove and I held my gun at the ready on the top of the pick-up, it was all very dramatic but was perhaps the turning point. There were of course repercussions. The unruly mob did as they were told and appeared terrified of the young manager and indeed his gun. The mob crossed the bridge. The vehicle we parked in the centre. I shouted at the mob that they could re-cross the bridge after 2pm. If they tried to cross before then, I would shoot them, and I meant it. My poor driver, who seemed to have entered into the spirit of this wild day, was despatched to fetch me some breakfast and get himself something. The head servant who was Nepali and did not want to miss out on the happenings, shortly arrived on a bike with a carrier on the back, with breakfast. He was dressed in immaculate white with his normal black cap and served breakfast on the top of the pick-up. In the meantime the other side of the bridge had not gone into complete retreat. They struck camp, re-erected the Communist party flag on a high bamboo pole and started their chant of "free India, kill the manager and burn his vehicle". Breakfast was eaten and developments awaited. Sure enough and within the hour the Communist Party Land Rover arrived with their leader, who went into consultation with the mob, and after lengthy discussions, one Communist Bengali was seen to be walking across this long bridge. I let him come within firing range of my 12 bore gun and shouted in English "Stop". He continued to waddle across this long bridge shouting "I want to talk to you." I raised my gun and told him in my best English "Come any further you bastard and I will shoot". He ran for it, returned to his Land Rover and departed. There would be dreadful further trouble, but we had won, so to speak, like Horatio, the major and most important conflict. Everything returned to normal except that we seemed to have regained more control.

After a cursory enquiry by the local police inspector the matter was dropped. Not long afterwards Mangroo refused to obey an order and the many workers in earshot waited to see the outcome of this impasse. Glendinning admits somewhat ashamedly: "The old theme of prestige or caste was once more at trial. Mangroo stopped work, and with his shifty brown eyes and foxy face grinned at me. Violence is rarely the correct way to solve a problem; however on this occasion it was resorted to. The incident was regrettable, dangerous but maybe justified? Mangroo was picked up by his white shirt and his face slapped, which made his nose bleed. No-one moved, no voice spoke, and on my return to my bungalow, and to this day, I remember washing the blood off my hands in the bathroom, and with trembling fingers changing my clothes."

Not long afterwards a further infraction of the rules gave Glendinning the legitimate excuse he needed to fire Mangroo and no more was heard of him.

The most interesting thing about this exchange, besides its author's tendency to see things in terms of slightly self-deprecating caricature, is that nothing happened. There was no actual physical clash between "Horatio" and the ranks of Indian Tuscany, no casualties and no collateral damage were suffered by either side – Mangroo's nose, Glendinning's conscience and a few bamboo poles apart. As Indian independence approached, Raj and Revolutionaries alike recognized that there were ritual exchanges and mutually recognized boundaries that could not be crossed with impunity, at least not until after independence had been achieved. And not always then.

"The problem is that these tribal people are backward and don't want to work. They are like herds of sheep and must be treated sternly. The worst thing you will find is that the men are drunkards, *matal* who will use every excuse to miss work. So the manager who is mai-baap has to be alert to these tendencies ... and problems. The women are not such a problem though. They are good disciplined workers but the men are real *badmashes* [bad-hats, petty criminals]." These are not the words of some nineteenth-century British diehard but of a young Marwari pontificating on how his family's tea gardens in Assam should best be run. (The Marwaris were, and are, a major force in the commerce and industry of Bangladesh and in the early days played a key part in financing British planters who had cash-flow difficulties.)

During the inter-war period many Indians had been recruited to junior positions in tea-garden management, and in some cases groomed as potential managers. At a lower level, educated members of the appropriate castes had risen to senior clerical, accounts and medical posts. However, only exceptionally were Indians to be found in more senior positions in British as opposed to Indian-owned companies. This was to change decisively with the calling-up for military service of the majority of the younger British tea-garden managers and assistants during the Second World War. By 1941 more than six hundred (35 per cent of the total British employment on Indian tea gardens) had answered the call to the colours. By 1942 this had risen to over 50 per cent and the invasion of Burma by the Japanese early that year further increased the drain, as engineers, doctors and ordinary planters were diverted to running refugee camps and building roads and airstrips for the military. With one, medically exempt exception, none under 30 remained in post.

This greatly accelerated the already well-established process of Indianization as, of necessity, junior Indians stepped up into positions of authority and responsibility. A novice Indian assistant could find himself running a large garden and a Brahmin clerk the whole of a company's administrative machine. On the whole competently filled, these positions would not be lightly surrendered after the war. In any case British-owned tea companies were finding it increasingly hard to recruit young Britons. The pace of transition received a further boost in 1955 with an agreement between the Indian Tea Association and the now independent Indian Government, to reach a target of a third of all senior posts being in Indian hands by the end of the decade. As it transpired, this rebalancing of authority improved relations between Indians and the mainly British senior staff who remained on the gardens and in the head offices, thus reinforcing the argument that differences had not been so much about race as economic status and power. Today all full-time tea-garden employees in India are Indian.

While it is not surprising that the surviving "old stagers", who had virtually run the industry in the last three years of the war, were disinclined to give up their old ways and attitudes, it is more puzzling as to why so many of their Indian successors and colleagues adopted a not dissimilar approach to their workforces. Under the Raj the managers and their foremen (the *babus*) had been of different races. The new Indian managers may have felt less secure in dealing with their fellow countrymen without resorting to an older, colonial style of management. As Piya Chaterjee puts it: "[These] aristocrats of new and old empires, [who] wear the jeans of the new and accent their talk with the old. Their schools are prestigious British Indian models of Eton. They embody the Raj's pedagogies with a postcolonial twist." Perhaps this was not so surprising. During the war many young and impressionable Indians had no one to look up to as mentors and role models but older Britons, some of whom still clung to outdated views. As one of these confessed: "After Independence and the Pakistan-Hindustan separation in 1947, everyone was feeling their way. In our little world of tea-planting, the old stagers and senior managers were to be shown not to be at their best. They remained with their attitudes of days gone by. It was not until the post-war recruits started to take senior positions that the delicate but most important relationship between Indian and English began to really improve."

The British who decided to "stay on" in garden management after independence, or, like my brother, went straight to it on demobilization from the army, were not best adapted to cope with the changing balance of power between workers and management, nor to being treated as foreigners for the first time, rather than as members of a ruling élite. It is therefore not surprising that, when Indian managers of the new breed found themselves in charge, some of them retained something of the mindset of men they had not only copied but often affectionately admired. Nor were the physical boundaries between men and masters on the ground readily abandoned. Thus was described one Indian-run tea garden late in the twentieth century:

Only if you look carefully from the distance of the road, will you notice rows of small, white-cement, two-roomed structures. These houses herald the "labour lines," where workers' families live. A brick wall behind the staff cottages separates the labour lines from road and staff cottages. A wire fence behind the bungalows similarly separates lawn from lines. Only those workers who serve in the bungalow – watchmen, maids, gardeners and cooks – are permitted entry across this border of wire. At night, the only areas lit are the perimeters of the bungalows and cottages: the labour lines, hardly visible even in daylight, lie silent and in almost total darkness.

In the early years of independence the planters' club culture was even more conservative than under the Raj itself. "Children must be neither seen nor heard in the club and strict dress codes are observed – only one drink allowed at the bar after tennis before changing into normal clothes. Nor is anyone expected to leave the club after dinner until the Burra Sahib has departed." Thus read the rules in one club with a predominantly Indian membership after independence. Perhaps this harking back – I found the officers of the Pakistan Army on the North-West Frontier in the 1950s more Sandhurst than Sandhurst – was no more than the looking back of a youngster to his parent on his first determined solo swim to the other end of the pool.

CHAPTER SEVEN

Coolies and Coolie-catchers

"They are docile and tractable, if not goaded too much; but this is not to be wondered at, when we consider that they are trained to work from six years old, from five in the morning to eight and nine at night ... in all kinds of weather ... examine the miserable pittance of food ... if late a few minutes, a quarter of a day is stopped in wages. These evils to the men have arisen from that dreadful monopoly which exists in those districts where wealth and power are got into the hands of the few." (1818)

"Upon my expressing indignation, he said, 'Damn their eyes, what need you care about them? How could I sell [to] you so cheap if I cared anything about them.'" (1824)

"Human beings living and sleeping ... with filth from overflowing cesspools exuding through and running down the walls and over the floors. It is utterly hopeless to expect to meet with either civilization, benevolence, religion or virtue, in any shape, where so much filth and wretchedness abounds." (1848)

"It is impossible to describe the wretchedness, dirt, and squalidness of thousands of famished and half-starved, drunken, dissolute vagabonds." (1849)

"[It was] so crammed with sleepers ... he believed there were 30 where 12 would have been the proper number ... that their breaths in the dead of night in that unventilated chamber rose in ... one foul, choking steam of stench." (1851)

"As, on the ruined human wretch, vermin parasites appear, so these ruined shelters have bred a crowd of foul existence that crawls in and out of gaps in walls and boards; and coils itself to sleep, in maggot numbers, where the rain drips in; and comes and goes, fetching and carrying fever, and sowing more evil in its every footprint." (1852)

"[Hours of work are] from 7 0'Clock in the Morning, until 7 0'Clock in the Evening, except at any busy period if required later; when such is the case, every [young] man ... to assist till the work is finished ... in case any person refuse to perform the duties assigned to him at his engagement, is insolent in his behaviour, wilfully transgresses the rules, or commits any flagrant breach of duty, he agrees to be instantly discharged, and to accept such wages as shall be due to him up to that time only." (1853)

"If work dried up, or was seasonal, men were laid off, and because they had hardly enough to live on when they were in work, they had no savings to fall back on." (1861)

These quotations are not descriptions of workers' conditions in the tea gardens of the colonial powers in the first two-thirds of the nineteenth century, but in Britain during that time. I have prefaced this chapter with the words of leading British philanthropists and writers so that an account of the treatment of plantation workers in the same era – an era of exponential growth in the international tea industry – may be seen in the context of contemporary mores, rather than through twenty-first-century eyes. Not until 1842 was it illegal in Britain to make women and children work down the mines; not until 1871 were all factories inspected to ensure minimum conditions; not until 1920 was the full-time employment of children under 14 prohibited; and we have yet to institute, in practice, equal pay for women doing the same job as men, or anything like meet the European Union working-hours directive of 34 hours a week.

In the Netherlands the civil code of 1838 made no legislative provision for relations between masters and men. These were based solely on the notion of a contract freely entered into by both parties.

In the event of any dispute, all the cards were held by the master, who was free to fire an employee without notice and whose word was taken as gospel in any dispute about wages, terms or dismissal. Only if a worker was on a fixed-term contract was he entitled to six weeks' pay – if he could get it – when dismissed before the term of the contract. These principles would apply, in an even more lopsided way, throughout the nineteenth and a large part of the twentieth centuries, on the plantations and tea gardens of the Dutch East Indies. An enquiry in 1859 into child employment in the Netherlands found that almost half a million children between the ages of six and 11 were employed in various ways. In 1874 Samuel van Houten introduced an Act to prohibit for the first time the employment of children under 12, except in agriculture and domestic work. But it was laxly applied and found wanting until 1889, when further legislation embraced agriculture, gave some protection to those under 16 and created an inspectorate to oversee the new laws. Until 1872 it was a criminal offence for workers to strike and even then they could still be sued in a civil action for withdrawing their labour. Not until 1890 were women at work afforded some protection, and safety rules in factories were not legally imposed until 1895.

During the second half of the nineteenth century and the first 40 years of the twentieth there evolved, by fits and starts, a recognition that employees were beings no less human than their employers and were morally and legally entitled to humane treatment. In parallel it slowly became apparent to more far-sighted capitalists that profit and people-care, far from being mutually exclusive, were synergistic. Their ledgers and accounts books increasingly demonstrated that a healthy, well-fed (and later better-educated) workforce which felt itself fairly treated and fairly paid yielded better commercial dividends in the long run than one which was exploited and abused. These changes came about at different paces in different places at different times.

In the hundred years from the beginnings of commercial tea cultivation in India in 1839 to the outbreak of the Second World War, there is a counterpoint between the laissez-faire attitude of many planters and planters' organizations of all nations, and the belief of a small but growing minority that the state should intervene in labour relations to protect the health and welfare of ordinary workers. Sometimes one theme dominates, sometimes the other. The discords between them could be harsh but, by the mid-twentieth century, in those situations for which the former imperial powers had been responsible, a more or less harmonious resolution had been achieved. Nor was it always the mother country, rather than her colonies, that led the way, particularly in such matters as paid sick leave, maternity leave and holidays. In few occupations was the transformation of the labour-relations ethos more important than in the tea industry. Growing and manufacturing tea is one of the most labour-intensive of all agricultures. (Harler calculates that, on a yearly average, 3.75–5 adult-equivalent workers are needed per hectare of tea bushes, whereas coffee requires an annual level of one per hectare.) Even in countries such as India and Ceylon, where tea harvesting is seasonal and there are relative peaks and troughs of labour requirement, there is a year-round demand for a substantial workforce. Only bearing all these considerations in mind can we fairly assess worker–management relations in the tea industry.

The three great tea-exporting economies of the second half of the nineteenth century, those of Ceylon, India and the Dutch East Indies, faced different problems in recruiting and managing their tea-garden coolies.

In Ceylon the indigenous Sinhalese peasants were smallholders cultivating their own quite profitable plots and with no wish, on both economic and cultural grounds, to hire out their labour to foreigners. From the outset they were inclined to look down on the landless foreign immigrants who did so. The coffee crop that the planters (nearly all British) were growing, before it was superseded by tea, required intensive harvesting for only some six to eight weeks of the year and otherwise little attention. Nor was the processing of the coffee beans difficult, labour-intensive or time-sensitive. It was, therefore, well suited to the short-term hiring of a migrant labour force, much of which would return home, cash in hand and smile on face, when the harvest was gathered. The planters found just such a labour force conveniently to hand in the Tamils of southern India. But neither its modest size, nor its migratory pattern, was of any use once tea, with its much greater and more consistent hunger for labour, had replaced coffee by the 1870s.

In India, for the first hundred years of tea cultivation, the pace of development completely outstripped the availability of labour to undertake it. In Assam and Cachar, the northern districts of India where tea cultivation first and most substantially took root, the sparseness of local population also meant that tea-garden labour would have to be imported. This time, however, the potential work-force lay not across a few miles of water, but many hundred difficult miles away in Bengal and Bihar, or else nearer, but involving a no less difficult journey, from Nepal or Nagaland. Later, in southern India, though the population of Tamil Nadu was adequate in itself for the task of tea growing in the Nilgiris, the large-scale drain of Tamils to Ceylon – in 1847 47,000; 1891 235,000; 1921 500,000; 1931 700,000 – also presented recruitment problems. Only Darjeeling, with its proximity to the ample labour pool in Nepal, was spared a labour shortage. There, one solution to such shortages – and not only for Darjeeling – was identified from the outset. A Colonel Lloyd, complaining he could not get coolies to build the military sanatorium on which he was engaged, was bluntly told: "His Honour in Council is compelled to think that your want of method and arrangements in the particular of supplies and shelter will have been the main cause of this difficulty, of course; without assurance of food, clothing and shelter adapted to the climate no one would voluntarily take employment under you."

In the Dutch East Indies there was no shortage of people living within the immediate vicinity of the tea gardens, but it was a popu-lation which, while perfectly willing to do paid labouring for short spells, would undertake it only in so far as it did not interfere with its own, more satisfying, smallholding cultivation. The combination of wage-earning and subsistence farming had the opposite balance to that in Assam, where immigrant coolies had a small plot added to wage payment as a means of tying them to the garden. In nine-teenth-century Java and Sumatra the demands of subsistence farming came first in both time and importance, and in most cases it was wage-earning that was supplementary. When, to augment unreliable local labour, the Dutch, and their not infrequent British partners, tried to recruit from the neighbouring British colonies – in particular Malaya and Singapore – they had first to satisfy the British authorities that their working conditions would be satisfactory. Having recently, in 1877, introduced a labour inspectorate in India, the British placed a labour agent on their side of the Malay straits to ensure the maintenance of these minimum standards. They also refused the Dutch permission to recruit coolies in India unless they allowed another British agent to operate in Sumatra. This the indignant Dutch refused to do. For them the challenge was to keep the noses of their coolies to the tea bush for more than a few days at a time. For the British the challenge was to recruit and then get the coolies alive to the tea gardens and keep them alive once they got there. It soon became self-evident that this was more cost-effective than repeatedly having to find, transport and train new ones. The challenge for the coolies was to survive.

The first British tea planters in India made the mistake of relying exclusively on Chinese labour and expertise. The Assam Company had engaged, as interpreter and adviser, Dr Lumqua, a Chinaman, who had been on the original Tea Committee. He died in August 1840, but not before he had warned his new employers of the likelihood that his fellow countrymen would try to cheat them. The first Chinese tea makers and cultivators, other than the 18 taken over from the Government of India at the time of Lumqua's appointment, had been recruited by the Assam Company in October 1839. By the end of 1840 some four to five thousand had been signed up, despite C.A. Bruce's warning in January of that year that too many were being taken on and that the few capable ones he had could soon teach the Assamese to cultivate and make tea. Within a few years it was recognized that, although much was to be learned from the Chinese in the manufacturing process, their method of plucking was quite inappropriate for the Assam tea bush as its configuration was very different from that of the bush in China.

Many Chinese recruits never even reached their intended garden destinations. Some got lost or strayed en route. Others were so riotous and troublesome that they were sent packing and shipped back whence they came – not without argument between the Assam Company and the Government as to who should pay for their transport and provisions. Those arriving in January 1840 were involved in a fracas in which several villagers were wounded. The young assistant in charge snatched them from the hands of the local police. But when he and nine Chinese were returned for trial, on Company orders, all were acquitted for lack of identification of the actual culprits. No doubt to the Indian police "all Chinese looked alike"! The local police must have felt doubly aggrieved at being fined 10 rupees for false arrest, as well as having seen men they knew to be collectively guilty escape scot-free. When Chinamen did reach the gardens they were no less troublesome, as J.W. Masters reported to the Company in 1840: "You will please to observe that these tea makers are very great gentlemen; even those who receive but Rs 3 per month consider themselves so, and object to do anything else but make tea. When spoken to, they threaten to leave the service if they are insulted by being asked to work."

At the London AGM of the Assam Company in May 1841 the directors were compelled to admit they had been wrong to recruit so many Chinese tea makers so hastily, rather than rely on the local Assamese acquiring the necessary skills. The Chinese had been "procured at great expense ... and heavy wages ... These men turned out to be of very bad character. They were turbulent, obstinate and rapacious. So injurious did they seem likely to prove to the other workmen employed by the company, that their contracts were cancelled and the whole gang, with the exception of the most experienced tea makers and the quietest men, were dismissed." Bruce had been proved right and, as soon as the Chinese tea makers who remained had taught their skills to local Indians, he begged the Board to get rid of the lot of them.

There were several reasons why creating a skilled Assamese workforce was no easy matter. In granting the Company's charter, the Government had banned the cultivation of *Papaver somniferum*, the opium poppy, but the majority of Assamese remained addicted, and unscrupulous planters sometimes used small gifts of opium (or brandy or rum, "the more fiery the better") to secure the compliance of those working for them. On top of the lethargy induced by drug taking, local villagers were inclined to work on the tea plantations only when the cultivation of their own crops was not a priority. Nor were locals accustomed to working only so much as was necessary to meet their basic needs inclined to become regular, season-after-season employees. Consequently much managerial time was spent teaching batch after batch of raw recruits the art of plucking.

The indigenous population in the main tea areas of Assam and Cachar was sparse and disinclined to abandon a relatively trouble-free, subsistence-level life on soil of "exuberant fertility" for more arduous paid work on a tea garden. As an 1868 Commission of Enquiry into the labour situation in the tea districts put it: "The wants of the people are few, and easily supplied. The climate is enervating. The people are naturally indolent, and largely addicted to the use of opium. They will work only under the pressure of urgent necessity."

Necessity usually only made its presence felt as a result of debt incurred to the local moneylender in order to buy livestock or pay a bride-price. The coolie then soon found himself faced with an even more urgent need to break free from the exorbitant rate of interest on the loan. As one shrewd observer, a Captain Phillips, explained: "In cases such as these they go to the tea-planter as their last resource, execute an agreement of service, receive an advance of twenty or thirty rupees, and in five cases out of ten never make their appearance at the garden again until they are compelled to do so as the result of an action against them for breach of contract." The Catch-22 for the planter was that, by the time he had transported the necessary witnesses and a lawyer to the magistrate's court, the cost of bringing the case far exceeded the sum owed by the coolie. He, in any case, by now no longer had the means to repay the advance, except by falling back into the clutches of the moneylender.

It soon became apparent that coolies recruited from Chota Nagpur, Bihar and elsewhere beyond the tea districts were more industrious and reliable than locals, and that Nagas and Nepalis were particularly adept at the jungle clearance that was the pre-requisite of extending the planted area.

The problem with bringing up coolies from beyond the tea districts was the cost of recruiting and transporting them, and, owing to inadequate commissariat and medical provision, the high proportion that fell sick and died, or deserted, en route on the long voyage by boat up the Brahmaputra and then overland to the gardens. For example, not a single coolie survived an outbreak of cholera from one large batch recruited by the Assam Company in 1841. This high wastage not only meant that supply failed to meet the demand of an industry expanding so rapidly but troubled the consciences of the more compassionate planters and officials. Nor, in the early days, could sufficient supplies of rice be guaranteed with which to feed them even when they reached the tea garden to which they had been allotted. Cultivation of their own food had first to be undertaken by the self-same coolies before they could be profitably employed producing tea.

By 1859 the tea planters of northern India had recognized that the *ad hoc* recruitment of coolies, either locally or from other parts of the country, was failing to meet their ever-growing needs. They tackled the problem in a variety of ways, the two most significant of which, covering by far the greater part of the immigrant labour force, were the use of licensed contractors and the use of their own garden *sirdars* (headmen).

At first all contractors (mostly Calcutta-based, Hindu and Muslim Indians, as well as a few Britons) were untrammelled in their methods of recruitment and the subsequent treatment in transit of those recruited. Thus numbers, rather than quality, was their criterion. The Labour Commission of 1862 noted that "all parties considered their duties and responsibility discharged when the living are landed, and the cost of death adjusted". Coolies entered into a contract at the place of recruitment before they had even seen a tea garden and the contractor usually got paid per head, "dead or alive", which was just as well for him since at this time anything from 10 to 50 per cent of those recruited died en route. Recognition of these abuses led to the Bengal Act of 1863, which prescribed that the majority of contractors should be licensed. (This and subsequent Bengal Acts of the next 50 years were, in fact, legislation of the Government of India. At this time control of Assam came under the regional government of Bengal. For a detailed account of this labour legislation see P.J. Griffiths's *The History of the Indian Tea Industry*.)

The conditions of the licence were that every intending emigrant should be medically examined and that the terms of his contract (which, in any case, was not to exceed four years) should be made clear to him and entered into in the presence of his own district magistrate and the newly appointed Superintendent of Emigration. The steamers carrying the coolies up the Brahmaputra also had to be inspected and licensed, and minimum standards of provision and hygiene were enforced as far as was practicable.

The planters argued that, since roughly a thousand pounds of tea had to be plucked to recover the cost of bringing even a moderately capable coolie up from Bengal, they had every reason to want them to arrive in good condition. In 1877 Henry Cottam, an Assam planter, pointed out that on the river journey "sheep are provided at the best price, good vegetables, medicines and sundry medical comforts are to be expected at the planter's expense ... Mr Edgar [a Bengal Civil Service Inspector] dwells on the ill-treatment of labourers and the insufficiency of food. He cannot understand that it is a most ruinous policy for a planter to ill-treat his men, on whom his very bread and butter depends." More scathingly, Samuel Baildon protested in the same year that "one of the last orders causes the planter to clothe his coolies on the way from Bengal to Assam. Labourers now arrive in red flannel jackets. Spurs will be added in due course! The comfort and well being of the working classes in England is quite a secondary consideration to the British Parliament, as compared with the paternal supervision of the Indian Government to coolies. Labour is too valuable to the planter not to take good care of it." In fact, the "red flannel jackets" were probably the surplus red greatcoats of the British Army with which many planters provided their coolies.

That these new standards were frequently evaded – either by unlicensed contractors legally outside the scope of the 1863 Act (the same result was later achieved by "doing a Dhubri", that is, waiting to sign up recruits until they reached Dhubri in Goalpara, on the west bank of the Brahmaputra, which was outside the jurisdiction of the Bengal Acts) or by being ignored – is evident from the comments of one medical official five years later that controls that allowed "a large percentage of cripples, idiots, lepers and people in far advanced stages of chronic diseases to come up here as labourers was nothing more or less than a farce". Even those who survived the journey were often not up to the job, one planter informing an 1868 Enquiry Commission: "Out of a hundred men not more than thirty or forty were healthy, useful men. I believe that they were originally bad, and not that they became ill on the voyage up. No sufficient care was ever taken in the selection."

As their business grew the labour contractors became very wealthy. One of them owned the first motor car in Purulia, a major recruiting town, and had petrol brought up the 150 miles from Calcutta at 10 rupees a gallon (about £44 at today's value). Such was their success that they could afford to employ licensed sub-contractors, *arkattis* – literally, pilots, but more commonly and abusively known as "coolie-catchers" – even more unscrupulous than themselves, to do the actual recruiting. *Arkattis* were despised even more than their bosses as they lurked in those places where drink, gambling and plain poverty made men and women desperate for employment on any terms. That a significant proportion of those entrapped in this way were physically or socially quite unsuited for the exacting and egalitarian work of a tea garden was a matter of indifference to the *arkattis*. They were described by police inspector Harrington Tucker, who had to deal with the consequences of their activities, as "the scum of the country, and unscrupulous to a degree ... who resort to every vile practice to obtain their ends". For those so dragooned it was almost "impossible for them to refuse the required consent".

Some of the more enlightened planters adopted an alternative method of recruitment through the *sirdars* on their own gardens. A *sirdar*, himself often only recently recruited and so still having strong home connections, would be dispatched to his home village with a float of 10 rupees or so to distribute as largesse. There, because known and very likely respected, he would not find it hard to persuade other members of his extended family and his former neighbours to commit themselves to joining him in Assam or Cachar. The *sirdar* would then return to the garden, collect an advance for those recruited, go back to the village and there get them to sign their contracts under the same safeguards of consent and medical inspection as required at the coolie depots used by contractors. There was, of course, always the risk that a *sirdar* would pocket the advance payments and vanish, but this was relatively rare, and most returned to collect their final recruiting bonus. Back on their gardens, though they might provide advice and discipline in a purely domestic capacity for their former fellow villagers, they now had no further responsibility for the conduct of their recruits, who were subsumed into the normal operational structure of the tea gardens.

There were many advantages to this system of recruiting. The *sirdar*'s personal experience permitted him to describe a garden's work regime and physical condition, as well as the temperaments of those who ran it. Even allowing for his motive for painting things in a rosy light, being forewarned diminished the risk for the new recruits of unexpected shocks on arrival at the garden. Fewer footloose and irresponsible, unattached young men – who might well have abandoned wives and families to debt – were attracted to the garden payroll because coolies recruited by *sirdars* tended to come as family groups who willingly migrated to an occupation that offered good employment to the women and children as well as to the men. Moreover, until well into the twentieth century children working in tea gardens could expect, more or less automatically, to move to full-wage status when they became adult. This gave greater stability to a workforce that had no reason to leave since, in effect, the tea garden had become their home village. Such continuity of skill and knowledge on the one hand, and security of employment on the other, were of mutual benefit to planter and coolie alike. Critically, given the high tea-garden mortality in the early decades, members of family groups, when taken ill, would have someone to nurse them and someone else to sustain an income, whereas single men were often left to die untended from lack of anyone willing and able to look after them full-time.

That officialdom also recognized the benefits of having balanced family units working on the tea gardens was soon apparent. As early as the first Bengal Act, the Superintendent of Emigration could refuse to send a batch of coolies up-country unless it consisted of one female for every four males to "facilitate stabilisation of the

labour force, and the promotion of community life on the estates".
If a single woman presented herself for recruitment at a coolie
depot, the immediate suspicion was that she was either running
away from husband or parents because of ill-treatment or had been
booted out. As a result married women were not allowed to volunteer unless their husbands also did so, nor could unmarried women
without parental consent. Although this was only a rule agreed by
the planters, rather than a law, to break it was severely frowned
upon. It certainly seems to have worked. By 1888 the ratio of men
to women recruited as coolies had fallen to four to three.

The *sirdar* system could also lead to abuse. On most gardens the
European manager or assistant would personally supervise the
weekly payday and see that the money due was placed in the hand
that had earned it. In the case of most children, and even of many
women, the likelihood is that the family's total wage was given to
the (male) head of household, or at least handed over to him as
soon as it was received, though I am unable to find more than anec-
dotal evidence of the extent of this practice. In Java, Jacobson had
been most insistent that "This paying to the women and children
must not take place by an increase of wages being given to the men;
they must themselves receive daily some trifle, that they may be
enabled to meet their own little wants."

It was quite common in Ceylon for alternate months' wages to
be paid to the *kangany*. In theory this was supposed to reduce the
coolie's debt to his overseer; in practice it gave ample opportunity
for the *kangany* to cheat the illiterate coolies by pocketing the
money. It was this kind of abuse that prompted a police superintendent in the coffee-growing era to compare the condition of
plantation workers to slavery, and 60 years later, in 1908, a planter
could still say: "The kangany system is slavery, I will call it nothing
else. He will not allow ... a cooly to leave his force if he can help it
– and if the Superintendent does not interfere then that is slavery."

On some Indian gardens also, wages were paid by making a
single payment to the various *sirdars* for onward distribution, and
not all of the coolie's share was always passed on to him or her.
Such a defalcating *sirdar* exercised his petty tyranny on the tea
garden where young Hetherington was assistant manager at the

start of the twentieth century. "There were endless stories of fines for nothing (the KB pocketing them), of people taken by force to his house at night and hammered, and of women being insulted and threatened with assault. The people say he has caused absconding and if he is sacked many will return. He has been behaving like this for several years and stole more tickets previously, as Allanson [Hetherington's predecessor] seldom went to *gunti* [roll-call]". Such dereliction of duty by a *sirdar* was the exception. In this case, as in many others, the paternalistic approach had its advantages. Having got to know and trust Hetherington, and confident in a British sense of justice, the abused women coolies were able to report the *sirdar* to him, the offender was dismissed and the victims recompensed. From 1915 onwards only *sirdar* recruitment, or close variations of it, were permitted in northern India.

A third recruitment system, that of the *maistri* (recruiting overseer), prevailed in southern India until the 1930s. Here, too, the demand for labour exceeded the supply so that it had to be recruited from further afield – though not from so far away as in northern India. The situation was complicated in the independent Princely States, such as Mysore and Malabar, from which much of the workforce was drawn. In these, farmers and landowners advanced money to agricultural labourers at a rate of interest that meant they could seldom earn enough ever to repay the debt. Although slavery had been made illegal in British India in 1843, these peasant labourers were no better than serfs who remained bound for life to their employers. (The Act making slavery illegal in the British Empire had been passed in 1833. India was almost the last British possession to implement this imperial legislation. The slave trade as such had been abolished by the British Parliament in 1807.) In order to be free to work elsewhere, they had first to be freed from the bondage of indebtedness and, to the chagrin of their former employers, the planters paid for this freedom. A committee of enquiry in 1896 expressed the view that, in repaying these debts, the planters had helped to break "the system of hereditary serfdom … and the depressed conditions of labour".

There were two kinds of *maistri*: those, like the *sirdars* in the north, who recruited from their own village districts; and those, akin to the nefarious *arkattis*, who recruited wherever they could find vulnerable men and women gullible enough to succumb to their blandishments.

The *maistri* had to be advanced cash with which to pay advances to his recruits. But, in areas of the subcontinent which were patchworks of districts under direct British rule and others in which local princes enjoyed self-government, it was easy for him to make off with the cash and slip into a neighbouring territory under a different jurisdiction. Once there he was beyond legal reach – rather as the rustlers in a Western would slip across a state line in the USA. The coolie, in turn, could do exactly the same with the money given him by the *maistri*. Not until well into the twentieth century was legislation enacted in British India that was also acceptable for adoption by the Princely States. This was to make criminal arrest and recovery at least possible – if not always very practicable. A significant difference between the *maistri* and the *sirdar* was that the former supervised those he recruited, with whom he rarely had any personal ties, in their work on the tea garden. He was thus both recruiting sergeant and RSM, a gang boss who exercised great power over those he had recruited, and frequently abused it.

Nevertheless, the legislation enacted by the British authorities in India, and its increasingly effective enforcement, though it was sometimes evaded and sometimes misguided, did gradually eliminate the worst abuses and minimize the suffering on their migration of those recruited as labourers for the tea gardens of India.

In Ceylon the *kangany* system of labour recruitment was similar to that of the worst kind of *maistri* system, the only difference being that the *kangany* had to cross the narrow Palk strait to gather his Tamil workers, to the great annoyance of the planters of southern India, who were competing for the same labour. In 1904 one indignant planter described the *kanganies* as "sordid, unfeeling, reprobate, degraded, spiritless, outcasts" and went on to deplore the fact that, even in the lowland areas where local labour was available, planters preferred to employ the more easily exploited Tamils. K. Jayawardena, writing almost 70 years later, more objectively describes the system thus:

The planter gave the *kangany* a sum of money for every worker he brought to Ceylon (head money), and he was also paid a daily bonus for each worker who turned up for work on the field (pence money). In the early years of Indian immigration, the *kangany*'s duties included the issuing of rice to workers, settling family disputes and sometimes running a shop. But the most important role of the *kangany* was his powerful position as intermediary between the plantation management and the workers. The need for direct recruitment by the *kangany* disappeared when the Indian workers became permanently resident, but the patriarchal role of the *kangany* and his position as moneylender and shopkeeper continued. ... The bond between the *kangany* and his gang of workers arose out of the workers' indebtedness, and they, according to the Controller of Indian Immigrant Labour reporting in 1932, were "born in debt, lived in debt and died in debt".

Tamil coolies arriving in Colombo by ship underwent no quarantine, so any diseases they carried went up into the tea-growing highlands with them. A more effective filter, from the planters' point of view, was the much more common route whereby the coolies arrived at Mannar – the nearest point to the coast of India – before setting off on the long trek on foot to central Ceylon. Despite the fact that, as early as 1867, the planters in southern India had established a hospital on the Malabar coast, with the honourable intention of weeding out the sick before they embarked, the state of medical knowledge at the time meant that inevitably they were never completely successful and cholera, in particular, would soon be rife on the far shore. (The aetiology of cholera was not understood, even vaguely, until Dr John Snow closed a contaminated London water-pump in 1854; and that of malaria remained a mystery until well into the twentieth century.) Over the next 40 years, to their credit, the planters of both countries expanded and improved these rest and medical facilities, but with relatively little impact on the incidence of mortality. Those who were actually sick on arrival in Ceylon were put into hospital, but those in whom the disease was latent went undetected until it surfaced and killed them. Complacently, Sir West Ridgeway,

Governor of Ceylon in the last decade of the nineteenth century, wrote: "It would seem at first sight as if under these circumstances the chances were remote that more than a small remnant of a gang of fifty or sixty persons would reach Matale, but, heavy as the mortality was, the great bulk of the coolies did reach their destinations, and each of them as a rule free from disease. The sick were abandoned either on the road, or at some of the established halting places. The rest of the gang pressed on and in this way the disease was gradually eliminated." No concern seems to have been expressed for the unfortunate inhabitants of the villages in which the cholera cases were dumped to die.

Problems also arose because of the immense growth of Ceylon's population through immigration. In one central province the population grew by 80 per cent between 1860 and the census of 1881, and of the new total between a fifth and a quarter were Indian Tamils. (By 1963, with the province in question only half its previous size, the population had risen 400 per cent and the density per square mile was almost 16 times its level of a century earlier.) While the rapid spread of plantations gave work to many of these new people, the jungle clearance entailed was both psychologically and economically damaging to the indigenous Sinhalese and reduced their capacity to fend for themselves. That virtually all the labour used on the tea estates was imported created great bitterness, the consequence of which can still be seen today in the enmity between the indigenous population and the Tamil Tigers.

One other way of recruiting coolies in the early days of tea planting in India and Ceylon was to steal them from your neighbours. There were a variety of ways in which this could be done. Simply hijacking them physically en route was one much favoured in the early days and led to some bloody clashes between coolie-catchers, including some British kidnappers. Another way was to bribe an especially devious contractor to deliver coolies to your garden, for whom another planter had already paid him; or else you could entice workers piecemeal from other estates by offering better pay and conditions: neither difficult nor particularly reprehensible in view of the pitifully low baseline from which their employment started. Eventually planters recognized that the tit-for-tat exchanges that arose from these practices were helpful to no one, so, initially by rules of the various planters' associations and later by legislation, coolie stealing was generally abandoned. If coolies did break contract – or "abscond", as managers who thought of them as property preferred to call it – and move to another garden, it was obligatory for the recipient to either return them or compensate the former employer financially on a collectively agreed basis.

At the end of their contracts coolies were theoretically free to change employers if they wished, but seldom did so. Not until the Act of 1932 were planters free to recruit by any method they wished – and even then still under the supervision of government officials – and coolies correspondingly free to offer their services in any of the various ways available. Having recruited and trained them, planters naturally wished to keep them rather than start all over again with raw recruits. A number of less than honourable devices were too often used to secure this continuity. A planter might make a substantial advance shortly before a contract ended so that a coolie had either to abscond, with all the risks that entailed, or sign up again. Another planter might sign up husbands and wives for the first time on contracts that were not concurrent. At the expiry of the first the coolie who wished to remain with his or her spouse would face the choice of expulsion from the garden or signing another non-coterminous contract. Then the cycle was repeated for the other spouse. If coolies often stayed reluctantly from a mixture of indebtedness, management pressure and financial inducement, the decision to remain on a particular garden could no less often arise from genuine contentment with personal or family pay and conditions.

So: when the coolie, his wife and children were eventually working on the tea garden in India or Ceylon for which they had been recruited, were they better off than they had been in their home villages? Sometimes yes, sometimes the same. But sometimes they were plunged into conditions so appalling that even the most hard-hearted advocate of laissez-faire was shocked into recognizing that government intervention to secure minimum standards was desirable.

CHAPTER EIGHT

Ma-bap

"The valleys of the Berhampooter [Brahmaputra] and the
Soorma, in which the tea districts are situated, possess all
the conditions calculated to render them unhealthy. With
a low elevation, subject to great inundation, having a heavy rainfall,
and a high temperature, abounding with swamps and jungle, they
may be described as hotbeds of malaria." The Government of
Bengal's Commission of Enquiry of 1868 into the tea gardens of
Assam, from which this finding comes, had been prompted by
genuine concern at the high levels of mortality among imported
coolies in the early years of the industry. Even by the fairly callous
standards of the day they were unacceptable on grounds of humanity.

The Royal Commission of 1906, looking back to the records of
the 1860s, was horrified to discover that of nearly 85,000 coolies
working on the tea gardens of Assam and Cachar, over a three-year
period, at least 30,000 – more than one in three – had died. A
survey of 1868 had arrived at a mortality rate of 26 per cent on the
gardens of north-east India. Using the yardstick of the Bhutan war
of 1864–65, the Commissioners pointed out that only 16 per cent
had died during that campaign – other than from fatal wounds,
which were relatively few. Such a difference was, even then, a cause
for recrimination and concern. The difference was almost certainly
due to a number of factors only partly evident to the Commission.
However arduous the military campaign itself, the native soldiers
would have been well clothed and equipped, been fed by a well-
organized commissariat and cared for in sickness by at least a

rudimentary medical service. In examining the contrast in the mortality rates, a modern statistician might also have wanted to take account of the difference in altitude – most of Bhutan lies at over two thousand metres – climate, and the prevalence of potentially fatal disease.

The central point of the 1868 report – that it was the quality of care that made the basic difference – is reinforced by an analysis of the spread of the mortality figures, garden by garden, that made up the overall 26 per cent. It ranged from 14 per cent in the lowest case to 56 per cent in the highest. The lesson was clear. On the best tea gardens, humanely and efficiently run in order to produce and sell tea, the death rate was only a quarter of that on the worst, run by speculators interested only in producing a plausible "shell", with minimal capital outlay on food and facilities, that would enable them to make a quick (and usually very large) buck by selling on. In Ceylon the death rate on tea gardens, despite the cholera weeding out the weakest intending workers on their way there, was three times that in the general population in 1891, and still double in 1920.

The 1868 Commission ascribed high mortality to three factors (in addition to those connected with recruiting and transport discussed earlier): poorly built and unhealthily situated housing on swampy, edge-of-jungle land; contaminated drinking water; and inadequate medical treatment. To these must certainly be added malnutrition and overwork. From the 1860s, Indian governments and conscientious planters would strive to improve conditions, while greedy managers and owners made corresponding efforts to resist them. The divide between the two approaches was marked. The 1868 Commission, after heaping criticism on the worst gardens, praised the best – most of these were in Cachar rather than Assam – and "found conditions [of coolies] in many gardens all that could be desired. Happy and contented, surrounded by their families, earning good wages and possessing numbers of cows and goats; their daily task was light and when they were sick they were treated with the greatest care." Overall mortality declined significantly where humane standards prevailed. On Lakhimpur gardens in Assam, between 1865 and 1871, it fell from 12.3 per cent to 2.2

per cent, the best result in the region, and in Assam as a whole it was just under 3 per cent by 1904–5.

Why did these improvements in the levels of sickness and mortality come about? What had changed the impact of the main causes of death?

The Commission of 1906 marked a significant watershed in the condition of tea-garden workers. Before then the careless or exploitative planter still comprised a significant proportion of the managerial community; after that date he was in a rapidly diminishing minority. By 1906 the tea-garden coolie was significantly better off than the poorer *ryot* (peasant) in the wider Indian world. Until this watershed conditions had improved slowly but spasmodically; thereafter change was accelerated by the effect on the imperial powers of two world wars and the parallel growth of nationalism, and, to a lesser extent, trade unionism. As if in recognition of the changed climate in which coercion would no longer pay dividends, the Commission urged planters to improve wages, allot land generously and get away from barrack-like housing.

The main physical reasons for the improving life and health expectancy of the tea-garden coolie in the colonial period were corresponding improvements in his nutrition and in the medical attention he received. Others, such as the statutory right to one paid day off in seven and improved hygiene and housing, also contributed to this process. That an overworked coolie was an inefficient coolie became apparent to even the most conservative of planters. William Roberts, the successful and pragmatic manager of the Jorhaut Company's tea gardens, declared, as early as 1867, with only the faintest air of surprise: "The payment of wages to the labourers for Sundays, on which days they are allowed leave of absence under the *Cooley Act*, will absorb a large sum of money. It is evident, however, that the health of the coolies has been improved by this indulgence, and that it has made them more contented and happy. The rate of mortality has also been considerably reduced; and in this way a satisfactory equivalent is apparently realized in return for the outlay of money."

If overwork hampered productivity, the enfeeblement caused by malnutrition did so even more; a fact recognized quite soon by the majority of the pioneering tea planters. J.W. Edgar, principal author of a perceptive report on labour conditions in Assam in 1873, speculated that "even as early as 1862 the number of imported labourers far exceeded the supply of food available for them, and I attribute much of the sickness and mortality of those years to want of food sufficient in quantity and variety to enable the cooly to resist the effects of the climate, deficiency of means of communication, and the imperfect machinery of distribution in sparsely-inhabited jungles like those of Assam and Cachar". In citing the problems of communications and distribution, Edgar put his finger on a major factor contributing to the numerous regional famines in the next hundred years at times of general plenty in India. Throughout that time the tea industry helped to alleviate malnutrition and hunger among its employees in two main ways, one incidental the other deliberate. The need to improve communications to get tea out meant that they were also improved to get food in during times of shortage. The supplying of cheaper rice to coolies was not just a matter of subsidy, but of organization and effort. Right up to, and particularly during, the Second World War this was a major burden on the industry, but one willingly, if self-interestedly, undertaken. When the fall of Burma to the Japanese in 1942 cut off a major source of imported rice, and the demands of military campaigning drained from north-east India other essential nutrients, such as fish, eggs and ghee (clarified butter), it was the Indian Tea Association that appointed honorary purchasing officers throughout the region. These were instrumental in preventing starvation on the gardens, though famine struck many other parts of India in 1943. This additional workload was taken on at a time when a large proportion of the British male management had either volunteered for war service or been called up. Of course, in sustaining a healthy workforce the planters were also securing the supply of tea so essential to the British war effort!

In 1909 Dr C.A. Bentley, reporting to the Calcutta managing agency of Duncan Brothers on the health of workers on a large estate in the Dooars, observed: "99% of hill coolies and 96% of plains coolies had the enlarged spleens that indicated malarial infection. This in turn led to a 25% incidence of anaemia, predominantly among females. If repeated long bouts of malaria prevent one or both adults from working, the frequent course of events ... would be the death of the wife and one or both children and the bolting of the husband ... there are many days of labour lost before death finally occurs." Of 89 cases of pneumonia Bentley investigated retrospectively, 24 had died. No wonder he considered a quick look-over by a "*babu*" doctor to be "not a system, [but] only medical hide and seek ... As regards European supervision of coolie treatment it is obvious under the present arrangement such a thing is practically impossible ... At present medical treatment is made too difficult for the babu doctors, too difficult for the coolies, and too doubtful in efficiency."

Healthy diet and regular rest enabled the coolie better to resist the killer diseases that had cut such a swath through his ranks year on year, but it was European and American advances in the aetiology and best treatment of malaria, cholera and blackwater fever, and recognition of the debilitating effect of the numerous parasites to which the coolie was vulnerable (Bentley's report claimed that only one coolie out of six hundred was not infected with hookworm), that made the biggest impact on happiness, efficiency and life expectancy.

The most important medical breakthrough came as a result of the compelling need to keep free from malaria the soldiers of an overstretched British and Indian army fighting the Japanese on the frontiers of the dominion. The customary febrifuge of quinine was replaced by mepacrine (also known as quinacrine), a drug soon taken up on India's tea gardens with excellent results. On one garden the number of malaria cases treated monthly fell from 150 to eight. When, after the war, mepacrine was replaced by paludrin, and coolies' houses were regularly sprayed with DDT, malaria became virtually an affliction of the past.

These advances in knowledge and pharmacology would have been of little use without that enlightened self-interest that saw the advantage, as well as the humanity, of making tea-garden Indians – and Tamils, and Javanese – equal beneficiaries in them. The gradual change that brought this about was a classic "push-pull" case. On the one hand, the push of a growing sense of nationalism in the native populations and the increasing ability of labour to organize and demand effectively; on the other, the pull of an ever-increasing body of men – and women, for many compassionate memsahibs played a part in the change – who sincerely believed they owed a duty of care to the men, women and children who worked for them. The seeds of this change had been sown by enlightened individuals in the liberal tradition long before it became the moral norm, or was effected by external pressure. It was an attitude epitomized in the sentiments expressed by the Assam planter David Crole when he wrote in 1897: "I am sure that a policy of reasonable kindness and conciliation is never thrown away on any sentient being, much less on one of our own species, even though he be of another race."

The changing approach to labour management was exemplified by a planter quoted approvingly by the 1906 Commission who allowed his coolies "to live anywhere outside the lines they like. They build their own houses and I supply all the materials and pay them for a reasonable time while doing it. They consider this a great privilege. They can make a small vegetable garden round their huts and this has been a great success." Recognition that greater freedom of choice was good for the psyche also played its part in the improved health and happiness of coolies. Attitudes had changed considerably since 1877, when Henry Cottam pontificated: "It is the opinion of many planters in Assam that the excessive mortality of coolies en route is mainly caused by over-spending on the steamers ... The arrangements for [the coolie's] comfort on the tea garden generally are so complete that it would be next to impossible to find fault. If the Bengalie coolie is not happy with his lot it is not the fault of his employer." But at the same time he shared the opinion of another planter, who wrote in 1866 that "six feet by eight feet should be large enough for two coolies living together, [which] is better than they are accustomed to in their own country". Hull, a Ceylon planter, took a more enlightened approach and proposed "Different apartments; each apartment being ten by twelve feet square, opening into the general verandah, which should be five or six feet in width, and extend along the entire building. Two or more persons will generally occupy one room of the above dimensions, provided they are of the same caste; it is much the best plan, however, to leave the coolies to make these little dispositions and arrangements among themselves. Each married couple should, of course, be allowed to appropriate a room to themselves."

Today we may find the working and living conditions of the "Bengalie coolie" unacceptable but this should not obscure the fact that, by the outbreak of the First World War, on the majority of Indian tea gardens they were superior to those experienced in the villages of India, Ceylon or Java, or indeed in the tenements and terraces of industrialized Europe of the day.

Did a coolie on a colonial tea garden get a fair day's wages for a fair day's work? This may seem a simple enough question, but the ramifications of the methods of remunerating him on the tea plantations of India and Ceylon make it much harder to answer than would at first appear. On these tea gardens payment was based on time-measured piecework calculated in tranches. That is to say, estimates were made of how long it should take a reasonably skilled and diligent coolie to accomplish any particular task; and then a calculation would be made of the part of that task, or tasks, that he or she could complete in a "working day". The "working day" varied between three and six hours, but was usually between four and five.

This basic task, the *hazri* (Hindi, "average"), was supposedly designed to provide only a minimum wage, fixed for most of the nineteenth and early twentieth centuries at five rupees a month for men, four for women and from one to two and a half for children (who might start work as young as five or six). The minimum wage on the tea gardens in north-east India was established by law in 1865 on the theoretical basis of a nine-hour day and a six-day week. Government inspectors were appointed to oversee its terms, but the coolie was still closely tied to his garden and could be imprisoned for persistently refusing to work or for any other breach of contract. The planter also had the right arbitrarily to arrest "absconders" – defined as those absent without leave for more than seven days – and local hillmen were paid a bounty for catching and returning a fugitive coolie. The bounty was deducted from the "absconder's" pay.

The minimum wage was abolished in 1870 but reinstated in 1882, together with increased powers for the inspectors of labour welfare and a subsistence-level payment in time of sickness. Most of this and subsequent wage and labour legislation was applied on the basis of "a sensible misinterpretation" of the extant Act. The last vestige of the 1882 legislation did not disappear from the statute book until 1926, when the planter's right to arbitrary arrest and the penalty of imprisonment for a coolie's breach of contract were rescinded. From a combination of Government legislation, progressive thinking coupled with enlightened self-interest on the part of the majority of planters, and the rise of Indian nationalism and trade-union activity, the tea-garden coolie became increasingly free between the world wars to place his labour where he could get the best terms. It is perhaps significant that, despite legislation giving him the right, after three years' service, to return home at his employer's expense, only a relatively small proportion of a workforce of almost three-quarters of a million chose to do so and not to return.

After the *hazri* had been completed, the coolie was theoretically free for the remainder of the working day, either to opt for further work at a higher rate, known as *ticca* (Hindi, "piecework") – or appositely in some districts as *doubli* – or to go home to cultivate his or her plot, or to do anything else they wished. In practice, particularly at busy times such as harvest, great pressure was put on coolies to undertake as much *ticca* labour as their managers required. Others, usually on short-term contracts of some kind, might undertake *ticca* willingly in order to save up sufficient to return home. It was not uncommon at the busiest times to see a line of lanterns wobbling across many gardens as male coolies rose before dawn to complete their allotted *hazri* hoeing in order to join the women plucking during daylight hours. There was also a bonus for exceeding the plucking quotas, known as "leaf pice". (Four pice to the anna; sixteen annas to the rupee. [Now 100 paise = 1 rupee.] In the 1890s a rupee was worth from 1s. 2d. to 1s. 4d. For comparative-value table, see p.377.) A good male worker could expect to earn as much as eight rupees a month. In the thirty years to 1905, during which both wages and prices remained fairly static, a family of husband, wife and three working children could expect to earn 15–20 rupees a month. In Victorian Britain, likewise, many mothers and children were expected to contribute to the family budget by their labours.

Inevitably there were a number of variables in setting the *hazri*, the assessment of which was left to the individual manager on the grounds that he alone knew the circumstances and difficulties of each job. Was the soil to be hoed heavy or light? According to the market, was fine or coarse plucking required? If the former, the *hazri* must be set so that the plucker was not tempted to pluck harshly in order to earn a better wage. Nor could these assessments remain static. Fairness might dictate that the *ticca* task be made less burdensome to a new recruit and increased as his or her skill developed, or be made lighter when, for example, growth on the bush was light and increased when the flush was heavy. From 1882, government inspectors were empowered to check the *hazri* tasks on any tea garden and, if they thought them unfair, to reduce the amount of work needed to fulfil them. It was a legal requirement for the *hazri*, or the proportion of it earned, to be entered into the *hazri* book, the wages ledger, but for many years the *ticca* did not have to be, so it is quite difficult, even from such original records as survive, to measure the precise earnings of tea-garden coolies in India and Ceylon until relatively modern times.

Nor can the living standard of the tea-garden coolie be measured by the pay alone. Through a mixture of legislation and good practice, the planter was also supposed to supplement garden wages in a number of ways. He had a legal obligation to provide rice at below market prices, when these were high, and minimal medical facilities. He also usually undertook to provide cloth, or subsidize it, and to provide housing, or the time and materials for its construction by the coolie. It was customary also for the planter to grant to each family a small plot of land on which to grow vegetables. This was either rent-free or offered for a nominal rent in order to pre-empt any claims for ownership.

The provision of subsidized rice was crucial to the coolies' survival. Typically, at a time in the 1880s when the market price was two rupees a maund, the coolie was able to buy it for one rupee. It is hard to see how coolies could have survived the famine of 1856 – which killed one and a half million people in Orissa and Bihar – or the 1920–21 depression, for example, without these subsidies. But for any additions to the nutritional value of their diet, in the shape of vegetables, fruit or meat, they would have had to rely almost entirely on their own efforts, though some managers did ensure that these were available cheaply in the local bazaar. It may well be argued that the payment of better wages would have obviated the need for such a complicated and exploitation-prone system of paying coolies. A purely monetary system might also have made it harder for plantation owners to deny them a share of the prosperity of the better years, though in defence of the planters it should be said that, in poorer times, many of them took cuts in salary when market conditions forced them to lower wages.

From 1865 coolies were entitled by law to one day off a week, usually a Sunday, and in the majority of cases they were paid the flat *hazri* rate for that day. In practice, many coolies, when they felt they had earned enough for their basic needs, simply failed to turn up for work on other days as well. The Assam branch of the Indian Tea Association calculated that, in 1901, the average coolie did tea-garden work for only 17 days of the month: a preference for leisure, family life and home cultivation that many a present-day European might be well advised to emulate. The 1931 Royal Commission on Labour confirmed that this 30 per cent level of absenteeism from the notional working-week still obtained.

Most importantly, it was laid down in 1861 that every tea garden employing more than three hundred people must have a "doctor" and a "hospital". Initially the latter tended to consist only of a group of small and simple huts, separated to facilitate isolation in cases of infectious disease. A high proportion of the first *babu* doctors were insufficiently trained and were sometimes tempted to sell patients the food provided free by the garden, rather than giving it to them. These shortcomings were quickly recognized and by 1867 each group of gardens usually had a qualified European doctor to oversee the work of the *babu* doctors.

The better planters exceeded these minimal requirements; the worst evaded them in a variety of ways, some subtle, many less so.

Among the most common means of exploitation were unfairly hard definitions of *hazri* and *ticca* tasks. Arbitrary deductions were made from the amount of leaf weighed by subtracting the nominal weight of the basket or cloth in which it was delivered for weighing from the amount credited to each coolie. All garden managers did this as a matter of standard industry practice. This deduction was effected by means of "distorted scales": scales adjusted by the manager to show less than true weight and whose recording face was often turned away from the coolie. To be credited with 1lb of tea plucked, the coolie would have to put considerably more than this weight of leaf on the scale. These adjustments regularly added as much as four ounces to the pound (25 per cent) and could add as much as eight (50 per cent). (My father was particularly proud that he was instrumental in getting distorted scales abandoned in 1939.)

If leaf had been plucked in wet conditions a similar arbitrary deduction would be made for the supposed extra weight of the additional moisture. Planters claimed that they judged these deductions as fairly as they could, and no doubt many did.

The coolies devised their own methods of tipping the scales, as it were, in the other direction. Most commonly, the women did so on the way to leaf weighing by "taking a rest" beside a convenient ditch in which their leaf got an "accidental" weight-enhancing wetting. If caught, they would excuse themselves by saying they had slipped and fallen into the water. Another trick was surreptitiously to insert small amounts of twigs or coarse leaf into a basketful of finer leaf so as to increase its weight. If the coolie was caught doing this, the manager would usually make her – it was most often a woman – spread the leaves out on a cloth and pick out the offending elements before being allowed to weigh in, thus losing valuable earning time. Some managers, more harsh than others, might deduct part or all of the day's pay for such offences.

In the factory, where *hazri* and *ticca* also applied, the most common petty crime at which coolies were caught was stealing small amounts of the poorest-quality tea, or tea waste, for selling either in the market for consumption or to one of the illicit local dealers who used it for turning into caffeine, a perfectly respectable chemical by-product produced on a larger scale by three or four reputable firms. If caught stealing from the factory, coolies could expect to receive the customary thrashing. Depending on the vigilance and brutality of the manager in question, this could be a greater or lesser deterrent.

There are too many variables between gardens in the many aspects of tea cultivation – soil, climate, bush quality, prevalence of plant diseases in the area and so on – to make any direct correlation between the quality and humanity of the management and the productivity of a garden in any particular case. However, it is easier to relate management attitudes at the cusp of the nineteenth and twentieth centuries to the well-being, and indeed the life expectancy, of a garden's coolies. Sir Henry Cotton, the Commissioner for Assam in the 1890s, made this connection in a report to the Government in India in 1901. To put his sharp criticisms in perspective, it is as well to preface his findings with his view of the planters of Assam at the end of his term of office in 1899: "On the whole he thinks it creditable to the European management that cases of collision should be so few ... the regrettable habit of giving a cuff, or even a kick or a blow with a cane to natives of the labouring classes ... is undoubtedly on the wane and is probably less common among them than among other members of the European community, for their action is tempered by self-interest." Exactly how the planters would have put it themselves – and many did.

If Sir Henry was initially biased toward the planters, once freed from the restraints of office he soon became disillusioned by what he saw and heard during his enquiries, referring to "managers having deemed that they were justified in making deductions right and left so long as they kept their labourers in good condition like their horses and their cattle". He was particularly severe on the practice of keeping down the mortality figures by cancelling the contracts of "sickly and unfit labourers, and others where deaths had been treated as desertions for the same reason". Cotton's findings make clear that there was a definite, if not quantifiable, link between levels of wages and welfare and the incidence of mortality – and possibly the agricultural out-turn – on any given group of gardens. It is evident that the morbidity on gardens that were genuinely developed as business enterprises was very much lower than on those speculative ones that were only nominally cultivated. The perpetrators of the Nowgong scam (see Chapter 16) saw as much as 40 per cent of their workforce die from disease and neglect in a six-month period in 1865 and again in 1866. It is harder, without diary-like details, to explain the dramatic fluctuations at this time on any given garden – as, for example, that in Sylhet (now in Bangladesh), where in 12 months the mortality fell from 57 per cent to just over 18 per cent.

The Viceroy, Lord Curzon, who had been sympathetic to the Commissioner's initial concern for coolie welfare, was less impressed by Cotton's total volte-face in the space of two years. When Curzon was also lobbied by the Indian Tea Association, and ridiculed in *The Times*, he seems to have instructed his officials gently to rebut the good Sir Henry. They wrote accordingly: "More than half a million emigrants drawn from the very poorest classes of India are indebted to the industry for a much more liberal supply of food and clothing than they would have expected to enjoy in their own homes." They found "that the relations between the great majority of planters and their coolies are of a kindly nature, [and] that the planter takes a humane interest in the well-being of the families amongst whom he lives. Instances of oppression are unhappily not altogether rare, and the Governor-General in Council entirely sympathises with the desire of the Commissioner that they should be severely dealt with. But he sees no reason to find in them a stigma which should apply to the planting community as a whole."

The Indian-owned and edited newspapers, on the other hand, were more than willing to stigmatize the planting community as a whole, and all too often did so. The more conscientious planters must have been wounded and angered by the repeated attacks on the whole industry in editorials in the Indian press by editors who had never even visited the tea districts. A typical "scandal" story in the *Madras Mail* of 11 September 1890 claimed that the low level of births in Dibrugarh was due to women workers being forced to have abortions so that their labour should not be lost. Such gibes must have been doubly hurtful when most tea-garden employers were way ahead of their industrial and farming counterparts in Europe in the provision of maternity leave with pay, and dietary and medical support for pregnant and post-parturition coolie women. H.J. Lawrie firmly rebutted the charge and challenged the paper to send someone to visit him so that he could demonstrate that "there is no garden where a woman is not given a month's leave before, and one month after, her confinement. For this period she draws half pay. This is the minimum amount of leave; on many gardens she is allowed to remain on leave as long as she is not strong enough to work."

Attacks such as the *Madras Mail*'s prompted the chairman of the Indian Tea Association to point out in 1899 that such libels were not only an obstacle to recruitment but encouraged "the public in England, through the medium of some Parliamentary busybody, [to] become imbued with the idea that the planter of India is the equal of the old slave driver of Virginia". He urged that his audience "boldly claim for planters on every opportunity we can that they are indeed the benefactors of the country and the people".

If Lord Curzon and his administration did not endorse Cotton's latter views, it was clear that the Indian coolie did. When Cotton next visited Assam after publication of his report he made an almost royal progress, cheered on his way by thousands of coolies carrying banners welcoming "Mr Cotton, the protector of the dumb coolie". When his views were largely ignored Cotton returned to England in a huff, became a Liberal MP and continued to campaign compassionately, if not always entirely objectively, for the improvement of the working conditions on India's tea gardens.

The truth probably lies in some hard-to-determine area between the two viewpoints of Cotton and Cottam (see p.171). There were numerous further enquiries during the remainder of the Raj into labour conditions in the tea districts, but primarily in Assam and Cachar, the second of which was given a much cleaner bill of health. The conclusion of the 1926 Labour Enquiry Commission – that the tea-garden coolie was reasonably well off compared with the poorer agricultural labourer in the rest of India – is probably as near to the truth as we are likely to get so long after the conditions in question. While this report was still sharply critical of some

aspects of tea-garden life, it considered that, with family recruitment and land and leisure for the cultivation of domestic plots, it
now more closely resembled life in the better villages of India and
that "for the great majority of immigrants the change is for the
better" and that, for many, leaving normal village life was "an
avenue of escape from destitution and even servitude".

The ninth edition of *Encyclopaedia Britannica*, published in 1888,
explaining the poor prospects for tea cultivation in Australia and
America in its article on tea, put its usual unerring finger on the
inevitable tension between the rights of tea-garden coolies and the
commercial interests of their owners: "Cheap labour is the sine qua
non of success. Tea can be plucked in China and the British East
Indies for two or three pence a day in wages, and it is on such exceedingly moderate outlay that the margin of profit depends." Today we
might regard that margin of profit as inflated; not so in 1888.

In 1909 the organizers of a campaign to improve the pay and
conditions of coolies in India unkindly portrayed the European
planter as "a young man of athletic build and somewhat villainous
countenance, in fancy riding kit, with a large whip". Like most cari-
catures, this one contained more than a grain of truth in some
instances, but in many others it was a travesty. Although the plantation ethos, as exemplified by young men like Hetherington,
Ramsden and Taylor, appears at first sight to be that of the British
public school, in which prefects without a qualm cheerfully flogged
the smaller boys for the slightest misdemeanour, relations between
British and Dutch planters and their coolies were much more
complex and usually more enlightened than that. The more ignorant Europeans may have seen themselves as racially superior to the
Indians or Javanese who worked for them, but overall the abuses
that arose in plantation labour relations were not essentially about
race but about class and economic power, about a breakdown of
the quasi-parent–quasi-child relationship on which the running of a
tea garden was predicated by all parties.

Most of the economic, military and even physical power lay on
the expatriate side; but, well before the European imperial era,
villagers in India, Ceylon and the Dutch East Indies were already
accustomed to the kind of feudal relationship between themselves

and local native landowners and tribal chiefs with which the English farm labourer of the early nineteenth century would have been quite familiar. There were mutual obligations and benefits on both sides, but power all on the one. The essence of the planter–coolie relationship until well into the twentieth century was the concept that the Burra Sahib (in India or Ceylon), the Tuan Kebun (in the Dutch East Indies), the senior manager, was *ma-bap*, mother and father, to the coolies who worked for him. And, as with a parent, the power to reward or punish was in his hands. As the beneficent *ma-bap*, the manager and his European assistants were the source of numerous, but entirely discretionary, benefits for the "good" child (such as unofficial loans to tide coolies over misfortunes and temporary hardships) and arbitrary, and too often disproportionately excessive, punishments for the "naughty" child (such as thrashing or docking pay).

Ma-bap in Hindi, and its equivalents in Tamil, Javanese and so on, all denoted the mother–father role in which European planters were viewed until the second half of the twentieth century, not only by those who worked for them but by themselves. Moreover, many of the indigenous managers who took over after independence saw themselves in a not dissimilar role. From the feminine side of this hermaphrodite construct, care and consideration were to be expected; from the masculine, justice, discipline, protection and punishment. The plantation worker or coolie looked to the mother half for sympathy and social support, health care and financial help. To the paternal element he or she would look for hard, but fairly managed, tasks, the pay to which they were entitled, fair, unbiased judgements in disputes between themselves, and proportionate and appropriate punishment for the guilty party. In India the worker would go to his manager and say, "*Bichar kar do*" ("Please be judge of this"). The manager's ruling would be *hokum*, as binding as any law: a judgement that must be, and nearly always was, willingly accepted because cumulative experience suggested that this was the reasonable and prudent thing to do. The worker pledged an almost feudal fealty to his manager, who usually took his responsibility for the worker with an equally feudal sense of *noblesse oblige*. In 1857 Dr William Jameson reported to the Indian Government that the tea-garden coolie was: "Honest to a degree, they look to a European as belonging to a superior class as from him they are in the habit of getting justice and redress when it is called for. To maintain this high and proud position the European planter must always act with justice and probity to those acting under him."

Ramsden, writing about the period between the two world wars, described the symbolic way in which his arrival on a new garden in Assam was greeted: "They all salaamed deeply and some of the little girls ran up, knelt in front of me and touched the ground with their foreheads. This was not a gesture of obeisance or fear, nor done in the hope of winning favour. It was simply the coolies' way of expressing their allegiance ... I touched the little girls on the head when they got up, and the older people on the hands."

Symbolism was all-important in cementing the master–servant relationship, and in underwriting the often distant, but nonetheless very real, power that lay behind this thin scattering of Europeans among the seething multitude of the native populations in the plantation colonies. It was, for example, customary for an Indian coolie or *babu* to fold his umbrella, or dismount from his pony or bicycle, when passing or speaking to a European. As late as 1900 failure to do so could still induce apoplectic threats from one who "met a Nepali who passed me without dismounting. If ever I see him again I will give him something to remind him." These particular marks of respect were also extended to wealthy or important native dignitaries throughout the East and dated back to pre-colonial times, when to be mounted, or protected from sun and rain by that rarity an umbrella, indicated power and the advisability of deference.

To arbitrate fairly, and thus sustain the British reputation for impartial justice, it was first necessary to understand and sympathize with the culture, customs and mores of the local natives. In India this could range from recognition that, because in Hindi there was no word for "thank you", its absence was not insolence, to knowing which tribe or caste you should recruit and instruct to carry out which specific task. It even encompassed knowing the circumstances and manner in which it was permissible, or not, to beat your wife. In 1902 Hetherington was asked to arbitrate on just such an arcane point when his overseer reported to him:

"There has been great trouble in the lines, your honour, Doorgacharan stripped his wife completely naked and beat her."

"Why did he beat her?"

"I don't know, but the women are very angry."

"Why are the women angry?"

"The women say, if you have seen one woman naked you have seen all women."

Ramsden's mentor warned him that "no European thoroughly understands the native. If you fondly imagine that you know from a native's words what is going on in his mind you're sure to be mistaken".

Europeans were, to a certain degree, above the law as it would have applied in their mother countries, but only to a certain degree. A missionary might be excused for murdering his wife's lover on the grounds that it "was only fair play", and as far back as 1877 Henry Cottam could insist that, while "the imprisonment of Europeans for assaulting natives under provocation would rouse the spirit of the British Lion in these parts ... he must be next to an angel who is not occasionally provoked into giving a slap", he was compelled to add in qualification: "but that serious and severe attacks will be punished has been proved since this was written". Despite objections from many in the European community – particularly where a case had been tried by an Indian magistrate or judge – several British planters were sent to prison for such assaults, though perhaps not for as long as they should have been.

The same nice distinction, between what was then regarded as reasonable chastisement and brutal assault, obtained on Dutch tea plantations. In the Dutch East Indies the long association with tea from Japan meant that several Japanese were employed as managers and assistants during the colonial period. The trial of one of them in October 1926 made clear that in the Dutch East Indies, too, there were limits to discipline that must not be exceeded. Kozo Oriuchie was found guilty on 12 counts of repeatedly beating his workers with a rattan stick and ordering his overseers to do the same; for locking up workers for weeks on end (except to leave for work) in a hut two metres square by two metres high. He had stripped several workers naked and smeared their bodies with horse dung, which he also forced them to eat along with human faeces. He was sentenced to a stiff term of imprisonment, which was first reduced to 30 months and then commuted to a fine.

Right up to the end of the colonial period the *ma-bap* relationship between a manager, or his assistants, and tea-garden workers, whether in India or Indonesia, Ceylon or East Africa, remained largely unchanged. In his excellent book *Tea Addiction, Exploitation and Empire* Roy Moxham describes how, in the 1950s in Nyasaland (now Malawi), he was still adjudicating "in many cases of theft, adultery and assault. Local custom was that all but the most serious cases were settled by the payment of money. Jailing an offender, so that he was precluded from earning the money to pay compensation, was regarded as absurd. This made my role relatively easy, especially as the parties had come to me voluntarily. Only very occasionally was it necessary to send them to the police, a chief, or a magistrate." However, after the elections of 1961 fewer and fewer cases came to him and most were heard, in equally paternalistic style, by officers of the Malawi Congress Party.

There was a hierarchy from top to bottom in tea gardens everywhere, starting with the manager and ending with the newest and worst-paid woman or child worker. What is remarkable is that this hierarchy, and the means by which it was enforced, was not only considered right and proper by Europeans but was, by and large, accepted as equally natural, if inevitable, by the natives who worked for them. There were a number of reasons for this, chief of which was the infinitely greater economic and physical power of the plantation owners. The hierarchy and its mechanisms were often both imposed and welcomed by those senior natives who most benefited in terms of income and status from imposing it: labour recruiters, overseers, clerks and medical orderlies. The European planters both acquiesced in and supervised this native hierarchy beneath them, through which alone their limited numbers were enabled to exercise control of their enterprises. As one of the early planters in India put it: "The best manner of treating your head natives in Assam is either to trust them thoroughly allowing them to cheat when they will take care nobody else does, or else go into every minute thing yourself."

Hard as the lot of the tea-garden coolie in north-east India may have been – and it was undeniably hard at times – it cannot be denied that, from the earliest days of the industry, both the central and the regional governments in India took a serious and genuine interest in his welfare and that of his family. This chapter has concentrated so far on the circumstances of tea-garden labour in north-east India, but a similar pattern, *mutatis mutandis*, applied in general to the rest of India and to Ceylon. However, in the Dutch East Indies at the time, and in East Africa from the 1920s, very different conditions and practices prevailed. In East Africa the pattern was one of long-established villages in the vicinity providing their "spare" labour for work on neighbouring tea gardens. Families would have their own houses and their own land, run and cultivated by the women of the family. It was the men and boys who worked on the tea gardens. But because commercial tea cultivation had not got meaningfully under way until the dying decades of the colonial period, the problems of transition to modern work patterns and labour relations were not so traumatic.

This was not the case in what is now Indonesia, which saw the earliest attempts at commercial tea growing outside China. Whereas in most of the Indian subcontinent shortages of local labour had to be offset by immigrants eager – if sometimes misguidedly – to better themselves by tea-garden work, in the Dutch East Indies, where there was a plethora of natives in the plantation areas, the problem was to get them to work regularly and consistently in the paid cultivation and manufacture of tea.

The Dutch plantation economy of the colonial era was managed at least as brutally and arbitrarily as the British, if less homogeneously. In Java, where over 80 per cent of Dutch tea was grown, labour was drawn from a plantation's nearest local villages. Population density was much greater than in Assam, and villagers were already accustomed to contracting out their labour to Dutch growers of spices and palm oil. In Sumatra plantations, including the few tea plantations, employed indentured and contracted workers, mostly from Java, in gulag-like conditions. Contract coolies worked for at least 10 hours a day, seven days a week and 52 weeks a year, for wages governed so as to be only a little higher than the current price of rice. "On the one hand, there was a multitude of coercive measures used to retain workers through debt; on the other hand, labouring and living conditions which underscored the transiency and expendability of the same population. Cramped and poor housing, widespread disease, high adult and infant mortality, along with verbally and physically abusive disciplinary measures were features of a system which in the end could hardly reproduce itself." A native writer, Tan Malaka, put it even more bluntly: "The class which toils from dawn to dusk; the class which earns a wage just sufficient to fill the belly and to cover its nakedness; the class which lives in a shed like goats in a stable; and is arbitrarily flogged or sworn at and damned to hell; the class which could at any time lose wife or daughter should the white boss lust after her ... that is the class of Indonesians known as contract coolies."

Javanese coolies were, however, much more free to come and go not only than their fellow countrymen employed across the straits but also than their Assamese counterparts. Javanese tea workers, like many coolies in Assam, not only had small plots of their own to cultivate but, by the twentieth century, were not even precluded from growing tea on them for sale to European markets. This was a privilege somewhat restricted by the fact that the control of both prices and channels of distribution lay in the hands of the large European-owned estates that dominated the tea business in the Dutch East Indies. Since Dutch tea gardens tended to be significantly larger than their counterparts in India or Ceylon, a gap was left between these and peasant smallholdings into which a number of Javanese and Chinese entrepreneurs soon slipped on a modest scale.

Whereas many Dutch planters complained about the intermittent application of the Javanese coolie to garden work, J.I.L.L. Jacobson typically saw from the outset in 1847 how it should, in fact, be turned to the planter's advantage: "When they go away, others coming in their places; they very soon learn the work; and then when the whole of the people are acquainted with it, this changing of people rather turns out to the advantage of the planter." Once all the local villagers had been taught the same fairly simple basic techniques for plucking and processing, then the rotation of work squads could actually enhance productivity. It gave the coolies ample rest in which to enjoy their own cultivation with their families and to restore their vigour for the more intensive work of the plantation. By returning to an independent existence at the end of every stint in the tea garden, the coolie also relieved the planter of much responsibility for his health and welfare.

Jacobson also recognized the psychological benefit to be derived from establishing regular and predictable patterns for these cyclical changes: "Men employed in the mere cultivation, must be liable to be changed without further notice being given; in ordinary changes, as for instance, factory work, five days' notice must be given to the heads; and regarding new applications, eight must be given; there must be fourteen days' likewise notice given of the number of people who will be required for the harvest time; further, the planter should keep a statement thereof, with the names and list of work done according to the forms laid down."

For similar reasons he insisted that, whether the coolies lived in the village or on the plantation, "the planter must always take care that they all likewise have a small garden attached; and that they are provided at the proper time with buffaloes, and as far as practicable, with *sawas* or *tipars* [wet and dry rice paddies, respectively]: this binds the people, in a great measure, to their lands." Sadly his successors would, in the main, conspicuously fail to see the wisdom of his advice. It would be the best part of a century before the tea planters of Java generally realized that the high levels of mortality, caused by neglect of Jacobson's simple principles, were not only morally reprehensible but counter-productive. Between the world wars there was a growing acceptance, in Java and Sumatra, as in India and Ceylon, that a stable, permanent workforce which was *senang* (content) was desirable; that coolies working willingly because they were fairly rewarded for their labour and well treated would produce more tea more cheaply than those driven by fear and abuse. Gradually "naked force made way for more restrained methods of labour control in subsequent decades; physical violence did not disappear, but was used in less extreme ways".

This enlightenment would in the end prove too late in the Dutch East Indies, as in India and Ceylon. For better or worse, *ma-bap* would be replaced by the confrontation between workers' unions and plantation owners, legislation in the place of paternalism. Nationalism and the movement for workers' rights under the law and enforced by the state would become the "unstoppable force"; what had once been the "immovable object" of capitalism backed by imperial power would be so weakened by war – and in the case of the Dutch colonies by defeat and occupation both of them and of the European mother country – that it became a "push-over".

9

Coolie Power

"The independent European public does not, however, wish to monopolize authority, to the exclusion of the many native gentlemen perfectly competent to look after the interests of their race and country."

That simple truth was understood by the Assam planter Alexander MacGowan almost a century and a half ago. It took two world wars and worldwide revolutions in thought and deed to advance that truth to its logical conclusion in self-government. A change in labour relations took place on colonial tea gardens as the dialogue between employers and trade unions, which had been the custom for so long in Europe and America, replaced the old paternalism of *ma-bap*. Where *ma-bap* worked well, as it did on many colonial tea gardens, trade unions had little appeal and made little impact before independence. Where it did not, because of needlessly harsh management or politically motivated agitation – or both – unionization was both necessary and inevitable.

An anonymous pre-war manager of P&T, a Dutch-owned tea plantation in Java, was fairly typical of the twentieth-century planters who believed in their role as mother-father to their coolies. (Bought by a consortium of Englishmen in 1815 as a general plantation, P&T became an Anglo-Dutch enterprise in 1910.) He did not regard himself as bound by the various labour laws of the country in which he worked – let alone those of his mother country – on the grounds that his employees were better off under his personal rule. He believed that taking "into account how many advantages the Landowner has given the population and what large sums he has expended towards this end and still is spending, then it must be acknowledged that the deviations which the Landowner still permits to be practised do not weigh against the great advantages which on the other hand the population enjoys". The author of the privately published history of the firm, writing in 1943, then adds: "If one enquires in a friendly way of the population, which I have done myself and also caused to he done secretly by others, whether they like to retain the present conditions or whether it is their desire that the Landowner should strictly adhere to the regulations, there is not one who desires an alteration in the existing conditions."

But alterations in the Dutch East Indies there would certainly be, and brought about by outside events unforeseen by either managers or coolies. In February 1942 the Japanese invaded and occupied the whole of the islands. Two significant changes followed. A land-allotment programme, tentatively begun by the pre-war planters and furthered by the occupying Japanese, gave rise to a massive squatter movement on plantation land. This not only led to a shortage of plantation labour but bestowed on the Javanese coolies, to some degree, the economic independence enjoyed by their forebears in the days before contract labour.

The second major change also came about by a rather tortuous route. When the British "liberated" what is now Indonesia on behalf of the war-shattered Dutch, they were surprised and shocked to find themselves not welcomed as liberators but resisted as occupiers by the very forces they had armed to resist the Japanese. When the Dutch eventually took over military responsibility, and tried to extend their control from the cities to the countryside, they met with unexpected armed resistance from republican militias largely based on those very plantation coolies who had been their pre-war employees. These formed the nucleus also of a vigorous trade-union movement which prospered still more after independence in 1952. However, the success of squatters and unions alike was short-lived. Following the right-wing military coup of 1962, the squatters were turfed off their land and the left-wing unions that supported them were banned. In Indonesia an autocratic state chose to equate workers' legitimate economic demands with revolutionary subversion, treated protesters as criminals and greatly curtailed the activities of labour organizations. By 1970 many coolies found themselves back on the plantations working for pay and conditions no better than those they had received before the war. The tea-garden owners, on the other hand, as earners of much-needed hard currency, were back in favour.

In India and Ceylon, what might be termed the *hap-hazri* approach to wage payment, based on task achievement, gradually gave way to the concept of a fixed day's wages for a fixed day's work. Pay was still loosely related to skill and seniority, and a coolie could still be docked part of his wage if his work was not up to scratch, or he was unduly late or absented himself. The minimum wage had been nominally in force again in India since 1882, but it was dropped altogether in 1915. From then until the visionary Royal Commission of 1931 there was something of a free-for-all in wage determination. The Commission proposed an independent, though voluntary, wage-fixing scheme for the whole industry to be determined and imposed through a wages board or boards. On such a board there would be not only officials and employer representatives but – a truly radical proposal – representatives of the coolies as well.

While acquiescing in principle, the Indian Tea Association (ITA), which had been founded in 1881 to represent the interests of the planting community as a whole, entered three caveats: that for the sake of consistency the Government should set up an effective statistics-gathering body on whose evidence decisions could be made; that each wages board should be limited to covering only an area in which conditions were broadly comparable; that as labour was insufficiently organized its interests should be represented by officials.

Two years earlier a tentative start had been made to the creation of a trade-union movement in India with the setting up of the Estates Staffs Association of Southern India, primarily as a welfare organization. The potential for worker organization had been demonstrated long before in what was probably the industry's first strike, in Sylhet in 1848, in protest at a three-month delay in paying coolies' wages. Cash-strapped planters had been using these delays to ease their own cash-flow problems. Much more dramatic were the violent and widespread pay protests during the 1921 depression, when wages shrank to a level which left coolies considerably worse off than they had been during the First World War.

An incipient, if only partial, change in planters' attitudes at this time can be detected in A.R. Ramsden's retrospective analysis of these strikes: "There were only three reasons for actual strikes out there in Assam. The first was bad economic conditions, such as occurred in 1921, when the price of food was not reduced sufficiently to meet the cut in wages after the last war. The strikes then were really serious and a number of Europeans lost their lives in the accompanying riots, but from the coolies' point of view they were absolutely justifiable. The other two reasons are unjust severity in handling the labour force, and the converse – being too soft with it." When Ramsden tried to discuss the implications of the dire economic situation in a rational way with some of the older planters they just told him to "have another peg and shut up". During the 1920s the British Trades Union Council and the All India Trade Union Council sent delegations to encourage and advise the embryo tea-garden unions. The latter council's representative was briefly imprisoned for his pains. Owing to the combination of lightning strikes and a price recovery in the tea market that had eased the pressure on tea companies hit by war and economic stagnation, tea-garden wages by 1930 were roughly double what they had been in 1920.

The fissiparous nature of the Indian trade-union movement was not conducive to good industrial relations as the Communist, Socialist and Congress-backed unions competed for membership and influence. Splinter group splintered from splinter group, until in one small region of southern India alone there were no fewer than 55 trade unions. But it should not be presumed that all the labour ferment on Indian tea gardens between the world wars was necessarily irresponsible. Many union leaders recognized that, for the well-being of their members, a reasonable balance had to be struck between the aims of men and managers. In 1948, in the immediate aftermath of Indian independence, a union in Cachar issued some sensible advice to its members:

> The Manager is the representative of the employer. The gardens are not yet our national property. They belong to the employers. How the gardens should be run is decided between Managers and

Dutch East Indiamen, pioneers of the 17th-century tea trade from China to Europe.

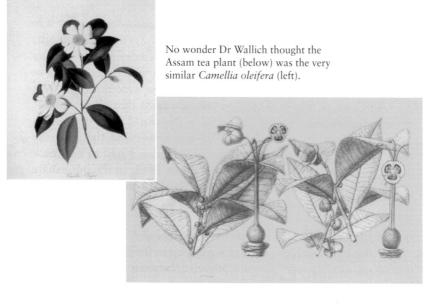

No wonder Dr Wallich thought the Assam tea plant (below) was the very similar *Camellia oleifera* (left).

A London opium den. Most Chinese addicts died within three years.

Baisao: Japanese philosopher and tea seller who kept things simple at his open-air itinerant tea stall.

Above: A British tea merchant in Canton deals with one of his suppliers in a tea-packing depot.

Below: The medicine America had to swallow as punishment for the Boston Tea Party was the blockade of Boston port.

Above: *Ariel* and *Taipeng* dash up the English Channel for home
on the last day of their 99-day race, 6 September 1866.

Below: "Steady on, Spencer, with the milk – Rosebery has not had a drop yet."

Above: Eighteenth-century tea drinking and manners in the West.

Below: Nineteenth-century tea drinking and manners among Afghan tribesmen in the East.

Right: A Japanese tea house in all its artistic and aesthetic simplicity.

Below: Garways, the famous early coffee shop, rebuilt and renamed Garraways after it was burned down.

GARRAWAY'S COFFEE-HOUSE, CHANGE-ALLEY, NOW BEING DEMOLISHED.

In the late-eighteenth century teapots were used to illustrate everything from saucy stories to moral tales – in this case a contemporary version of the Biblical story of the prodigal son.

Left: The bold women who manned the tea cars in World War II got their restorative cuppa to wherever it was needed!

Left: Tibetan monks – probably the world's champion tea drinkers – sup their own soupy version.

Below: Early tea caddies had locks: their contents were often worth more than the containers.

employers and we merely carry out instructions. The primary objective of the Manager and the employer is to earn more profits. There are two ways to do this. The first one is by way of producing more tea and good quality tea and selling at a high price. The other method is to under-pay the workers and *Babus* and thereby increase profits. The Union and the *Panchayats* [local councils] have been set up to prevent their taking recourse to the second method. The Union will fight for proper wages but simultaneously it is the duty of the workers to improve the productivity of the gardens.

This echoed the dialogue of pre-war years in which a planter could say in defence of his laissez-faire attitude: "Is it not ridiculous to suppose that owners would wilfully maltreat their servants, knowing that everything depends upon them being in a good state of health?" Only for it to be answered by the equally subjective, but equally true, observation of an Indian worker on a badly run tea garden: "This garden's sorrow is great. This is our garden. When the sahib goes after six or seven years to another garden, it is we who will remain here. This is why *sewa* [service] to the tea bush is so important. If we don't do this, one day, we won't eat."

The ITA also foresaw the population explosion that would become a serious problem in post-independence India. The planters seem to have sensed this intuitively from the teeming human fecundity about them. If coolies were to get into the habit of working a full six-day week throughout the month, then fewer would be needed to work the tea gardens and factories. What was to be done with the surplus labour? Would resentment arise from the inescapable break with the tradition by which child workers and the children of garden coolies, on attaining adulthood, were automatically offered work on the same garden? Would such a large pool of discontented unemployed not only create severe hardship but pose a threat to public order? The Indian Government took little notice of the situation there and then, but eventually, late in the 1950s, the problem was tackled from the other end, as it were, through a (fairly ineffectual) campaign of birth-control education and subsidized condom distribution.

A similar improvement in productivity in Ceylon had the same effect of creating unemployment with the added hardship for most coolies that as "foreigners" they had even fewer rights than their Indian counterparts. Moreover, the Tamil unemployed were seen as a threat to the increasing numbers of urban Sinhalese unemployed, who feared that, despite the coolies' lack of relevant skills, they might offer competition for scarce jobs.

By the 1920s in India, politics, economics and labour unrest had become interwoven, not just on the tea gardens but throughout the country. No doubt the genuine economic hardship being experienced in that decade made coolie ears more receptive to the tempting sounds of political agitators. They now not only struck in situations in which there was no apparent economic motive, but many were also selling up their meagre possessions and leaving the gardens altogether at the instigation of Gandhi's Quit India campaign. To the coolie, the *Satyagraha* which Gandhi advocated, with its return to the simplicities of traditional village life, was "holding fast to truth"; to the planter and the official, it was a subtle form of civil disobedience. All too foreseeably, the self-control of the Mahatma, who pursued a purely passive form of civil disobedience himself, was beyond the volatile passions of almost all those at whom his exhortations were aimed. In 1937 the Government of India tried to create a safety valve by allocating specific seats to tea-garden coolies in the Assam and Bengal regional legislative assemblies, but there was too much steam in the boiler. Two years later strikes spread rapidly from the railways and the oil industry to the tea gardens, and they were often violent.

Shortly after the outbreak of the Second World War the regional assemblies were suspended and, under the Defence of India Act, the country was governed by administrative fiat. It is greatly to the credit of tea-garden workers, and of Indian political and trade-union leaders, that when the seriousness of the Japanese threat was perceived, strikes were taken almost totally from the agenda. In Assam, between 1942 and 1945 there were only two. In the early days of Indian independence the residue of this good will kept strikes in the tea industry to a minimum. In 1950 they accounted for less than 0.05 per cent of working days, and in 1953 for only three seconds lost a day per employee. Such restraint was too good to last.

The new Congress-led government wanted to flex its unfamiliar legislative muscle, and to earn respect from those international organ-izations, such as the International Labour Organization, on which it was now directly represented, rather than by British proxy. The old informal relationship between planters and coolies, under which the great majority on both sides had kept the tacit rules without compul-sion, was superseded by a whole statute book of legislation. It is hard to say how much effect this depersonalization of the rules of engage-ment had directly on labour relations, but from the mid-1950s onwards they became increasingly confrontational, and frequently violent, despite the fact that an ever-growing number of the senior garden managers were now Indians.

In 1971 a number of Indian managers were beaten up by their workers in the course of a wages disputes. In 2000 security guards at a tea garden owned by the industrial conglomerate Tata fired on the coolies and killed one of them. In 2001, when a protest meeting over security guards beating a worker got out of control at a Birla-owned garden, the manager panicked and shot four of the protesters. The coolies, not entirely unreasonably, then beat him to death. My purpose in reciting these various incidents is only to reiterate my argument that, during the British period, serious conflict was rarely prompted by race, but was then, and continued to be after indepen-dence, about economic power and the maintenance of privilege.

If further evidence is needed that it was economic rather than racial attitudes that lay at the root of planter–coolie conflict in India, it may be provided by a comparison of the very different reports of two Commissions of Enquiry, both headed by Indians, which exam-ined labour conditions in 1944 (under the Raj) and in 1948 (after independence). The report of the Rege Commission of 1944 endorsed the stricture in an earlier publication: "A system of wages which requires the worker to depend upon the earnings of his wife and children or upon a subsidiary industry just in order to earn the necessaries of life, not to talk of decencies, luxuries and savings, can scarcely justify its existence from the point of view of social welfare or national economy."

The Deshpande Report of 1948 was more thorough and analytical than that of the Rege Committee, and provided a factual basis on which minimum wages could justly be calculated. The inquiry covered

43 gardens in Assam and Bengal. Family budgets were drawn up, dietary needs were studied, incomes were examined and the composition of the average family was analysed. Deshpande took a more realistic view than Rege of the fact that, on a tea garden, the earning unit is not the individual but the family. He concluded that: "In the present stage of our economic evolution, therefore, it may not be entirely unjustifiable to maintain that in determining the family wage the earnings of the other members of the family, including the wife and others, should be taken into consideration."

If the combination of productivity-created surplus labour and recession had caused problems in India, the situation was twice as serious in Ceylon, where the principal victims were foreigners. The recession was met not just by reductions in wages, but by attempts to ship the surplus Tamils back to India. In 1930 the first batch, of twenty-five thousand, was summarily deported. The Government of India responded with unexpected helpfulness by restricting further emigration to those who had already worked in Ceylon or who had immediate family there. A second batch, this time of twenty-seven thousand, was dispatched two years later and, under pressure, more returned voluntarily in the ensuing few years. When, in 1939, Ceylon compelled another seven thousand to go back, India's attitude changed. Its government banned all movement of coolies between the two countries, thus cutting off those in India from their jobs in Ceylon and those in Ceylon from their families in India.

The Second World War erected a further barrier to free migration and after it, when the two countries had become independent, Ceylon legislated to force all coolies to chose between retaining citizenship of India and applying for citizenship of Ceylon. This might have been a reasonable choice had the Ceylonese Government not made it so difficult for the still largely illiterate Tamil coolie to attain its citizenship. (Compulsory vernacular education for children had been introduced in 1920, but was not always implemented.) Continuous residence was one condition that was unlikely to be often fulfilled by a people for whom keeping up family ties with India had been important. India's subsequent refusal to recognize as citizens those Tamils who had not succeeded in becoming citizens of Ceylon left many thousands in a limbo of statelessness. In 1964 the two governments eventually agreed that, over the next 15 years, a little over half a million coolies, "together with their natural increase", should be returned to India while three hundred thousand would be granted Ceylonese citizenship. The fate of the remaining one hundred and fifty thousand was put off, so that they became, to all intents and purposes, stateless, with the vulnerability to exploitation that implies. The lot of the Tamil tea-garden coolie was made even more onerous by the hostility or indifference of the substantial number of mainly urban, middle-class Tamils, who were already citizens of Ceylon and who feared to provoke the resentment of their Sinhalese neighbours by espousing the coolie cause. Ten years later, in an arbitrary deal between the two countries, the remaining stateless Tamils were allotted equally to the two countries. This was shabby treatment of those who were, in many cases, the third and fourth generations of the men and women who had made tea Ceylon's greatest asset. That this ethnic cleansing was largely due to pressure from Sinhalese politicians exacerbated ill-feeling between the two communities.

Since the 1970s Sinhalese politicians have deployed the "swamped by foreigners" vote-catching ploy with which the British public, in its own backyard, has become degradingly familiar in the twenty-first century. Resistance from the 1920s onwards to the enfranchisement of tea-garden Tamils and to the formation of tea-garden trade unions was prompted by recognition that these reforms would make such ethnic cleansing harder to achieve.

The customary way for a coolie to express a grievance before 1931 and the formation of the All Ceylon Estate Labour Association had been by way of an individual petition, and every garden had its professional petition writer. These petitions might be submitted to a magistrate or to K.P.S. Menon, whose role, as Labour Agent, was to stand up for the Indian Tamils on the tea gardens. Menon was a feisty character who, when asked by the planters to ignore such petitions, flatly refused. All too often, however, a petition would find its way for adjudication into the hands of the very garden superintendent against whom it was directed: a travesty of justice, as Natesa Aiyar never tired of pointing out.

The trade-union movement in Ceylon began in 1931, when Aiyar, an Indian Brahmin who had been the Indian member in Ceylon's

Legislative Assembly since 1926, formed the All Ceylon Estate Labour Federation. But he had already been an increasingly sharp thorn in the side of both planters and British officials since 1925. In an editorial in the *Citizen* newspaper, which he had just launched, he had cheekily warned that Britain's troubles in India, Egypt and Ireland showed that the "present condition of the Empire was shaky". This he followed up with a provocative pamphlet entitled "Planter Raj" which attacked the oppressive regime of the British tea planter. Although the radical views expressed in these publications were shared by those Sinhalese who also wanted to be rid of the British, the urban trade unions, almost exclusively Sinhalese, were more concerned with keeping their members' depressed living standards at least better than those of their tea-garden fellow workers than with collaborating with them for a common purpose.

The police urged the government to prosecute Aiyar for sedition, but the Colonial Office in London thought it wiser just to keep an eye on him. Meanwhile the planters went to great lengths to curtail his influence. Had he visited plantations to harangue and recruit, the planters were ready to prosecute him for trespass. He outwitted them by going round the gardens as the sidekick of a cloth merchant who had legitimate business there.

Worried by the impact on the coolies of that "immoral publication", the *Citizen,* and later the English language *Indian Estate Labourer*, the planters launched their own Tamil weekly, the *Oolian.* This masqueraded as what the *Times of Ceylon* called "an organ for fostering better understanding between planters and labourers". It highlighted Aiyar's Brahmin status as separating him from the coolies, failing to recognize that his readiness to cross caste lines to help the lowly coolie was central to his appeal. The paper accused the union of collecting subscriptions that were spent on high living, while tactlessly dismissing the coolie himself as "an ignorant individual who would give his last penny to hear some maniac get on to a platform and run others down". Not content with demanding that Aiyar be "securely shut up for some time", the *Oolian* dismissed hanging only because it was too good for him and his union colleagues "lest they pollute the very rope from whose end they might sway".

Kanganies, who recruited and controlled the lives of the coolies, were the planters' most effective weapon against the unions. Condemned by Aiyar as no better than the slave traders of Africa, they willingly used their hold on most coolies to dissuade them from joining the union. Even this might not have been effective in more propitious circumstances for the reformers. Aiyar was eloquent, charismatic and well organized, so that he soon had the coolies, as the planters recognized, "seething with discontent"; a discontent that could have been mobilized to improve their pay and conditions, but for the recession. The cuts in wages and the threat of deportation made the ordinary coolie more than ever reliant on the good will of his tea-planter. By 1933 the first attempt at mobilizing tea-garden labour had petered out. It would not revive until after the Second World War and the granting of independence.

Two reforms that should have enhanced the well-being of the tea-garden coolies were initiated in Ceylon in the face of strong opposition by some planters, though others saw both their virtue and their necessity. In 1921 the Planters' Association decided to remit the *tundu*. This was the system whereby a coolie who incurred a debt to his employer – and nearly all of them did – took the debt with him wherever he went. This was not only a crippling, and almost invariably lifelong, burden, but tortuously complex for the planters to administer. At this time the debt had reached the considerable sum of £4 million, so, in deciding to wipe it out, the planters, as with most reforms, combined altruism with self-interest. Unfortunately the altruism did not extend to abolishing the discharge certificate as well. By tacit agreement no Ceylon planter would take on a coolie from another plantation who did not have such a certificate. If the original employer wished to keep him he could do so easily just by procrastinating until the wageless coolie had no option but to sign up for another term.

Although many Tamils returned cyclically to Tamil Nadu on the Indian mainland, they invariably came back to the same tea garden. Thus the labour force on each side of the Palk strait tended to be a cohesive but inward-looking community with a stable – and therefore more easily managed – population. New wives might join, but it grew otherwise only by natural increase. This stability was anchored in a predominantly non-monetary system of paying coolies similar to that in India. By a combination of this and the certificate the coolie was effectively tied to his first employer.

Statutory, as opposed to voluntary, wage boards with coolie representation were first established in Ceylon in 1927. To the chagrin of the Ceylon planters this was largely in response to pressure from India, where no such legal obligation existed. The same legislation also regulated discharge certificates, imposed dates for payment of wages and banned the employment of children under 10. The new laws were not implemented until 1929 and had barely begun to improve coolie pay when, in May 1931, the wage boards cut the minimum wage in the light of the world recession. The boards did so again later in the year, despite opposition from all but one of the members of the relevant Labour Committee. When he visited Ceylon in 1931, Jawaharlal Nehru – destined to be independent India's first Prime Minister – attacked the reductions as "monstrous" and was justifiably indignant and argued that "to declare a dividend of 35 per cent and in the same breath to talk of lowering the minimum wage, seems to me to indicate a mentality that is dangerous to society. It is this mentality which always tries to pay the least possible wage and seeks to wring out the biggest dividends from the labour of these wage slaves. Labour must have a living wage ... if this cannot be paid by any industrial undertaking the sooner it shuts up the better." In fact this is exactly what happened, despite the second reduction of the minimum wage. Several plantations closed down, while others simply failed to pay even the reduced minimum and hoped to escape prosecution.

A third reduction took place in May 1933, resulting in a total reduction in wages of between 25 and 30 per cent. Although the price of rice also fell by 29 per cent in the same period, it was by no means the only element of the coolies' cost of living, albeit an important one. Even the threat of taking advantage of the offer of repatriation to India could do nothing to halt the decline. In the face of hostility from both their employers and the urban trade-union movement, the plantation coolies – uprooted, unskilled, poor, illiterate and of low caste – were helpless in the face of these external pressures. The trade-union movement on tea plantations more or less faded away and did not revive until 1939, when it recovered sufficiently to begin to secure decent conditions for its members. During the same period the increasing involvement of the native population in its own governance was no less influential, though the division between Sinhalese and Tamils in the labour movement would be tragically reflected in civil war once the global conflict was over.

The worldwide economic depressions and the poor prices for tea of 1921–23 and 1929–34 largely resulted in the negation of the gains of the intervening years. As a matter of expediency the minimum wages set by the new wage boards in India and Ceylon were either reduced or ignored. Large numbers of coolies were also laid off and greater emphasis was placed on increasing the productivity of those who remained. Nor were European managers and their assistants spared the axe at this time. The alternative to these measures would have been the bankruptcy and closure of many gardens and the loss of all the jobs on them. Quite a number did, in fact, go out of business. In such circumstances trade unions were severely handicapped in both recruiting and negotiating with managers, who often took the opportunity of redundancies to get rid of those coolies and *babus* whom they regarded as troublemakers.

Once independence had been achieved a paradoxical situation arose, in India and Ceylon at least. The new governments saw themselves as protectors of the workers – whose votes they would want at the next election – by means of labour legislation, while at the same time they clamped down nervously on the workers' own representatives, the trade unions, which were perceived as alternative centres of power. For example, no sooner had the new Congress government come to power in India than it banned the Communist Trades Union.

Greatly improved productivity in the cultivation of the tea bush, and mechanization and automation in the manufacturing process, also meant that far fewer coolies were needed to produce a given volume and quality of tea. As a consequence employers could afford to pay substantially higher wages to those who remained in employment. A female coolie in Ceylon, for example, could earn about twice as much in real terms in 1970 as she would have done in 1939, though perks, other than those that tied her to a particular tea garden, were often dropped or reduced. The corollary to this benefit for coolies in work was that those who would have been employed in less productive, more labour-intensive times found themselves out of a job at a time when indigenous industries were not expanding fast enough to absorb them. Although, in recent years, particularly in India, industrial growth has been very great, so has the natural growth of the urban population competing for those new jobs.

The genesis of the surge in productivity in the tea industry is the subject of the next chapter.

CHAPTER TEN

From Leaf to Lip

On the basis of their relationship to a presumed source of the ancestral tea plant round the headwaters of the Irrawaddy, three subspecies of tea have been named by more or less common consent: *Camellia sinensis* var. *sinensis*; *Camellia sinensis* var. *assamica*; and *Camellia sinensis* var. *cambodiensis*. We are closely concerned with only the first two. Of varieties – usually known in tea circles as jats (Hindi, "caste") – there are nine or 10. There are five Assam jats: Manipur, Burma, Lushai, light-leaved and dark-leaved, this last the producer of high yields of the best-quality tea. While the Assam hybrids do better in the plains of north-east India than China or Indo-China plants, they have their problems, as we have seen, particularly when crossed with the China variety.

Most China jats are self-fertile and, as good seed is not available, they are usually propagated from leaf cuttings in what is known as vegetative production (VP). This technique was pioneered by the Dutch in Java in 1912. China bushes and their hybrids constitute about half the world's tea plants today. As most Assam jats are self-sterile, they are nearly always propagated from seed grown in specialist seed gardens. In recent years both China and Assam plants have been successfully propagated by cloning from the best bushes, in order to keep exactly the desired characteristics and avoid any variation in the seed quality. This is is more usual for China jats as good seed is available from Assam bushes.

For the best-cloned plantations, yields of 1,000kg a hectare have been claimed. Such yields are not achieved without patience and ruthless selection. The starting point might be forty thousand bushes of fine tea. From these some two hundred would be chosen on the basis of their superior vigour, density and uniformity of yielding wood, diameter of frame, size and time of flush and erectness and pubescence of leaf (which latter gives the "golden tips"). These will be allowed to grow for seven or eight months, then leaf cuttings from each will be planted in two or three different types of soil. Six months later the poorly rooting clones are discarded. Now the total is down to a mere 50 or so bushes. These are allowed to grow and are plucked the following year when the leaf from each bush is made into tea. Of the original forty thousand bushes, no more than four or five now remain. From these super-bushes, or bush – for there is sometimes just one – others are propagated by VP or crossed with another clone, or clones, to produce seeds. Quality is checked by a mini-manufacture of the new bush's leaf.

Tea is a remarkably adaptable plant, hence its cultivated presence in more than 60 countries today. It can grow as far west as California (120° W) and as far east as Queensland (145° E), as far south as Corrientes in Argentina (27° S) and as far north as Georgia (43° N) – to which we must add, in 2005, Falmouth in Cornwall, at a little over 50° N.

Like many plants, tea prefers a friable, light loam with plenty of nutrients in which to grow. As Michael Faraday put it in a chemical analysis he made to oblige his friend Samuel Ball, "the general character of these soils seems to be that of a ferruginous clay, but easily crumbling, and falling down in water". However, tea can grow on poor soil and survive well even on rough hillsides and farm margins where other plants will fail. Ball also found that some of the best tea in China was grown on "soil which is very compact, a little muddy, black". Where it will not grow is in soil with any significant presence of lime, for tea prefers soil with a pH factor of 5 to 6, just on the acidic side of neutral (7 = neutral; below 7 = acidic; above 7 = alkaline). Otherwise (to quote Harler): "There is no scientific evidence in India, Ceylon, Java or Malaya to show that quality or flavour go with certain chemical or physical properties of the soil."

Again, like most other plants, tea flourishes best when weed-free, grass being the most inimical of weeds to the tea bush. But a plantation of tea bushes is not easy to keep free of weeds. In the early days planters in India and Ceylon tended to weed their tea bushes as they would their vegetable patches back in Britain by giving the ground a deep hoeing and a thorough digging. Where there was any kind of slope this simply broke up the soil into lumps that were too readily washed away from the roots. Once this was understood, a planter somewhere, or more likely one of his Indian employees, invented the *cheel* to prevent plantation workers hoeing too vigorously. Because this hoe's 25cm half-moon-shaped blade is set at an acute angle to the shaft, it can only be used as a light surface scraper. The use of this technique also greatly reduces the amount of manpower needed for hoeing.

A bush correctly (that is, lightly) pruned and selectively plucked will mostly keep itself free of weeds by occupying the near-surface soil with its roots. With the addition of green manure or sulphate of ammonia artificial fertilizer, the leaf-fall from the bush rots on the surface; the natural downward penetration of the decomposed matter provides all the necessary nutrients without the need for "digging in". One Ceylon planter even went so far as to have street sweepings sent in by train.

The tea bush does not have a particularly deep tap root – on average 90–150cm long and 7.5cm in diameter – and it is the lateral roots in the top 20–25cm of soil that are crucial in feeding the plant. If bushes are planted too close together their roots compete for nourishment. These red lateral roots have a corky layer with which to stabilize water balance and store food, mostly starch. Ideally bushes should be planted equidistant but for access by pluckers and mechanical harvesters a gap of 1.2 metres between rows and of 0.6 metres between bushes provides a continuous plucking table. But, as with so many horticultural ideals, there are swings and roundabouts. Experiments in Assam showed that the yield per bush was 75 per cent higher for the widest planting compared with that for the closest. That's the swing. The roundabout is that close planting gives bigger overall crops in the earlier stage of a new plantation because the centre of the bush grows more densely than the outer edge, so more bush centres means more leaves; twice the closeness gives a 50 per cent higher yield per hectare. But then we get back to the swings because a density of thirty-two thousand bushes a hectare gradually becomes less productive and in the longer run a density of sixteen thousand bushes an acre and then eight thousand gives a bigger yield. Hedge planting is also widely used for convenience of plucking and is essential if mechanical methods are to be used.

Another example of swings and roundabouts is the use of shade trees. The astute Bruce soon realized that, in certain circumstances, bushes shaded by certain trees – such as the sau tree (*Albizzia stipulata*) – that give a dappled light are protected from excessively hot direct sun, and this also allows grass and shrubs to grow beneath them. At night the leaves fold up, which permits the dew to reach the ground and the fallen leaves to make mulch. All of this can improve the productivity of the bush. It was the industry's own research station, at Tocklai in Assam, that in 1923 went about trying to give a measured answer to the question of whether or not shade was beneficial. In general, the requirement for shade may be determined by bush leaf temperature. Hadfield suggests that the rate of photosynthesis, and therefore yield potential, is inhibited above 34°C. As ever with tea, the empirical approach is the only valid one.

Tea bushes "flush" – produce new leaves and buds – in different seasonal cycles in different parts of the world regardless of the type of bush involved. Here temperature is the crucial determinant. In some locations tea is plucked all the year round, albeit with variation in quality and quantity at different times. In others the crop is seasonal, with a dormant "winter" period in growth during which no tea is plucked. This seasonality is determined by the conditions under which the bush is grown and these are defined as a combination of temperature at a specific season over annual temperature range plus seasonal rainfall and rainfall distribution over the year, with a minor input from the nature of the soil.

The latitude and height at which tea can survive govern the temperature range, but also its degree of exposure to direct ultraviolet light from the sun. A rise in temperature of roughly 1°C for every two hundred metres of height is probably less important than the fact that there is a much more intense exposure of the plant to UV with an increase in altitude. Whether this directly affects the flavour of the tea may be debatable, but there is no doubt that the teas with the best flavour are grown at altitudes of over nine hundred metres.

If the temperature range between summer and winter is greater than 11°C – as in north-east India, China and Japan, Caucasia and parts of East Africa and Latin America – there will be a dormant period in which there is no growth and no plucking. Where the seasonal temperature difference is less than 11°C – as in Java, Malaya and Kenya, for example – tea can be harvested all the year round.

China jats are better at enduring extremes of temperature and variation than Assam jats, and the hybrids between them can lead to a good compromise between hardiness and yield. In the former Soviet state of Georgia, the tea-growing area with the lowest temperatures, the effect of frost is tempered by a winter covering of snow; and in shaded hollows in India the thermometer can fall to –9°C, which shows that tea has some capacity for naturalizing itself to its conditions. Georgia's early tea planters modestly confessed: "It must be admitted that our tea cultivation is not on a very high plane."

Another element that determines whether or not tea can be successfully grown is the quantity and distribution of rainfall. This needs to be at least 100–125cm a year and some of this needs to fall at the onset of the growing season. The rainfall level during the dormant season in areas that have no winter growth is irrelevant: in some places it is torrential and in others negligible. On a hot day in Ceylon a hectare of mature tea can draw 25,000kg of water from the soil, equivalent to 0.25cm of rainfall; and in Assam water take-up under shade trees can even be twice that amount in a day. Excessive rainfall at the time of growth and harvest, however, can cause problems by waterlogging the ground and slowing growth, though this can be mitigated to some extent by efficient drainage. Such intensity of rainfall is not uncommon during the south-west monsoon in southern India and Ceylon.

The growth, and therefore the profitability, of a tea bush is strongly influenced by two other factors: plucking and pruning. When harvesting tea, two often conflicting considerations have to be reconciled: yield (or quantity) and quality (usually gauged in terms of flavour and strength). The plucking mantra of the purist planter for whom quality is all has always been "two leaves and a bud"; that is, the two leaves and the bud nearest the tip of each stem on a bush, known as "fine plucking". Such plucking stimulates growth lower down the stem so that the process can be repeated, perhaps a dozen times or more in a year.

The quantity/quality equation also depends on how often the leaf is plucked, this rate being known as the "plucking round". The length of the plucking round varies, depending on the type of bush, the conditions in which it grows, and the point in the seasonal cycle even on those plantations where the bushes are plucked throughout the year. The interval between plucking rounds can be as little as four or five days in, for example, Assam at the peak of the growing season. At altitude in Ceylon it can be nine to 10 days and as long as 20–30 days at the low point in countries where plucking is a year-round activity. As a rule of thumb, the longer the round the greater the yield, but there will be a corresponding drop in quality. Swings and roundabouts again.

On bushes with a dormant period in India, a *banjhi* (Hindi, "sterile") bud is formed at the tip of the stem while the plant regathers its strength. When growth resumes, some three months later, the *banjhi* swells before producing a narrow, unserrated leaf, no more than an inch long, called the *janum* (Hindi, "birth"), which in turn gives way to the *gol-pat* (Hindi, "round leaf"). This in Ceylon is called the "fish leaf". The harvestable bud and leaves follow. It is when a field of bushes shows the optimum number of stems bearing two leaves and a bud that it should be plucked if quality is paramount. With skilled workers plucking by hand, this process can be as selective as the current demands of the market require and a high quality can be sustained.

Where quantity is the more important consideration – sadly, usually the case these days – "coarse plucking" is adopted. This entails taking three or even four leaves as well as the bud so that the resultant crop will contain not only more larger leaves with less flavour but a high proportion of stalk, which must either be expensively removed or coarsen the flavour of the tea. Where the modern factory process reduces the whole crop to a small size for use in tea bags, this is not such an important consideration. Coarse plucking also lends itself much more readily to mechanical harvesting methods, using a variety of electrically or petrol-driven cutters similar to the domestic hedge-trimmer. As public taste has declined and labour costs have risen, mechanical harvesting has become increasingly popular in view of the fact that harvesting labour constitutes some 60 per cent of all labour costs. In high-wage economies, such as that of Australia, mechanical harvesting was inevitable from the outset of tea growing. Green tea does not require quite so much care in selecting the leaves to be plucked, so machinery is more appropriate than for the better black teas and yields are greater. In Japan, it is claimed, over 22,000kg a hectare have been harvested by mechanized means, though the same approach in China gives an out-turn 80–90 per cent lower.

Another disadvantage of drastic or "hard" plucking, as with over-vigorous pruning, is that it removes a significant proportion of "maintenance leaves", the leaves whose photosynthesis forms the crop. On the other hand, if plucking is consistently too light the bush will shoot up beyond the convenient reach of the worker who must pluck it. Where there is a dormant winter period, hard plucking can be more safely used.

Pruning serves two purposes: to foster growth and to maintain the bushes at the best level for swift and efficient plucking. Broadly speaking, there are three levels of severity. Light pruning, or skiffing, is little more than a tidying-up operation taking only 1–2cm from the top of the bush. Its main purpose is to keep a level plucking table and prevent growth-inhibiting congestion at the top of the bush. This may be carried out annually or even more often.

Maintenance pruning is more severe, taking the bush down to its basic frame by cutting straight across the top. This kind of pruning should be done when the bush is at its strongest after manuring, and avoid the dry season, as the plant will have to live off its starch reserve in the roots while it recovers. This kind of pruning should be done when the bush is dormant or least productive. The bushes in north-east India usually require maintenance pruning every three to four years. Whereas after skiffing a bush is quickly back into production, after maintenance pruning it will take between six and 10 weeks to get back to normal growth. The frequency at which this kind of pruning is needed varies according to geographical location and altitude. Bushes in north-east India usually require maintenance pruning annually, whereas at the highest altitude in Ceylon the cycle may be as long as six years.

Finally there is what is known as collar or medium pruning, done when bushes have become knotty, congested or diseased and yield poorly and so need to be taken down to within 10–30cm of the ground. It is even more important to carry out this intensive prune after fertilizing and at the kindest season. It will take the bush five or six months to get back into something like normal shape and productivity. Quite a high proportion of collar-pruned bushes will die, so the opportunity is usually taken to infill with new bushes, thus increasing plant density and potential yield.

I cannot resist concluding this horticultural interlude with a horror story or two. Although *Hemileia vastatrix*, the semi-smooth female killer, does not attack tea, this blight virtually eradicated coffee growing in Ceylon within less than a decade of its arrival between 1867 and 1869. Between 1870 and 1890 the coffee crop dropped from five million kilos a year to half a million. But tea has plenty of nasties of its own.

There are more than 150 pests which attack the tea plant, of which 125 are found in north-east India; and there are 380 funguses, of which half spread their spores in the same area. The roll-call is impressive. *Exobasidium vexans*, *Heliopeltis theivora*, *Poeciliocoris latus*, *Botryodiplodia theobromae*, *Aglaospora aculeata*, *Poria hypobrunnea* and *Pulvinaria floccifera*. A scary list in Latin, and not much less so in English, what with blister blight, tea mosquito, red spider or the tea-seed bug, diplodia and thorny blight. In Caucasia blights grey, yellow and brown have struck. And the various root diseases are even more colourful: charcoal stump rot, violet root rot, red root rot, brown root rot, black root rot, purple root rot and tarry root rot, to name but a few.

It seems surprising, in the face of so many hazards, that we get any tea to drink at all. It is perhaps less surprising that turning the plucked leaf into usable tea has not changed in its essentials since it was first achieved more than a thousand years ago, although the means of doing so today are more sophisticated. The manufacture of tea from plucked leaf still involves a sequence of five processes – withering, rolling, fermenting, drying and sorting – although the manufacture of green tea avoids the fermentation stage altogether and oolong reduces it considerably.

Samuel Ball, whom we met in Chapter 1, was a Chinese-speaking close observer of the methods still in use in the first two decades of the nineteenth century. I have here cannibalized his various descriptions:

[They] spread the leaves about five or six inches thick on bamboo trays in a proper place for the air to blow on them. Thus the leaves continue from noon until six o'clock, when they begin to give out a fragrant smell. They are then poured into large bamboo trays, in which they are tossed with the hands about three or four hundred times. It is this operation which gives the red edges and spots to the leaves.

They are now carried to the Kuo [a large wok made out of very thin cast iron. For green tea, a shallow cylinder with metal lugs for fitting into the top of the stove] and roasted; and afterwards poured on flat trays to be rolled. The rolling is performed with both hands in a *circular direction* about three or four hundred times; when the leaves are again carried to the Kuo; and thus roasted and rolled three times. If the rolling be performed by a good workman, the leaves will be close and well twisted; if by an inferior one, loose, open, straight, and ill-looking. They are then conveyed to the Poey Long, the fire fierce, and the leaves turned without intermission until they are nearly eight-tenths dried. They are afterwards spread on flat trays to dry until five o'clock, when the old, the yellow leaves, and the stalks are nicked out. At eight o'clock they are "poeyed" again over a slow fire. This exposure to the fire is simply to produce an evaporation of the exuberant juices acquired during rain; for in proportion as the leaves are full of juices, so is the pain and difficulty, and even expense, of manipulation increased. At noon they are turned once, and then left in this state to dry until three o'clock, when they are packed in chests. They are now fit for sale.

Elsewhere, Ball describes the roasting process in greater detail:

To recapitulate concisely the different processes to which black and green tea are submitted. The leaves of black tea are exposed to the sun and air on circular trays, and treated as hay, during which an incipient saccharine fermentation is supposed to take place in conjunction with a volatile oil. Various modifications of flavour are thus produced by the management of this fermentation; a loss of tannin takes place by the conversion of a part of the tannic acid into sugar. During this change the leaves become flaccid, and slightly tinged or spotted with red or brown colouring matter; and give out a peculiar odour, approximating to, or, as some think, identical with, the odour of tea. A certain change in this odour is carefully watched by the workmen, this being an indication that the roasting must not be delayed. They are then roasted in an iron vessel, and afterwards rolled with the hands, to express their juices. The roasting and rolling are repeated so long as any juices can be expressed from the leaves in the act of rolling. Finally, they are dried in sieves placed over a charcoal fire in drying-tubes, during which the leaves are occasionally taken from the fire, and turned until completely dried. This "drying tube" is an hourglass-waisted long woven basket into which the sieve of tea is placed. The basket is then placed over a low charcoal stove on the ground. The leaves are later taken out of the drying tube and rubbed and twisted between the hands. This process is also repeated two or three times. It is in this last stage of the process that the leaves turn black, though this change of colour is mainly due to the process of manipulation previously to roasting, and not to the action of heat.

The leaves of the green teas are roasted, also, in an iron vessel, but as soon as gathered, without any previous manipulation, all heating or fermentation of the leaves being studiously avoided: they are then rolled as black tea, and finally dried in the same vessel in which they have been roasted, by constantly stirring and moving them about. They are also fanned to hasten evaporation, and the drying and formation of the peculiar characteristic colour of this tea, which it gradually acquires in the process, and which resembles the bloom on some fruits.

In much more recent times, even if neither plucker nor weigher was trying to cheat, the repeated handling of the leaves – from bush to a cane basket with a rough inner surface; from basket to weighing scales; from scales to a heap on the factory floor; from the heap to the *chung*, or withering platform – gave the leaf a rough ride. Damage and delay introduced uncertainty as to the degree of uncontrolled fermentation that might already have taken place. By replacing baskets or cloth bags with nylon mesh ones in which the tea can breathe; by using a portable weighing gantry and hand-held computers to log the weight plucked by each individual coolie; by packing the bags straight on to a truck for the journey to the factory; and by emptying the bags of leaf straight into a withering trough as and when required – all such refinements not only bring the leaf for manipulation in a more pristine state, but the flow of raw material is more even and thus more efficient.

Mechanical withering in revolving drums was tried in the 1950s, but, although it could cut the time needed for this process by as much as 85 per cent from the usual 12–18 hours, by doing so it curtailed the chemical reaction involved in withering: the breakdown of proteins and carbohydrates into amino acids and less complex sugars and the concentration of caffeine and polyphenols. So it was not widely adopted. Withering in open troughs, pioneered in the 1960s by Williamson Magor, was an improvement in terms of duration and efficacy on both the *chung* and the drum. But the great variations in temperature and humidity, often almost from minute to minute, in most tea-growing areas of the world necessitated using fans to blow air over the troughs. However, since this significantly affected only the exposed surface of the leaves, they had to be either spread in a very shallow layer that demanded excessive space, or constantly turned by hand, which involved more labour. Both solutions entailed more cost. The eventual answer was to enclose the withering trough completely, sustain a constant ambient temperature and draw a flow of air at the requisite temperature up or down through a 12-inch-deep layer of leaves. I say "requisite" because, despite every refinement of mechanization and computing, the planter's skill and experience are still crucial in gauging the moisture content of different leaves in the light of seasonal and daily weather conditions at the time of plucking.

Growing demand for an increasingly homogeneous product means that the usual range of ratios between raw leaf and the withered state (from 2.8:1 to 3.1:1) can broadly be pre-programmed. Nevertheless, there remain the fine adjustments in temperature and rate of flow to achieve the desired outcome that require human input. There remained one other minor problem. The traditional bamboo or hessian base of the withering platform was replaced with wire to ensure greater uniformity of interstices, but wire rusts and the fractured pieces were not always drawn out of the tea by the magnetic extraction used. The customer whose wake-up mouthful of tea was punctuated by a piece of wire would not be a happy one. The use of a plastic mesh ensured this did not happen.

After this first stage the leaf is now flaccid and ready for the next: rolling, which both dries the leaf and twists and curls it. This ruptures the cells of the leaf and so releases the catechins and enzymes which react with the air to cause oxidation. The degree of leaf distortion obtained in rolling dictates the time needed to infuse the tea to get the best results: the greater the twist the longer the infusion needed.

Mechanical rolling could be said to have started in a pair of planter's trousers. A planter in Cachar called Nelson asked himself whether the slow and costly process by which his coolies rolled the leaves by hand against the surface of a table could be speeded up by placing another table upside down on top of the first and rotating the whole. The problem was to prevent the leaves being forced out at the sides by the rotary motion. This is where the trousers came in. Having made bags from the legs of an old pair, he filled them with leaf, made the upper table heavier by the weight of a couple of coolies and bade the others push it from end to end and side to side in a circular motion. It worked, but I doubt if the *dhobi wallah* (washerman) was too pleased with the state of the trousers. There were various developments of Nelson's device: one of these, Greig's Patent Link and Lever Tea Roller, rolled two bags at once; it could be worked mechanically, requiring only one man to operate it, and it rolled between two and a half and five times as much in an hour.

Today the base table is round with a cone rising from the centre and "spokes" radiating from the cone. On top of the base an inverted, lidless box presses down while the two planes rotate elliptically in opposite directions. The leaf, fed automatically into the space between the two planes, is twisted and curled by its movement over the cone and spokes. The coagulated lumps of leaf are then broken up and sifted. The smaller finings pass to the fermentation room and the coarser are rolled again.

To understand the urge to mechanize processes, such as rolling, it is only necessary to consider the long-winded and labour-intensive method, as described by Edward Money, that was previously hand-rolling.

> The leaf is rolled by a line of men on each side of such a table (4.5 feet is a good width for it) passing up from man to man, from the bottom of the table to the top. The passage of each handful of roll from man to man is regulated by the man at the end, who, when the roll in his hand is ready (that is, rolled enough), forms it into a tight compressed ball (a truncated shape is the most convenient) and puts it away on an adjacent stand. When he does this, the roll each man has passes up one step … There will be some coarse leaves in the roll which cannot be twisted. These, if left, would give much red leaf in the tea. They should be picked out by, say, the third or fourth man from the head of the table, for it is only when the leaf has been partly rolled that they show. The man who picked out the coarse leaf should not roll at all. He should spread the roll, and pick out as much as he can, between the time of receiving and passing it on.

With more than 60 per cent of tea output now needed for the ubiquitous teabag, the CTC (Crush, Tear and Curl), Rotorvane and Lawrie machines in their many variations have replaced conventional rolling. The McKercher CTC machine that, with its siblings and descendants, dominates tea manufacture today had already been invented by 1931. The basic CTC machine consists of serrated metal rollers operating like an old-fashioned mangle, but one in which each roller rotates at a different speed. The most recent versions, with their hundreds of cutting edges intersecting in the annular and helical grooves, just cut and curl. These machines all compress and turn the leaf in a continuous process that distorts it so as to mix the enzymes and catechins, expose them to the air and thus trigger the oxidation of the polyphenols.

A tea leaf contains chemicals known as flavonols, which undergo oxidation during manufacture. These largely determine the character of the tea made. At the same time polymerization takes place to form the more complex molecules that are the main constituents of finished tea. The distribution of these soluble and insoluble polymers is determined by the length and temperature of fermentation and influences the colour, strength and briskness of the tea. The soluble-range red polymers are theaflavins, the dull-brown, insoluble ones the thearubigins. A high level of theaflavins is crucial to good tea, and if the thearubigin level is also high, so much the better. A high thearubigin but low theaflavin level makes dull tea, while low levels of both produce tea that is thin and grey.

Now the all-important process of fermentation is under way and the leaves start to turn a coppery brown and their essential oils begin to emit a fragrant scent When the degree of fermentation needed for the type of tea required has been achieved, the leaf has to be dried again, but this, too, can now be done by drying machines using direct heat in vibrating fluid bed driers, the largest of which can dry 450kg of tea an hour.

The fermentation process, which ideally takes place at 25–28°C, presents yet another swings-and-roundabouts challenge. Flavour builds between the first and third hours of fermentation and diminishes thereafter; but good strong liquor requires at least four hours of fermentation. The characteristics of the leaf used, and of the other leaves it is to be blended with eventually, and the balance between flavour and strength required in the end product, will determine the duration of the fermentation stage.

After it has been dried – very much as described by Ball – the tea is sorted into various sizes depending on its intended use. Early mechanization involved a sequence of progressively finer sieves. The Trinnick automatic sorter used today is but a more complicated multi-sieve sequential sorter. The belt-fed flow of tea passes over a series of sieves each with a smaller aperture size than the one before it. The sieves are so pitched that the selected leaves are fed by gravity into an appropriate bin. Thence the selected leaves go, with the minimum of re-handling, for re-drying, so that the moisture content is no greater than 3 per cent. This is important because the tea may have to be stored for as long as 12 months before dispatch to the market. In many cases this actual re-drying is avoided by using dehumidifiers to maintain the stored tea in a moisture-free atmosphere. In the same fight against tea-spoiling moisture, most major manufacturers have now adopted vacuum packing.

The Chinese were developing various ways in which to mechanize the production process by the nineteenth century, and planters in India, brought up in the burgeoning steam age, were trying to apply the new technology from the 1840s. As Bruce had prophesied, "it might be left to the ingenuity of an Englishman to roll, sift and clean the tea by machinery". By the end of the nineteenth century mechanization had developed to a stage from which it was to make no further advance until after the Second World War, at which time many of the machines installed 50 years earlier were still going strong. But major changes were afoot.

In the age of mechanized tea production, the chief engineer became the highest-paid man on the plantation, if not the top of the social pile. One London office described a clutch of five new assistants as consisting of "three engineers and two gentlemen". More important even than the chief engineer was (and is) the native *"mistri"*, or blacksmith, who was crucial to keeping wheels turning and pistons reciprocating. With no theoretical training, these supreme pragmatists had the knack, almost instinct, of keeping complex machinery working. (In 1967, in a remote part of Afghanistan, my Mercedes estate suffered a total breakdown of its automatic gear. In three days the local *mistri* had dismantled it, figured out the way it worked, repaired and reassembled it so that it required no further attention when driven all the way back to England.)

All this mechanization was fine for the engineer and the *mistri*, but not so good for the thousands of coolies whose jobs disappeared. The first of William Jackson's mechanical rolling machines was installed in 1871. By 1913 eight thousand of them had replaced

1.6 million coolies. Similarly, the first mechanical sorting apparatus, introduced 10 years later, enabled eight women and eight boys to do the work of 90 women and 10 men. Modern sorting machines come in different configurations but all of them do no more than copy the movement of an old-fashioned sieve in skilled hands. In an expanding industry many of these superfluous skilled hands from the factory were re-employed in the labour-intensive and (despite improvements in mechanical plucking) essentially manual tasks of cultivation in an industry that in 2004 had 2.49 million hectares under tea, of which China accounted for half.

The advances of science have been welcomed the world over, but most tea planters would endorse Henry Cottam's view in 1877 that "the manufacture of tea is not acquired by reading alone, but by a great deal of practice and strict attention to the details of the manipulation". They would also, with a certain degree of justifiable satisfaction, understand Alexander MacGowan's astonishment, on considering the process of tea manufacture in 1861, that "this turmoil seemed quite incompatible with the peaceful product whose grateful and refreshing qualities fortunately survive the rough passage which calls them forth".

CHAPTER ELEVEN

The Art of Stowage

Ariel – Captain's log September 6th 5.55:

Rounded to close to the pilot cutter and got first pilot. Were saluted as first ship from China this season. I replied, "Yes, and what is that to the westward? We have not room to boast yet. Thank God we are first up Channel and hove to for a pilot an hour before him."

Taeping reached Gravesend fifty-five minutes before us. We avoided anchoring by getting a tug alongside to keep us astern. Proceeded with first tug ahead, as the flowing tide gave us sufficient water to float, thus reached Blackwall and East India Dock entrance at 9 p.m. Could not open the gates till tide rose higher.

10.23 p.m. Hove the ship inside dock gates. *Taeping* had preceded us up the river, but, having farther to go, did not reach the entrance of London Docks till 10 p.m. and, drawing less water than we, also dock having two gates, they got her inside outer gate, shut it, and allowed the lock to fill from the dock, then opened the inner gate so she docked some twenty minutes before us – the papers have it half an hour, for the sake of precision.

Probably the best-known event in the transport of tea from China to London was the "race" between five Tea Clippers – *Ariel, Taeping, Serica, Taitsing* and *Fiery Cross* – that left Foochow on the same tide on 28 May 1866. The first two docked in London within half an hour of each other 99 days later; the third, *Serica*, only two hours after that on the same tide. In fact this iconic moment had far more significance as a sporting and wagering event than it did in the development of tea-trade transport. The reign of the Tea Clippers lasted less than 20 years, between the first such passage in 1850 and shortly after the opening of the Suez canal in 1869, and had far less impact on the transhipment of tea than is commonly supposed.

In many ways the more arduous part of tea's journey from leaf to lip – both in China and, later, in India – was its overland passage. But before it could go anywhere, thousands of loose and disorderly leaves had to be packed into containers that could be easily manhandled. When tea first came to Europe it did so in such small and valuable quantities – no more than a few pounds at a time – that the essential thing was to pack it in such a way as to guarantee its arrival in pristine condition. It would, in any case, have been en route for anything from 14 months to two years, such was the protracted nature of leaves' travels. As soon as this tea reached one of the three Chinese ports – Amoy, Canton and Foochow – from which tea ships departed eastwards and westwards, it was packed in glazed jars to render it impervious to damp and salt water, and the lids of the jars were sealed with wax to render them airtight. These early small consignments usually arrived in reasonable condition. If they had not, it is hard to see how the fashion for tea drinking among the trend-setting wealthy could have caught on. The same elite also took a fancy, for display, to the elegantly shaped, blue-and-white or five-coloured porcelain jars in which their tea came.

However, when tea travelled out of China overland to Mongolia, Tibet and Russia, it was required in far larger quantities. You did not get twenty thousand Tibetan warhorses in barter exchange for a few spoonfuls of tea. Many thousands of pounds went northwards in the shape of bricks of tea that had been wrapped in wet yak skins, which had then shrunk to form an almost unbreakable 27kg pack that protected the contents from the rocks and thorns into which the beasts carrying them (two packs to a yak) bumped as they grazed. Until the opening of the final stretch of the Trans-Siberian railway in 1896, brick tea was also carried by sinuous camel trains of two or three hundred animals across the Gobi desert on a 16-month, four-thousand-mile journey to the cities of northern Russia. The last of the camel trains left China in 1900. At their peak they had been transporting up to 117 million pounds of tea a year. On the early part of its journey this "caravan tea" – a romantic title that gave it strong appeal in Western Europe (Edward Bramah wittily explains this fallacious fascination as due to a belief that "several weeks of sea voyage deteriorated the tea more than several months of contact with hot camel") – was escorted by armed guards to protect it from brigands in the territories through which it passed, where brick tea was a medium of exchange. This was particularly necessary at the end of the nineteenth century for the numerous trains of two to three hundred yaks which carried the 4.5–6.5 million metric tons of brick tea that wound their 12-month-long way to Tibet's spiritual capital, Lhasa.

The journey from the country of the "Bohea" hills in Fukien province south to Canton, where eager European agents awaited the new season's crop, was only a little less hazardous and difficult – if shorter. Even so, a tea chest of bamboo, lined with waxed or rice paper, and travelling some twelve hundred miles, could take several months to arrive in Canton. Its first stage was by human portage. For ordinary tea two tea chests of bamboo would be suspended from the ends of a yoke of a kind with which a European peasant would have been familiar. Where top-quality tea was concerned, the belief that any contact with the ground was deleterious had led to the design of an ingenious, bamboo carrying frame in the shape of an isosceles triangle. The two long sides consisted of two-metre poles strapped to the sides of the tea chest so that a dozen centimetres or so of each pole protruded beyond the end. The coolie stood inside the gap between the chest and the apex of the triangle, formed by tying the two poles together, with the chest resting for comfort on a small, flat piece of wood across his shoulders. Thus, on the frequent occasions when the coolie needed to rest on the steep climb up mountain passes, he could take the weight off his shoulders by placing the ends of the poles vertically on the ground so that the chest still did not touch it. While resting at an inn, he would have propped the frame against the wall with the same effect.

At such transfer points as Hokow on the Kin-Keang river or on one of the other small rivers in Kiangsi province, the chests were transferred to flat-bottomed boats, rather like large-scale punts, carrying 100–150 chests. Where the rapids were too fierce to be shot safely, or the water was too shallow for the boat's draught, the cargo would be taken on to smaller boats or be portered round to the next calmer stretch of river. On the border between Kiangsi and Kwangtun provinces, the tea was again switched to porters – who were preferred to pack animals because "they were cheaper to feed". Thence, once over the next range of mountain passes, the tea chests were again loaded on to small boats, before one final transfer to what British sailors called "tea wagons": large boats capable of ferrying five hundred chests to the chosen port. At every stage of its journey the tea would have been subject to provincial border duties, which added considerably to its cost before it reached the godown, or warehouse, of a member of the Hong.

Duties in Canton could amount to as much as £710 on a single shipment, so a foreign agent would be anxious that every leaf of his dearly obtained cargo should reach its destination in good condition. His nightmare was that the whole lot would be lost at sea. In both these respects he was largely dependent on the Chinese stevedores who loaded the East Indiamen, and later the Tea Clippers, in which his tea would travel. From the author of *Notes on Stowage* (1894) these men met with nothing but praise: "Chinese stevedores cannot be surpassed in the stowage of tea cargoes; they thoroughly understand their work. A good stevedore will go into the holds and tell you within a few chests what the vessel will stow." But before the tea chests could be stowed the ship's main ballast had to be correctly placed. This consisted of about 100 tons of pig iron (ingots) topped by 150–250 tons of shingle. Shingle was used because the ballast had to be impervious to water to avoid the risk of damp being drawn into the tea by the heat it generated. *Notes on Stowage* also urges that tea be packed well clear of "sugar, safflower, rhubarb, India rubber, rapeseed, hides, turmeric, drugs of any sort or other cargo likely to create strong fumes or of a nature or tendency to injure the flavour of the tea".

The coarser shingle was levelled smooth and planked over in such a way that the even surface followed the slightly curved contours of the beams and decking in order to maximize the number of chests that could be stowed. Once the base layer was complete, the next – a carefully measured chest-height deep – would be layered in the same way, level by level, until the cargo came up flush with the deck. At each level, dunnage (packing) in the shape of fine shingle would fill in the gap, only two to six inches wide, between the outer chests and the sides of the ship. Different teas came in chests of different sizes which – although complicating the Rubik's-cube challenge of stowage – made possible use of virtually 100 per cent of all available space. If silk were also in the cargo it would be packed in the midst of the tea chests. In order to make sure that as many chests as possible were crammed in, they were hammered into place with a wooden mallet with a head the size of a small cask. More spectacularly, "when stowing the last chest in an early tier, a Chinaman, rather than strike it with any hard instrument, walks off to a distance, and running back jumps into the air and falls in a sitting posture on the chest, which is thus sent uninjured into its place".

While most of this technique was developed to service the Tea Clippers, the principles also applied to the East Indiamen, in whose ballast large quantities of porcelain cups (and some teapots) were almost always found until the mid-eighteenth century, when they became something of a glut on the market. Just how effective and durable such porcelain ballast could be was shown when the Dutch ship *Geldermalsen*, which sank in a storm in 1752, was recovered in 1984 with practically all her porcelain intact.

Precision in stowage was not only important for economic reasons but because if badly done it could adversely affect the trim of the ship. This, quite apart from the risk to vessel and crew, could knock as much as 5 per cent off its sailing speed. In the days when a premium was being paid for early-arrival tea, that could add a week to the voyage, perhaps delaying landfall until after earlier cargoes had already depressed the price.

So skilled were the Chinese stevedores that probably not untypical was a reported instance of eight thousand cases of tea and 1,141 bales of silk being loaded on one Tea Clipper in just 17 hours over a two-day period. English dockers, not to be outdone, once unloaded fourteen thousand chests from one of the star Clippers, the *Fiery Cross*, in just over a day. Again, this was probably not so unusual, though in post-Second World War Britain such indecent haste would certainly have caused a dock strike.

The British East Indiamen plying the China trade from the mid-seventeenth to the mid-nineteenth century hardly ever exceeded five hundred tons – cargo capacity was a little less than half a ship's tonnage – and could take anything from two to four years to make the complete round trip of London–Canton–London. They seldom completed more than half a dozen such trips before they were sold off as no longer fit for the job. Dutch-built vessels, being usually a little larger – 750 tons perhaps – and more durable, were much in demand second-hand from nations that could not build their own. By the end of the eighteenth century an East Indiaman could have a burthen of as much as fourteen hundred tons. East Indiamen sailed in convoys and were armed with cannon, and their crews with small arms, lest they be attacked by the pirates that infested oriental waters. However, the main reason for groups of vessels leaving the Thames together was to be sure of being in time for the season's tea in Canton and of catching the favourable monsoon wind home.

There were no tea races until the 1850s. The economics of the trade meant it was much more important to sail with a full cargo, which could take time to acquire, than to beat a rival ship to Europe. Indeed, it could often pay fortuitously to be a late arrival. What was crucial in terms of timing was not to miss the end of the north-east monsoon for a fair wind home and thus be confronted by the adverse south-west monsoon. In such circumstances ships almost invariably stayed in Canton for another, expensive nine months before sailing for home, with a much-deteriorated cargo of tea.

The Tea Clippers that briefly succeeded the Indiamen were American-designed and built, and were the progeny of the ships that had run rings round the British fleet in American waters during the war of 1812. The Clippers were designed to do what their name says: "clip" time off the duration of the fourteen-thousand-mile voyage between China and Britain. In practice the amount by which they reduced the journey was not always as much as is usually supposed, but the shock, in 1850, of the Clipper *Oriental* arriving in the Thames only 97 days after leaving Hong Kong spurred several British shipyards, such as Robert Steele & Co. of Greenock, to develop their own improved versions of the American design. The shock was the greater because much of the tea the *Oriental* carried belonged to English merchants who had paid a 50 per cent freight premium just on the promise of a faster voyage. It was British Clippers – and the few Americans that took advantage of the ending, in 1849, of the restriction on foreign vessels trading to British ports – that briefly dominated the China trade. The fastest journey between the two countries was made by the *Sir Lancelot* in 88 days, but a hundred days was more usual. This was only a 9 per cent reduction on the average time of 110 days taken by the dumpy East Indiamen, shaped as they were like brandy glasses amidships. But for the absurd obsession of the London tea merchants in the 1850s and 1860s to be first with the new season's teas, and the premium prices they were prepared to pay, such a margin would not have been economically significant.

Beautiful as they undoubtedly were, the Clippers, with their low sterns, were inherently unstable and vulnerable to a following sea. They were even more vulnerable to the opening of the Suez Canal and the improvements in coal consumption and propulsion (particularly the screw propeller) that quickly made the voyage from Britain to China and back both much quicker and much more economical. While early coal-guzzling steamers also had to go round the Cape, and required several costly coaling stations at various points along the route, there was not much to chose between them. However, within a few years of the opening of the Suez Canal the larger, steam-driven ships could not only carry more tea but were able to make the round trip in 120 days and so were capable of making two or three complete voyages a year instead of only one. In 1882 the SS *Stirling* took just 32 days to reach London from Hankow. The demise of the sailing ship as the carrier of choice for tea was graphically described by Captain Henry Davies in the late 1870s:

> There were eight or ten of our clippers anchored there, waiting for tea – glossy black sides, brasswork gleaming in the early sunlight, yards squared by lifts and braces, house flags fluttering at the main, and the glorious red ensign at peak or staff. Some of the ships had been there many days, ours only a few. Enter the s.s. *Aberdeen* of

Aberdeen, under her own steam. She anchored below all of us and was admired by all, I think, for she looked very smart in her green dress. But although we all admired her, I think we resented her intrusion into what had been our freehold and domain for long, long years. She was optical proof to most of us that the day of the tea clipper proper was swiftly drawing to its close. And when, at dawn on the fourth day, she hove up by steam, the rattle of her cables and windlass sounded the knell of our lovely vessels as tea carriers, for she had gobbled up all there was in the godowns, except ours (for we were loading for the Cape), and left the fleet waiting for their cargoes which she had swallowed whole!

There is a sad postscript to the brief and spectacular reign of the Tea Clippers, the last of which, the *Cutty Sark*, is being restored – funds permitting – in London. Four of those which took part in the classic race of 1866 – the *Ariel, Taeping, Fiery Cross* and *Serica* – met tragic ends. The *Ariel*, on its way to Australia, crammed with hopeful immigrants, disappeared at sea with the loss of all hands and passengers. Of the other three, one foundered, one burned and one sank (as did several other Clippers).

The seabound part of tea's journey from India, Ceylon or Java to Europe in the nineteenth century was shorter but no different in essence from that from China. In later years there were endless arguments about freight rates for tea, and shortages of shipping – especially during the world wars – and threats and attempts by the planters to set up rival shipping lines of their own, which never came to much. After the Second World War the British shipping monopoly for tea was broken and local shipping lines took an increasing share of the trade.

But before a single leaf can be conveyed anywhere, it has to be packed in a more manageable form. In India the earliest solution was to copy the Chinese chest, even to the colourful outer paper wrapping. This soon gave way to chests made of hand-sawn planks of local teak or sal – exceptionally hard woods – lined with sheet lead from England, which might weigh as much as 40lb a chest. Such a chest was certainly robust and, once soldered shut, usually airtight. But a container comprising 30–40 per cent of the gross weight, coupled with a shortage of means of transport, scarcely made economic sense and could not be made in sufficient quantity to meet the demands of an expanding industry. Moreover, thieves soon learned the trick of extracting the nails from one side panel, removing it, prising open the soft lead, taking out some tea and sealing the chest up again. Because of the usual great variation in weight, the theft was undetectable.

Having to use such a heavy chest made it important to pack as much tea into it as possible. In China this was achieved until well into the twentieth century by the insalubrious practice of barefoot coolies stamping down the contents – occasionally, as a gesture to hygiene, wrapping their feet in a dirty cloth. Today tight packing is achieved by the use of vibrating machines to shake down the leaves. When the turbulence of the oceans had the same effect on chests in the old sailing ships, it was assumed by the recipients that they were being short-changed.

At first the shortage of suitable local timber for chests in India could be made up by importing teak from Burma, but this did not suffice for long, and almost any timber the planter could get his hands on – pine, mango, simul, much of it still green – was pressed into service. As a result, an increasing number of chests either broke and spilled their contents, or rotted and spoiled them altogether by contamination. Complaints were numerous about "the extremely bad packing of chests from many well known gardens, not only with regard to the quality of the wood employed for the boxes, but also with reference to the slackness of the contents".

A solution was discovered at the very end of the nineteenth century, when Williamson Magor imported a sample plywood chest from Russia. The principle of making plywood by cross-laminating very thin layers of a pliable wood, such as birch, had long been known. However, not until 1900 was a method developed, by the Acme Tea Chest Company, of doing this mechanically so that chests could be mass-produced.

The classic tea chest (24 × 19 × 19 inches) consisted of six birch-wood-ply sides, "flat-packed" from Finland and Estonia, to be assembled and strengthened by nailing internal battens along all the adjoining sides of the cube. It was then lined either with tinfoil –

soon vetoed by the American Food and Drug Administration – or aluminium foil, with a thin inner lining of paper rather like baking paper. In a standard 110lb tea chest over 90 per cent of the weight could now consist of tea not box.

Though three-ply birch proved ideal for strength and lightness, an early problem arose when the humidity in the tea-producing countries caused the layers to separate. Fortunately an Estonian firm developed a new casein-based glue that solved that problem. The various firms initially involved combined to form the Venesta Syndicate, supplying tea chests to India, Ceylon, the Dutch East Indies and wherever else they were needed. At its peak the industry was making some 10 million chests a year. But when, during the First World War, the Germans occupied Estonia and the Bolsheviks later stopped the supply of birch from Russia, the supply of chests collapsed. Similar occupation of the chest-producing countries had a similar effect in the Second World War, and the substitution of less satisfactory American and Canadian maple or walnut was short-lived, owing to Britain's shortage of both dollars and shipping.

The result of these two hiatuses was to stimulate the birth of a native plywood tea-chest industry in India. But poor quality and limited capacity – no more than 1.5 million chests a year, when India alone needed more than four million – created the ironic situation of planters having to revert to making their own chests from local wood. Worse, the demand for aluminium for war production meant that the chests were once more lined with lead, by now recognized as a possible health hazard. Other gardens in India and Ceylon resolved the problem by packing their tea in gunny-bags: a glimpse of things to come. After the Second World War, environmentalists, too, began to challenge the impact of tea-chest manufacture, pointing out that a year's demand of 10 million chests entailed cutting down 4,500 hectares of forest.

After the war the quality of India-made tea chests steadily improved, but the government of independent India foolishly restricted the import of chests to save foreign exchange without calculating how much sterling was lost through the consequent drop in exports. The problem was not solved by legislation compelling tea companies in India to buy 26 locally made chests for every one imported. Two new factors now meant that the days of the tea chest were numbered – and great would be the grief among removal men, children's den improvisers and impoverished students.

Pallets and containers were already changing the mode of goods transport in the 1950s. There was a brief reprieve for the chest makers when they adapted to the brick-shaped (24 × 20 × 16 inches) requirements of the pallet assemblers for a uniform cubic stack. But even this shape was not so convenient as the thick-paper 25kg bags that the Ceylon tea planters had been the first in the industry to introduce in 1975, albeit 50 years after their adoption by many other industries. It is a nice touch that Ceylon was also the last to let go of the tea chest for some of its best teas. Today all Kenya's teas, and most of those from India, Ceylon and Indonesia, are packed in paper sacks. With the chest's demise went one of the tea trade's best advertisements. As early as 1912 the ITA had seen the potential of promoting its wares on the sides of tea chests, just as their predecessors had done on the sides of teapots. Although they had to amend "Pure Indian Tea" to "Pure India Tea" (owing to misunderstandings in America), tea chests bearing the latter inscription – or its equivalent for Ceylon or Java – rapidly became the outward manifestation of tea worldwide.

In some cases the new paper or hessian tea sacks were loaded straight into containers at the garden for onward travel by truck, on roads which would have been impassable only a few decades earlier, for loading on to container ships. Most tea companies, however, are content to deliver their paper sacks of tea to giant container depots, such as the one at Gauhati, where they are transferred to containers in garden manifest order, loaded on to rakes – flat-bed rail wagons taking 80 containers each – for the journey to specially designed container ports to be craned straight on to container ships. These are unloaded a few weeks later at equally specialized container ports, in Europe and America, such as Felixstowe in East Anglia (where a cargo that once took recalcitrant British dockers several weeks to unload by hand can be disgorged and on its way in less than a day).

Ceylon and Java tea gardens, though mostly at altitude, were never so far from the coast as to cause serious problems in reaching the docks for shipment abroad. For India it was very different. One Assam planter writing in 1975 published a tell-tale table of how journey times between Calcutta and Dibrugarh had changed in less than 120 years:

    1859 mostly river journey Calcutta to Dibrugarh = 3 months
    1860 River steamer = 3 weeks
    1904 Assam Bengal railway = 3 days
    1975 by air = 3 hours.

In the early days of Assam tea growing, the modest quantities produced were often taken down small tributary rivers by canoe or shallow-draught "country boat" to the Brahmaputra for onward carriage. Wood-built country boats could carry 150 chests, the later, iron-built ones 300–650. However, in the dry season the smaller rivers were no more than stony gullies. Then coolies, who could carry only one heavy chest between a pair of them, and elephants, whose howdahs could take only six – both equally scarce means of transport – had to be used, for neither the bullock cart of later years nor the roads to carry them existed. As the needs of the planters grew, they (ever practical) came up with the elephant-powered wagon. Though this was expensive to build, it carried 54 chests at a time. But none of this land transport was any use in the rainy season, when everything just got bogged down.

The only three "main" roads linking Calcutta and Assam in 1800 were all virtually impassable during the monsoon rains, and not until the 1860s did either local or central governments in India pay much attention to their improvement. Before then it was considered a matter for the planters to undertake road repairs and building if they wanted better links with the outside world. Road building in areas such as Darjeeling was no easy task. One six-mile stretch necessitated building three hundred bridges. Roads in the tea-growing hills of southern India were equally rare and difficult to construct. Nor were there, in this case, any rail or river alternatives. So planters sent out their tea by porter and pack pony along bridlepaths and bridge tracks and aerial ropeways. Similar expedients were necessary for the many high-altitude gardens in Ceylon and Java, though the distances involved were not so great.

Once such major rivers as the Ganges and the Brahmaputra had been reached, transport became a little easier, though the many way-stations needed to service boats and people were expensive to maintain. That far-sighted Governor-General, Lord William Bentinck, had initiated a river-steamer run on the Ganges in 1834, when such vessels were in their infancy. This prompted both British and Indian companies to offer private steamer services. These sail-assisted river steamers towed "flats" – large, shallow-draughted barges for both goods and passengers – and required skilled pilotage as the course of the river bed shifted year by year. The upstream journey on what (a few government staff and packages apart) was virtually a tea-industry service could take as much as three months from Calcutta to Gauhati. Downstream travel, at a cautious speed, was not a great deal quicker. Although the number of steamers and the frequency of service increased progressively during the second half of the nineteenth century, they did not do so sufficiently to satisfy the needs of the planters who, encouraged by men like Henry Cottam to "rouse yourselves and shout for a railway", had ever-larger quantities of tea to get to Calcutta for shipment home.

And railways – today still one of the best networks in the world – they got. In 1845 the first survey was made for the ambitious Trans-India railway: afterwards, in part owing to the urging of the planters of southern India, the first 20-mile stretch of the Great India Peninsular Railway out of Bombay was opened in 1853. The commercially essential, 740-mile Assam–Bengal railway, completed in 1904, was a remarkable feat of engineering, accomplished in part thanks to the skills of the many Cornishmen who worked (and died) building the hundreds of masonry bridges needed.

Tea was opening up the subcontinent: both road and rail expansion in India largely resulted from a combination of planter pressure and the Government of India's growing recognition of the potential fiscal and commercial importance of the tea industry. Moreover, the psychological boost which better communications gave the isolated planter was as important to his productivity as was the better means of transporting his tea.

Sadly, the partition of British India in 1947 into the independent sovereign states of India and Pakistan proved a serious setback to what had been the increasingly well integrated and efficient transport system on which tea relied so heavily. The physical sharing out of staff and rolling stock would have presented problems enough, but these were multiplied tenfold by the mutual animosity of the two states. Pakistan's refusal to permit the transit of traffic from Assam and Cachar across what was then West Pakistan (now independent Bangladesh) prompted India to undertake one of the most challenging feats of railway engineering in any country at any time: a link from Assam to Calcutta that passed only through Indian territory. The need was all the more pressing as Pakistan had also blocked the river traffic by which tea from northern India habitually flowed to Calcutta. Crucial supplies were flown in by more than eight hundred emergency air-lifts, but this did not resolve the problem of getting the tea out. Sensibly, by 1950, the two governments recognized the mutual destructiveness of such policies and the blockade was ended. By this time the Assam–Calcutta railway had been completed in only 254 days. In the first monsoon only one bridge was washed away and that was soon replaced.

Just how great an accomplishment this railway was is perhaps best conveyed by a report in 1955 by the chairman of the ITA, which showed how damaging inclement nature could be in the tea districts of India:

> Torrential storms with rainfall that on one day exceeded forty inches; landslides and the blocking of rivers by the debris; and then the bursting of the dams so created; bringing to sections of the Dooars devastations of such completeness that no one who has not visited the area can imagine the havoc which has been caused. The Assam Rail Link was breached in forty-four places; bridges were washed away; and on one occasion a locomotive was carried a quarter of a mile downstream by the force of the current. A thousand acres of tea lies buried in sand, while, most tragic of all, nearly 150 people were drowned on two [tea] gardens which stood in the way of the turbulent waters as they carved out a new channel. The Railway was out of action for three and a half months.

Throughout the eighteenth and nineteenth centuries ever-larger docks accommodated ever-larger ships and turned them round faster. Increasingly grand and capacious warehouses received ever greater quantities of tea as the commodity awaited the final stage of its wholesale journey from leaf to lip: the tea auction. When tea first came to London the quantities were small and no haste was necessary at auction, which took place "by the candle": bids for a lot of tea continued to be taken until a candle had burned down a marked inch. It was not long before the volume of tea for sale rendered such a leisurely approach impractical and the practice with which we are familiar at auctions today superseded it. Bidding at tea auctions soon became brisk and competitive and, as we have seen, sometimes an exercise in machismo rather than commerce.

One sale catalogue, for 2 April 1838 – for China tea only, of course – showed nine selling brokers offering more than 12.5 million pounds of tea, in 176,424 packages. Rather a lot of candles! When Indian, Ceylon, Java and other teas came to what was one of the world's two international tea markets (the other being in the Netherlands), they slotted into the London pattern without fuss. The buyer used to have 90 days – known as the "prompt" – to take and pay for the tea he had bought. This gave him, if he wished, what amounted to extra warehousing and a three-month, interest-free loan. Today the interest-free prompt is only 42 days, with a further 14 on request on which interest is charged. The fifty-sixth day is known as "Deal End Day".

The other unusual feature of the London tea auction was that quite often the same firm of brokers would act for both the seller and the buyer without any apparent conflict of interest. This was not as odd as it might seem, for having "charactered" the tea beforehand, brokers in the same firm would be in a unique position to match the taste requirement of the one with the tea of the other. The selling broker would usually also have at the auction a "market man": a broker who would bid against the other buyers, if possible until a satisfactory price was reached. When a similar practice was uncovered in the antiques business it was condemned as a "ring", but the two Monopolies Commission investigations of the industry in 1956 and 1970 gave it a clean bill of health, despite this seemingly cosy arrangement.

By the late 1960s the big six British tea-selling companies – Allied Suppliers (Lipton), Brooke Bond, CWS, Lyons, Meriden

(Typhoo) and Ridgway, all still limited companies – were buying more than 80 per cent of the tea sold through London. A hundred or so smaller firms accounted for the rest, many of them just to sell on to other blenders and packers, often for them to re-export. As four of the big six were themselves absorbed by still larger concerns, direct deals with producers more and more replaced tea sold at auction in London. This, together with the tea producers themselves preferring to have auctions nearer home, brought about the demise of the London auctions in June 1998. The first auction outside London had been held in Calcutta in 1841, though regular auctions did not begin until 1861. It would be many years before its turnover exceeded that of London. In 2004 the pecking order is Mombasa, Colombo (opened in 1883), Calcutta, Gauhati and Chittagong (in 2004 handling 298, 270, 119, 110 and 53 thousand metric tons, respectively: 80 per cent of world exports).

However, London continues to be a considerable centre for the selling and buying of tea through a variety of private deals. Yet although these may seem more direct and efficient, they lack the competitive transparency of the old auction system. Nor is the quality of the tea sold scrutinized quite so ruthlessly as it was in the London auctions, where both selling and buying brokers employed highly experienced tasters to double-check the quality of each lot up for sale. With the tea-trade giants of the twentieth century buying in large quantities, more and more tea selling is done by direct, one-to-one methods. Regional auctions and regional deals mean that growers do not have to wait so long to get paid, and such new big consumers as Pakistan and Egypt have a shorter and less time-consuming link to their supplies than they had when these were routed through London. But the new auction centres are themselves under pressure. In the 1970s 85 per cent of tea (other than from China) was sold at auction. Today it is less than a third, as direct deals between producers and the big blenders and packers have become the norm. That the world's tea is no longer auctioned in London is a mark of how far the international tea trade has travelled in the 350 years since that first jar of chaw made its way to England.

CHAPTER TWELVE

A Matter of Taste

Recipe for a perfect cup of tea for two:
In a double steel or silver infusion basket or tongs, place two rounded caddy spoons of finest Assam leaf.

In a single basket, place one rounded caddy spoon of best Darjeeling (or *genuine* Earl Grey) leaf. Always leave plenty of room for the leaves to expand and move.

Warm a small (500ml), white, globe-shaped teapot. (This configuration best retains the heat.) The pot should be warmed by placing near the fire or on a moderately hot stove or by pouring in a small amount of boiling water. Warm two attractive tea cups (150ml) in the same way; and don't forget the saucers.

To a clean, empty kettle add about 600ml (there's a planet to save!) of fresh, well-oxygenated water, preferably from a spring or bore-hole but if from a chlorinated mains supply use a good filter first.

Bring toward the boil and shortly before it reaches boiling empty any hot water from the teapot.

Place the two infusers in the teapot. As the water hits boiling point – and not a second later – fill the teapot with all but the last drops.

Immediately place the tea cosy – as crazy as you like, as long as it blocks heat loss – on the teapot.

Five minutes after filling the teapot, take the double (Assam) infuser out of it. Tip any hot water from the teacups and pour in such milk (if any) and sugar (if any) as experience has shown each drinker to prefer.

Seven minutes after filling the pot take the single (Darjeeling) infuser out of it; this optimizes the infusion time of the two different leaves.

Pour at once so as to fill each cup to within a centimetre of its rim and replace the tea cosy. Sip the tea slowly and savour it. Don't gulp!

The tea will not "stew" as there are no leaves in the pot, so the second cup should be nearly as enjoyable as the first.

This just happens to be the author's favourite way of making tea – for which today's hectic life seldom leaves time – but, as Lu Yu reminds us, there are ten thousand teas. (The British Standards Institute's attempt to arrive at a definitive method of tea brewing in 1980 was greeted with hilarity by tea men and tea drinkers alike.) The actual origins of infusing, boiling or decocting the dried leaves of *Camellia sinensis* in hot or boiling water and drinking the result-ant liquid can only be guessed at. Perhaps somewhere, sometime, some five millennia ago, half a dozen bronze axes cut into the trunk of a tree. It could not have been a very big tree – maybe seven or eight metres high and 30cm thick – for soft, bronze axes don't cut bigger trees that easily – but it fell with a satisfying crash. It may have lain for a few days in the sun to dry out before being taken "home" to burn. The women and children of the group probably stripped off the small branches for kindling. Perhaps the leaves, now well withered by the sun, were tossed into the pot of perpetu-ally boiling water on the grounds that nothing must be wasted that might be worth a try for food. And they tasted and it was good. The first tea had been brewed.

Or maybe the leaves of a tea bush may once have been plucked and chewed and a few handfuls kept for later. Those leaves, left accidentally in bright sunshine for a while, would have turned into basically brewable tea leaves; freshly plucked and unprocessed tea leaves are of little use for making tea. (Some the author made in this way tasted like boiled grass or out-of-date camomile and was not much more refreshing than hot water.) The sun-dried leaves might then have been tossed into a crude cooking pot to avoid waste, and the resulting brew, proving tasty and stimulating, was then repeated and its preparation gradually improved.

The drink of tea was probably discovered by just such a combination of accident and primitive pragmatism. But this is all pure speculation, if more probable than some of the subsequent myths about tea's origins (see Chapter 13). So what concrete facts have we? Botanical evidence suggests that tea's trees and bushes – tea grows in both forms – originated along an arc pivoting on the northern border of Burma and stretching from Yunnan in the east of China to Assam in north-west India, and have been growing there for from a quarter to half a million years. Evidence as to when man first made culinary use of them is no more precise.

On the outskirts of Beijing, at Zhoukoudian, there is an ash pit six metres deep, all that is left of a very large ancient hearth. From the remains in it we can infer that Peking Man (400,000–250,000 BC) roasted meat and boiled water to purify it. Even today the Chinese prefer warm water, which they regard as healthier than cold. We also know, from these and similar remains elsewhere, that Early Man immersed a variety of leaves in boiling water to make herbal infusions. Ancient writers comment frequently on the bitterness of tea, which may indicate that the earliest practice was to use leaves straight from tree or bush, though sun-withered tea also tastes slightly bitter. Again speculation relies on only shreds of evidence. That the boiling of water for infusions and the existence of tea plants coexisted in time and location is the only basis we have for inferring that tea was brewed some five millennia ago. Until tea leaves are discovered that have clearly been immersed in hot or boiling water, and which can be accurately dated to such early times, we cannot know, even roughly, when tea was first drunk.

We do know that there are written records indicating that it was certainly a known drink some time between 1000 and 500 BC. Claimants for the Indian origin of tea cite the story of how Prince Siddartha brought tea to China in 519 BC when he was taking his teaching there from southern India, and it is in connection with Buddhist temples in China, and the duty of their monks to be vigilant, that we find the earliest records of the cultivation and imbibing of tea. The admirable Emperor Asoka (reigned 270–237 BC) certainly did dispatch many monks to teach Buddhism in the countries adjacent to his Indian kingdom, probably including northern China. But although early Chinese histories acknowledge that "during the reign of the Emperor Xuan WuDi (515–500 BC) the venerable Bodhidharma came to Northern Wei from Southern India to teach Buddhism" they make no mention of tea anywhere.

Another claim for tea's Indian origin is based on the assertion that the monk Wu Li Zhen, alias Gan Lu (sweet dew), a Chinese missionary to India, took back some tea plants to cultivate in his home province of Sichuan. In the early twentieth century the travelling tea man James Hutchison gave an interesting account of a visit to the temple, sacred to Gan Lu, on Mount Mung-Shan, where the seven venerable bushes of legend were supposed to have been planted. He did indeed see seven bushes; and various monks told him that the "benignant leaves of this fragrant and immortal tea" were between two and two and a half thousand years old and had been brought from India and "hand planted" by Gan Lu himself. Now, they said, the bushes were plucked annually by a local dignitary for sending to the Emperor, who had them made into the ink with which he signed the death warrants for condemned criminals. As is so often the case, there appeared to be some confusion as to who had done what. A parchment at the site gave a date of AD 25, which could not have been right; while a nearby stone monument referred to the event taking place in the Western Han dynasty (206 BC–AD 24). In any case botanically knowledgeable colleagues at the Linnaean Society tell me it is highly unlikely that the same bush could survive for two thousand years.

During the Eastern Han dynasty (25 BC–AD 220) a retrospective *Manual of Rituals of the Zhou Dynasty* (794–221 BC) specifically refers to tea in religious rites in which it heightened alertness and so allowed discourse with the gods, and also promoted the drinker's own health. Confucius (551–479 BC) also appears to have been familiar with tea drinking. In his *Shih Jing* (Book of Odes) he asks: "Who can say tea is bitter?" But, in comparing it with another herbal infusion, it is possible that he was referring to a similar herb rather than tea itself. Tea also features in the westward journey of Master Lao, the founder of Daoism, in the sixth century BC. When Lao finds himself weary from crossing the high Han Pass, a student offers him a cup of tea to "strengthen and refresh" him. This gesture has entered into Chinese culture – and hence into that of the West – in the custom of offering visitors, even strangers, a cup of tea first thing on arrival. Rather less attractively to present-day Western thought, it established the convention in the East of inferiors serving tea to their social superiors: a practice that also found favour in the upper echelons of eighteenth-century and Victorian England.

Though it is impossible after such a lapse of time to be precise, it does appear that by the sixth century BC, when Buddhism came to China, both the medicinal and the pleasurable properties of tea were already well established. Lu Yu (AD 733–804) was certainly convinced of this earlier familiarity when he wrote the seminal *Chajing,* or *Classic of Tea.* During Lu Yu's lifetime tea was numbered among the items that were taxed, so suggesting that it was sufficiently widely available for the levy to be worth collecting.

We saw in Chapter 1 how the demand for tea in Europe and America developed gradually into the enormous trade of the eighteenth, nineteenth and twentieth centuries, and how William Melrose's first task in meeting his part of that demand was to "character", or taste, the tea before buying. To this day the process remains crucial to ensuring that we get the tea that suits our taste.

The tea taster is, to my mind, a much more sophisticated artist than the wine taster. In the course of a working day he may have to pronounce on as many as 250 different samples, measured against his knowledge and memory of over two thousand different teas. He will not only have to distinguish between and analyse a whole gamut of intrinsic qualities in each, but, if they are destined for blending, consider their potential compatibility with perhaps 20 others. Most importantly, he will have to value the tea so that, in maintaining consistency for a particular blend, the buying merchant can mix teas at an overall price that yields the expected profit. As a background, the taster will have to have a particular knowledge of the requirements of the broker or merchant on whose behalf he is working at the time, and a general knowledge of wider market trends, the precise conditions in which the tea was grown and transported, and even of the politics and economy of the country whence it came. He will also know that his verdict may well be cross-checked against that of other tasters, both at the producer's end and in the auction house.

In very general terms, tea divides into three taxa or broad categories: fermented, unfermented and semi-fermented; or black, green and oolong. These categories may be found in two forms: whole-leaf of various sizes; and powder produced by various means and to varying degrees of fineness. Four broad qualifiers provide further precision: Flowery (F), Orange (O), Pekoe (P) and Souchong (S), which mainly denote the particle size, or grade, of the processed leaf. The etymology of the grades, from the original Chinese terminology, is revealing for the implication of what the user might expect from the tea. Pekoe is the European corruption of *"Pei Hao"* or *"Pac Ho"*, meaning white hair or down, and refers to the bloom on young leaf buds. Nowadays it has come to indicate what Bramah calls a "bold leaf size", eight to fifteen millimetres in length. Flowery, from the Chinese *"Tsai Haui"*, once referred to the Chinese predilection for scented teas, but Flowery Orange Pekoe now only means having a good aroma and a leaf size of five to eight millimetres. Golden or Tippy denotes the proportion of golden tips. Souchong is yet another European verbal mangling, this time of the Chinese *"Hsaio Chung"*, or "small sort". The small sorts are, in fact, fannings, the word for smaller leaf particles (about one and a half millimetres), usually those left over when the manufacture of larger leaf teas has been completed, but still often of good quality. Finally there is dust (a millimetre or less), the residue from the processing of broken and fannings, and ideal for use, with fannings, in tea bags and very often of perfectly acceptable quality, and moreover, the most profitable. A whole leaf base is assumed if no letter prefixes the grade. A prefix of B shows that a broken leaf has been used and a suffix of F that the tea consists of fannings. Thus, F.B.O.P.F. would indicate that the tea had been made using flowery, broken, orange, pekoe fannings.

Japanese tea is graded differently into three categories. The lowest is *bancha* – common tea – consisting of the tea bush's coarser leaves, which are picked late in the season. *Bancha* is the least expensive Japanese tea. The better tea for the general palate is *sencha* – literally infused or boiled tea – and is made from the young leaves picked in the first and most vigorous part of the growing cycle. The true connoisseur of Japanese tea, however, will settle for nothing less than "jade dew", *gyokuro*, the leaves of which are grown under shade in the hottest part of the growing season.

From this general background and his own experience the taster can form a very good idea of the life-history of any leaf from its particular garden to his broker's office, and he will have a fairly good idea of what kind of tea it will make. But he needs more, and for this he must go to the tasting room.

The tasting room should have the spotless orderliness of a regimental parade ground, with the serried ranks of teas and bowls, cups, lids and kettles all lined up under evenly shaded daylight or artificial light so that the eye is not deceived when assessing colour. In the furthest rank of the parade from the taster stand the tins of the various different leaves, one to a tin, with their lids open; in the next rank are the pure-white, porcelain pots in which the tea will be infused, as if in a miniature teapot, with their lids inverted upon them; the front rank is occupied by the white-china tasting bowls. The first officer on parade is the taster's assistant – probably a trainee taster himself – as one of them recalls:

> In 1951 I trained every morning at Plantation House with one or other of the senior tasters. I would start at 9.0 a.m. with one other trainee and the senior taster would appear in a white coat at about 9.45. In that 45 minutes I would lay out between 150 and 250 teas of many different types, but mostly from India and Ceylon. We would put the open tins containing the teas furthest back, then the small china pot with its lid, then the small china bowl. That done we would take a pair of small scales and place a weight equivalent to an old sixpence coin [about 3gm] on one side. Brooke Bond used a shilling [5.65gm]. Into the other scale we put a balancing amount of tea from each tin – depending on the size of leaf there would be a bigger or smaller heap. We put each heap of leaf into its corresponding pot.

Meanwhile the kettles, which have been filled with water, preferably fresh or distilled, both for uniformity and to avoid the taste-obscuring chlorine in mains water, are brought toward the boil, but no further. They should be of copper with tinplate sides and bottoms, as these are best for retaining the heat in the water, thus minimizing another possible variable. The "trainee" again:

> When everything was set up we would take an enormous wrist-breaking kettle, which had just come to the boil, and go down the line pouring quarter of a pint, as near as we could judge, into each pot to infuse the leaves – not forgetting to put the lid back on each pot. You would start a four-minute timer as you began – for some teas infusion time could be as much as six minutes. By the time you got to the end of the line the timer would ring and you would go back to where you started and go down the line again, tipping the liquor from each pot into its tasting bowl, but leaving the pot to drain. Then once more back to the head of the line to shake out the infused leaf – more or less drained by now – on to the inverted lid of its pot, which we put back, upside down, so that the leaf showed.

Now the tea taster can apply his art – and it is an art, not a science. Although some good progress has been made in Kenya and elsewhere in applying an "electronic nose" and analytical chemistry to the job of tasting, it cannot yet match the indefinable, neural cross-referencing between sight and smell, taste and touch, deployed by the experienced taster. There appears as yet to be no significant chemical difference between a good tea and a poor one, for, as Lu Yu says, "goodness is a decision for the mouth to make". Some tasters join the process earlier because they like to see the boiling water added so that they can observe "the agony of the leaves", that is the rate and way they uncurl. A tight curl will release the flavour slowly, a flat one more quickly, emphasizing strength rather than flavour.

Sight and touch are the first senses to be enlisted. The process of tasting begins with the taster shaking some dry leaf from each tin on to a plain white card in order to scrutinize the appearance of the leaf. Uniformity, or lack of it, between the leaves is also a good indicator of careful manufacture. If a tea of higher quality is required he will look for the quantity and distribution of the orange-coloured "tips". If this sounds easy, Lu Yu reminds the taster that it is not:

> Tea has a myriad shapes. If I may speak vulgarly and rashly, tea may shrink and crinkle like a Mongol's boots. Or it may look like the dewlap of a wild ox, some sharp, some curling as the eaves of a house. It can look like a mushroom in whirling flight just as clouds do when they float out from behind a mountain peak. Its leaves can swell and leap as if they were being lightly tossed on wind-disturbed water. Others will look like clay, soft and malleable, prepared for the hand of the potter and will be as clear and pure as if filtered through wood. Still others will twist and turn like the rivulets carved out by a violent rain in newly tilled fields. Those are the very finest of teas.

Next the taster picks up each small, damp pile of infused leaves on its lid – where their aroma is most easily discernible – and both sniffs them and visually examines them for signs of excessive, or insufficient, withering and fermentation. This done, the white-coated maestro gets to the nub of his task. Sight, smell and taste are now applied to the liquid tea.

First he studies the liquor carefully for its colour. If it is intended for blending, cold fresh milk will have been added. Milked Ceylon should be a golden brown, Assam a reddish-brown and Darjeeling a rather off-putting beige-grey – which is one reason I prefer my Darjeeling in a blend or without milk. For unmilked teas there are now also some other clues to quality. What is known as an "angel-ring" – a golden ring at the edge of a cup of hot, freshly poured tea – is one of these clues. Good black tea's tendency to "cream" or "cloud down" is another. Creaming takes place because, as black tea cools below 40°C, certain colloids separate out from the liquor, giving the tea an opaque appearance, rather as if a small quantity of cream had indeed been added.

Next the taster dips his spoon – probably silver for the taster and a baser metal for the mere assistant – into the tasting bowl, fills it, raises it toward his lips, just touching them, inhales deeply through his nose to sample the aroma of the liquor and then slurps, sucks in, the tea, rather than sipping it, to maximize the impact on his taste buds. The Chinese and Korean *gongfu* school of tea tasting, in whose ceremonies only one or two teas will be tasted, describes five stages in the actual tasting of a liquid tea: observe the colour; smell the fragrance; taste on the tongue; taste on the back of the throat; swallow and feel the aftertaste in the mouth. The professional tea taster, with dozens and dozens of teas to taste one after the other, cannot afford to indulge in the last of these practices, but more or less follows the others. He will let the hot liquid linger for a moment on his tongue, pass it up to his palate in the roof of his mouth, and slosh it round in the pouches of his cheeks, just like a wine taster. And now, again like a wine taster, to avoid blunting his taste buds, instead of swallowing he ejects the tea liquor in a fine stream into the wheeled spittoon at his side. In the larger tasting establishments there may even be a channel of running water beside the tasting table to serve this last stage more hygienically.

All this only takes a few seconds, for most tasters seem to think that undue prolonging of this stage blurs the original, instinctive analysis. The taster then makes his judgement and his valuation of each tea, in an arcane language, which I will not inflict on the reader, for a clerk to log, or enters it himself on his clipboard. To those in the know this entry will immediately convey all the various qualities of the tea in question, and, if it is for a blend, indicate with which other teas it might be married satisfactorily and within a pre-defined price bracket. The more advanced trainees – clutching their own personal tasting spoons – would be expected to tell the taster their individual verdicts before he declares his, and woe betide the tyro if his price is more than an old halfpenny a pound out.

Much work was done in the middle years of the twentieth century to try to standardize both terminology and tasting results, particularly at Tocklai, by extensive cross-referencing with tasters from all branches of the industry. Cynics have been known to observe that, where three tasters taste the same tea, three different assessments will result. However, in all but highly specialized instances regular cross-checks will largely eliminate a taster's personal preferences and any bias, and ensure that these are subsumed into a generally acceptable consensus. All this to ensure that what is drunk tastes as the drinker thinks it should taste.

But even with the most choice leaf in the world, if the drinker brews it incorrectly he will not get his perfect cup of tea. So once the favoured leaf is chosen the drinker's next task is to consider the water in which it will be made. In the "good old days", when tea could be bought only in leaf form, and usually from the local grocer, he and his customers would soon get to know which teas best suited the local water. Or the tea drinker could send a sample of the water from the domestic tap or spring for analysis to one of the quality tea specialists, such as Jacksons or Twinings, Fortnum and Mason or the Indian Tea Centre. They would advise him in some detail as to what teas or blends would give the best results with that particular water. Alas! – in the days of the mass market, the superstore and the tea bag, only broad, regional water variations are taken into account by the better wholesalers in supplying their customers. However, the discerning tea drinker, who sometimes wants to brew something special, can still discriminate by following certain broad guidelines about the water being used and experimenting within them to find the preferred leaf.

There are two general categories of water to consider, soft and hard. Rain water is naturally soft, but when it filters through chalk or limestone it becomes hard from the salts of calcium and magnesium it takes up. Sixty per cent of British water is hard. Hard water is of two types: permanently hard (non-alkaline) and temporarily hard (alkaline), which occur together in different proportions according to their geology. Calcium and magnesium carbonate are the main salts found in water which is temporarily hard. These will separate from the other elements in water when in solution, which is why, when boiled, they leave their "scale" in the kettle. The extent and rapidity of scaling is a good indicator of the proportion of this type of hardness in the water. The salts of permanent hardness are chlorates and sulphates and remain held in the water even when it is boiled. Teas from the Far East and Indonesia, the high-grown teas of Darjeeling, Ceylon and southern India, and the CTC teas of East Africa respond best in this kind of water. Soft water is found in areas of granite or other low-porosity rocks, and is usually drawn from fairly near the surface of the earth. It contains few mineral salts but may have a brownish colour from peat. For soft water, strong-liquoring teas from Java and Assam are best, though only experiment will determine exactly what best suits both the water and the individual palate. Tea made with soft water, or water that is almost entirely permanently hard, will have a bright tinge of red in it. Where the water is hard but the salts of calcium and magnesium carbonate predominate, the iron salts will give the tea a duller, yellower tone of the basic brown. If in doubt, brew Assam: the most versatile of teas, which will give you an acceptable cup, whatever the water, although it opens up its full strength best to soft water.

However carefully matched tea and water may be, the resulting cup will suffer if the tea is badly kept or the water brutalized. Lu Yu was so right when he wrote, most poetically: "When the water is boiling, it must look like fishes' eyes and give off but the hint of a sound. When at the edges it chatters like a bubbling spring and looks like pearls innumerable strung together, it has reached the second stage. When it leaps like breakers majestic and resounds like a swelling wave, it is at its peak. Any more and the water will be boiled out and should not be used." Excessive boiling deoxygenates water, and makes tea brewed with it flat and dull to the taste. Therefore, in making tea, do not boil the same water twice, but empty a kettle into a houseplant or the washing up and start again with fresh water. For the same reason, Lu Yu's suggested choice of water is misguided in part. He is quite right to assert that "tea made from mountain streams is best, river water is all right, but well-water tea is quite inferior" and properly adds, with due respect to the rules of hygiene: "If you must use river water, take only that which man has not been near; and if it is well-water, then draw a great deal before using it. If the evil genius of a stream makes the water bubble like a fresh spring, pour it out." However, he is on much less sure ground when he admonishes: "Never take tea made from water that falls in cascades, gushes from springs, rushes in a torrent or that eddies and surges as if nature were rinsing its mouth. Over-usage of all such water to make tea will lead to illnesses of the throat." In fact fast-flowing, tumbling water will be better oxygenated, and therefore make better tea, even than the "water from the slow-flowing streams, the stone-lined pools or milk-pure springs" that Lu Yu advocates. But good tea mostly depends on choosing a good leaf.

Crudely speaking, the less trouble taken to maintain the size and quality of the raw leaf during manufacture, the less the cost of processing. With the relentless onward march of the tea bag, and the cut-throat competition between supermarkets whose gullible customers' sole criterion for purchase is price, it is the teas at the bottom of the quality ladder that dominate the market in volume terms. Recognition of this fact, early in Kenya's relatively recent entry into tea production, led to the growing of leaf destined for the CTC machines that Crush, Tear and Curl whatever is fed into them. Ideal for tea bags, this tea makes a strong cup with dark colour, if little or no subtlety of flavour, and accounts for the fact that Kenya is now the world's largest exporter of tea.

However good the tea chosen, it will not remain good for long unless it is properly stored. In addition to the usual cool, dark, dry place preferred for storing most foodstuffs, tea also needs to be kept as nearly airtight as possible. When choosing a caddy it is as well to select one that has a heavy, close-fitting lid, and even a rubber seal similar to that on a Kilner jar. However well manufactured, tea leaves that are left exposed to the air for any length of time will resume, to some extent, the process of oxidization in their manufacture. Moreover, the essential oils responsible for flavour and aroma, being volatile, will evaporate if exposed to heat. It is said that an experienced taster can tell the difference between two cups of tea brewed from the same packet of leaves when the first was fresh and the second was made from leaves exposed to the air for 24 hours.

Black tea should, ideally, be drunk within a year of being plucked from the bush. Most manufacturers now try to extend its full flavour retention by packing it on the garden as soon as manufactured, or by using vacuum-sealed foil packs, or both. Once a packet of quality black tea has been opened, it is best drunk within two to three weeks. Green tea, while a little less prone to rapid deterioration, does quickly lose much of its valued vitamin C when exposed to air. This can be replaced by drinking it with lemon, though it seems pointless to obliterate the taste of the tea with such an acidic additive. A slice of the gentler citrus, an orange, is preferable. The merchants who sell leaf tea in quarter-pound packets are being neither commercially devious nor profligate with packaging, but are only trying to ensure that their tea is likely to be used up while it is at its best.

As a rule of thumb, the better the tea the shorter the shelf life. The first of the season's Darjeeling, for example, will probably keep six months from plucking; the coarser, end-of-season crop will keep for a year or more. While it is gratifying that many people are now abandoning the tea bag on at least some occasions during the day, it is as possible to go to the other extreme of nicety over tea as it is for a wine buff to become a bore in his pursuit of perfection. Germany brings in by air the first Chongton Darjeeling with the same kind of misplaced zeal with which the British pursue Beaujolais nouveau. But at least the Germans are getting a much more drinkable product. Silly prices – as much as £200 a kilogram – are still paid by some tea snobs for certain exclusive speciality teas, just as they were when it first came to England. But most tea drunk in Britain today is not from a single estate, or even a single region, but a blend.

Tea has been blended in Europe ever since the day it first arrived. We know that, as early as 1715, Twinings were offering customers at their coffee house in the Strand blends of bohea mixed with pekoe; congou with pekoe; congou with bohea; bloom green with imperial hyson. When Indian tea first came to England it was used to blend with China tea rather than drunk on its own. In the 1860s Mrs Beeton's famous book was recommending its readers to mix four parts of Indian to one of China. Not until toward the end of the century was it customary to drink Indian teas alone, or in purely Indian blends. There are currently the best part of two thousand different blends commercially available, of which Twinings still offer some 150. When tea was first offered in England for sale to the public in significant amounts, grocers would stock several teas and blend them to the requirements of their customers. However, the whims and changing fancies of his clientele often left the grocer with part of a chest, or maybe whole chests, of tea that had lost its flavour and was going musty, and this could not always be fobbed off on the poorer or less particular customers. By the end of the nineteenth century most of the larger tea merchants were blending in bulk for their grocers and other non-specialist retailers. This was more cost-effective and led to less waste and greater consistency of the blends within each delivery. As a consequence, there was less personality in the teas bought by most customers, though the blenders did try to adjust their blends to suit the characteristics of the region's water.

If the grocer now depended on the merchant, he in turn depended on his tasters and those of the brokers he dealt with to sustain the consistency of a particular branded blend over many shipments and many years. Some, like Typhoo yellow, sustained that consistency for more than half a century. If the broker failed to deliver the requisite balance of teas, the merchant might just blend whatever he had in stock and hope to get away with it. Packers and blenders were seldom also growers, lest they felt obliged to use inferior tea just because they had grown it.

The connoisseur usually blended tea for himself at home, and there are some exquisite examples of tea cabinets of the early eighteenth century with separate, tight-lidded compartments for the different teas and an inset glass mixing bowl for blending. Two or three different teas were usually accommodated, but some of the larger cabinets had partitions for as many as eight. Less ostentatious households might be content with two or three separate caddies. Many discerning tea drinkers still prefer to blend their own tea, but have to be mindful that certain teas do not blend together successfully. Great disparity in leaf size means the blend will not remain uniformly mixed for long, as the smaller particles sink through the larger. If a large and a small leaf tea are mixed – Darjeeling and Assam, for example – then it is necessary to agitate the mixture with a fork every three days or so to bring up the smaller leaves again from the bottom of the caddy. When infusing such a blended tea, of which the constituents may have different infusion times, it is as well to allow the brew to stand long enough to extract the full flavour from the slowest-releasing leaf in the convoy.

There are really only two basic ways of turning tea leaves into tea – though in parts of south-east Asia they do cook and eat them as if they were a kind of spinach. Tea can be brewed by decoction, or by infusion or steeping. The whisking of powdered tea is really only an accelerated form of infusion.

Decoction involves boiling up leaves and water together in the same vessel, the relative proportions and the boiling time governing the concentration of the tea essence thus produced. The weaker tea may sometimes be drunk straight away, particularly if the mixture also involves other ingredients, such as milk, herbs and spices, as found in the delicious Indian *masala cha*. More often it is anticipated that a strong essence will be diluted later with hot or boiling water.

The samovar, the self-boiler, is the quintessential utensil for this decoction approach, with its pot of concentrated tea at the top, its boiling vessel for the water and a tap in the middle and its own heat source – usually charcoal or a spirit lamp – coming up from below through a central pipe. Caravan tea from China was the preferred leaf source at a time when the advent of the samovar changed the social life of Imperial Russia. Even mealtimes were adjusted to accommodate its central role. So deeply a part of the Russian psyche has the samovar become that it is as much a national symbol as the bear itself. It has outlasted the rise and fall of regimes of every colour and complexion. Samovar tea even inspired the great Pushkin to write "ecstasy is a glass full of tea and a piece of sugar in the mouth". A favourite Russian way to drink tea was to suck it up from the glass – the most common tea-drinking vessel – through a lump of sugar. One explanation for the Russian preference for tea glasses is that the first china teacups had inside at the bottom a picture of the citadel at Kronstadt, where they were made, which could be seen if the tea were not strong, and therefore black, enough to obscure it. Dishonest vendors, who watered their tea and served it weak, switched to glasses on which no pictures could be painted.

Infusion involves placing tea leaves (or powdered leaves) in the serving vessel, which will not itself be directly heated, and pouring hot or boiling water on them. After the elapse of anything from one to 15 minutes, depending on the tea and the taste required, the resulting brew is poured into drinking receptacles and it is in these that additives such as milk and sugar are mixed. It is this process that is described at the head of this chapter.

The infusion of green tea in China and Japan took on a ritual intensity whose significance we shall examine in the next chapter, but its disciplines were equally aimed at producing as good a cup of tea as possible. One school of thought insisted that, after the boiling water was added to the leaves in a small china pot, the brew should be allowed to infuse only for as long as it took the maker to inhale and exhale slowly three times. The liquor was then poured into small, handle-less cups to warm them, before being returned to the pot for a second three-breath-cycle infusion. The tea was now ready to drink, its strength depending, I suppose, on the pulmonary capacity of its maker. If more tea was wanted the leaves would be discarded and the process repeated, though in more frugal households the same leaves might be used several times. Samuel Ball puts in nicely when observing the wealthier Chinese household of his day: "The wealthy Chinese simply infuse the leaves in an elegant porcelain cup, which has a cover of the same material; the leaves sink to the bottom of the cup, and generally remain there without inconvenience, though occasionally some may float or rise to the surface. To prevent this inconvenience, sometimes a thin piece of silver, of filigree or open work, is placed immediately on them. Where economy is necessary to be studied, the tea-pot is used."

In Japan the green leaves are often steamed, rather than dry-heated, in manufacture. This lends the tea a delicate flavour less sweet than China tea. Tea is also made in Japan from brick leaf reduced to a fine powder (*tencha*) by pestle and mortar, particularly for use in tea ceremonies. Depending on whether thin tea (*usucha*) or thick tea (*koicha*) is required, boiling water and tea powder are whipped up together in a bowl in appropriate proportions until the brew has a frothy head, when it is drunk down to and including the dregs.

Chinese green teas come in many varieties and there are many poetic names for them: sparrow's tongue, falcon talons, grey eyebrows. The most common way in which the Chinese ring the changes on basic tea is to scent the leaves with a wide range of aromas. The Ming emperors, who it seemed did not care for the traditional bitter taste that their predecessors had considered the mark of a good tea, developed scented teas across a great range of flower aromas. Each blend was made with the same one-to-three, flowers-to-tea ratio. Ideally tea-bush flowers would have been used, but since this was impractical – if tea was to develop for harvesting – jasmine and rose became the most common substitutes, as their natural fragrance is similar. Dates were another popular additive, providing both fragrance and sweetness. Good scented tea should balance fragrance with flavour but all too often scenting was used to disguise inferior quality. Suspicion that this might be the case prompted the wealthier Chinese to despise scented teas, particularly jasmine, as "servants' tea".

The most popular of these today is Earl Grey, a tea whose connection with the eponymous Prime Minister of the day (1830–34) is tenuous indeed. Grey himself had never been within many thousand miles of China and gifts would hardly have been exchanged at the highest level between two nations on the brink of the Opium Wars. A wide variety of scented teas was being shipped to England from Canton at that time, and genuine Earl Grey – that is, tea scented with oil extracted from the peel of *Citrus bergamia*, a tangerine-sized orange – would have been one of the most attractive. It was almost certainly a marketing ploy to make a gift to the popular premier and then associate his name in this way with the product. There were no scruples in those days about using the names of prominent people without their permission. The more popular the tea became the harder it became to sustain its quality by using oil of *Citrus bergamia*, which was expensive to extract. A variety of substitutes was soon in use, including an extract from the herb bergamot, with which the original is often confused. In much Earl Grey today the flavouring is chemical, though it is still possible to get Earl Grey as originally conceived.

The emperors and courtiers of the Manchu dynasty (1644–1911), even a century after coming to rule most of China, ignored even the best green tea, which they could so easily have used their great wealth to obtain, in favour of their traditional black tea. I suspect the reason for this was largely psychological. The most valued – and expensive – drink in Manchuria was ginseng, greatly coveted for its rejuvenating powers, as it still is today. In appearance, brewed ginseng looks very like conventional, strong black tea, though its taste and smell were very different, and European travellers often confused the two. While the Chinese wanted their tea to resemble as closely as possible the green jade they esteemed so highly, the Manchu wanted theirs to look like ginseng – black gold – for the same reason. This black tea they drank with milk: a practice which would come eventually to dominate the tea-drinking habits of the British Empire, especially India, and continental Europe. In France, during its brief flirtation with tea drinking, the fashion of adding milk was mistakenly known as *thé à la chinoise*. The Manchu emperor Qianlong (1736–95), though an art collector and calligrapher of refined taste, had his tea "infused with as much milk as water" and thus proved the blameless progenitor of the gruesome Indian practice of boiling up together in the same pot of water leaves and very sweet condensed milk. Fairly sickening to the European palate though it is, I can vouch for the fact that this mixture is highly restorative and invigorating.

In 1904 James Hutchison published a report on a visit he made on behalf of the Indian Tea Association to study the cultivation of Formosa's oolong tea. He seems to have carried out his observations in a state of paranoid scepticism. His nerves were constantly set on edge by reports that the northern tip of the island, in the lowlands of which oolong was grown, was beset by head-hunters. His scepticism was provoked by the claim that the best oolong, *pe-mun-kaw* (white-haired monkey), was literally harvested by monkeys. These were supposedly goaded into hurling down branches from tea bushes clinging to places inaccessible to man, and for this were rewarded with opium. It is just possible that this claim was not quite so outrageous as Hutchison believed. My original inclination to pooh-pooh the idea was recently somewhat modified by a report from the Congo alleging that the large native rat has been trained to detect landmines by a very similar process of conditioning with food and drugs – albeit one with rather more drastic consequences of failure for the animal. But alas! – the whole "monkey-plucked" tradition was probably just a clever nineteenth-century Chinese marketing ploy.

Poor Mr Hutchison had no sooner returned, with his head still in place, from these nerve-racking experiences in Formosa than the

ITA landed him with the job of trying to persuade the Tibetans to import and drink Indian tea rather than their customary Chinese supplies. The Tibetans, copious drinkers of tea, were potentially a lucrative market, but the difficulties were well-nigh insurmountable, and Tibetan taste in tea matters proved most particular. In his report of 1906 Hutchison gives a graphic account of how the Chinese catered for that taste:

A liquid paste made from grinding softened glutinous rice (*Oryza glutinosa*) is then boiled up into a dark brown sticky mass which is mixed with the poor quality leaves to make them stick together. For better quality tea steaming alone is sufficient to give them adhesion with the addition of a little pig fat to prevent foaming. ... The mixture is then rammed into a wooden frame or hollow bamboo with a 17lb rammer and left for three days for the bricks to set before being opened and re-packed. A seven-man team can produce some 400lb of tea a day by this method. The bricks are then stamped with the Hong mark plus an emblem such as a Buddha or a dragon, and Tibetan writing. The bricks are then bound with string and re-packed. This is the most common way of making brick tea.

The bricks are then re-crumbled, placed in cold water and boiled with a little soda from the shores of Tibet's lakes, which gives the liquor a red tinge. The liquor is then strained slowly through a sieve of horsehair or brass (or these days, steel or plastic) into the *cha dong*, a long wooden cylinder closed at one end. Into this are then mixed *tsampa* (parched barley flour), salt and ghee (clarified, and usually rancid, butter). The mixture is then churned vigorously to make a rather oleaginous tea soup. The churning of the *cha dong* may well be accompanied by the Tibetan tea song:

From the Chinese country comes the tea flower beautiful.
From the northern plain comes the small white salt.
From the Tibetan country comes the yak butter like gold.
The birthplace and dwelling place are not the same –
But they all meet together in the little belted churn.

On the Assam border with Tibet a variant occurs before the solids are added. This method involves heating simultaneously two brass pots of water and an empty earthenware pot over the fire. The tea brick is then crumbled and sifted into the latter. Into this about a third of a litre of cold water is poured through a sieve full of ashes to make potash water. The brew is then boiled until it has evaporated. A small spoonful of hot water is then added and allowed to evaporate in the same way, the leaves being continuously stirred the while to prevent them sticking or burning. This is repeated two or three times. Hot water from the second pot and a little salt are then added and the liquid is brought to the boil before being added to the *cha dong*. For a European, Tibetan tea takes a fair amount of determined getting used to, but it is a very sustaining and warming drink, and a crucial part of survival at the high altitudes and low temperatures of Tibet.

Hutchison's endeavours to sell Indian tea to the Tibetans were fruitless. The Chinese held on to their market, as they have since held on to Tibet itself, by a combination of military threat and well-placed propaganda. Whether from practical experience or brainwashing, the Tibetans were convinced that Indian tea was not only disgusting but also actually poisonous, and would have none of it.

No less disgusting to the true tea lover is the accidental invention of the American tea merchant Thomas Sullivan, who must have been one of the very few men to make a sow's ear out of a silk purse. The well-known tale of how he economized by sending out his samples in small silk bags instead of in tins, only for his customers to put them unopened into their teapots, makes an amusing, if no doubt embroidered, account of the birth of the tea bag in 1908. Its subsequent proliferation to command the largest slice of the Western tea market may be less amusing to the tea connoisseur, but has been one of the great commercial successes of the throw-away, convenience century. No mess, no time-wasting, no teapot – and often no flavour, for the tea bag is the natural home of the finely cut leaves and dust that make strong liquor but are usually light on flavour: a case of the kick without the horse. In America today the proffered cup of tea will almost certainly have been made with leaves and water together in a mug and "nuked" for a few seconds in the microwave. The Japanese have compromised by selling empty, self-seal tea bags, into which the drinker puts the leaves of his choice.

The tea bag was much slower to catch on in conservative Britain. Tetley was the first to try in 1935 in America, but tea bags did not become popular in Britain until the 1950s. Founded in 1837 by two Yorkshire pedlars, who had done well out of hawking tea, Joseph Tetley & Co. moved to London as wholesalers in 1856 and into America in 1888. Later the firm was bought by Lyons, itself taken over in 2000 by the Indian Tata group's tea operation. The round tea bag with two thousand holes appeared in 1992, though Tetley's rival Typhoo claimed you could get more holes – and hence better infusion – in a square. I have never counted them! Environmentally conscious firms, such as Twinings and Clipper, have gone in for biodegradable bags with no whitening chemicals, which accounts for their slightly grubby look. Nevertheless, commercially speaking, the tea bag has been the saving of the international tea industry in its competition with the wide range of convenience, ready-to-hand, alternative drinks now available. Tea bags have also helped to make the china mug a more socially acceptable vessel for tea drinking.

Instant tea has been another, but much less successful, attempt to compete in this market. The powdered green tea in use in China, probably as early as the seventh century AD, could claim to be the original instant tea. An Englishman, J.W. Brown, used concentrated tea liquor, sugar and evaporated milk to create an instant paste in 1895, but it did not catch on. It was the appearance of Nescafé in 1938 that triggered the race in the 1940s and 1950s to find a tea equivalent, as Nescafé's convenience threatened the market. In the end all instant teas are variations on brewing, concentrating and drying by one means or another – and pretty unpalatable to my mind they are. They are mainly used in various concoctions: principally the iced tea and canned-tea drinks popular in the United States. Canned tea, particularly oolong, became another fashion fad in the late 1990s on the grounds of its supposed slimming and health-giving properties, and its portability as a street accessory. The Far East and inevitably the United States are the main markets.

The appeal of instant tea is its novelty, speed and convenience – particularly the absence of residual mess – all important factors in sustaining tea in the marketplace where the flibbertigibbet inconstancy of the over-affluent young plays such a crucial role in determining sales volume. Instant tea has less than 4 per cent of the British market and its proportion is mercifully declining, though it still has a role to play in the nigh-undrinkable outpouring of many vending machines. Sadly, the tea lady and the tea trolley have vanished from almost every workplace in favour of the vending machine (of which Japan has over two million).

Stopwatch-happy time-and-motion experts had worked out that, by the time the workers had walked to the trolley or canteen, queued, drunk their tea and walked back to their posts, a good 15 minutes of production time had been lost. Nor was taking the tea trolley to the worker deemed any more efficient. In one medium-sized office the bean-counters calculated that by the time the tea lady had been paid for making, moving, serving and clearing up, each cup served was more expensive than in the best restaurant. When the biometricians threw in their twopenn'orth to argue that tea breaks did not appear to raise blood-sugar levels, and therefore energy and concentration, the tea lady was doomed and the vending machine installed on every corridor and corner. This stratagem was disguised as giving workers more choice as to what, when and how often to drink, but entirely overlooked the psychological boost given by social interchange (otherwise known as gossip) round the trolley, and the jungle-drum value of the peripatetic tea lady. Moreover, where the tea from the trolley had almost always been free, workers resented the fact that they now usually had to pay for a less than agreeable cuppa, though the quality has improved in recent years. My sympathies are with the vending-machine bandit who, when drawing a cup of tea, discovered that he could also get a free cup of coffee by switching the indicator over from tea to coffee just before the stream of water for tea finished. Sadly that and other machine-defeating trickeries have been foiled by ever more complex electronic circuitry. Yet, happily, there is still a massive underground of smuggled tea and kettles in the corner of most offices.

North America is also the main consumer of iced tea, though

cold tea in an old cider bottle was certainly the favoured refreshment during haymaking on many British farms until recently. It is
an Englishman, Richard Blechynden, who must take responsibility
for devising iced tea. Compassion for the perspiring visitors to the
Indian Tea Pavilion at the World's Fair in St Louis in 1904
prompted him to brew tea overnight for serving cold with ice
during the next day. The stand was well patronized as more and
more thirsty Americans discovered what a refreshing drink cold tea
made from good leaves could be. The process has been taken to its
logical conclusion by Botanica, an American firm that produces a
frozen mixture of tea, fruit juice, herbs and soy for later reconstitu-
tion into a cold drink.

North Africans drink mint tea only by a fortunate misfortune. In
1854 British ships with cargoes of Chinese green tea (Indian was
still in its infancy) bound for Scandinavia and the Baltic states were
refused permission to dock and unload. Somewhat aimlessly, it
would seem, they found themselves back in the Mediterranean.
Why did they not try to unload in London, I wonder? Putting in at
the ports of Morocco, to their pleasant surprise they were able to
sell their entire shipment to various enterprising local merchants. It
happens that mint, a native herb along the Mediterranean littoral,
was already used as an infusion and by a happy chance the combination of the two leaves created the delectable drink so well known
to tourists to North Africa.

To make a superior mint tea, the best Chinese green leaf should
be placed in a brass or china pot and immersed for a few seconds
only before the water is drained off. Fresh, good-quality mint leaves
(*Mentha viridis*) should then be layered over the moist China leaf in
the pot and a very small quantity of sugar added. The tea maker's
acting and gymnastic powers are now called into play in order to
produce the *keshkusha*, the characteristic froth on top of the tea,
which is to mint tea what a good head is to the best cappuccino.
The froth is produced by raising the pot high above the tea maker's
head and pouring it vigorously into a second receptacle placed at
waist level. The rising and falling pot, and the stream of opalescent
liquid that ties it to the stationary one, resemble a youngster playing
with a yo-yo. Once the upper pot is empty, the roles of the two

receptacles are reversed, and the cycle is repeated until sufficient *keshkusha* has been achieved to satisfy the maker's artistic sensibilities. In this way, even tea that has lain dormant for a while is reoxygenated and a palatable drink still results. It is through the froth that the tea should be drawn up to the lips by sucking, not sipping: literally a lip-smacking gesture of appreciation. A guest – even a patron of a tea or coffee shop – is expected to drink three cups and while the first may be a little bitter, the next two will be progressively sweeter and mintier as more sugar is added and the tea concentrates. The number three seems to have ritual significance among tea drinkers, for Lu Yu also recommends limiting oneself to three cups "unless you are quite thirsty", and that you should sip, not gulp, for tea "is the very essence of moderation and helps to still the six passions".

Today the countries of the Maghreb and Sahel drink more green tea than anywhere else in the world except China.

However, before getting bogged down in the minutiae of tea making, it is as well to recall the words of the sixteenth-century tea master Sen no Rikyu: "Tea is nothing other than this: heat the water, prepare the tea and drink it with propriety. That is all you need to know."

CHAPTER THIRTEEN

The Buddha's Eyelashes

The first retrospective claim for the discovery of tea making comes on behalf of a Chinaman named Shen Nong, the so-called "Divine Farmer", who is reputed to have tried decoctions and infusions of more than three thousand plants in the third millennium BC – many at his peril – and in this way also discovered tea. Another version claims that the leaves fell accidentally into his pot of boiling water; and yet another holds that it was the aroma of a burning tea bush – presumably one he was using for fuel – that alerted him to the possibility of tea. Whether Shen Nong actually existed is a matter of debate. Perhaps he is only the conflation of a number of early herbalists, as Robin Hood is of a number of English outlaws.

Many of the myths about tea are connected with the early days of Buddhism and involve the accidental discovery of, or self-sacrifice for, a means of ensuring wakefulness during meditation. Reputedly Bodhidharma, the founder of Zen, on failing to stay awake through a self-imposed vigil, grew so angry that he cut off his eyelids, threw them into a cauldron of boiling water and drank the resulting infusion only to find it an effective and stimulating anti-somnific. (Surely anger, even with himself, seems an unlikely emotion for Buddha?) Another, more benignly, relates that, as Prince Siddhartha – as a Buddha more properly, Sakyamuni – was nodding off during a similar vigil, some of his eyelashes fell into the cauldron with similar results. Yet another version is that, just when weariness overcame him, green leaves sprang spontaneously from a (tea) bush and by chewing on the leaves he kept awake. (The author's experiments with chewing newly plucked leaves revealed no such anti-somnific effect.)

The common theme of all these legends is wakefulness: the very word "Buddha" derives from the Sanskrit for "awaken". Being awake in the broadest philosophical sense is inevitably connected with the desirability of being, and thus of staying, awake in the physical sense. Tea, being the best and most harmless means of sustaining wakefulness, thus became linked with the Buddhist practice of meditation. It is in connection with Buddhist temples in China and the duty of their monks to be vigilant that we find the earliest records of the actual cultivation and imbibing of tea.

The subject matter of the first unequivocal and detailed record of such practices, Lu Yu's book *Cha Ching* (*The Classic of Tea*), was broadly grouped into four categories: the history, much of it mythological; cultivation and manufacture; methodology and necessary utensils for brewing tea; and the spiritual and medical benefits. It is arguable that the juxtaposition of these elements under the aegis of such a revered figure in tea hagiology was partly responsible for the ritual and mental rigidity that would become later a characteristic of Chinese, and more particularly Japanese, society from the seventeenth century onwards.

Lu Yu's contemporary the Taoist poet Lu Tong (d. 835), having drunk seven cups of tea (a porcelain handle-less cup held only about 2.5 fluid ounces) which progressively stimulated his physical, mental and spiritual sense of well-being, then composed the often-quoted "Tea Song" or, in full, "Thanks to the Imperial Censor Meng for his Gift of Freshly Picked Tea". For the Taoists, tea symbolized the abstract essence of being. "Teaism was Taoism" in disguise. But in one line of the 'Tea Song' we can also find the worm in the apple: "My bramble gate closed tight against vulgar visitors." When ritual tea drinking spread to Japan in the twelfth century this attitude would lead eventually to an elitist exclusivity that reinforced the country's social divisions and suspicion of foreigners.

Chinese Buddhists, on the other hand, saw tea differently. During the Northern and Southern Sung dynasties (960–1279), temple monks regularly offered tea to the Buddha as an element of their religious and meditational practice. The idea developed, in keeping with the Buddhist notion of the universality of all things, that tea embodied that essence of being and so could not be separated from it. In other words, providing your guest with a well-made, elegantly presented cup of tea was no more nor less important than attaining enlightenment. One could not be distinguished from the other.

It was around the time Lu Yu was writing that tea first found its way from China to Japan, significantly in the hands of Buddhist monks. Some scholars put this as early as the sixth century AD, others the eighth. In 815 the Emperor Saga is recorded as drinking tea at his court, but after his death the habit seems to have retreated to a few obscure Buddhist temples. Not until the twelfth century does the transfer really take root, with the return to Japan in 1187 of the monk Eisai (1141–1215) from his travels in China with tea seeds, which he grew at his temple in Kyushu.

Eisai, who founded the Rinzai sect of Buddhism, in his book *A Record of Drinking Tea for Good Health* gave advice on its medical uses "not as a stimulant during meditation, but as an esoteric ritual conducive to the harmonious functioning of the bodily organs". Eisai was a practical man, who recognized the importance of giving the spiritual a little material impetus when the opportunity offered. A distinguished shogun, Minamoto Sanetomo, so overindulged at the dinner table that he thought he was about to die and begged Eisai to pray for his recovery. Eisai had the sense to back his prayers with several draughts of the tea grown at his temple. So grateful was the shogun to be relieved of his suffering that he became a highly effective proselytizer both for tea and for Eisai's book. As a result tea gained widespread popularity among Japan's upper classes.

Another shogun, Ashikaga-Yoshimasa, in 1477 even employed a professional priestly tea master, Shuko, to oversee the correct serving of tea at his palace. Out of the rituals that Shuko developed, there came his prescriptive *Rules for the Tea Ceremony*. It was this text that inspired the greatest of the tea masters, Sen no Rikyu (1521–91), who lived in one of the more turbulent periods of Japanese history. Japan at this time was not only undergoing a contentious period of national unification but had to come to terms with the impact of the first foreigners to sail into its ports looking for trade and, worse, for converts to their religion. From this turbulence Rikyu sought refuge in *Chanoyu* (literally, hot water for tea), or rather in its rituals of *Chado* (the way of tea). These involved everything from games, in which the participants tried to identify different teas – much as *les chevaliers du taste vin* still do today with wines – to the display of aesthetically pleasing and valuable paintings and ceramics to the accompaniment of arcane music. At its best this combination of faith and art led to creations of exquisite beauty, which perhaps have their closest European parallel in the religiously inspired painting, sculpture and music of the Renaissance and in England the poetry of Donne, Herbert and Vaughan. At their worst they led to sterile snobbery. More than three hundred years after Rikyu's death the novelist Natsume Soseki has one of his characters say: "Those who take part in the tea-ceremony are really only tradesmen, merchants and the like who have not the first idea of what the words 'artistic taste' mean."

In reaction to the over-elaboration of *Chado* in his day, Rikyu devised his own simplified Reformation version, *Wabicha*. He protested against a pretentious and extravagant practice which, instead of leading to serenity and purity, only bred worry and care. *Wabicha* emphasized the need for a kind of rustic simplicity. Paradoxically, this did not prevent Rikyu becoming involved in helping the military dictator Hideyoshi stage one of the most spectacular tea parties ever, in 1587. Almost a thousand guests were treated to a display of Hideyoshi's most treasured and valuable artistic possessions and were expected to bring one of their own as a gift. Among the wilder extravagances was a portable tea house the walls of which were lined with gold leaf, with gold utensils to match.

Rikyu does seem to have been something of a hypocrite, enjoying the good life while exhorting others to simplicity, and the Emperor eventually gave him an unrefusable invitation to kill himself. After composing a poem and smashing his favourite tea bowl, he duly did so. "There are many ways," he said, "to put into practice in our own lives the teachings of the great masters of the past; in Zen, truth is pursued through the discipline of meditation in order to realize enlightenment, while in Tea we use training in the actual procedures of making tea to achieve the same end."

Unfortunately, this latter emphasis led eventually to the triumph of ritual over spirituality.

In setting out the steps for making tea in such minute detail, Chinese monks had begun the process that turned the pragmatic "how to" manual into the "must do" of a religious rubric. By the seventeenth century, during the Ming dynasty in China, the distinction in Japan between a cultured, intellectual elite who had mastered these prescriptions and "tradesmen, merchants, and the like" became ever more marked: the *ya* (elegance) of the elite contrasting with the *su* (vulgarity) of a bourgeoisie that aped their practices. The literati patronizingly condescended to the nouveau riche by allowing that the vulgar objects they so promiscuously acquired could, in the skilled hands of the initiate, be arranged to become *ya*.

In any set of beliefs that becomes increasingly precious and prescriptive, schism is inevitable. Narrower and narrower differences of detail lead to ever more bitter disputes as to who has the "true way". So it was with *Chanoyu* and *Senchado* (the way of steeped tea) after Rinzai brought back the rules of the former to Japan with his packets of tea seeds. This dichotomy accounts in part for the ambivalent attitude of Japan to China. Until the nineteenth century Chinese culture and aesthetic values represented the highest levels of sophistication for the Japanese intelligentsia. *Chanoyu* was an essential part of that sinofication. The Japanese elite of priests, samurai and aristocrats was expected to be able to read and write Chinese and to possess Chinese artefacts. This marked them out as different from the common people, who had neither the time nor the wealth to indulge in such esoteric pursuits. In parallel there was a growing resentment that something so central to Japanese spiritual life and social hierarchy was of foreign origin. Japanese resentment at Chinese cultural hegemony would culminate in the First Sino-Japanese War of 1894–5.

Although by the end of the sixteenth century educated Japanese were familiar with the tenets of Confucianism (and Taoism), they soon rejected its concept that authority should be based on morally superior behaviour and not on might and birth. This rejection coincided with three centuries of Japanese isolationism that began with the expulsion of all Westerners from the mainland and, revealingly, the labelling of all foreigners whencesoever they came as *Tojin*, people of China. A shrewd observer of Japanese customs, the Portuguese Jesuit Joao Rodrigues, noted early in the seventeenth century that the Chinese themselves "do not observe any particular ceremony, nor do they set aside a special place for the pastime. They boil the leaves in the water. In fact this way is also practised in Japan by peasants and lowly people."

It was the greater availability of home-grown leaf tea from the early eighteenth century onwards that made the alternative of brewing *sencha* and the practice of *Senchado* not only popular but briefly paramount among the poorer classes in Japan. Yet even *sencha* contained within itself the chemistry of petrifaction. When in 1774 Daiten translated Lu Yu's work into Japanese as the *Detailed Explanation of the Classic of Tea*, what had been intended only as a useful guide to tea preparation soon became yet another sacrosanct text, ignorance or contradiction of which instantly marked you out as not of the elite. Phrases such as "One could behold the nature of a person's heart from the things they possess" and "Looking on things that are vulgar and not elegant is annoying" inevitably added to the sense of superiority of the cognoscenti. For the next two hundred years that elite made every effort to maintain its position by emphasizing its *ya* as opposed to the *su* of the common man.

In about 1800 the celebrated Japanese intellectual and feudal lord Sessai (1754–1819) insisted that if you were not floating downriver in a boat composing poetry, and indulging in painting, calligraphy and purist music, then at least your tea-room table must be equipped with brush, paper, inkstone, ink, musical instruments, at least one painting, carefully arranged flowers and a figurine of such a *Senchado* saint as Baisao (who would have turned in his grave at such distortion of his simple teaching). More than a century later Okakura Kakuzo claimed in *The Book of Tea* (1906): "Tea provides a situation, a quiet and peaceful environment for a man to meditate. Teaism is the discipline of the mind, body, heart and spirit. It is a cult founded on the adoration of the beautiful among the sordid facts of everyday existence."

Despite the ultimate prevalence of *Chanoyu* there was, nevertheless, a continuing counterpoint to this elitist snobbery and the proponents of simplicity did not give up without a fight. *A Miscellaneous Record of the Old Man of the Pines* epitomizes both the artistry and, even in *Senchado*, the incipient exclusiveness of Japanese tea poetry:

> *Sitting by my gate I await* famous *visitors* [emphasis added].
> *Then I sip the cup to bring forth poems and literary grace.*
> *My activity incites the competition of heavenly deities who*
> *Send down heavenly flowers [snow].*

The author of these lines, Ingen, was an influential Chinese monk who went to Japan in the middle of the seventeenth century. He was followed by his even more gifted Japanese disciple, Gettan Docho, who took up the cause of the reformist *Senchado* in its struggle with *Chanoyu*, arguing that only Obaku monks and recluses (there is a strong hermitic element in both codes) stick to the ideals of *Senchado* in preferring fine-tasting leaf tea brewed simply in a kettle at home. The drinking of tea for pleasure, as well as for enlightenment, was a characteristic in the mid-seventeenth century of the Obaku monks, of whom another tea master, Kyorei Ryokaku, observed that they drank *sencha* and eat cakes at "odd hours" between meals and in the evening, and as a result were fatter than monks at other temples.

Ingen – whose personal teapot, respectfully preserved in the collection of the temple Manpukuji, which he founded in Uji as his Obaku Zen sect headquarters, is virtually identical in shape and colour to the "Brown Betty" of working-class Britain of the nineteenth century – also wrote this early pastoral account of tea cultivation:

> *The fertile land stretches up to my home.*
> *Field after field of tea creates broad green spaces.*
> *The locals trade it to make a living and care for the tea plants*
>   *as if they are precious jade.*
> *They cultivate them and trim them diligently, and fear the possi-*
>   *bility of frost coming at night.*
> [...]
> *Spring thunder awakens the insects and the tea shoots emerge.*

Crowds gather, picking tea to the beating of drums.
The tender leaves fill the baskets and are selected, roasted, and
  prepared with great care.
The first cup is offered to the shogun.
Who can resist the famous teas, "Sparrow's Tongue" and
  "Dragon's Body"?
The teas "Falling Mortar" and "Jade Dust" appear light gold.
The fire roars in the brazier signalling that springtime is filling
  the room
In the iron kettle, the water boils into bubbles shaped like duck
  eyes.
[...]
Yet rural recluses also appreciate tea.
These humble men do not approve of attending expensive tea
  gatherings;
They prefer simplicity and dwell in mountain huts.
[...]
Tea is brewed strong and drunk to moisten the bowels.
After three cups his spirits are elevated,
And he leans on the windowsill to listen to the reed flute.

Although these early Japanese Zen monks "appreciated tea" to "elevate their spirits", *Chanoyu* was becoming an ever more prescriptive ritual in the hands of wealthy Samurai and others who were more interested in *Chado* as a means of displaying their treasures than as a path to spiritual enlightenment. It was in reaction to this excessive ritualization that, around 1735, Baisao, a non-practising priest then already aged 60, took to peddling *sencha* in and around Kyoto. This he did, he said, to atone for his inability to attain the spiritual heights of Buddha, Confucius and Lao Tse. An eclectic, he subscribed to none of these philosophies alone but drew on all in his efforts to return those he met over the next 20 itinerant years to the original simplicity of *Senchado* and the pleasures of *sencha*, which he would advocate in such equally simple poems as:

Setting up Shop at the Rengeoin
This place of mine, so poor

I'm often even out of water;
But I offer you an elixir
To change your very marrow [emphasis added].
You'll find me in the pines,
By the Hall of a Thousand Buddhas,
Come take a drink – who knows?
You may reach Sagehood yourself.

From the accounts of his friends, disciples and portraitists a picture emerges of Baisao as a formidable but endearing personality. Imagine a stooped old man wearing the traditional Taoist "Crane" robe of white trimmed with black (the colours of the Japanese crane): "He has white hair and a beard and is a bright faced person of extremely calm temperament. The clothes on his body are modest and dishevelled. From his tendency to drink too much *sake*, at one glance, you can discern his character."

He stands beside his portable tea stall, *Tsusentei* (The Pavilion along the Pathway to the Immortals), and lowers a bamboo basket to the ground. He calls it *Senka* (Den of the Sages) and it contains his simple wooden utensils for making and drinking leaf tea. On the other side of the stall he sets down a bamboo tube and plants a banner which bears the characters *Sei-fu*, "pure elegance". He asks his customers to drop whatever they can afford, even if it is only a single *sen* (the widow's mite), into the bamboo tube, for he puts no fixed price on his tea, which is spiritually priceless. Equipment unloaded at some scenic spot, "he would set up his brazier, then ladle the pure stream water into the teapot with his gourd dipper, and before long the steam from the simmering tea would begin to rise curling and billowing into the skies. As he fanned the fire in the brazier, a wonderful aroma filled the air. Those who came to partake of his tea marvelled at its exquisite sweetness."

When Baisao died, cocking a last snook at *Chanoyu*'s veneration of the utensils of ancient tea masters, he burned all his wooden pedlar's equipment to prevent this happening in his case. With the ambivalence that runs through *Senchado* and *Chanoyu* alike, as it does through all religions, he left a few of the more choice and valuable items of his domestic tea service as legacies for his friends.

During his lifetime Baisao published *A Collection of Documents from the Plum Mountain* (1748), the first formal polemic deriding *Chanoyu* and exalting *Senchado*. It took its title from the place where MyOe, Eisai's friend and fellow priest, had first cultivated the leaf tea used in *sencha*. This work contrasted the essential spirituality of *Senchado* with the cognitive materialism of *Chado*, whose priests and practitioners merely imitated the ceremonies of the ancients, without their spiritual content, in order to set themselves apart from the general run of society, and who were as far from the ethos of the great philosophers as "heaven was from earth". Baisao's influence continued long after his death, at the age of 88 in 1763, with the coincident publication of his *Verses of the Old Tea Pedlar*. Soon after his death the *Senchado* that Baisao promoted was turned into a formal tea ceremony and remained popular until the mid-nineteenth century. When Japan later wanted to distance itself from China, *Chanoyu* was promoted as a more purely Japanese tea ritual and the ceremonial popularity of *sencha* steadily declined. Paradoxically, *sencha*'s appeal as a drink among the ordinary people of Japan increased, as it did among the people of China.

In both China and Japan quasi-religious rituals filtered down into the social practices of the upper classes. The Japanese are more closely associated with the tea ceremony than anyone, though many other nations have their own tea ceremonies. In Japan, at the most refined level, the ceremony is a culinary, classical ballet, in which traditional gestures convey thoughts and feelings generally recognized by the aficionado, and in which minutely differentiated variations in execution demonstrate the creative artistry and aesthetic interpretation of choreographer and dancers. There is a succinct description in Patricia Graham's book *Tea of the Sages* of such a ceremony, one that has remained largely unchanged from its early beginnings to this day:

After all were settled, the person who actually prepared the tea arrived with essential utensils in hand, and the ceremony began. Bowls with sweets were passed around as the tea was being prepared, coals in the clay brazier were stoked, and the kettle was filled and heated. The tea caddy was ceremoniously wiped with a silken cloth, and a measured quantity of tea leaves was placed in a teapot that was then filled with hot water from the kettle. As the tea was steeping, a tiny set of five matching porcelain cups and saucers, plus one plainer cup (from which the server later drank her serving of tea), was ritually washed and set out. Finally the tea was poured and served to the five most distinguished guests. Attendants appeared from the adjoining rooms with cups for the rest of us. A second round of tea followed; this time a small side-handled teapot (*kyusu*) was passed around and we filled our own cups. During these preparations, we chatted with the host, sometimes jokingly, as we admired the tea utensils, the painting in the tokonoma [a small alcove a few inches above the floor], and the flower arrangement. All too soon the cups were cleared away and cleaned by the server as we watched. She then prepared for the next visitors.

In the ordinary Japanese household the formality of the ceremony is less important than the warmth of the hospitality and the mutual enjoyment of the art or music with which it is often accompanied. The tea ceremony in Japan also provides an occasion to develop business and political contacts and influence, and is still much used for this purpose. How well a visitor "plays away from home", where he is surrounded by carefully presented evidence of his host's wealth and culture, in what is essentially a ritual game of one-upmanship, can significantly affect his future. Not so long ago and in very much the same way, the dinner-table manners and conversation of the British would-be diplomat or military officer could determine his chances of being recruited.

In China itself, the etiquette prescribed during the Song dynasty (960–1279) for paying a visit only by appointment to dignitaries and other important persons gave way under the Ming to a more informal "drop-in" culture. The visitor would hand the gateman his large, red visiting card, probably with a tip (tea money) discreetly tucked into the same hand, and be admitted. (Russian slang for a tip is still "*goryachi na chai*", "hot for tea", and in Britain beggars still ask passers-by to spare a few coins "for a cup of tea".) If the host were too ill or too busy to receive, it would be incumbent on him to invite his visitor to return at some specific date and time. Whether the meeting took place *ad hoc* or by appointment, tea must at once be given to the visitor, whatever his status or the purpose of his visit. Not to be offered tea was a grave snub and would provoke the indignant report on the supplicant's return home: "He didn't even offer me a cup of tea." This complaint can be heard to this day in the Anglo-Saxon world.

Such rebuffs were rare in China, but the number of times tea was poured for the guest was also an indicator of the degree of warmth and welcome with which he was being received – or the importance of the visitor to his host. Inferiors would boast to their friends that an important mandarin had served them with a second cup, or even a third, the usual maximum. (The Briton's "nice cup of tea" offered for comfort, condolence or commiseration is the progeny of the Chinese "tasty tea" or "fragrant tea", poured as a mark of respect or congratulation on these occasions.) Normally an interview between inferior and superior would last for the time it took to drink a single cup of tea: 10 minutes at most. During this time the visitor was expected to state his business and get his answer. If no second cup was offered it was the tacit sign that it was time for him to leave. In the early Qing dynasty (1644–1911), if the host touched his *zhong* to his lips a second time without drinking it also meant it was time for the guest to go. (Chinese tea-ware had reached its apogee in the Ming dynasty [1368–1644] with the creation of the *zhong*, a porcelain cup with a slightly flared lip, a lid and a separate, matching saucer.)

These rituals applied mostly to official rather than domestic visits, and were much speeded up when the Ming did away with the "farewell cup".

More informal tea drinking took place in numerous tea houses throughout China, where soothsayers did a brisk trade telling fortunes from the leaves in a person's *zhong*. If we are tempted to scoff at the credulity of these tea patrons we would do well to observe that the ancient practice of tasseography – foretelling the future from the pattern of tea leaves in an empty cup – still has a considerable following today, as it did in Alexander Pope's time: "*Matrons, who toss the cup, and see / The grounds of fate in grounds of tea.*"

Woe unto tasseographers in this day of the tea bag and the leaf-less teacup! Like any other pseudo-psychic form of fortune telling, tasseography is a combination of psychology and chicanery, and anyone who believes in such a farrago of nonsense is in no position to mock the ancients.

The satrapies of China in the eighteenth century also had their rituals. Recording what he saw during an embassy to Peking in 1729, during which he went into Mongol country, the Russian diplomat Timkowski was most impressed, not only by the games he had been invited to watch but by the prize-giving ceremony that ended them. This took place "in a richly decorated tent", full of idols and incense and with the Mongol chief enthroned. "Brick tea in silver cups was brought in, and presented to the Koutouktou and his sister. The former, after having tasted it, returned it, and gave orders to pour a part of it into each tea-pot. As soon as this was done, a cup of this tea was presented, first to the Koubilgon and the Dalama, and then to all the persons of distinction. As for those who had no cups, some of the tea was poured into their hands. Prizes were then distributed."

No less impressed was Captain Turner on his mission to the Tashi Lama in Tibet in 1783 when taking tea with a local Raja. A servant poured hot tea, from what sounds like a silver and gold ornamented teapot, into his own cupped hands, and "hastily sipped it", in the traditional gesture of assurance against poisoning. Then:

> The Raja held out upon the points of the fingers of his right hand a shallow lacquered cup of small circumference, which was filled with tea. Three cups had been sent, and were set down before us; the Raja directed his servant to fill them. Also: still holding the cup in his right hand, he repeated, in a low and hollow tone of voice, a long invocation ("We humbly beseech thee! That we and our relatives throughout all our life-cycles may never be separated from the three holy ones. May the blessing of the trinity enter into this drink. To all the dread locality, demons of this country, we offer this good Chinese tea! Let us obtain our wishes! And may the doctrines of Buddha be extended."); and afterwards dipping the point of his finger three times into the cup, he threw as many drops

upon the floor, by way of oblation, and then began to sip his tea. Taking this as a signal, we followed the example. Having at last with a tolerable grace swallowed the tea, we yet found ourselves very deficient in the conclusion of the ceremony ... The Raja, with surprising dexterity, turned the cup as he held it fast betwixt his fingers, and in an instant passed his tongue over every part of it: so that it was sufficiently cleansed to be wrapped in a piece of scarlet silk, which bore evident marks of having been prepared for this purpose.

Turner was hooked and soon "habit had not only rendered this composition agreeable to our tastes, but experience most fully proved that warm liquids, at all times, contribute to alleviate the sensation of fatigue. I was never more disposed to praise the comfortable practice of the country, having constantly observed that the first object of attention with every man at the end of a long journey is to procure himself a dish of hot tea".

The patterns of social, religious and medicinal use of tea in China and Japan reinforced and epitomized certain psychological characteristics of those two nations which in turn fed back into the rituals and beliefs connected with Chinese and Japanese tea drinking. It was a circle whose circumference was limited by their deliberate isolation: hubristic in the case of China, paranoid in Japan. Even the forceful commercial, military and technological intrusion of the West since the mid-nineteenth century has not entirely dissipated these separatist characteristics. This intrusion came about only gradually as Europeans, sip by sip, became aware of tea, then acquired a taste for it that developed before long into an insatiable popular thirst that necessitated ever-closer links with China.

CHAPTER FOURTEEN

A Nice Cup of Tea

For a seventeenth-century Englishman, and indeed any European, China *was* silk and tea and porcelain, and the greatest of these was porcelain. Jane Austen's General Tilney could declare as much as he pleased in 1818 that he "thought it right to encourage the manufacture of his country; and for his part, to his uncritical palate, the tea was as well flavoured from the clay of Staffordshire, as from that of Dresden or Sèvres", but to no avail. The fact remained that porcelain cups and teapots were not only very beautiful but best for serving tea as they retained no lingering taste of any previous contents. Tough and of low conductivity, translucent and hauntingly blue, the porcelain imported in large quantities by the East India Company "provided Europe not just with ornamental novelties, but with useful decencies".

These "useful decencies" were also significant status symbols. It was socially important to show off the latest designs, so a brisk trade in Chinese tea-ware developed in the footsteps of tea drinking. As La Rochefoucauld observed in 1784, tea drinking "gives the rich an opportunity to show off their fine possessions: cups, teapots, etc., all made to the most elegant designs, all copies of the Etruscan and the antique". This in turn prompted serious efforts by Europeans to reproduce techniques that the Chinese kept such a closely guarded secret. Others, mostly British, tried to develop alternatives that were as attractive and effective as Chinese porcelain. One obvious short cut was to have your tea-ware made in prestige-bestowing silver, the earliest example of which appears to be a silver tea kettle in Norwich Castle Museum that dates to 1694.

Some scholars have argued that Chinese porcelain came to England in the first instance as ballast only because the handle-less teacups could be stacked with the base of one lodged tightly in the mouth of the next – "mother and child" as the Chinese called it – to provide compact and tidily stowed weight just above a ship's keel. For every ton of cargo, mostly tea and silk, six tons of ballast were required to trim the ship. Some was still conventional ballast – shingle, iron and suchlike – but a substantial part was in the form of porcelain and red stoneware. But the directors and captains of the East India Company were not fools. They realized that tea cannot be drunk without teacups and that these could provide some of the ballast and saleable drinking vessels at the same time. In any case the argument did not apply to the *zhong* with its lid and saucer, nor to the teapot with its handle, which had to be packed and stowed carefully and separately.

When porcelain first came to England, in the seventeenth century, it was as much desired by aristocrats and wealthy merchants for its oriental exoticism as for its function. It was also very expensive. Though small at first, this was still a business growing fast and worth having, so potters across Europe were soon trying to emulate and displace Chinese porcelain. As cups and pots became chipped by use and washing, they were passed on to – or "acquired" by – servants and retainers, whose master's prestige required their replacement by the latest versions, thus increasing demand and the volume of trade. Moreover, as tea grew in popularity and fell in price, so the volume of imported porcelain increased and its price declined. In 1712 a 216-piece porcelain dinner service cost £5 10s. and in 1723 large batches of teapots were being imported at a penny-halfpenny each. One estimate is that by 1791, when the East India Company stopped importing porcelain, some 215 million pieces had been brought into Britain. This was still not enough to furnish the 5.5 million people (some two-thirds of the British population) now drinking tea. Tea-ware, for the middling and poorer sort, had increasingly been provided by English pottery, first English porcelain itself, then uniquely English forms of tea-ware.

In 1707 the German alchemist Johann Böttger, who had been trying to turn base metal into gold, and the famous physicist Ehrenfried Walther von Tschirnhaus were brought together by the Elector of Saxony to make rubies for him. In this, of course, they failed. What they did produce, at the very high temperatures at which they worked, was red-stoneware pottery identical to that being imported, along with porcelain, from China. This they called jasper, the name by which Wedgwood later sold his famous pottery imitating classical, carved cameos. Working from this basis they had produced hard porcelain itself by 1709 and shortly afterwards opened the Meissen pottery. Böttger, who seems not to have taken himself too seriously, stuck a notice over the pottery door: "God the Creator has transmuted a maker of gold into a maker of pots." Meissen "pots" were to make a great deal of gold and cast their spell over the whole of Europe for the next three hundred years.

Despite extensive espionage and the luring to England of potters from France, Germany and Belgium, it was not until 1729 that Samuel Bell of Staffordshire took out a patent "for making red marbled stoneware with mineral earth found within this kingdom which being firmly united by fire will make it capable of receiving a gloss so beautiful as to imitate if not compare with ruby". Sadly for Mr Bell, his stoneware, though attractive, did not have the durability of that precious stone, and like all his fellow potters he was faced with the challenge of matching Chinese porcelain's immunity to the impact of boiling water on cold receptacles. Nicholas Crisp broke both his health and his bank balance striving in vain to produce a successful substitute for "the porcelain ware of China [which was] free from these imperfections". He wrote with feeling in 1753 that "it must be considered as a great Acquisition to this Nation, could a domestic Manufacture be introduced, that might supply the place of this foreign Commodity". In 1760 the firm of Robinson and Rhodes was still covering itself against its teapots "flying", or shattering suddenly. Their advertisement, claiming that their "English China of the newest improvement [would] wear as well as any foreign", added the rider that they would "change [it] gratis if broke with hot water". As late as 1780 the manager of the famous Derby pottery lamented that its teapots were still "flying" and "the disgrace is worse than anything, and it looses [sic] the sale of many sets". Although several modifications were made to its soft paste, Derby teapots continued to "fly", to the chagrin and discomfort of not a few scalded maids and mistresses.

William Cookworthy had already taken out a patent for a hard paste in 1765, the formula for which he may well have learned from Andrew Duche, a visiting American potter from Georgia, a couple of years earlier. Duche, while prospecting for gold in Virginia, had been struck by the quality of *unaker*, the pottery vessels of the Cherokee Red Indians. His curiosity led him to the discovery that its raw material was a mixture of china clay (kaolin or alumina) and Cornish stone (granite with a high percentage of feldspar known to the Chinese as *petuntse*), both of which were to be found in plenty in Britain, chiefly in Cornwall. Although Cookworthy's very high wastage rate – a result of firing at the high temperatures (1,350°C) required for Chinese porcelain – meant his enterprise failed, the patent was bought out in 1781 by the New Hall pottery and was in general use once the patent restriction expired in 1796.

The breakthrough in the manufacture of characteristically English porcelain tea-ware came in the late 1740s when Thomas Frye applied for a patent, granted in 1749, for "calcining animals, vegetables and fossils" for mixing with soft paste clay to make china. This was bone ash, the critical ingredient in the uniquely English bone china. Frye, an artist and engraver of some repute, had become manager in 1744 of the Bow pottery on the Essex, rather than the London, side of the River Lea. There, by adding bone ash to his soft paste mix, and by reversing the traditional method by setting the second firing of the lead-glazed items at a lower temperature than the first, he created the first viable English porcelain. Samuel Richardson's panegyric of 1748, in which he claims "the tea cups and saucers" made at Bow, in east London, are thought "by some skillful persons ... to be little inferior to those brought from China", was either prophetic, or Frye had been using bone ash for some time before he applied for his patent. Frye, "who spent fifteen years among the furnaces till his constitution was near destroyed", died in 1762 and was, as his epitaph rightly proclaimed, "the inventor and first manufacturer of porcelain in England": an achievement for which Josiah Spode the Younger, who perfected the use of bone ash around 1800, often gets the credit.

English potters had already come up with their own unique contribution to the art of ceramics by 1743. (The earliest extant example is in the British Museum.) English cream-coloured ware was made by giving biscuit-fired (1,180°C) white-salt-glazed stoneware a lead glaze and a second firing at earthenware temperature (1,060°C). Because it was tough as well as attractive, and because it was so brilliantly perfected and marketed by Josiah Wedgwood from 1765 onwards, English creamware began to be preferred to the aesthetically more sophisticated, but less durable, output of Delft and other Continental potteries. By the end of the century English firms were publishing their catalogues for it in French, Spanish, German and Dutch, but, more importantly, had taken over the British market, so that Chinese and European porcelain was only in demand among connoisseurs, collectors and those who wished to be thought of as such.

It could be argued that it was the pursuit of a better teapot that largely created the heyday of the British pottery industry and the glories of Spode and Wedgwood, Worcester and Derby. It was certainly the development of a durable, relatively inexpensive, teaware by English potters, over a hundred-year period, that was as much the catalyst as the fall in the price of tea for the runaway spread of tea drinking in Britain in the nineteenth century.

A typical tea service in the early eighteenth century was presented on a tray, then confusingly known as a tea table. It might have consisted of a silver teapot – with a spirit lamp underneath to keep the water hot – or a porcelain teapot and a metal tea kettle similarly heated. A jug with a lid and a heat-insulating wooden handle would have been for hot water, or possibly hot milk. Milk, hot or cold, probably makes its first English appearance in the late 1650s or early 1660s. Garway's extravagant advertisement of 1657 refers to milk, which was probably added at source in the coffee house before being delivered to the drinker. With the domestication of tea, milk began to have its own containers to meet individual preferences for its addition. In these situations it would have been served in a small jug – some with, some without lids – or a small bottle. In 1698 Lady

Rachel Russell sent "a little bottle to pour milk out for tea" to her daughter as a present, and clearly regarded it as a novelty.

The tea leaves themselves would have been kept in a caddy, or caddies, which, since the contents were as valuable as the containers, would have been locked against pilfering servants. In wealthier households, where pride and etiquette demanded the offering of a choice of teas, there would have been a tea canister: a multiple tea caddy of six or eight compartments. These were of fine workmanship in mahogany or other valuable wood, and inlaid with mother-of-pearl, ivory or tortoiseshell. The leaves might have been scooped out of the caddy with a spoon in a shape of a shell, which emulated the larger shells sometimes placed as scoops by the Chinese in chests of tea. The short-handled spoon, with the wide, shallow bowl of today's caddy spoon, did not appear until the second half of the eighteenth century. There might also have been a "mote" spoon for removing the "motes", those floating bits of stalk and leaf, from many a cup of tea. The mote spoon – I can find no reference to "beams" – had a heart-shaped, perforated bowl through which the liquid could drain but in which the bits were retained, and a long, pointed handle for clearing out the teapot's spout. Around 1896 a hinged upper half was added to the basic mote spoon to create the infuser, whether of silver, steel or wire-mesh, which plays an important role today for the tea lover who eschews tea bags.

Sugar was added to tea in Britain from its first drinking. It was either scraped off a sugar loaf or was offered as somewhat irregular lumps in a covered dish from which it was extracted and put in the cup by silver tongs, or "nips". Both milk and sugar would have been daintily stirred in with teaspoons resting in a spoon boat and there would have been another bowl for slops. Cups and saucers would have been placed separately on the table. Until well into the eighteenth century the cups would have been without handles, in pursuit of both orientalism and economy, as cups with handles were harder to make and easier to break.

The origins and purpose of the saucer have been both a mystery and an embarrassment to many. The saucer is supposed to have been devised in the eighth century by a Chinese lady who found her handle-less cup too hot to hold. She placed it on a small dish, whose rim she could grasp, and when it started to slip, stuck it down with wax – which would surely have melted with the heat? The first authenticated appearance of a saucer is sometime in the twelfth century at the Chinese Emperor's court, when it was definitely an integral part of the tea bowl. Not until the sixteenth century did the saucer assume its present guise as a shallow, concave dish, made as a pair with its cup, which sat comfortably on it. Separation of cup and saucer found its way back from Europe to China and caused problems of etiquette on both continents.

Were they for bearing the cup or for drinking from? Were they for keeping the tea warm or for preventing slops spoiling the tea table? As ever, the Chinese had resolved this dilemma long before Europeans were even aware of it. It had briefly been the custom in the Song dynasty to drink from the saucer, but generally tea was drunk from a cup placed on a saucer and often with a lid, thus enabling it to act as cup or teapot, or both. Robert Fortune experienced this dual use on his venture into China in 1848:

> The lady of the house set a teacup before each of us, into which she put some tea, and then filled each cup up with boiling water. I need scarcely say she did not offer us any sugar or milk. Other tables were crowded with people, most of whom were coolies going to Chang-shaii with tea, and whose chests nearly blocked up the road in front of the door. We drank our tea, which I found most refreshing, in its pure state without sugar and milk. Now and then some one connected with the house came round and filled our basins again with boiling water. This is usually repeated two or three times, or until all the strength is drawn out of the leaves.

In Russia and America, France, the Netherlands and Scotland tea was often drunk from the saucer rather than the cup. In Russia, Catherine the Great (reigned 1762–96) "dined at two ... and drank tea at five". I infer, from the mimetic practice of aristocratic ladies of the period, that she did this from the saucer, without milk and with a sweetener, such as jam, taken as a side dish, not put into the tea. A Swedish traveller in America comments rather scornfully on noticing women drinking from the saucer that "when the English women drank tea, they never poured it out of the cup into the saucer to cool it, but drank it as hot as it came from the teapot". In India, however, English women seem to have been in the habit of drinking tea from the saucer, perhaps to cool their tea in a hot climate, though the perspiratory effect of hot tea would have been more effective. In a Zoffany *alfresco* family portrait of the Dashwood family in India (about 1780), the hostess is shown pouring tea into a saucer, but who is to say this is not for the dog in the corner of the picture? The French in Pondicherry also seem to have dispensed tea throughout the day, from breakfast to eight in the evening, apart from siesta time, to an "ever changing circle of visitants". Talk at the tea table "provides the sole source of conversation because once the vessels of Europe have left, people no longer have anything to say, unless love has provided some adventure".

Teapot design also laboured under many constraints. A teapot must optimize space and volume for good infusion, while minimizing surface area for heat retention; it must be large enough to serve a reasonable number of guests, while not being too heavy for the hostess to lift elegantly; it must have a heat-proof handle that is in balance with a well-shaped spout that pours near-boiling water safely and does not drip. Not surprisingly, when British manufacturers began to make their own teapots they copied the basic pear and globe shapes of the Chinese and Japanese.

Potteries would try to get the edge on their rivals by making their pint teapots hold more than a pint, so the purchaser was never quite sure how much he was getting. Standardizing was further complicated by the industry's eccentric quantifying, in which a dozen only meant 12 if a vessel held exactly a pint. (Six pints and you only got two to a dozen, a third of a pint and it was 36!)

Although the later versatility of English china gave rise to a whole range of bizarre and grotesque teapot shapes, in the end the basic cylinder, cone or, predominantly, globe dominated the tea table. Such odd variants as Wadham's with a heated iron rod in the middle to keep the water hot, or mistress Sarah Guppy's teapot complete with an internal wire basket for boiling eggs, never caught on, though variations on the integral infuser have been with us ever since

The more guests you wished to entertain, the larger your teapot or tea kettle might have to be, until even the most muscular hostess baulked at the weight. The answer for large gatherings – such as the temperance gatherings of the nineteenth century or the WI-run fêtes of our own time – was the tea urn. This was a giant tea kettle on a base that could be rotated with a tap at the bottom, amidships. The device was not, in fact, a tea urn but a water-heating urn, from which boiling water could be comfortably drawn to a whole series of teapots brought to it for the infusion of the leaves. The tea urn has remained virtually the same since its invention, only the method of heating has changed from the central red-hot iron or spirit-lamp flue to the modern electric hob or gas flame. By the 1830s much of the actual brewing apparatus had lost its cachet and been relegated to the kitchen, whence the maid would bring the pot of already brewed tea to drawing room or dining room, thus saving the society hostess from being overshadowed by a cumbersome urn. In the drawing room itself simplicity prevailed in what was, until the twentieth century, the simplest way of preparing a simple, refreshing, hot drink. Its rampant growth made it a natural target for government greed.

CHAPTER FIFTEEN

Tea and Taxes

O nly "baccy and booze" have ever been more heavily taxed in Britain than tea, and more tea was probably smuggled than of either in the eighteenth and nineteenth centuries. As import or excise duties rose, and with them the price of tea, so did smuggling and adulteration. When imposts fell, and with them the price of tea, legal consumption increased and, often, so did revenue to the Exchequer. (The table on p.377 shows some of the main fluctuations in tea tax over the past 350 years.)

The taxation of tea went through eight general phases. The first, from 1660 to 1690, entailed an excise duty on liquid tea which only served to exacerbate the gustatory hazards of early tea making. In 30 years it rose 300 per cent, from 8d. a gallon to 2s. a gallon. The keeper of the coffee house was not supposed to serve the Stygian essence lurking in the old barrel in the corner until the "gauger" (customs officer) had estimated the amount in the barrel, which would be liable to tax. Since he made only two rounds a day, much tea, stale or untaxed, was served, depending on the disposition of the proprietor. This expensive and inefficient method gave way to an import customs duty of 5s. per pound of dry tea leaf from 1690 at levels varying from 5s. to 1s. It went up by 1s. a pound in 1695 to finance "the reduction of Ireland"; the first but by no means the last time tea tax would be enlisted to fight a war.

During this second phase, by re-exporting tea, the original importer could reclaim the duty paid. No sooner did re-exported tea reach Europe than the bulk of it was promptly smuggled back to Britain at a substantial profit. In 1723 Robert Walpole, George I's chief minister, thought to tackle the problem by replacing the import duty by an excise duty of 4s. a pound, payable only when the importer withdrew the tea from a bonded warehouse. Although re-exports did fall in this third phase, the measure simply served to show that this particular device was but one in the smuggler's extensive bag of tricks – which we shall open later. Nevertheless, it was obviously a useful one, because when the draw-back was re-introduced in 1768, the volume of "re-exports" doubled to 10 million pounds.

Any attempt to quantify an essentially clandestine activity must be treated with caution, but one careful scholar has calculated that between 1730 and 1739 two-thirds of British tea was smuggled. The same source puts the proportion over the following 10 years at 71 per cent. However, in 1745 Henry Pelham, one of Walpole's successors, cut the excise duty to 1s., whereupon legal imports trebled to 2.4 million pounds, with a corresponding cut in smugglers' profits. I infer from this that before the Pelham cut as much as 90 per cent of British tea was being smuggled in.

This third-phase respite was short-lived, as the tax on tea was steadily raised during the duty's fourth phase to finance first the Seven Years War (1756–63) and then, from 1773, resistance to America's struggle for independence. (The precedent had been well set in 784 when the Tang Emperor taxed tea in order to raise an army to suppress rebellion.) Possibly through a mixture of patriotism and pusillanimity – smuggling became more hazardous at sea in wartime – the proportion of smuggled tea fell steadily; from half in the 1770s to a mere 5 per cent between 1790 and 1800. The crucial moment for the smuggler came in 1784 when Pitt the Younger decided to cut the excise duty levied on tea, which by then had risen – with encouragement from the brewers – to an astronomic 119 per cent *ad valorem*. But when a series of bad harvests also pushed up the price of beer and ale to a point where few labouring families could afford them, Pitt reduced the tea tax to 12½ per cent, and replaced the lost revenue with the window tax, which was to blight both British architecture and the health of the poor until its repeal in 1851.

Richard Twining, a member of the third generation of the family, who had campaigned vigorously against the tea tax, reported an average fall of 3s. a pound in the price of tea in 1785. In 1783, with all tea still coming from China, the British had already switched their preference from green tea to black, which now made up two-thirds of imports. The cheapest black tea (bohea) cost from 5s. to 8s. a pound, including tax; the most expensive green tea (Hyson) from 12s. to 18s. a pound, including tax. Pitt's Commutation Act had cut the ground from under the smugglers' feet. It was rumoured that several swarthy, seafaring types, seen at the tea auctions immediately following the Act, were smugglers incognito trying to bid up prices to protect their stocks. A more likely explanation for the time-lag in price reductions is the natural "pipeline" delay in the impact of any fiscal measure. Legal imports almost doubled from six million pounds in 1784 to 10.8 million in 1785, and Richard Twining was selling bohea that year at 2s. a pound and best Hyson at between 6s. and 10s. The Commutation Act was an unusually well prepared measure in that the Excise men carried out a survey in 1783 to ascertain how many licensed tea dealers there actually were – licensing and inspection had been introduced in 1750. The survey identified 33,778. Within half a dozen years of Pitt's measure their number had almost doubled to 62,065. When, in 1869, tea licensing was finally abolished, 194,798 "had their letters up". The Wine and Beerhouse Act of the same year brought that trade under the magistrates, and when the spread of off-licence sales encouraged grocers to sell liquor, pubs briefly tried to retaliate by selling leaf tea.

Although smuggling continued in the next phase, and even picked up somewhat after 1815, it never again reached the levels of the mid-eighteenth century. Phase six occupied the remainder of the nineteenth century, during which excise duty fluctuated between 4d. and 1s. 1d. a pound, depending on the revenue needs of the government of the day, and is notable only for the two cuts made by Gladstone in 1863 and 1866, which may have been prompted by his own gargantuan consumption of tea. (He was even reputed to keep warm tea in his hot-water bottle in case he felt like a cup in the middle of the night.) After the second of these cuts in duty, British tea imports exceeded 100 million pounds for the first time.

The need to finance yet another war against claimants for independence – this time against the Boers in South Africa – added 2d. to the tax on tea and in 1905, although the war was over, the duty rose another 2d. This was too much for the nation's tea lovers and on 18 January 1905 the Anti-Tea Duty League was formed at a well-attended public rally. The League mounted an effective campaign of lampoons and lobbying during the 1906 General Election campaign, carefully differentiating among its targets. It appealed to the Liberals, who wanted "a free breakfast table"; to the Conservatives, who wanted total Empire free trade but tariffs for everyone else; and to the small Labour group, which objected to a "penny tax on a penn'orth of tea". I like to think it was the natural free-trade instincts of the great new Liberal reform government of 1906 that lopped first two pence, and then another penny, off the duty on tea. It did not rise again until the exigencies of yet another war, in 1914, made it a tempting target once more. This twentieth-century phase of fluctuating tariffs ended in 1929 when Winston Churchill, as Chancellor of the Exchequer, abolished taxation of every kind on tea for the first time since it was first imported to Britain.

By 1932, in its eighth and final phase, tea tax was back again, together with "Empire Preference": an excise charge of 2d. a pound was imposed on tea grown in the Empire; 4d. was charged if it came from elsewhere. The duty on Empire tea fluctuated between 2d. and 6d. until 1949, when the tariff on the newly independent tea-producing members of the Commonwealth was reduced to zero. An unwelcome and unforeseen effect of Empire Preference was that it made those discriminated against, such as Java and China, redouble their efforts to export to America and look to markets nearer home in Australia and New Zealand, which were largely lost to tea from India and Ceylon. The last tax burden on tea imported to Britain was abolished in 1964 and there has been none since.

Just as resistance to tea taxation and the resort to smuggling in eighteenth-century America led to contempt for the law, and eventually revolution, so the scale of tea smuggling in eighteenth- and nineteenth-century Britain may have contributed to an increasing lack of respect for the law and a loosening of the ties of civic responsibility. Not only was it illegal to smuggle brandy and tobacco but the commodities themselves were potentially "sinful". Brandy could lead to drunkenness, violence and poverty; tobacco, considered by many a dirty habit from its first introduction, whether smoked or sniffed, was thought to encourage sloth and idleness. While some of the early opponents of tea, such as Jonas Hannaway, ascribed to it similar vices, the great majority saw it as a harmless indulgence. Oblivious to tea's mildly addictive quality, most people considered its taxation mean-spirited and unnecessary. It was almost a duty to smuggle tea, and the great majority of the British people, from parson to pauper, aristocrat to artisan, fulfilled that duty with enthusiasm.

The smuggling started before the tea had left the Canton port of Whampoa; indeed, it had even started before the East Indiamen left England. All members of every ship's crew – from captains to cabin boys, seamen to supercargoes (the men in charge – nominally at least – of *all* commercial transactions on a venture) – stocked up with their own tradable goods or silver dollars to exchange for tea, primarily, but also for porcelain and silk. As early as 1674 the East India Company estimated that its ships' complements took on board £45,000 in trade goods and £90,000 in silver; in 1717 it was reckoned that 20,000lb of private tea was still being conveyed in the Company's ships. The defrauding of the Company seems to have got steadily worse. William Hickey, returning from India in 1770, watched amazed as his captain transferred 68 chests of tea at a prearranged rendezvous in the Channel with his smuggling confederates, receiving £12,024 for his trouble.

When the Indiamen arrived at Whampoa, their official agents negotiated for legitimate cargo in Canton in competition with ships from Sweden and Denmark, the Netherlands, Portugal and France, all trading legitimately in China but with every intention of dealing illegitimately once they returned to Europe. Most of their cargo was destined, once unloaded in their native ports, to be smuggled straight into England. These large cargoes of tea were broken up into smaller lots for crossing the Channel in everything from small luggers to 24-gun merchantmen of as much as three hundred tons. I like the one named *Brotherly Love*, captained by a Francis Coffee.

Seven years after Hickey witnessed his smuggling incident, the East India Company was still bewailing the fact that, according to one tip-off, each Indiaman had between three and four hundred chests of unauthorized tea on board. In 1785, well past the peak of smuggling, about 250 vessels were still engaged in it.

The Excise men did their best to catch the smugglers at sea – which was a lot safer for the officers than trying to apprehend the felons on dry land, where the odds were stacked against them. In 1733 they managed to seize 54,000lb of tea – perhaps about 8–10 per cent of the smuggled total for that year – but usually the smugglers were too numerous, too nasty and too nippy for them. Moreover, by contracting out much of the revenue patrolling to privateers, the government was usually just adding to the smuggling fleet. In September 1747 the most notorious set-to between Excise men and smugglers began, when, for a change, one of these privateers, the *Swift*, intercepted the *Three Brothers* and confiscated 38 hundredweight, or nearly two tons, of tea. (For a graphic and gory account of the whole incident, see Roy Moxham's *Tea Addiction, Exploitation and Empire*, pp.9–14.) This they lodged in the Custom House at Poole in Dorset for, as they thought, safe keeping while the legal wheels slowly ground into action against the seven arrested smugglers.

The tea, neatly packed in canvas bags, had been stored barely two weeks when one half of a band of some 50 armed smugglers "liberated" the bags, while the other half blocked all the roads into the town along which the forces of the law might try to intervene. During the smugglers' fairly leisurely retreat one of their number, Jack Diamond, was identified by a villager, Daniel Chater, who was eventually persuaded to testify against him at Chichester assizes. On his way to court Chater was escorted by a single customs officer. (Why only one, I wonder?) When the two men stopped at an inn for a break, they were betrayed to the smugglers' gang by the landlady. With typical feminine ferocity, she and other local women urged the smugglers to "hang the pair of them". At first it was decided to wait and see what happened to Jack Diamond, so the smugglers rode off with their two captives; gouging them with their spurs, cudgelling them savagely and, by way of variation, crushing their testicles from time to time. Eventually the offer en route of a safe spot where smugglers were wont to bury their tea was an opportunity for complete revenge too tempting to resist. They buried the unfortunate customs man alive, then returned a few days later to suspend the informer over a well, into which they then dropped him, still alive, before piling rocks and timbers on his body. The newspapers of the day took the press's usual sordid delight in the details.

Provoked by the audacity of the raid on the Customs House, perhaps even more than by the brutal dispatch of the two men, the authorities relentlessly tracked down the perpetrators. Five of them were hanged for murder. Three more suffered the same fate shortly afterwards for their part in raiding the Custom House, thus re-inforcing the well-established principle that an offence against property is at least as heinous as one against the person in the eyes of the English law. The severity of the punishment did not deter British or Continental smugglers, for the rewards were too great. During much of the eighteenth century it was not only easier but more profitable to smuggle tea than it was to smuggle brandy or tobacco, and at its height as many as twenty thousand people were engaged in this traffic.

The brutality of many smuggling gangs, who often fought bloody, and sometimes fatal, battles not only against the revenue men, but against each other over "pitches" or contraband, did give the local magistrate pause for thought before he intervened – particularly if some of the smuggler's stock was stored in his cellars. Once the goods were ashore, trains of packhorses, often several hundred strong, would carry them inland for storage in cave or crypt, or gentleman's barn, while arrangements were made to "launder" them. Soon the contraband would be on its way in small lots to the thousands of legitimate licensed retailers – most of whom chose not to ask questions about the origin of the cheap tea – or in the padded jackets of the "duffers". These men and women would hang 30–40lb of tea about their bodies under a heavy coat – made of duffel, a coarse woollen cloth – and hawk it in small packets directly to householders. The daftest of all attempts to check these methods was legislation in 1781 banning the movement into

London of more than 6lb of tea at a time, or more than 40lb between any two points elsewhere. The smugglers just set up shops in the London suburbs to which 40lb lots could be sent and from which a stream of 6lb packets found their way into the capital.

In some parts of Britain smuggled tea was often all you could get. In Groombridge, near Tunbridge Wells in Kent, in 1737, the smugglers were turning over 3,000lb of tea a week, and it was said that all along the south coast of England there was nothing but smuggled tea to be had. One entrepreneurial smuggler from Edinburgh opened his own retail outlets for his contraband tea in many towns and cities in the north of England; and a M. Foucauld, a French smuggler who presumably did not trust the English distributors to play fair, had his own agents selling tea door to door in the west of England.

Perhaps if the gentry had resolutely refused to buy smuggled tea or to profit from it, the contraband business would not have flourished so. But they did not. The rot went almost to the very top. The Earl of Derby exploited his ownership of the Isle of Man – a favoured staging post for French smugglers – by levying a charge of 1d. on every pound of tea passing through Douglas harbour. Income from this source must have been substantial, for Hanway claims that he saw as many as 40 French vessels at a time choose "dark nights for their dark purposes" because it was "more profitable to smuggle to England than sell in France".

The problem was that most British people shared the view of Mrs Elizabeth Montagu, a lion-hunting blue stocking (1720–1800) who, having got her sister to bring in smuggled tea from France, asserted that "after I have paid you for it, I shall drink it with a quiet conscience". And we find parson James Woodforde calmly noting (*The Diary of a Country Parson* for 29 March 1777) that "Andrews the Smuggler brought me this night about 11 o'clock a bag of Hyson tea 6 pound weight. He frightened us a little by whistling under the parlour window just as we were going to bed. I gave him some Genever."

It was left to the curmudgeons and the Quakers to uphold the absolutes of conscience and the law. Rightly, if irrelevantly, Hanway declared: "Those who buy smuggled goods knowing them to be such, are, with regard to the injury they do their country, smugglers." William Tuke (1732–1822), a Quaker philanthropist who pioneered more humane treatment of the insane and was himself a tea and coffee merchant, only with great difficulty persuaded his fellow Quakers not to do anything "to the injury of the King's revenue or the common good, or to the hurt of the fair trader". Many a "fair trader" buying his East India Company tea, duly taxed, could not compete with the vast quantities of smuggled tea available at half the price round the corner. Many indeed went to the wall. They would have earned little sympathy from the Reverend Canon Sydney Smith (1771–1845) of Windsor, who "was glad he was not born before tea" and reckoned anyone who claimed never to have bought smuggled tea to be "a greater knave than his neighbours". For Smith the smuggler was a man who "might have been in every respect an excellent citizen had not the laws of his country made that a crime which nature never meant to be one".

Canon Smith probably heartily endorsed the opinion Charles Lamb expressed in his 1820s essay *The Old Margate Hoy*: "I like a smuggler. He is the only honest thief. He robs nothing but the revenue – an abstraction I never cared greatly about. I could go out with him in his mackerel boat or about his less ostensible business, with some satisfaction." The cleric might have been less sympathetic toward the next sentence of this kind and likeable man, who was himself employed as a clerk by the East India Company for more than 30 years: "I can even tolerate those poor victims to monotony, who from day to day pace along the beach, in endless progress and recurrence to watch their illicit countrymen – towns-folk or brethren perchance – whistling to the sheathing and unsheathing of their cutlasses (their only solace) who under the mild name of preventive service, keep up a legitimated civil warfare in the absence of a foreign one..."

But if everyone (outside government circles and the Revenue) loved a smuggler, everyone despised the tea adulterator. As with smuggling, adulteration operated at different levels of nefariousness and on different scales. At its simplest there was the maid who dried out a few used leaves and mixed them in her mistress's tea caddy to disguise her pilfering. The Chinese sometimes practised the same trick on a much grander scale. Infused leaves, or *"maloo"*, were collected from a multitude of teapots, dried in the sun and mixed in with the contents of chests of tea destined for export. This was almost impossible to detect before the days of regular official inspection as the adulteration was done after the tea had been "charactered" by the European agent. In 1837 the anonymous author of a pamphlet entitled "Deadly Adulteration and Slow Poisoning, or Disease and Death in the Pot and Bottle", having sarcastically castigated "the antemundane subjects of the Brother of the Sun and Moon", was honest enough to admit that there was also large-scale recycling of leaf in London itself: "Tea leaves are purchased from the London coffee houses and shops by a set of men who make their regular rounds for the purpose, to be redried and coloured. Their clear gains are £6 or £7, and this for morning work only." Even in mid-century Henry Mayhew, in his classic work *London Labour and the London Poor*, was claiming that 1,500lb of used leaves were being "reclaimed", dyed, dried and reissued every week and that no one thought the worse of those involved. London merchants often got the blame undeservedly for the poor-quality tea this could put in the customer's caddy, yet at least it was possible still to get some kind of tea from reinfusing used leaves. Although dishonest, this kind of adulteration harmed only the victim's purse, not his health.

Other forms of adulteration, however, could have much more serious consequences. It became commonplace among some British tea traders to bulk out expensive, genuine tea leaves with native leaves, twigs and other hedgerow rubbish that cost next to nothing to collect. The whole was then sold as if it were unadulterated tea. Some of the leaves used were relatively harmless (favourites were hawthorn and ash); others, such as belladonna, ivy and Robin-run-the-hedge – which had precisely the effect on the bowels that its name suggests – were not. (I wonder if Hanway's obsessive hatred of tea could have been triggered by an encounter with unrecognized Robin.) These miscegenated teas were known as "smouch": a term I should like to think derives from the German word *Schmutz*, dirt, and thus by sniggering association the modern usage of a kiss-and-cuddle session; but I fear it is more likely to have come from the Afrikaans-Dutch word for a pedlar or a cheat.

So damaging to the honest tea merchant had the practice of smouching become that in 1776 a law was hastily passed threatening a fine of £5 a pound, or imprisonment, for anyone caught trying "to dye or fabricate any sloe leaves, liquorice leaves, or leaves of tea that has been used". Like so much hasty legislation, it was ineffectual. There was no regular system of inspection and, even if adulterated tea were detected, it was almost impossible to prove where in the lengthy supply chain the offending material had been added. Matters were not improved by further legislation, with stiffer penalties, the following year. The Act (17 George III. Cap.29, for those who relish bureaucratic exaggeration) opened with the absurd suggestion that smouching was so extensive that it was denuding the woods and undergrowth of Britain. Richard Twining's sober *Observations ... on the Tea Trade*, as part of his lobbying of Pitt to cut the tea tax, shows the practice continuing unabated: "When gathered [the leaves] are first dried in the sun and then baked. They are next put on the floor and trod upon until the leaves are small, then lifted and steeped in copperas [ferrous sulphate, to give a greenish tinge to the leaves] with sheep's dung, after which, being dried on a floor, they are fit for use."

The McCavity of tea-leaf recycling in London was a Mr Heale, who set up in the street which was soon to become the heart of the international tea trade: Mincing Lane. He sold what he chose to call "British tea", which looked like Orange Pekoe but "had a faint smell in the pot". This was fair enough, as "British tea" largely consisted of the leaves of elm, rose and sloe, with a few stones and the odd maple seed thrown in for good measure – all indisputably British. Nevertheless, despite barrister Bompass's impassioned plea that Heale was being "oppressed", 11,000lb of the noxious stuff was burned publicly in 1833.

The Chinese were as active in this kind of adulteration as in recycling. They added warehouse sweepings mixed with rice-water paste, paddy husks mixed with china clay, soapstone and blacklead and *li* leaves to bulk out real tea – the latter inevitably known as "lie-tea". Not until the Food and Drug Act of 1875 was official tea inspection introduced. (Inspections ended in 1969, but it is this process that accounts for the small round aluminium disc still sometimes found in the side of an old tea chest, put there to seal the hole made by the auger.) Samples were then taken by boring a hole into the heart of the tea chest for checking. In practice much adulteration of this kind had been put paid to 50 years earlier.

"Honest" John Horniman was the son of a dypsomaniac, umbrella-making Yorkshire Quaker and had presumably fled south to the Isle of Wight to get as far away as possible from his father's fondness for the bottle. His experience of alcoholism may have accounted also for the fact that he became a small-time tea dealer on the island as well as an ardent and generous supporter of the temperance movement. In 1826 he had a brilliant idea for capitalizing on the British paranoia about adulterated tea. In that year he began to offer for sale ¼lb and ½lb packets of tea which had been hand-sealed in lead-lined paper packets and were guaranteed to contain only pure tea. Thrilled by the protection offered, the British public took to the new packet tea in a big way. Many grocers were less enthusiastic: some because they felt it intruded upon their personal service to their customers, others because it intruded upon their opportunity to cheat them. So Horniman's packets were sold at first through chemists and confectioners. These, together with the few grocers who stocked his product, he supported by advertising. Gradually demand became so great that Horniman not only had to move to London to cope with it, but was driven to invent one of the earliest forms of industrial automation: a machine for filling and sealing packets much faster than could be done by hand. In 1918 Horniman's was taken over by Lyons. Other tea firms, such as the Mazawattee Tea Company, soon followed Horniman's lead on an even bigger scale, so that by 1901 the grocers had been won round and packet tea outsold leaf tea. Smouch had kissed the customer goodbye – even if Chinese colouring and recycled leaves may still have crept into a few teapots.

CHAPTER SIXTEEN

Tea Mania

The British compulsion to gamble on everything from stocks and shares to snail racing created in the 1860s the dot.com boom and bust of its age: tea mania. Tea became as alluring as the South Seas Company had been in 1720, and just as irrationally. Some of those who sailed close to the wind, as most did, managed to stay just on the right side of the line and cruise on to great profits; others fraudulently crossed the line and capsized, taking many people's money down with them. The contrasting fortunes of the Assam Company (founded in 1839) and the Nowgong Tea Company (launched in 1864) are instructive in these nice distinctions in the heyday of British economic imperialism.

In 1839 the leading tea merchants in London, such as Twinings and Travers, did not wish to jeopardize their trade with China, yet they wanted to break the hold of the "Celestial Empire" which frequently severed the supply of tea to the "barbarians". So they participated in the formation of the Assam Company but kept a low profile during its inaugural meetings of 12–16 February 1839. The opening offered by the East India Company's declared intent only to develop tea experimentally, before handing over its resources to private entrepreneurs, was too good to miss. In advancing their case for the formation of a tea-production venture the founders of the Assam Company concluded their four-page "concise statement" (Victorian ideas of conciseness and ours differ somewhat) by stating that "it only required the application of European capital and enterprise to render it a great source of profit and an object of great national importance". The Company was formed with a capital of ten thousand £50 shares, the attraction of which was that investors would only have to part with cash bit by bit as and when called upon to "answer a call". Four-fifths of the shares were to be allotted in Britain and one-fifth in Calcutta, where there would be a separate board of directors. Of the British allocation 223 shares were not taken up and were subscribed in Calcutta, thus giving the holders in India a little short of the 25 per cent which under today's company law would be a blocking holding but was not at the time. The first "call" on these shares was for £5, and the first task for the Calcutta agent was to try to recruit C.A. Bruce to manage its estates, the Company having already failed first to recruit the Java tea pioneer J.I.L.L. Jacobson. Bruce declined, so the Company's first Superintendent of its plantations was a J.W. Masters. Bruce did eventually join in March 1840 but in a subordinate role.

The Assam Company had been beaten to the starting gate for a share of the Government's tea assets by the Bengal Tea Association. The BTA was remarkable for the fact that of its 18 provisional directors five were native Indians. Its condition for accepting merger with the Assam Company was that "the local management and direction be left entirely with the Committee here [Calcutta]" and that Board vacancies in London should be filled as a priority by Calcutta directors holding no fewer than 50 shares, of whom there were several. This was confirmed in London on 19 July 1839. Dwarkanath Tagore, ancestor of the Indian Nobel poet Rabindranath Tagore, and Maniram Datta Barua, a minister of the King of Assam, became the first and only Indian directors of the Assam Company until after Indian Independence. Among the numerous British merchants the Assam Company also numbered a Chinese physician, Dr Lumqua. Although the Government uttered the usual bland assurances about there being no intention to create a monopoly, one shareholder, who opposed the amalgamation, insisted with some justice that "it, notwithstanding, would all turn out to be humbug". The BTA stipulation, initially agreed by all involved, was to prove a source of great friction and mismanagement until the two Assam Company Boards were finally merged under the London aegis in 1864. The problem arose because the Deed of Settlement, to which all share-holders in Britain had to subscribe, necessarily spawned a Supplementary Deed to be signed by shareholders in Calcutta. This latter stated that the Calcutta Board was to conform to any directions given by the London Board. Those in London chose to interpret this to mean that Calcutta could do nothing without prior agreement from London. Calcutta took it to mean that they could get on with the day-to-day practical running of the business except where specific prior instruction had been given by London. Mistake after mistake was made by what proved to be largely two groups of commercial and agricultural tyros.

At the end of 1843 virtually the only two men who knew their business, Bruce and Masters, were sacked. It did not help that the Government proved very dilatory in registering the incorporation of the Calcutta arm of the Company in India and passing the Act incorporating the new combined company. This was not done until August 1845, when the Company's very survival was in doubt, but this restored the confidence of both Board and shareholders. The move was premature, it transpired, as was the transfer to the Assam Company that year of the remaining third of the Government's experimental gardens. The first two-thirds had been handed over in 1840, before the techniques of tea cultivation and manufacture in India had been even rudimentarily developed, and they were not much further advanced in 1845.

In the early days applications could also be made to the Government of India for virtually unlimited areas of "waste land", with only the occasional argument about whether or not a tract on which valuable timber grew could be construed as "waste". In the event applications were made by the Assam Company and others for acreage far in excess of what could be cleared and cultivated or for which there was neither sufficient seed nor labour. Other extravagances and miscalculations multiplied, such as the commissioning of a river steamer, the *Assam*, which could operate on the Brahmaputra with great difficulty and only after her engines had been reversed so that she could steam stern first with the long bow acting as an aid to steering. She was soon confined to the Ganges and tug duties in Calcutta harbour.

By the mid-1840s a plethora of European staff and inappropriate buildings had put the Company in serious financial difficulties, yet in 1845 it took out a bank loan of £5,000 to enable it to pay, yet again, a dividend out of capital of 2.5 per cent. On top of the excessive outflow of funds, nearly one in seven shareholders whose nerve had gone failed to meet their legally binding calls for further payments. (It should be remembered that not until 1862 was the first legislation introduced that began to offer the protection of limited liability.) Others simply sold at a loss even if it meant forfeiting the right to be on the Board. In 1847 the London directors even considered closing down altogether and invited the Calcutta Board to buy them out. London was "inclined to recommend to their shareholders the acceptance of any proposition that would give them a moderate sum per share, rather than depend on the distant prospect of a larger benefit". The Calcutta directors were unimpressed and persuaded their London colleagues to venture on another year's work. They did so confident in the knowledge that they had just appointed one outstanding man, Henry Burkinyoung, to take over in Calcutta and another, Stephen Mornay, to take charge in Assam.

The Company's first serious commercial sale of tea in January 1842 had consisted of 171 chests at an average of 3s. a pound. If the quality was not of the highest it was probably because the undoubtedly extravagant Superintendent, Masters, and his assistant, Bruce, had responded to London's directive to confine themselves "to the manufacture of common and good black and green teas ... experimental teas being no longer required". These instructions were based on the London directors' soundings of brokers and consumers, who had both suggested that what was wanted was tea that would "taste through hard water, sugar and milk". They therefore demanded "a stronger tea. The tea that would be most used would be that which would stand two liquorings far better than many of the articles from China." The early batches of the Company's tea would certainly have produced "strong liquor" even if it also had a rather bitter taste. At that time the tea bushes were being either pruned brutally and too early or not pruned at all. Weeds and jungle were allowed to choke them, and careless plucking and long, if unavoidable, delays before the leaf was processed all tended to produce poor tea with too much stalk and coarse leaf. On the one hand, both superintendent and managers were being told to produce as much as possible; and on the other, they were being criticized for poor quality even though much of the worst tea was being fobbed off on the army and foreigners or "sent to the American market as was suggested formerly by the Home Secretary".

So bad were conditions on the Company's gardens that Bruce should have been given credit for delivering tea at all. As it was, in 1843 he was given a ticking-off for poor quality. Not unnaturally he was incensed by reprimands from men sitting comfortably in Calcutta apparently oblivious to the dangers and difficulties of pioneering tea cultivation in Assam. The recent death of Colonel White in 1839 in the massacre of the garrison at Sadiya, where Bruce had his first plant nursery, would have made him even more sensitive to the disparities between the Calcutta "box wallahs" and those on a dangerous frontier of the Empire. Although he did not, as his superior Masters had done, resign in high dudgeon on receipt of these criticisms, he did write pointedly to the Board to express his feelings. He protested "at such censures being applied after all in the service have risked their lives in the performance of their duty; very discouraging and will not tend to make the assistants more zealous". The Calcutta Board was unmoved and instructed its Secretary to "intimate to Mr Bruce that it is expected that he will see the propriety of adopting a more respectful tone in his communications to the Board". By 1846 his tone had clearly changed insufficiently and, whether he was pushed or whether he jumped, he had left the service of the Company, though his opinion on various matters continued to be sought.

By this time the Company was in a bad way. Expenditure was out of hand, deliveries to London were unsatisfactory in both quality and quantity, and returns on investment were well below the predictions made in the prospectus and to subsequent shareholders' meetings. A Committee of Enquiry from among the shareholders was appointed at their request by the Board. However, as its membership and terms of reference were determined by the

Board, it unsurprisingly concluded "that without further effort it is not expedient to dissolve the Assam Company". Fortunately for the Company, it was rescued from this parlous state by the efforts of three very capable men.

When Stephen Mornay took over the superintendence of the gardens in 1847, there was no effective control of capital expenditure, wages and salaries. He applied a cost-cutting scalpel to all three with a ruthlessness that was just what the shareholders were looking for. One would not have expected this to endear him to his subordinates, but they continued to regard him with affection. He reduced the number of European managers and assistants to the bare minimum sufficient to oversee cultivation and manufacture. He cut the coolies' wages by 15 per cent, to just three rupees a month. He laid them off without compunction when there was more labour than work, and when there was more work than labour forbade them to cultivate their own rice paddies. To some extent he had no choice but to treat all employees at every level unsympathetically because ready money for buying supplies and paying wages was so short that the latter were often three months in arrears, with workers and managers alike often obliged to cheat the company to try to make ends meet. When, in 1852, the Board in Calcutta reprimanded him for his harsh treatment of a subordinate he resigned in a huff.

In January 1848 Henry Burkinyoung, a director based in India who had owned a music shop in Calcutta and also served a short stint as Secretary to the Board, was appointed to the then novel post of Managing Director and at once began to take the same kind of grip on the Company's sloppy Calcutta administration and accounting practices that Mornay had taken on plantation management. Consequently this aspect of the Company's cost effectiveness also improved greatly.

But if the Company found itself making profits in the 1850s it was mainly due to the horticultural and actuarial genius of a third employee, an experienced sugar planter named George Williamson, who was appointed Superintendent in 1852. He based the improvement he achieved in the cultivation of the tea bushes on a simple tenet: if you wanted a sustained output of tea throughout the growing season you must first let the bushes grow by ensuring that the early pluckings were light. In 1848 only some 500 acres were under cultivation and the bushes were so drastically plucked early in the season (March–April) that subsequent growth was curtailed. Thus the monthly average of 30,000lb at the start of the harvesting year did not rise above 35,000lb during the May–July peak and fell to below 23,000 in August–September. Williamson realized that selective plucking – just the two leaves and a bud at the tip of each shoot – from the start of the season not only improved the quality of the tea by reducing the proportion of coarse leaf but also increased the overall output. This, of course, meant a later start to the season, but when his directors expressed their anxiety about this Williamson reassured them by pointing out: "Injudicious and ignorant plucking may seriously injure the plant and even cause its death by rendering it more liable to be attacked by white ants and worms." So acreage and output steadily increased from then on, and with them profitability.

Williamson's second seminal innovation was the recognition that only by an accurate system of measurement of output could you ascertain which innovations worked and how well, and which did not. His first report, dated 16 February 1854, lucidly sets out the need to quantify each season's output in terms of both out-turn per acre and cost per pound of finished tea: a yardstick by which achievement is still measured.

Yet the very men who overcame the Company's first crisis were, in part, responsible for its second. The dividends in the 1850s and early 1860s increased steadily, even though no profit was made until 1853. Dividends rose from 2.5 per cent in 1850 to 12 per cent in 1862, although – a sign of the recklessness to come – in the first three years they were paid out of capital or bank borrowings. It should also be borne in mind that at this time tea from Assam still represented just 1 per cent of the total imported to Britain. In 1863 profits of almost £65,000 led the Board to declare a 25 per cent dividend, and although the profit had halved by 1865 the dividend level was maintained at 20 per cent. Then with a thump the whole edifice came tumbling down after heavy losses in 1866 and 1867 (almost £77,000 in the latter year), and no dividends were paid again until 1869. The reason was greed on all sides. The key lies in a passage of Williamson's 1854 report that follows directly on his shrewd analysis of labour shortage as the main obstacle to profitable growth. It refers to increasing competition because "many private persons are now settling in the province and engaging in the cultivation of tea and the other more valuable products". The temptation to cash in on this situation was too much for the very men who had identified it. Among these was Williamson himself and indeed other directors of the Assam Company, including the Managing Director, Henry Burkinyoung, who played a leading role in the Jorhaut Company, founded in 1859, while he was still a director and an officer of the Assam Company. This led to a censure of Burkinyoung by the London Board and an acrimonious if rather feeble defence of his conduct by the Calcutta director. Williamson had already resigned as Superintendent on 25 October 1858, only to reappear in the identical role for the Jorhaut Company on 20 February 1860.

By the 1860s the practice of running private ventures alongside one's corporate responsibilities was rife, with even junior assistants venturing on their own account. These private investments were often on land adjoining that of the employer company and into which it might reasonably have hoped to expand. With the Assam Company showing an 11 per cent return on capital and an average dividend of 18.4 per cent between 1861 and 1866 it is not surprising that others blindly sought to plunge their snouts in this trough and thus became ready prey for the fraudsters who accompany any such outbreak of greed. The seemingly happy state of affairs up to the mid-1860s hid for a time the parlous state of cultivation and manufacture (which fell steadily from 1863) and of deliberate fraud involving the then Chairman and Honorary Managing Director of the Calcutta Board and at least the apparent connivance of Burkinyoung. Not that the Company's own overall conduct at the time was beyond reproach. Prompted by the high levels of profit from 1855 onwards, the Company began to buy up land wherever possible under the Government's absurdly generous scheme which allotted vast acreage for nominal deposits on long rent-free and low-rent terms. Nor did the Company hesitate to sell off at exorbitant prices the poorer sections of any surplus land which it had acquired on the cheap. The Secretary blandly declared that "The Company would not need to show the returns. The prospective buyers and speculators, not knowing, thought the properties much better than they were."

The doctoring of the books and delaying of financial reporting to London had disguised the true and sorry state of affairs for a while until the appointment of W.J. Judge, the new Calcutta Chairman, to investigate the situation. His enquiries revealed such gross malpractices as recruiting and transporting labour at the Company's expense, only to have the coolies delivered to competing gardens, and using the Company's flats (river barges) to carry tools and supplies for rival companies. As a result of these revelations the Calcutta Chairman and the Deputy Secretary were dismissed in the spring of 1862. Burkinyoung was also implicated and eventually forced to resign at the Annual General Meeting in August. Judge, a lawyer by training, so impressed the two Boards by his forensic investigation that they appointed him to a role for which he had no skills or experience: that of overseeing the remedying of the inefficiencies on the gardens themselves. We have seen already with what results.

Such was the momentum of "tea mania" that by 1865 20 new companies had been registered in London and Calcutta, and many more were unregistered or simply private concerns. These new enterprises needed experienced managers and a large proportion of those trained by the well-established concerns were enticed away. Moreover, the new regulations governing the conditions and payment of labour, and the rising price of supplies, inflated the costs of production and diminished the real margin of profit. In such a climate senior people were appointed by the Company's Boards in London and Calcutta with extravagant encomia as to their skills and experience, only to be sacked for incompetence a year or so later.

A report by one shareholder into the Company's affairs written in mid-1866 concludes: "we cannot work the concern except at a loss, the sooner we get rid of the whole thing the better. I for one am not prepared to ... throw good money after bad." The Board had already appointed H.G. Bainbridge to report on the Company's gardens, which he did in April 1866. Some of the Calcutta shareholders, no doubt apprehensive as to what he might discover, objected to his appointment and disparaged his qualifications. The London directors wisely ignored their Calcutta colleagues and went ahead with the appointment. Bainbridge did a thorough, merciless job. His verdict was damning, as well as revealing the very different attitude toward the "natives" since the Mutiny in 1857. He described the gardens' past management system as one "of complete disorder and native dominance". The previous Superintendent was "a man quite unfit for such a charge, half a native himself in feeling, he allowed natives to get the upper hand and he will yet be a source of great trouble to us; he has a bungalow close to Nazira, and he has Gardens close to ours on one side, and Mr Vangulin on the other, and they have an agent and ally in Mr. Lumpinyoung [sic], whom I have ordered out at once, but as a road only divides us from the Bazaar which is Government property, all the discharged vagabonds have a harbour of refuge close by."

Bainbridge's comments on the staff were equally illuminating. "There can be no doubt that for many years the Assam Company has been but a halting place and training school for all the fortune-hunters of Assam who have no sooner learnt or imagined they have learnt, the work before them at the expense of the Company, than they have left the service to establish factories of their own in the immediate neighbourhood, and thus the Company has for years been breeding and nursing a host of future enemies. I attribute this greatly to the mode of payment of employees; the combined salaries and commission amounted to a considerable sum, but the salaries were low and the commission high, and consequently an inferior class of men were alone attracted to the service."

He followed his report with a letter on 11 May 1867 that was equally critical of the very men the Company had appointed to turn things round: "I am afraid you have been horribly deceived in your people. Mr. Judge sat in this house and mostly read magazines, and drew Rs.25,000. Mr. Staunton picked up what he could by corresponding with subordinates and other such dodges, and since 1865 his little game has been to get for himself the Chief Superintendent's billet. The wheels within wheels I shall hope to expose gradually."

At the June 1867 shareholders' meeting a proposal to appoint a

Committee of Enquiry consisting largely of dissident shareholders was substantially supported but defeated. However, at this stage the Board decided to dispense with the services of several officers of the Company in India and to put its affairs in the hands of Schoene Kilburn, one of the managing agencies that were now playing an increasing role in the Indian tea industry. "There was not a shilling of ready money in the hands of anyone on the island," wrote one banker of the planters of Ceylon. It was this lack of liquidity that made many tea-garden owners in India and Ceylon call in a managing agency. These had the funds and the experience to both alleviate cash-flow problems and oversee the operation of a garden right through from planting to London auction. So tight was the grip of the agencies that both before and after independence in both countries legislation was introduced to restrict their power. By the end of Mrs Gandhi's premiership, apart from one or two major firms, such as Balmer Lawrie and Andrew Yule, all the agencies were in the hands of natives of India and Ceylon.

Because so many companies were going bust in the slump of 1866–67, the Government allowed holders of undeveloped land to relinquish it rather than pay the balance due and to consolidate what they had already paid as deposit on all areas as payments on the ones they retained. The more prudent and tightly managed approach, and the appointment of yet another batch of managers who turned out, this time, to be competent, retrieved the fortunes of the Company once more and it went from strength to strength thereafter and is still going strong today.

That difficulties were to be met in a completely new venture was to be expected, but that the Assam Company should survive and eventually flourish was more surprising in view of the collapse of so many other tea companies in the 1860s. The Company's first period of failure (1846–50) arose from ignorance and inordinate expectation; its second (1866–70) from corruption and incompetence. In both instances it was saved from disaster by the efforts of capable men. Although there were occasionally individual cases of corruption and more than a few of incompetence in the Company's first 30 years, the general intent was both honest and consistent. Which was more than could be said for the Nowgong Tea Company.

Sometime in 1863 G.R. Barry (who later was briefly a Liberal MP), together with John Phillips and James Herriot, two planter-speculators involved with tea in India, acquired a number of tracts of jungle in eastern Assam with a view to offering them to investors as thriving tea plantations. In November of that year and in the following year some token clearance and cultivation of the land was undertaken. Barry then initiated the drawing-up of a glowing prospectus for a seemingly attractive venture through the proposed Nowgong Tea Company which claimed:

1. That the Company was formed for the purchase "of thirteen valuable and extensive Tea Estates, already in profitable cultivation".

2. That the whole of the lands were held direct from Government, and were freehold.

3. That of the 12,000 acres "2,182 acres are planted in tea gardens, varying in growth from one to five years".

4. That the plantations were, in respect to soil and position, second to none in the Province, and were calculated to produce during the first year of the Company's operations (1864–5) returns sufficient to yield 10 per cent, on the paid-up capital.

5. That the Directors had "provisionally secured the property upon very favourable terms from the proprietors."

6. That the vendors had "stipulated that 6,000 of the shares are to be allotted to them; 6,000 of the remaining shares have been already subscribed for, leaving 6,000 shares available for the public".

7. That "the factories have the advantage of being traversed by good roads and navigable rivers".

There was no documentary support nor corroborative statements to support these claims and it was to transpire that none of them was true.

Investment was invited, and in October 1864 a company was formed with a view to purchasing and developing the gardens owned by Barry and his friends. The Nowgong Tea Company of Assam was so named after the principal region in which its estates would lie. The agreement for the purchase of the gardens was signed on 16 February 1865 by Barry as chairman and director of Nowgong. He also signed for the three vendors. Quite improperly, Barry's solicitors acted both for vendors and purchasers.

There now took place a significant exchange of telegrams between Calcutta and London:

15 March 1865: Herriot (Barry's co-vendor) to Barry: "You must cancel the sale of our gardens. No cultivation as old as two years."

17 March: Barry to Herriot: "Sale cannot be cancelled – The agreements are signed – possession must be given."

The next day Forbes, the Company Secretary, ostensibly having brought the matter to the Board's attention, telegraphed to the Calcutta lawyers to confirm Barry's instructions, but not until 23 March did the Board formally confirm Barry's action.

The gardens were duly conveyed and the company appointed a Mr Phillipson, a neighbouring garden manager, to receive the properties on the Nowgong Tea Company's behalf and to report on them. The gardens themselves were to be managed by the two vendors in India and the whole project was put under the superintendence of Phillipson. However, the first doubts began to make themselves felt with Phillipson's report written on 20 October 1865 but not received by Nowgong until 23 December. In it Phillipson found "a very serious falling off of the quantity of land under cultivation [20 per cent, in fact], and that the gardens in other respects differed from those originally agreed for." He concludes pointedly: "All statistics given above ... were given me by the vendors and for their accuracy I do not vouch as I had no means of verification and I consider it would be more satisfactory to engage a competent European surveyor to proceed from Calcutta and make a proper survey ..."

Phillipson's report was considered by the Board on 5 January 1866 and then by a subcommittee of all the directors other than Barry. On 26 January a letter was sent to Barry that was originally minuted thus: "They regret much to find the great difference that exists between the ages of the plant as made over, and that stated in the Prospectus – *a difference so great as to alter the whole character of the scheme and prospects of the Company, and which, in their opinion, would justify their repudiating the bargain altogether*", but the words here italicized were erased from the minute book and not communicated to the shareholders at their meeting on 9 March. On the day before that meeting Forbes received a letter dated 7 February from Nowgong's agents in Calcutta. "With reference to Mr. Phillipson's Report, we are now very much afraid that it cannot be relied on as correct." The directors' report to shareholders mentioned neither Phillipson's qualification on the source of his figures nor the agents' reservations. Even the Board minutes for 10 and 15 March have been tampered with to elide them – though they do indicate that the agents' letter was read. Unless Forbes (at Barry's bidding?) deliberately withheld the letter until after the shareholders' meeting, it is hard to imagine that it was not drawn to the directors' attention immediately upon receipt.

Should the agreement between Nowgong and vendors have been repudiated on receipt of Phillipson's report – or at least the shareholders asked for their views? The later Committee of Enquiry thought so, but the Board agreed that "in consideration of the several claims of the Company against the Vendors for deficient area, &c., &c., the Vendors agreed to accept £112,000 in lieu of £163,000, this arrangement to be a full settlement, acquittance, and discharge of all differences now existing between the parties". This decision was put to the shareholders as part of the directors' report, signed by G.R. Barry, as chairman, at the General Meeting of 9 March 1866. (Sometime between 27 February, when Barry signed the report, and the meeting on 9 March at which a William Moran is shown as chairman, the latter seems to have taken over in that role.) The report concluded by informing the shareholders:

[The] Directors believe that they may state with certainty the following facts: – that the properties of the Company are well situated in a populous district, where labour will become every year more easily available, and that the lands which are conterminous with one another, and which are of much greater extent than set forth in the Prospectus, have been admirably selected for the purpose of Tea cultivation; also, that the varieties of the plant are the best possible, and the bushes have been put in at distances which give many more per acre than was the case in the old mode of planting, when they were six feet apart every way. The price which has now been paid for the property will enable the Directors to pay the Vendors, and to carry on the cultivation with very moderate calls. Arrangements have been made for efficient super-intendence, and your Directors trust that in a few months your properties will not be inferior to any in Assam.

On the strength of these assurances the shareholders were content and Barry was paid the first instalment of his money, £15,000 in cash, and in June issued with £45,000 worth of debentures, which he was not supposed to receive until all the transaction had been satisfactorily completed. A reference to £29,000 of these was struck out after Barry's man, Ward, had persuaded the auditors that the conveyance of the estates was even then under the pen and so no reservation was necessary. On 28 June Barry resigned from the Board.

Meanwhile another time bomb was ticking under the speculators. John Phillips had resigned on grounds of ill health in August 1865 as manager of the gardens, but his replacement, Alex S. Lindeman, who had also taken over the general superintendence from the discredited Phillipson, was not in place until 23 December. Barry and his colleagues were to hide behind these three months of undoubted neglect to excuse the even more grave deficiencies that Lindeman's own subsequent report was to highlight. It was written on 23 March 1866 but not received in London until 7 May. On going over the several gardens "he found, to his surprise, that they were in extent not anything like what they have been described to be in Mr Phillipson's Report, and that the vacancies (unplanted areas) among the plants were far more numerous than had been stated in the Report." In fact 1,727.5 acres had now shrunk to 689 and 807,000 nursery plants to 548,000. On top of these quantitative deficiencies there was a glaring qualitative one. A tea bush does not contribute significantly to a garden's crop until it is at least three years old and the prospectus claimed that the gardens being bought "have many such". Phillipson had downgraded the total number of bushes claimed by 21 per cent and emphasized that, far from being mature, these were all new or one-year-old plants. Lindeman was even more harsh and vouchsafed for the existence of only 31 per cent of the original claim. He pointed out that, allowing for vacancies as well, barely a fifth of the supposed original acreage actually carried bushes.

Lindeman did put forward a number of mitigating circumstances in respect of Phillipson's shortcomings: "The land was measured by natives, who in many cases cultivated it by contract, and who gave in erroneous statements, and a good deal of what was planted being choked by the jungle, has entirely disappeared." Later he adds: "Gardens once neglected for some time require a deal more care than those that have continuously and regularly been attended to." He then sets out the programme he proposes to remedy the situation at a cost of a further £40,000.

About the end of April, Frederick Campbell, a professional surveyor, was engaged to survey the gardens, and the result was to corroborate the measurements made by Lindeman. Campbell pointed out, "as a great fault to these gardens, that they are scattered over a large extent of country, which renders their efficient superintendence difficult, and is against their economical management". He also considered "the quality of the soil inferior" and "condemns the variety of the plant", which, he says, "is chiefly China". Campbell summed up his report by saying that, "throughout his experience, which extends over the length and breadth of Assam and Cachar, he has never met with a property encumbered with so many disadvantages, or, for its extent of so little value". His report was even more pessimistic than its predecessors as the following table shows. It indicates the number of acres bearing bushes of each stage of maturity, shown on the left, after vacancies – patches without bushes or where bushes have died – have been subtracted.

	Prospectus	Phillipson	Lindeman	Campbell
New		400	375	
1 year		440	1351	11
2 year		902	0	732
3 year		440	0	
Total	2182	1721	685	743

Real Extent of Tea 444 362
(i.e. total area bearing bushes less the vacancies or patches where none are growing)

This report was received by the directors on 28 July 1866, though they may have been aware of the gist of its contents before that from their Calcutta agents since it was being discussed openly in Assam in June. Lindeman, though he regarded some of it as "too depreciatory and condemnatory", had to admit that "there is much he has said cannot be denied". Indeed as far back as 20 June 1866 he had asked Nowgong's solicitors in Calcutta for a salary rise in the light of the fact that the tea yield, on which his commission would be based, would be barely a quarter of that forecast in the prospectus.

Barry and his co-vendors naturally denied both blame and liability but, "having regard to the large stake in the company held by themselves and their friends", offered to buy and transfer to Nowgong a further 600 acres in the same area. This "stake" was not as large as might have been assumed for, of the six thousand shares for which the vendors were supposed to subscribe, they had taken up only 3,151. Nor had the "6000 shares already subscribed" been taken up. Barry's offer was not without some very sticky strings; it was conditional on Nowgong merging with the Eastern Assam Company (not to be confused with the Assam Company). This was astute on two counts. First, it made it look as though the vendors were doing everything in their power to secure Nowgong's future; and secondly, the Eastern Assam Company was an almost identical set-up in terms of shareholders, directors and garden vendors as Nowgong. A look at the arithmetic shows that the vendors had already made more than they stood to lose from any call on them as debenture holders. If the companies were wound up, they would gain even more.

Faced with these two damning analyses at their half-yearly meeting on 27 September 1866, the directors, in their report to shareholders signed 20 September, pusillanimously declined "to take upon themselves alone the responsibility of abandoning the enterprise" or to support Lindeman's recovery programme. Indeed they admitted to the meeting of 9 March that "they had not sufficient grounds for the favourable statements in their report". Nevertheless, they had already paid a 10 per cent dividend on 4 July, *after* both Phillipson's and Lindeman's reports had come into their hands. Not surprisingly the shareholders, with the consent of some rather apprehensive directors, appointed a Committee of Enquiry – unusual in that it contained a woman shareholder among its members – to look into the affairs of Nowgong and confer with the Board. The Committee was chaired – driven might be a better description – by Dr T. Leckie, the most vociferous critic of Nowgong's Board. Barry, in a pre-emptive move, immediately volunteered to appear before the Enquiry. However, when he attended on 3 October, chaperoned by his solicitor, and saw that the interview was to be recorded by a shorthand writer, he declined to speak and withdrew. The remaining Nowgong directors, themselves likewise under the shadow of indictment, also clammed up when the Enquiry met them with its preliminary findings. They claimed that they had agreed to be consulted not questioned.

The Committee of Enquiry itself could by no stretch of the imagination be considered unbiased. Its members all stood to lose considerable sums if Nowgong collapsed or failed to make a profit. By now it looked as though a call of at least £1 a share would be required to get Nowgong back into the originally forecast levels of production, and not a few shareholders had already failed, for want of means or will, to meet their obligations to date. It is clear that the Committee's chairman, Leckie, was no less biased and influential in regard to the report of the Committee than Barry was in manipulating the shareholders and the initial board of directors on behalf of the vendors.

In a memo solicited by the Enquiry dated 16 October 1866, C.S. Leckie – an experienced planter and presumably related to the Enquiry chairman – wrote:

> In my opinion, the estates ought *not* to be retained, and that it would be better to abandon them, than to attempt to continue their cultivation ... I do not think that the estates ought ever to have become the property of the Company ... Indeed, it may almost be said, that when there was plant there was no labour, and when there was labour there was no plant [there were 875 coolies when there were few bushes and only 581 coolies when there were more]. ...

> I read Mr. Phillipson's as the Report of a brother planter of the

Vendors, who did not feel at liberty to be instrumental in letting them miss the advantage of a singularly profitable bargain, but who neither wished to be the medium of binding the Shareholders to what he saw, as a very bad bargain indeed.

Mr. Lindeman's Report bears unmistakable evidence of a desire to be accurate, [but], I read [it] as the opinion of a conscientious man committed to an engagement, and not wishing to do otherwise than try to make the best of it for all concerned ...

Mr. Campbell on the other hand is in every way independent, and I look upon his views as those of one who did well to be angry at having to examine and describe a property which to him seemed in every way unattractive. Mr. C. can have had no interest, so far as I can imagine, to do otherwise than speak out as to what he saw ...

[The prospectus forecasts] *385,080* lbs. as the produce of 1865; or allowing for the season being an unfavourable one, only half that quantity, or, say in round numbers 200,000 lbs; in place of which, the out-turn of the season was nil ...

I doubt if any man acquainted with Tea cultivation in Assam could be found to purchase [the gardens] at any price; and I think I may venture to say that it would be possible by the outlay of £15,000 rightly expended, over a period of three years, in the formation of a new garden in a suitable locality, to have a much better property than the Nowgong estates now are.

The Enquiry's report, presented to a reconvened shareholders' meeting on 30 October and reflecting Leckie's views, convincingly demonstrated the falsity of the prospectus and that the directors had concealed critical evidence of its misleading nature from the shareholders.

It condemned "the all pervading influence of Mr Barry in his double capacity of vendor and Chairman of the Directors ... himself signing the report which so entirely misled the shareholders". Probably correctly, the Committee was advised that this dual role "would be looked on by a Court of Equity with the greatest disfavour and suspicion".

The report concludes:

The Committee is of opinion that the property could not be worked so as ever to become profitable. Already in the first 18 months of the Company's existence, the sum of £40,000 has been expended on the gardens and on office expenses, and according to Mr. Lindeman's estimate a further sum of £40,000 would be required for the gardens alone during the next two years, and even then with favourable weather, the yield of Tea for the year 1867 would be only 900 maunds [74,000lb]. In fact, the expenses of working the property would be so enormous, to say nothing of the original outlay, that the Company could never compete with other proprietors in the manufacture of tea.

The Committee having therefore been driven unwillingly to the conclusion, that the property of the Company must be looked upon more in the light of an encumbrance than an investment … [i]t will be for the Shareholders now to decide, whether they will adopt the line of policy indicated in this statement of the result of the Committee's deliberations, or whether they will prefer to pay up (without question or dispute), the heavy calls requisite to meet all the debentures, as well as the large sum yet needed to bring the gardens into a really productive state. If the Shareholders decide on the former course, it will be for them to consider how far such a policy can be carried out by means of the present Board of Directors.

This report was handed to the vendors on 27 October 1866. The Committee of Enquiry clearly did not intend that they should have a reasonable opportunity to respond. By offering not to pursue the directors' own derelictions, it persuaded the Board members to resign and join in the campaign against the vendors. This probably accounts for the refusal of the directors to make minutes, letters and other documents available to Barry, though as a former fellow director he was arguably entitled to them. He complained, with some justification, that "it was a packed Committee in every sense of the word, containing the names of those who have been most hostile, and most active for months past, and who had been concerting and meeting together for the purpose of opposition, and whose names were all selected at a previously held private meeting". One of its members had even publicly called Barry a "wholesale swindler", for which he threatened to sue, but, as far as I can ascertain and for obvious reasons, he never did so, preferring briefly to take shelter behind parliamentary privilege as MP for County Cork for a few months.

Notwithstanding the unfairness of the tactics of both Nowgong and the Enquiry, the vendors' defence was unconvincing. The gist of it was that other tea company prospectuses were couched in similar terms, as indeed many were, and no less speciously; that plants once they were a year old were customarily counted as "profitable" though they yielded nothing; and that the roads "were the best in Assam". Barry and his colleagues echoed the Nowgong director's claim that "bad seasons, rise in cost of provisions, of coolies, and of everything else are misfortunes which it is impossible [they] could have foreseen". Barry denied the right of the Enquiry to ask about his private share dealings through employees of the company whom he had put in place.

The vendors' reply piled on the agony and the crocodile tears:

It will be seen that such a frightful season had never before been known in Assam. An outbreak of epidemic cholera carried off 300 men out of 600 in some three months time. Fever also appeared, and not only the factory coolies, but whole villages fled. For the purposes of the Bootan war, seizures of men as camp followers and carriers of baggage were made, and added still more to the panic which prevailed. The Managers were all ill, as well as the five assistants – one, the Manager's brother, died; another assistant went mad, and had to be sent home; and a third had to go to sea. A perusal of the letters in the Appendix will show that such a state of things existed that the plantations were literally abandoned for two or three months and *overrun* with jungle. The Vendors in India have asked the Directors again and again to cause inquiries to be made, and they will find all this to be strictly true, and that their own Manager would not but be able to admit it. The loss which has occurred, serious and heavy as it is, has been caused by one of those misfortunes to which all speculations are liable, and is the more to be regretted that it occurred at the unfortunate time of the year it did, during the rains, when the jungle grows so rapidly. But to attempt to make the Vendors liable for losses which have occurred within the Company's own management, from six to nine and twelve months after they had received possession of the gardens, is simply absurd, and is what the Vendors never could consent to.

One plea by the vendors is both significant and true: "Dozens of Tea Companies have wound up, or been put in liquidation during the last six months in India and in England, owing to these causes and to some of them running short of capital, so that there is at the present moment a perfect panic about Tea properties. The number of factories being closed will, however, reduce competition and rates, the Vendors believe, will very soon fall again to the old scale, which admitted of handsome profits."

It is also true that, in jungle country, gardens can rapidly revert to nature, but since the garden management had been appointed by the vendors it is more likely that there never was the degree of sound cultivation claimed. After a lapse of 140 years the truth of the matter cannot be entirely clear and probably would not even have yielded to professional investigation at the time. However, overall there is little doubt that the vendors grossly misled the investors as to their considerable profit, nor that the majority of Nowgong's investors tried to evade their legitimate obligations. The investors went away poorer and wiser men; the vendors richer and probably more careful of how they attempted to gull the public in future.

Throughout the 1860s, stimulated by such examples as the Assam Company and Nowgong, the argument raged as to whether the new concept of limited liability gave too little protection to the public or too little encouragement to the entrepreneur. On one side of the argument the financier and banker William Newmarch asserted: "If a person is foolish enough to take shares in a concern about which he knows nothing, and about the directors of which he knows nothing, he must take the consequences." Speculation was compared to alcoholism, a weakness to be cured by individual self-discipline. On the other side of the argument the magazine *Temple Bar* was typical when it complained that, for the last three years in the business community, "Dishonesty, untruth, and what may, in plain English, be termed mercantile swindling within the limits of the law, exist on all sides and on every quarter." More than a third of the companies formed between 1856 and 1865 had folded within five years. When on 10 May 1866 Overend and Gurney, a major discount house, suspended payments it brought some two hundred companies crashing down in its wake. It was in such a climate that the shareholders of Nowgong, justifiably angry, desperately tried to get out of further calls on their financial resources.

This typical "South Sea Bubble" style of story was indeed repeated many times over during the "tea mania" of the 1860s which followed the rapid increase in the demand for Indian tea and the genuine opportunities for greatly expanded tea production in Assam. Naivety and greed on the one side; deviousness, if not downright dishonesty, on the other, led to many a repetition of the Nowgong debacle during the decade of tea mania. Fortunately this chaotic spasm was then followed by better-informed cultivation and a more orderly and sensible pattern of British investment in the tea industry of India.

CHAPTER SEVENTEEN

With a Pound of Tea

Pigs, pianos and pensions: the pig was superseded by an elephant; the pianos played the opening bars of a harmonious fortune; and the pensions landed several people in Queer Street. All these featured among the exuberant outpouring of gimmicks and gambits by which the rapidly expanding tea industry promoted its wares at the end of the nineteenth century.

The pensions were perhaps the most astounding example of ill-thought-out or fraudulent publicity stunts embarked on in pursuit of the fortunes to be made from tea. Many of Nelson & Company's 250,000 customers had been enticed by its offer of a £25 annual pension for life to widows who bought its tea. By the time it had nineteen thousand widows entitled to pensions, it was clear that the company could no longer meet its obligations out of its rapid growth and it went down in a welter of lawsuits with assets of only £20,000 and liabilities of £30 million.

The pianos and the pigs, or rather the pig, led on to fortunes. The most flamboyant of all the tea tycoons was Tommy Lipton (1850–1931), who had paraded a pig along the streets of his native Glasgow to draw attention to the quality bacon available in his first shop, which he had opened in 1871. Before he was 40 he was a millionaire, but not a leaf of tea had yet passed across the counters of his three hundred shops. In 1890 his even larger chain sold six million pounds of it. Lipton – partly from a desire to sell groceries cheaply to those who were as poor as he had been when he started out, but more, I suspect, from being among the first to recognize the value of "pile 'em high, and sell 'em cheap" tactics – decided that the same principles should apply to tea. He was sure that he could retail tea for 1s. 7d. a pound that usually sold for 3s. and still make a profit if he cut out the middlemen: the London tea merchants who had courted him so assiduously for access to his chain of shops.

The man who caused a traffic jam with his pig, offered a 35-ton cheese to the Queen, paraded his tea on elephants, and also on the sandwich boards of men dressed as Indians, and in a convoy of 40 lorries preceded by a pipe band, believed the secret of success lay in being seen and heard in every way at every opportunity. Although the genteel and established thought him brash and vulgar, which he was, his approach worked. "Lipton's" became a household word synonymous with "tea". I cannot help thinking that he laid on the rough-diamond façade a bit. He must have been piqued by the kind of snobbery typified by the Kaiser's scathing remark that the Prince of Wales "had gone boating with his grocer", an attitude that made Lipton withdraw his application to become a member of the Royal Yacht Squadron rather than be blackballed. He was, and always felt, more readily accepted in America, that land of the vulgar and the brash, where commercial success is seen as the acme of human achievement.

It is clear from the autobiographical *Leaves from the Lipton Logs* that this son of an Irishman had no need to travel to Blarney to get either his gift of the gab or his elasticity with the truth. It is equally clear that he was a genuine visionary. If Tommy Lipton had a dream image in his head of a smiling Tamil girl plucking tea that would come straight from his tea garden to the customer's pot, he also had the drive and, by 1890, the capital to turn the dream into reality. Sending his agent, Frank Dipluck, to reconnoitre in advance, Lipton, under the guise of a holiday to Australia he never intended to take, travelled to Ceylon in 1890 and bought up five of the few remaining former coffee-estates-turned-tea-gardens for what were still relatively knock-down prices. Star among these was the spectacular Dambatenne estate. He loved to stand his guests at the precipitous edge of its 1,830-metre elevation and embrace with a sweep of his arm the thousands of acres of tea gardens below – most of which did not belong to him – as if they were his personal empire. Exaggeration was Tommy Lipton's stock in trade, and if people chose to infer the impossible – that every leaf in the millions of packets of Lipton's tea came from his own three thousand acres, or that he was so virile he had to shave three times a day – he was not going to disabuse them. The *Mona Lisa*-like smile on the face of the Tamil girl on every packet may have been his way of enjoying the joke that made him, for a while, the most powerful man in the British tea business.

What Lipton saw, well before almost anyone else, was that if Ceylon tea in general prospered he would prosper, too. The Ceylon tea planters had already decided in 1892 to levy a cess (short for "assess", a compulsory financial levy based on annual tea production) on their members to promote the sale of Ceylon tea abroad, particularly in America, so Lipton had little difficulty in persuading them to put up the money to make a splash at the World's Fair in Chicago in 1893. The Ceylon tea pavilion, built in Colombo and shipped piecemeal, was exotic and magnificent and the popularity of Ceylon tea grew rapidly. In 1888, Ceylon had exported only 24 million pounds of tea; in 1893, 80 million pounds were shipped; and in 1898, at 120 million pounds, the island colony was already closing the gap on the exports of its main rival, India, which it would overtake in 1965.

If the affection of the British for the eccentric Irishman with the white, bushy moustache, spotted blue bow-tie and professional-looking yachting cap was a little patronizing, the Americans took to Tommy Lipton unreservedly. Perhaps this was also because he had bummed around their country as a teenager doing odd jobs and had got to know and like them. Four times he spent a great deal of time, money and energy trying – unsuccessfully – to win the America's Cup, one of the great international yachting prizes, and thus became in the United States the epitome of the "sporting" British loser. Perhaps this nautical fame made up for early humiliations as a cabin boy on the Glasgow–Belfast ferry steamer. Since he appears to have had no other obsessions or pastimes but yacht racing – though he had a reputation as a "ladies' man" but never married – and since his pursuit of the trophy gave his tea a high profile in America, his boastful exaggerations could be forgiven.

Indeed it seems as if the great British public was prepared to forgive this showman anything. Although Lipton was a genuinely generous man, his acts of benevolence were usually also undertaken with an eye to the publicity they attracted. He could be devious and unscrupulous in his promotional activities, but even when it was proved in court that his employees had been bribing army quarter-masters to place contracts with Lipton's, no stigma seemed to attach to him, although his unfortunate minions, acting no doubt, as the judge said, on implied if not direct instruction, were sacked and the senior army officer in question was jailed for six months. When in 1898 he decided to float his company the share placement was 35 times oversubscribed.

Tommy Lipton would probably have been happy to have had carved on his tombstone, by way of epitaph, the cartoon that showed him framed by a teapot with heraldic bearers, sinister, of four pretty girls, dexter of four elderly spinsters. The motto of the former ran, "We love you for your success, we love you for your title"; and of the latter, "We love you for your tea." You can still buy tea bearing the Lipton's label today, but your money now goes into the pocket of Unilever, which took it over in 1972.

Two years before the Lipton's flotation another tea giant went public, this one sadly no longer with us under any guise. When, in 1873, a Plymouth retail chemist, John Boon Densham, decided to bring his four sons into the business and branch out into tea, a great firm was born. (Densham's original partner had been a Mr Lees, possibly the Indian tea pioneer of the 1850s and 1860s W. Nassau Lees, in retirement in England.) Densham and Sons – devout Baptists all – not only preceded Lipton's but outstripped it, and their eventual success was almost entirely due to the commercial nous of the youngest son, John Lane Densham. Until his father's death in 1886, John jnr. had been the Joseph of the family, tricycling round Plymouth delivering to the family's customers. Wisely, his three brothers decided to make him a partner.

John's first achievement seems to have been to coin what became one of the best-known brand names in tea. Mazawattee – an entirely made-up name that perfectly combined the slightly bizarre and unusual with an implied exotic superiority – became the leading brand of packet tea sold in Britain. Apparently John shut himself in the Guildhall library with a Hindi and a Sinhalese dictionary and came up with the hybrid "Mazatha-Wattee", or "luscious growth". (The credit for coining the name is sometimes also given to D.F. Shillington, a tea buyer for Harrison and Crossfield.) It was a printer who added his finishing touches by suggesting that the tongue-twisting "*tha*" in the middle be dropped. I am surprised that John's linguistic skills should have been such as to have mastered both these languages – or at least to have done so without help – sufficiently to create this hybrid. But whatever its genesis, Mazawattee became such an alluring name that Denshams' had to go to court on several occasions to stamp on such attempts at "passing off" as Mallawattee.

Like Lipton after him, John believed in prolific advertising. Soon the Mazawattee lace-capped granny, and her equally be-capped granddaughter, were to be seen side by side on the lids of tins, on enamelled station advertising plaques and in cheap book advertisements happily drinking their cups of John's tea. Such (by Victorian standards) titillatingly risqué cartoons as the one showing a lady upbraiding a porter because she had alighted at the wrong station on account of the proliferation of signs saying either "Gentlemen" or "Mazawattee" were all free grist to Denshams' promotional mill. No doubt potential customers were equally charmed by the three jolly "niggers" who also featured in the firm's advertisements and would today be thought as politically incorrect as the chimpanzees' tea parties later used in television advertisements for Brooke Bond's PG Tips.

Denshams' tea brand was among the first to exploit the health-promoting qualities of its tea, though modern science might suggest that ¼lb bags of tea consisting of 2¾oz of tea and 1¼oz of lead-foil lining were a greater hazard to health – not to mention to integrity – than any possible toxin in tea. Nor did John Densham overlook the free advertising provided by his own publicity stunts. In May 1891 he highlighted the quality to be found in Mazawattee by buying a consignment of "golden tips" from the Gartmore estate in Ceylon for the absurdly high price of £25 10s. a pound. A sample of this widely publicized purchase was thereafter hallowed in a glass case at the company's headquarters in Mincing Lane. Mazawattee also entered into an absurd contest with Lipton's as to which company paid the most tea duty to the Crown in "a single week". When Mazawattee won the first round with a cheque for £63,147 2s. 10d. – I love the precision of the pence – the company ran off thousands of copies and placed them on the seats of every form of public transport it could reach. Lipton's responded with a bigger cheque still, only to be topped once and for all by a Mazawattee cheque for almost £86,000. As one newspaper pointed out this was clearly a ridiculous claim. With duty at 4d. a pound this would have meant Mazawattee was taking over five million pounds of tea a week out of bond. Once the trick of accumulating payments had been shown up, it was dropped, but the champion cheque also found its way into a glass shrine in Mincing Lane.

But Denshams' would not have been so successful for so long merely on the strength of good publicity. Very soon after leaf from Ceylon first came to the London auctions on 28 October 1878, John was the first to see the advantage of allying his brand with tea from this single reputable source, and of automating his packing lines to cut costs and increase the rate at which tea was packed. Before John Densham died, Mazawattee was the most popular brand of packet tea. Later Mazawattee was among the first to install automated tea-bag-filling machinery and for a while was the largest tea wholesaler in the world.

Yet such was the driving force of John jnr. that his advancing years, ill-health and too heavy a work burden were reflected in the fading fortunes of Mazawattee. Denshams' began to diversify in too many directions. Some, such as the manufacture of brightly decorated tins for tea and biscuits, at least had some connection with tea. Others, such as branching into coffee and cocoa, were in direct competition with the firm's main product, and still others, such as confectionery, were simply irrelevant to the core business. Most damaging of all was the decision of the two senior Denshams' managers, McQuitty and McLean, into whose hands the reins had been entrusted in 1906 in John's absence abroad, to launch a massive expansion into retailing. Within a matter of months 70 shops had been opened and a further 98 equipped at a cost of

£178,000. This both upset Mazawattee's established grocer outlets and overstretched the company's already strained financial resources. John, who was in South Africa, in his new role as roving ambassador to the 36 countries in which Mazawattee was now sold, was alerted to the danger by other worried directors and shareholders. He hastened back to England, persuaded an Extraordinary General Meeting to sack the two managers, and resumed executive control of operations himself. But he was no longer the force he had been. Although many of the Mazawattee ship's leaks were staunched, it remained a slowly sinking craft, which finally went to the bottom. Denshams' business was largely obliterated by German bombing in 1943 and after the war the firm was taken over by Burton Sons and Saunders and what had once been the best-known Ceylon tea brand in Britain disappeared.

Such was the reputation of Ceylon as a source of top-quality tea that several small firms tried to capitalize on the aura created by Lipton's and Mazawattee. These were relentlessly prosecuted, but apart from a £10 fine for one company, which used the name of an actual estate on its packets, the charges failed. The lawyers had a field day. What exactly could be called Ceylon tea? How much must a packet contain before the claim could be made legitimately? Several firms, including at least one reputable one, got away with including a very small proportion in a blend with Indian or China in packets that nevertheless claimed to be "Pure Ceylon Tea". As the prosecuting counsel in one case pointed out, "by paying close attention to the label, and perhaps with the aid of glasses, the words 'blended with India and China' might be discovered, but they were so hidden by a signature, one flourish being scrawled heavily through them, that the words denoting a blend were certain to escape the eye of the purchaser".

The line between sharp practice and keen marketing has always been a thin one, but most of the ingenious gimmicks devised to sell tea managed – sometimes only just – to stay on the right side of that line. The anonymous author of The Tea Purchaser's Guide (1785) warns his readers of a variety of traps into which they might fall: "Contrast the price of one set of advertisers with the other; the former vends the best Hyson at 13s. per lb. Let those be asked if they are warranted to be imposed on the public by selling at such an enormous price; and the other is selling at 1s. 4d. per lb, when the most inferior quality at the late India sale, sold at eighteen pence per lb exclusive of duty." He concludes that one is a rip-off and the other an adulterated fraud, and that the Government itself is capable of dirty tricks: "There are few persons in the metropolis, except in the tea trade, who have the least knowledge of the immense quantity of damaged teas sold by government. In their bad state they were little better than dirt, and so exceeding disgustful to the eye that none would have thought them worth acceptance." Though Elizabeth Gaskell's Miss Matty in *Cranford* was taking honesty a little too far when she "plaintively entreated some of her customers not to buy green tea – running it down as slow poison, sure to destroy the nerves, and produce all manner of evil", she provided an antidote to those exaggerated claims which culminated in the late nineteenth and early twentieth centuries in the deliberate exploitation of health anxieties and the offering of a particular brand of tea as the remedy.

The very first tea advertisement, printed in the *London Gazette* for the first week of September 1658, which had to compete for attention with the news of Oliver Cromwell's death, set the trend in offering for sale "a China drink, by all physitians approved". More than three hundred years later John Sumner (1856–1934) and J.R. Brindley (d. 1919) saw the advantage of securing for their new Typhoo brand the approval of "all physitians" by sending out free samples to some four thousand doctors and then claiming to have their endorsement on the tacit grounds that they had not refused it. This certainly paid off. When, during the First World War, all tea had to be pooled in one amorphous blend, it was pressure from the medical profession that earned Typhoo exemption.

The evolution of Typhoo into a leading brand was a combination of chance and clever exploitation of the kind of anxieties provoked by a typical later *Daily Chronicle* "scare" story in 1914 claiming that the tannin in tea was bad for the "nerves". John Sumner's sister, Mary, suffered from indigestion whenever she drank a cup or two of her customary brew. I suspect that, as in the case of Jonas Hanway, the irritation of Miss Sumner's digestive tract may have been due not, as she claimed, to the tannin in her tea, but to the adulterants which were still sometimes finding their way into black tea from China. Whether or not this was true, Miss Sumner attributed her distress to the excess of tannin in the tea she had been drinking. By chance, in 1905, she then made herself a pot from what appears to have been Broken Orange Pekoe fannings and suffered no ill effects. The much smaller leaf would have been less susceptible to the kind of toxic colourants the Chinese sometimes added to larger leaf tea.

Mary Sumner drew this apparent benefit to the attention of her brother John, who ran the family's grocery shops in Birmingham. At her urging he decided to try selling 30 chests of her particular tea on the strength of its claim to be free from dyspepsia-causing "injurious gallo-tannic acid". It wasn't true, but it worked. When Sumner asked his bank for a loan to finance expansion of this side of his business, the manager not only refused but demanded he clear his existing overdraft to boot. A true entrepreneur, Sumner sold off the grocery side of the business, paid off the bank and, no doubt with some relish, closed his account, to gamble everything on being a successful tea merchant. His gamble paid off. His first year's profit in 1906 was only £181 2s. 7d., but 61 years later Typhoo's profit was a few pounds short of £4 million.

John Sumner's success was more due to his business acumen than to his sister's fortuitous, and erroneous, claim. It was also due to taking into partnership J.R. Brindley, the proprietor of Priory Teas, another small Birmingham company, who had shown a real flair for publicity. Brindley had already persuaded the French balloonist Lamprière to fly over the city dropping leaflets promoting his tea, and he followed this in 1896 by offering a hundred pianos worth £40 each to customers who bought its tea. The local grocery trade was sharply divided between those who put a piano in the shop window and those who fulminated against the whole concept.

As any professional marketing man would confirm, a rose by any other name would *not* smell as sweet, because the sniffer would not be expecting it to. The right name is half the sale's battle. Who thought of Typhoo as a brand name, we do not know, but it may well have been Brindley. Typhoo Tipps, with its easily pronounceable hint of the Orient in "Typhoo" and the tacit claim to quality implied by "Tipps", evolved by stages. First it acquired the "h", then it replaced the dot between "Ty" and "phoo" by a hyphen, then it dropped the hyphen and finally, in the 1940s, abandoned "Tipps", of which the second "p" had arisen in the first place from a printer's error which the partners had shrewdly ignored.

Typhoo was also skilfully promoted. There were a number of fairly commonplace give-aways – tennis rackets, rubber mats and so on – which could be obtained in exchange for a given number of Typhoo packet labels. Even more enticing were the individual picture cards, like cigarette cards, that were to be found in each packet and each of which was part of a series. To be sure to complete each series you had to buy more than the corresponding number of packets of Typhoo, but at least if you own a complete set today it will be worth more than the occasional sovereign to be found in the rival packets of Mr Francis of Oswestry, which more usually yielded a 3d. piece – or nothing. Another tea retailer, Robert Eadie, offered a free teapot to the first ten thousand people to buy ½lb of his tea; for ¼lb you got only a cup and saucer. Everything from an antimacassar to a baby's chair was to be had for those tempted to buy this or that brand of tea. It is perhaps indicative of the shoddy nature of many of these give-aways that the catch-phrase "given away with a pound of tea" has come to imply something worthless that would not otherwise be worth having. However, one at least certainly was worth having and remains indispensable to the London visitor to this day. In 1851 the small firm of Sidney, Wells, Manduell & Co. gave away a *New Map of the Principal Streets of London for 1851*, the precursor to the *London A–Z*. The same firm had the cunning idea of inviting subpostmasters to act as agents for its tea and of getting the "letter-carriers" to act as door-to-door salesmen, to the annoyance of Post Office and public alike. But it survived for another 40 years.

Another much-practised sales device is the loss-leader, which is older than may be supposed. One of the most common items used in this role for the sale of groceries today is sugar. And so it was in Dr Short's day. In his famous *Dissertation on Tea* of 1730, he points out, albeit in a tone of surprise, that "should they sell sugar at or under Prime cost, to get off their Tea, an industrious man may raise a very handsome fortune in no very long time". Today it is tea itself that is the most common loss-leader.

In Typhoo's case these promotional devices and loss-leaders were backed by some high-powered advertising. As Typhoo consisted of fannings, it was bound to produce more cups to a spoonful of these small leaves than could be obtained from a large-leaf tea. Typhoo's advertisements showed a level spoonful of Typhoo giving the same number of cups of tea as a heaped spoonful of a rival tea. The leaf weight, of course, would have been the same, but no mention was made of that. If the promotional touch was due to Brindley, the mastery of logistics and quality control, the sourcing and packaging of the tea and the positive cash flow were the contribution of John Sumner. He was one of the first to appreciate the advantages of vertical integration and control of the supply chain. He was not the first to recognize the value of the association in the public mind between quality tea and Ceylon, but whereas Lipton's boast that he cut out the middleman and supplied tea straight from his own garden to the drinker's cup had been a gimmick, Sumner was content to get his cheaper tea from many sources in Ceylon, over which he exercised a ruthless quality control. When, in response to complaints that there was some tannin in Typhoo, one of his hawk-eyed buying brokers spotted that certain consignments had been adulterated, Sumner sailed for Ceylon immediately. Some rough language and the eventual suicide of the culpable managing director and the problem had been solved.

Sumner implemented a system of buying, blending, quality control and packing in Ceylon that reduced his costs considerably. Moreover, Typhoo was packed in standard cartons rather than the conventional thick-paper bags, and these in turn were put into chests of a size suitable for forwarding to retailers. Ensuring that the tea was not touched again in its journey from the Colombo dockside, via steamer, harbour lighter and English canal barge to the Typhoo warehouses in Birmingham, both kept the price down and gave confidence to the consumer. It is no surprise that one of the first firms to ship its tea on pallets in large containers through the port of Felixstowe in the 1980s was Typhoo. By then, however, it was a part of the food giant Premier Brands, which had swallowed it up, along with other famous tea names such as Melrose and Glengettie.

Sumner also wisely kept out of the very retail trade in which his tea empire had its origins, supplying only to wholesalers and solely against cash-with-order. The first outlets for Typhoo had been chemists and other health-connected outlets, which could capitalize on Typhoo's supposed health advantages; but long before Sumner and Brindley's firm was taken over, there was scarcely a grocer's in the land where a packet of Typhoo could not be bought off the shelf. And Sir John Sumner had his philanthropic fame and a knighthood to prove it.

Britain in the nineteenth and early-twentieth centuries was a country where fortunes were made and great mansions built, good works were undertaken and knighthoods received by the tea tycoons on a scale only matched by the cotton kings and the iron and coal masters. The dominance in the British wholesale and retail tea business of religious nonconformists, particularly Quakers, with their close ties to the Temperance movement, is matched only by the Frys, Cadburys and Rowntrees in chocolate and confectionery. Then shall their names, familiar in our mouths as household words – Lipton's and Horniman, Twinings, Brooke Bond and Typhoo, Mazawattee and Lyons, Ridgway and Cassell – be in our flowing cups freshly remember'd. Sadly, all these, without a single exception, have either vanished altogether or been swallowed up by giant corporations with as much relish and as little effort as one of their own delicious cups of tea.

Ridgway survived some 160 years as an independent brand name and was also the first to embark on selling tea in Britain. Thomas Ridgway, in partnership with Arthur Dakin, had started trading in tea in Birmingham's (old) Bull Ring and in Derby at the enticingly named Sign of the Golden Canister. These first ventures were a financial failure and Ridgway and Dakin stayed in business only by compounding with their creditors. Ridgway was not deterred by this set-back. Anticipating the growing demand for tea that would result from the ending of the East India Company's monopoly in 1834, he moved to London in 1836 and set up there as Ridgway,

Dakin and Co. He advertised his intent to establish "an extensive tea concern founded on the principle of a small profit and large sales. But as great professions, without proof, can entitle us to no confidence we shall state at what prices we can supply you with the best quality, for ready money only". The lesson of the need for positive cash flow learned, tea competitively priced, and Dakin having departed, the firm, now known just as Ridgway, flourished and soon excited the envy of critical rivals. Ridgway rebuked them in the robust advertising style of the day: "It is evident that such attempts at misleading the Public can only arise from a consciousness, on their parts, of the want of either resources or merits of their own, on which to found any claims to confidence, and are the highest tributes that can be paid to the general acknowledged excellence and cheapness of our Tea. Such proceedings further exhibit a surprising lack of talent and common prudence, inasmuch as it is clear that so many anxious imitators and copiers confess by the act their hopeless inferiority to the original." From this basic platform Ridgway became one of the leading players in the tea business, but, despite being appointed tea merchant to Queen Victoria – which gave it cachet and a special niche in the American market – and despite becoming a limited company in 1896, was eventually taken over by Tate and Lyle and was finally swallowed up by Premier Brands in 1987.

Another old firm to have survived more or less intact sprang not from individual entrepreneurial drive but from collective need. The English and Scottish Joint Co-operative Wholesale Society (CWS) was founded in 1863 to supply the necessaries of life as cheaply as possible to poorer members of the community and to distribute its profits among its member-customers. Tea was, of course, one of those necessities by now. As the membership grew, so did CWS's buying power and consequently its competitive selling price until it became one of the half-dozen dominant players in the tea market, particularly with its quasi-medicinal Prescription Tea, and, later, straightforward TV advertising.

What television advertising was to the second half of the twentieth century, exhibitions were to the final decades of the nineteenth. Nor were they much inferior to the commercial television of the 1950s and 1960s in providing "opportunities to view". Six million people passed through the Great Exhibition of 1851 at the Crystal Palace in Hyde Park, almost a third of the population of Britain (though many will have visited more than once), and 28 million saw the World's Fair in Paris in 1889. Here again Ceylon beat India to the draw by securing the exclusive tearoom concession in the British section, though not without anxious moments caused by attempts to lure away the traditionally dressed attendants as servants. Such was the impact of the extended experience of a visit to an exhibition that the word-of-mouth effect was probably much greater and more sustained than that of today's 15- or 30-second TV advertisement. Moreover, before the days of cheap foreign travel for ordinary citizens, such exhibitions provided them with a glimpse of the exotic lands from which their tea and coffee, their sugar and cotton, originally came.

On the other hand, the competition to attract attention at an exhibition was just as intense as it is in a seven-minute TV ad break. The Crystal Palace offered thirteen thousand exhibits, Paris over sixty thousand. So much care had to be taken to make an exhibit stand out from its rivals. India, Ceylon and the Dutch East Indies did this by recreating something of their mysterious worlds in replica temples and palaces, made from native materials and manned by natives in their most extravagant costumes. Most effectively of all, they provided the leg-weary and thirsty exhibition-goer with a place to rest and drink a cup of the very best tea, either free or very cheaply. This was the case at the London Health Exhibition of 1884, where the Indian Tea Association managed to get in first with the claim to the tearoom. No doubt its representatives were slightly taken aback to see some of the self-appointed tea experts taking the leaves out of the teapots to examine them, and to hear some of the less expert asking for "Darlington" (Darjeeling) and "Catcher" (Cachar) tea.

These high-impact one-offs had to be supported by more sustained exposure at a lower level of intensity. The stream of give-aways was backed up by advertising hoardings – particularly those eye-catching coloured enamel ones at railway stations – and elaborate advertisements in newspapers and magazines, often given a further boost by celebrity endorsement. This is one of the older forms of advertising, and in the days before the Advertising Standards Authority, or its equivalent elsewhere in Europe and America, there was no legal restraint on what could be claimed in an advertisement, provided it was not libellous or fraudulent. This meant that anyone's name could be taken as much in vain as the advertiser thought to his advantage. In pursuit of prominence there were many outrageous acts of identity theft. Particularly cheeky was one by a minor brand, Avoncherra, that depicted Gladstone presiding over a meeting of his entire cabinet, every man of which is drinking Avoncherra tea. The Grand Old Man is seen admonishing Earl Spencer, "Steady there, Spencer, with the milk, Rosebery has not had a drop yet." Whether this promoted the sale of Avoncherra among Tories is doubtful. Another shows Queen Victoria presenting Princess Mary and the Duke of York with a packet of Mazawattee's Gartmore Golden Tips on the occasion of their marriage in 1893.

The search for competitive edge over rival brands gave rise to some dreadful doggerel. A trite play featured a Mrs Love-a-cup. In David Lewis's Manchester department store (not to be confused with the John Lewis Partnership) in 1959 a singing teapot urged the passer-by, in a song specially composed many years earlier, to buy "Lewis's Beautiful Tea". David Lewis's business also provides the best example of the reverse: using tea, sold for minimal profit, or even at a loss, to entice purchasers for other goods. Its celebrated India–Ceylon blend, "beautiful two-shilling tea", which was soon selling at the rate of 20,000lb a week, was situated strategically near the entrance to the store on the ground floor in order to draw customers in. It was flanked by haberdashery, dress fabrics and umbrellas, and used to promote velveteen at the same price per yard.

If tea could be used to promote things quite other than tea, so could teapots. In the Norwich City Castle Museum there is a fascinating array of examples of how this poster site in the middle of the tea table was exploited to promote other ends. Some of these were just for fun – the saucy image of the "Miller's Maid grinding Old Men Young", for example – and, like the many colourful and sometimes bizarre designs, were intended just to sell teapots. Others exhorted the pourer to respond with anything from votes to virtues. I do not know what household would have required all six teapots necessary to depict the six stages in the story of the Prodigal Son, but many a home must have been graced by the teapot exhorting the beholder to "Let your Conversation be upon the Gospel of Christ". A sure antidote to the usual gossip. Others put forward the virtues of various candidates at parliamentary elections and were used in substantial numbers at political rallies and teas. One of the more popular was one that declared for "Wilkes and Liberty", deployed during the great radical's election campaign of 1768 when he was returned as MP for Middlesex.

Lewis's two-shilling tea was also a good example of another crucial element in successful marketing: pitching the price right. A quality tea at 2s., the lower end of the quality price bracket, did just that. But the past master at pricing was probably John Cassell (1817–65). As was so often the case in the eighteenth and nineteenth centuries, tea and Temperance went hand in hand yet again. Born in an alehouse in one of the poorer parts of Manchester where the problems of drink were rife, Cassell became, like his contemporary Horniman, a fervent and eloquent supporter of the Temperance movement. In his passionately conducted campaign against the evils of alcohol, Cassell saw tea as a valuable weapon in the struggle to oust the demon drink, provided it could be offered to the poor – and the not so poor – in quantities and at a price that suited their respective budgets. By marrying into a modest amount of money he acquired the means to test his theory. Shrewdly, he also saw the value of the high-profile name recognition that could attach to British enterprise after Hong Kong became a Crown colony in 1843. So he called his company the Hong Kong Tea Company, though neither product nor company had anything to do with that shameful prize. Cassell offered his fairly basic tea blend, at competitive prices, in simple tinfoil packets that ranged in weight from 1oz to 1lb. Thomas Hardy claimed that his mother was a Cassell's tea devotee "because it was the only packet she could get for a shilling". Despite his success as a tea wholesaler – seven hundred retailers were offering Cassell's tea at its peak – it is as a book publisher that the name of John Cassell is best known. The story is that he bought a printing press on which to print the labels for his tea packets and rather than see it stand idle much of the time, also put it to work printing the *Teetotal Times*. From there to wider publishing was a natural step.

Another name that began in tea but subsequently became far more famous for other things is that of Tesco. Jakob (Jack) Cohen (1898–1979) – later Sir Jack – as an astute young East Ender in 1924 saw a job lot of tea on offer at 9d. a pound by the small east London firm of Torrington and Stockwell. He snapped it up, repacked it simply in ½lb bags and sold them at 6d. a time. Soon he was doing such a roaring trade that he was buying 50 chests at a time. He already had a grocery store which he had set up in a similar fashion in 1919, using his Royal Flying Corps demob gratuity of £30 to do similar deals buying job lots of fish paste and golden syrup and selling them on for a modest profit. But it was the tea deal that saw his enterprise take off. For want of a name, he combined the initials of the man who sold him his first tea, T.E. Stockwell, with his own to form "Tesco", though I doubt if even the ambitious Sir Jack envisaged the day when a third of all Britain's grocery sales would pass through stores bearing this name.

Arthur Brooke (1845–1918) was different from the other nineteenth-century tea tycoons in that he grew up in the business. His father, Charles, was a tea wholesaler. In 1869, after a false start in the cotton industry and a £1-a-week apprenticeship with another tea firm, Arthur decided to set up his own retailing business, but sell only tea, coffee and sugar. He was another who recognized the importance of the right name, both for his brand and for his firm. Brooke Bond & Co. would become one of the leading tea firms without there ever having been a Mr Bond. It just sounded more respectable and confidence-inspiring for there to be more than one partner, so Mr Brooke invented one as entirely fictitious as the James of that ilk. Brooke's successors also grasped the value of leaping on the tea-equals-health bandwagon. Taking a leaf out of Typhoo's book, they launched their own "Digestive Tea" in 1932.

In 1945 the Ministry of Health outlawed all advertising that claimed health benefits unless they could be proved scientifically and clinically. The three big companies that had used just such claims dutifully complied, but each with their own particular slant. The CWS re-branded its Prescription Tea with the old-fashioned, slightly medical-sounding name "99". Typhoo felt sufficiently sure of its ground simply to comply. Brooke Bond, however, adopted the "we are transparently honest" technique. Its packets baldly stated: "Brooke Bond do not claim any medicinal nutritional or dietary value for their tea." But the name had been subtly changed to Pre-Gestee, thus tacitly implying its previous claim. By a nice irony, those claims for the health benefits of tea that had been made with a mixture of blind faith and tongue in cheek for 350 years could be made again, hand on heart, in the 1990s, as a result of the work referred to in Chapter 3. Brooke Bond reverted to the slightly pompous jargon designed to impress the uninitiated. Britain's number-one brand – now familiarly known by its metamorphosed name of PG Tips – claimed: "Tea is a natural source of powerful antioxidants called flavonoids. Increasing evidence shows that these antioxidants, found in both tea and fruit and vegetables, form an important part of a healthy diet."

If the efforts to promote their brands of tea by the forceful tea entrepreneurs and their successors were spurred on by competition with one another, what motivated their principal sources at the other end of the supply chain? For India and the Dutch East Indies, Ceylon and later Kenya – as tea-exporting countries to whose economies it was important, even vital – was competition or co-operation the answer?

CHAPTER EIGHTEEN

A Million-plus Cups a Minute

A million cups of tea are drunk every minute of every day. But tea, while mildly addictive, is not essential to human life, other than as one of several means of ingesting water. The demand for it is, therefore, an artificial one. However, the economies of two countries – Ceylon and Kenya – are heavily dependent on tea exports, and in four others – India, Indonesia, China and Japan – it plays a major part in the economy both as export and as part of the internal economy. In a handful of others, from Argentina to Vietnam, Georgia to Rwanda and Turkey, it is playing an increasingly important role, either by creating exports or saving on imports.

In 2005 there were 2.5 million hectares under tea producing 3,430 million kilos of tea a year, of which 46 per cent was exported. The International Tea Committee forecast for 2016 is for 4,000 million kilos to be produced. (To prevent this chapter suffering a severe case of typographical measles I have confined myself mostly to general comparisons and dealt mainly in round figures. The statistically minded can find salient figures on p.379.)

Tea-producing countries today fall into four broad categories: those that once supplied most of the world's tea and now drink most or all of what they grow (India, Bangladesh and Pakistan, China and Japan); those that have always supplied the world with nearly all the tea they grew, and still do (Ceylon, Kenya and, increasingly, Indonesia and Vietnam); those that have grown, and usually still grow, tea almost entirely for their own consumption

(Turkey, Iran and Brazil); and those that grew, or are growing, relatively small amounts of tea almost entirely for specialist export (Argentina, Taiwan and Rwanda). Before looking at these four groups it is useful to consider two factors that have influenced the international tea trade for at least a hundred years.

There has been a strong difference of opinion between those who thought they had more to gain from promoting tea consumption in general and those who thought their commercial interest best served by promoting tea from their own country alone. The difference was exacerbated by the difficulty of keeping in balance supply and demand of a commodity for which extra output took years to bring to fruition. Too much tea, and prices and profits fell; too little, and the poor-quality tea that got used, together with the availability of an increasing number of cheap alternatives, meant the consumer lost confidence and sales were jeopardized. This has been the central dilemma for the world's tea industry for the past 140 years.

Opinion has swung at different times, and among different tea producers, between belief that demand was infinitely elastic, and so production could race ahead unchecked, and fear that demand was static or even shrinking, so that the only way to sustain prices and profits was to restrict production. Unfortunately, there was seldom simultaneous agreement among producers as to which of these two approaches should be followed. Over the years one country's pursuit of increasing export demand for its tea has usually been at the expense of others. There have been a few times when India and Ceylon have undertaken joint promotion campaigns, and even once or twice more coordinated campaigns have been tried by the main producers for tea *per se*. Equally, attempts over the past 70 years to regulate supply to match actual, rather than illusory, demand have been both spasmodic and were based, until relatively recently, on insufficiently accurate data. Restrictions have been more or less effective when all the main producers agreed at the same time that they were each producing too much tea; but completely ineffectual when even one of them has seen clear national advantage in ignoring such restrictions and pursuing headlong growth – which has been the case in all but a dozen years in the past century. In the past 50 years tea production has quadrupled.

In the last two decades of the nineteenth century the newly domi-nant tea power India and its rising competitor Ceylon sought to expand sales of their tea beyond the still steadily rising but ulti-mately finite British market. North America was the prime target but there were hopes, too, of selling more tea to continental Europe. Ceylon had been the first to levy a cess on its tea planters, and did so in 1892 with legislative backing. The substantial funds raised were managed by the Committee of Thirty ("the Thirty"), repre-senting planters and officials, which sent out sales ambassadors to Europe and America. India followed suit, though its levy was volun-tary and evaded by a quarter of its planters. The ITA dispatched J.E.M. Harington in the 1890s on a grand sweep of Europe which took him to Russia, Turkey, Greece, Italy, the Netherlands and Germany. He started out with high hopes, but by 1909 had little evidence for his claim that "there is all over the continent an undoubted tendency towards the increasing use of tea".

Harington's highest hopes were for the Dutch market, where he felt the tea habit was already well established. He was right. It was – but for tea from the country's own colonies in the Dutch East Indies, with which it had established the oldest tea-trading centre in Europe at Antwerp. This left little room for tea from elsewhere. In neighbouring Belgium two ladies opened a tearoom in 1908 "in the Indian style" with the help of subsidies from the ITA. However, the two proprietors fell out – the subsidy no doubt all spent – and the venture closed. Indian tea had no better luck in Italy, where, in 1888, a Signor Consolo tried to sell tea in "Naples, Rome, Florence, Bologna, Leghorn, Milan, Turin, and Genoa, but found no encouragement whatever to induce a shipment of Indian teas, unless in very small quantities to arrive about the month of October, when Italy is frequented by many English, American, Russian, and other visitors".

Harington also had hopes for Germany, where he distributed samples, circulars and postcards, employed men to wear sandwich boards carrying coloured posters and backed this campaign with newspaper articles and advertisements. Indian tearooms were opened in Berlin and Hamburg, and demonstrations by Indians, splendidly clothed in native costume, were staged in 40 of the country's major cities and towns. The indefatigable Harington, perhaps mistaking civil gestures for concrete intention, felt that the formal adoption of tea as a permissible alternative to coffee in the German Army was a sign of good things to come, but he was soon obliged to admit that "he had made no real impression in the German market".

A Mr Ryan tried a more direct approach on behalf of Ceylon by presenting the Kaiser with 5,000lb of its best tea, and urging upon him the "advantage of Ceylon tea as a beverage for the troops, and [pointing out] the success that has attended the Campaign in the Sudan, where it is understood that tea was largely drunk, and materially assisted in connection with the brilliant military operations in that territory". The Kaiser's response summed up the situation: "I wish I could get my soldiers to drink more tea instead of beer, [but] they like beer best." This failure was perhaps just as well, for who knows what the outcome of the First World War would have been if it had been Fritz rather than Tommy drinking tea!

Ceylon tea fared better in the hands of a Swiss salesman, a Mr Rogivue, who sold over a million pounds of it in Europe between 1890 and 1896 and was well rewarded with nearly £3,000 in cash and kind. To the chagrin of the Thirty he then transferred his allegiance to India, denied that "he had been crimped by anybody" and asserted that he did not need "the permission of the Thirty Committee or of anybody else".

Reports from tea's governing bodies in India and Ceylon make it clear that attempts at this time to sell tea to Persia, Afghanistan, China, Turkestan and Tibet had been equally fruitless. But what of America? Here the ITA and the Thirty were faced with deciding whether to compete or cooperate. As the editor of the *Ceylon Observer* admitted in 1894, "The danger is of India and Ceylon going on separately in a peddling way and creating suspicions of each other." They vacillated between the two – despite the obvious lesson of the figures. While they worked hand in hand between 1891 and 1896 sales of Indian tea rose almost four times to 5.2 million pounds and those of Ceylon more than four times to 4.3 million. But when the ITA proposed a combined effort, Ceylon's planters felt "that the control of the Ceylon arrangements and the settlement of their precise nature will have to remain in Ceylon". So while they continued to coordinate to some extent, they did not combine.

The ITA was lucky to be represented in the United States by the shrewd and energetic Richard Blechynden, whom it ended up treating shabbily. Blechynden had masterminded the Indian presence at the Chicago World's Fair in 1893, where the Indian tea pavilion was

> entered through a lofty gateway surmounted by four minarets, and is profusely ornamented in an elaborate arabesque design. The gateway, as is customary in structures in this style, forms the principal architectural feature of the building, and it is here that the ornament is most fully carried out, and reinforced, by paintings in vivid oriental colours, in strict keeping with the design followed, the whole having a rich and harmonious effect. On either side of the entrance are arcades, lavishly decorated with relief work, brackets, and ornamentation ... The whole of the interior of the building was draped and decorated with carpets, rugs, *phoolkaries*, silk saries, hand-printed cloths, trophies of arms and armour, niches, and brackets supporting Indian and Burmese gods, and other figures, and the whole effect was at once rich and artistic to a degree.

Many cries of "Gee!" but only modest sales of tea – Light of Asia from Darjeeling gardens and Star of India from Assam – until Blechynden thought to sell it iced in St Louis the following year.

The Indian pavilion had indeed made an impression, but Blechynden soon realized that in such a sensation-hungry society as North America the impact of the exotic would soon diminish. So he refocused India's money on various forms of more conventional media exposure and on supporting the "speciality men" who sold tea to the retail trade, which, it had been decided, should be the sole means of selling Indian tea to the US market.

In what may have seemed at the time a good move, the ITA decided in 1899 that it need no longer promote its tea because of the effect of the new American war tax (arising from the conflict with Spain) and of more stringent inspection of imported tea, which might exclude some from Japan and China. It further concluded that "there are now so many well-established and powerful Agencies at work in the United States and Canada, whose interests it is to push British-grown Tea, that the Committee consider the further expansion of the trade may safely be left in their hands". Instead the ITA gave the Ceylon tea representative £2,000 to promote its tea alongside its own. That year each sold some 8.5 million pounds. Poor Blechynden was sacked. By the 1980s Americans were drinking 36 billion glasses of the iced-tea drink he had invented, which was nearly four times as much as they drank of the hot version.

The First World War put an end to the marketing activities in Europe and North America of the ITA and the Thirty. It also induced in their planters a dangerous complacency through the certainty of exclusive export sale of their tea to the British Government at a reasonable profit for the duration of the conflict. The Dutch saw this as an opportunity to increase their sales to America. They seized it with vigour and success.

For a few years after the First World War, as world tea consumption increased substantially, the complacency of the war years continued. High dividends were paid, and although prices fell this was offset by increasing the area under tea. But by 1925 the cloud on the horizon had become visible to even the most myopic, and India and Ceylon both reduced the amount of tea they offered at the London auctions. Prices recovered a little for a few weeks but soon dived again, so, in September, the ITA persuaded its members to cut back production by 41 million pounds. This time it was the Dutch planters who refused to follow suit, so prices fell again and, to the distress of those who depended on them for their income, more and more tea companies paid no dividends. In 1931 the ITA again suggested restraint in the shape of a moratorium on production during August, when leaf would be plucked for the health of the bushes but destroyed. Ceylon declined to play ball.

By 1933 it was clear that the free market could not solve the problem and this time the Dutch – faced with the additional obstacle to the sale of their tea presented by Britain's introduction of Empire Preference – took the initiative. The governments of India, Ceylon and the Netherlands (which still treated Java and

Sumatra as a traditional colony) agreed to fix enforceable production export quotas based on the previous quantity and quality of tea produced, and to halt the spread of new planting. They also generously but, it would transpire, unwisely exempted the new tea estates of East Africa, still at this time owned by British tea companies of India and Ceylon. This feeble foal would grow rapidly into a Trojan horse.

The agreement worked well on the whole and prices steadied. Due to end in 1943, it was extended because of the war but – disastrously for the tea business – it was not renewed in 1945. Worse, Kenya again declined to join the UN-brokered commodity agreement that might have replaced it. During these war years production and prices had been stabilized and profits were modest but at least assured, and no longer dependent on quality, which was allowed to decline. With the coming of independence to many colonies after the war, the costs of production rose sharply. Machinery that had been kept going with "string and sealing wax" had to be expensively replaced and the governments of independent India and Ceylon, and later Indonesia, naturally wanted for their own people an ever bigger slice of what they mistakenly saw as an infinite cake.

Some slight recovery in the market occurred after the end of rationing in Britain in 1952 and the virtual disappearance from the export market of Pakistan (which would before long be a massive net importer of tea). However, there followed a drop in prices and a consequent drop in tea-garden wages, which managers rightly shared with their coolies. Equally abruptly and irrationally, prices took off again in a fit of panic buying in January 1954. They rose by 75 per cent in the three months to March, only to crash again even more spectacularly on "Wild Wednesday", 16 February 1955, when they halved in a single trading day. Then, once more, they bounded up, almost doubling between July and December 1956, as the Suez crisis rekindled panic buying. Clearly, neither governments nor private enterprise could conduct their affairs rationally in such an irrational climate.

During the Second World War the British Government had adopted the same stance as it had in the First, namely that tea should be given a high shipping priority as being essential to the war effort. However, the conflict with Nazism, and later Japanese imperialism, differed from the war of 1914–18 in its effects in a number of crucial ways. Tea rationing in Britain continued for another seven years after the war was over. It was the biggest market for India and Ceylon, but the British had tightened their belts for 13 years and got used to drinking less tea. The restrictive agreement on exports and expansion collapsed and was never formally resumed, though attempts to do so were made through the United Nations Conference on Trade and Employment (1947–48), to whose findings the Kenyans declined to subscribe. On top of this, a new generation in the West, for which tea drinking was not a deeply ingrained habit, had now a great variety of new drinks – from coffee to cola to Cuba Libre – to chose from as they grazed their much more itinerant way through life. Tea, despite the efforts of the marketing men, and whether iced or hot, was no longer cool. Since then the supply of tea has nearly always outstripped demand by a large margin, prices have fallen, costs – particularly wages – have risen and profits have been harder to come by, except for the relative newcomers in East Africa, Argentina and Vietnam, where land for expansion is plentiful or labour is cheap, or both.

So how are the four groups into which we divided tea-growing countries at the beginning of the chapter affected by these considerations today?

For almost a century China has been in a state of perpetual, and usually violent, turmoil: wars, civil wars and revolutions cultural, social and political. Now it has re-emerged into the community of nations as a major economic power, open once more to the commercial intercourse with the West in which it played such a major role in the nineteenth century.

If world tea statistics generally have not always been precise, in China they have varied between fragmentary and figmentary, for a number of reasons. A culture of secretiveness has combined with the practical difficulty of calculating the output of the millions of marginal peasant plots on which a few bushes and leaves, processed in the centuries-old way, have provided tea for a family and its neighbours, and which have never been entered, even in this most bureaucratic of societies, in any official's notebook. My guess is that this may add 10 or even 20 per cent to the figures for official production and home consumption of tea.

In 2004, according to its official figures, China (including for our purpose Taiwan's small contribution of excellent oolong after 1950) produced 835 million kilos of tea – a little over a quarter of world production – of which just over a third went for export. This now makes China only third in world trade terms, whereas in 1866 – before Ceylon even had a tea industry or India and the Dutch East Indies had made much impact – it was selling 132.3 million pounds to the (mainly British) "barbarians" and, apart from a little tea from Japan, had a monopoly of the international tea business. In their dealings with foreigners, the Hong merchants of Canton set standards of integrity for this most "my-word-is-my-bond" business that have largely obtained ever since. If a "chop" was rejected as substandard by a European tea merchant, it was taken back and payment reimbursed or credited without question. The only caveat was that the returned tea should be dumped at sea outside China's territorial waters, so that import duty did not have to be paid. Eventually the members of the Hong allowed the equally trustworthy British merchants to dump unacceptable chops in the Thames estuary and gave them credit or repayment on their word alone.

Today only 2 per cent of the international tea trade is in green tea. China supplies most of that, but almost no black. The main market is in North Africa, though its appeal to the West on health grounds is growing. The rest of China's tea production is drunk in China, most of it in the home. After Mao's revolution, public tea drinking almost vanished in China, condemned as "an unproductive leisure activity", but it is now making a slow comeback. China still produces the greatest variety of teas anywhere in the world – and many of the finest as well.

Not until 1888–89 was China, with exports of 92.5 million pounds, ousted by India (94.5 million pounds) as the main source of Britain's (mainly black) tea, and not until 1900 as the world's largest producer. The decline in popularity of China tea in Britain was aided by diatribes in trade journals such as *The Grocer's* article of 7 September 1881 which urged its readers not to buy such "horrible rubbish" lest people "give up drinking tea altogether if supplied with this poison".

The Grocer's powers of prognostication were not to be much relied on. Earlier in the year it had forecast that Indian tea would never top 40 million pounds as it was "too strong and rough to drink alone". Between 1874–75 and 1882–83 the price per pound of Indian tea fell by two-thirds. Such price changes have not been uncommon for this commodity. Indeed, in the 15-year period to 2005, the lowest average yearly price was only two-thirds of the highest. At its height in 1968 113,000 metric tons of Indian tea was being imported into Britain, which represented 27 per cent of British India's total production. (For ease of comparison, India, Bangladesh and Pakistan are treated together in this part of this chapter.)

It is hard to believe that in India, which today drinks four-fifths of the tea it grows, virtually none was drunk by its urban citizens, and not much by those in rural area, until after the First World War. Only when wartime restrictions on exports and the slump in sales in the mid-1920s had left planters with substantial unsold stocks did the Indian Cess Committee seriously turn its attention to the internal market. The sales campaign targeted three areas: industrial concerns, private homes and public places. Although it offered four or five months' free tea to canteens in mines, mills and factories, managers were chary of what might turn into an expensive and time-wasting concession to labour, so it was slow to catch on, but the tea break is now commonplace in Indian workplaces.

Sales to private homes frequently ran into the problem of perceived social and religious divisions between those selling and those being sold to. In Muslim homes, where purdah was practised, the women of the household would watch the sales demonstration from behind a screen and only well-educated women or very young men – regarded as little more than children – were allowed access. Within the Hindu community orthodox Brahmin families were friendly enough but were reluctant to accept tea from the hands of salespeople who might be of a lower caste and therefore render it unclean. Though many of the sales representatives could claim to be as good Brahmins as their potential customers, this carried little weight. Wealthy Indians in some towns seemed to accept free tea willingly, only to pass it on to their servants on the grounds that it had been prepared at the home of a socially inferior neighbour.

Despite these difficulties the seeds of future domestic tea drinking were sown, but the sales campaign had the most success in public places. While free cups of tea outside theatres in winter were never going to make a great impact, free or cheap tea along the length and breadth of India's extensive and busy railway network certainly did. On a long, hot journey in the 1920s and 1930s, where "air conditioning" for the privileged consisted simply of a box of rapidly melting ice under the seat, the tea offered by agile and prehensile platform or track-side vendors was not only welcome but usually tasted better than that to be had in the first-class dining car. The only surprising thing was that the rather naive Cess Committee was surprised when "it proved impossible to secure reliable accounts from vendors" or that "a considerable quantity of tea was sold and not reported".

The most successful element of the campaign was not a sales approach but – as is so often the case in selling anything – a decision about pricing and packaging. With the introduction of the pice packet – 5gm of tea (96 of them to the pound) for one pice – tea came for the first time within the budget of millions of ordinary Indians. At the time, the ITA ruefully concluded that "the result of three years working [did not] indicate the existence of a proper tea-market in India". How wrong they were! Though the picking up of export sales in the years just before the Second World War, when India and Ceylon were producing two-fifths of the world's tea and three-fifths of its exports, hid just how great a change they had set in train.

After India's independence there was far more governmental regulation of the tea industry for political reasons. The downside for tea companies was an even fiercer tax regime, starting with an export tax in 1947 – though the Raj had set the precedent as far back as 1916. By the 1970s combined national, state and local taxes took as much as 75 per cent of profit. For example, in 1972, sales that accounted for almost 90 per cent of India's production yielded a net profit, after deduction of taxes and duties, of only £10,675. This, coupled with restrictions on the repatriation of profits, caused British-owned tea companies to struggle more than they had done even during the war. They found themselves in the paradoxical position of having to "buy in" export quota so as to be able to send the lower-quality teas abroad. Fortunately for India, the growing dominance of the tea bag among the world's consumers meant there was a growing market for the poorer teas, which still gave a perfectly drinkable cup. By the early 1960s, of all Britain's foreign investments, tea yielded the poorest overall return.

Tea companies had to tread a careful path between conflicting political pressures. On the one hand, as Indian consumers became more discriminating they began to demand the very teas that had the strongest appeal abroad; on the other, India's desperate need for foreign exchange with which to buy the means for its own industrial take-off meant that the export market was vital.

Of the world's two largest major black-tea suppliers at the beginning of the twenty-first century, Ceylon is by far the older. It sent its first consignment of tea, 23lb of it, to London in 1873 and within 10 years auctions were being held in Colombo. A hundred years later the picture was not quite so bright. Immediately after independence in 1948, riots and violence on the gardens and the threat of nationalization frightened off many British plantation owners – even if they hastened the sale of many gardens to the Sinhalese. This was due to the disincentive for sterling-area companies to continue growing tea under threat of nationalization, to the ban on taking profits out of the country (often circumvented by increasing freight rates) and to pressure to provide more small plots for peasant agriculture. At this time Ceylon could not afford to offend its biggest customer, Britain, and did not have the money to pay proper compensation for nationalization, so the threat passed for the time being. But in 1972 two not unrelated changes took place. Pakistan replaced Britain as Ceylon's largest (and much nearer) customer and the island's tea industry was indeed nationalized. The next four years were a disaster from which Ceylon has not long emerged, although tea was re-privatized in 1976. In the decade to 1982 its exports fell by a fifth. The virtual civil war between Tamils (the plantations' core labour force) and Sinhalese (constituting the majority of the new owners) brought exports down still further, so that by 1983 they were only two-thirds of their pre-nationalization level. The acreage under tea in Ceylon declined steadily from 1980 until by 2000 it was only three-quarters of its previous maximum. For a country so heavily dependent on tea exports for the income to make up for its chronic shortage of food, this was a disaster. It became recognized as such by its government, which now encourages tea production once more. The recovery of recent years put Ceylon black tea back in second place owing in part, I believe, to its reluctance to change to CTC. It remains the largest exporter of orthodox black tea, which is the island's largest foreign-exchange earner.

Tea is a relative newcomer to East Africa: the region that now dominates world tea trading. In Malawi (formerly Nyasaland) tea was first planted by a Church of Scotland mission gardener in 1878. In Kenya tea arrived even later, when, in 1903, C.S.L. Caine planted a couple of experimental acres outside Nairobi. The big tea companies, Brooke Bond and James Finlay, were quick to step in and the first Kenyan tea was sold in London in 1928. When independence was granted to India and Ceylon, their sterling companies could see possible difficulties ahead so decided to balance their tea portfolios by expanding in East Africa, where labour was cheap and land plentiful. Today nearly a third of the world's tea imports come from East Africa, three-quarters of that from Kenya, which, bar a few pounds, exports its entire crop as CTC. But, almost uniquely, this production comes not just from the big producers. Two-thirds of Kenya's tea is grown, with government encouragement, by over a quarter of a million smallholders. The leaf they grow is processed collectively at cooperative or government-owned factories, with a corresponding beneficial effect for family cohesion and the spread of wealth in rural Kenya. Apart from its natural advantages, the country enjoys all those that benefit the newcomer in any business. It has more up-to-date equipment and scientific know-how than its older rivals and a large proportion of its tea bushes are in their prime. Although Kenyan labour is now more expensive than India's, it is more much more productive. It takes only two Kenyans to pluck a hectare of tea, whereas it takes three Asians, and this is only partly due to the longer growing season. Only tourism brings more money into Kenya than tea.

Tea in Java and Sumatra has only recently recovered from occupation by the Japanese in the Second World War and the expropriation of Dutch plantations in 1957–58. At that time the acreage under tea was less than a third of what it was pre-war. In 1950 the British drank only a twentieth of the 82.5 million pounds of Indonesian tea they had imbibed in 1930, and even in 2004 still less than a quarter.

Before the Second World War the Dutch East Indies was producing and exporting very competitively. At times Java's altitude-grown teas were fetching more at auction than their Indian and Ceylon rivals. When Empire Preference for tea was introduced in 1932 the Dutch were forced to sell even harder to non-preferential markets and it is these new markets that have restored Indonesia to the position of equal fourth-largest producer and, unlike Turkey, with which it shares that position, it now exports 60 per cent of what it produces.

In our second group, China and India were producing a little more than half the world's tea by 2005, but themselves drinking two-fifths of the world total. India still exported more than China, but Britain, which had once been its sole significant market, now ranked only fourth after the Commonwealth of Independent States, Iraq and the United Arab Emirates (these two neck and neck and the last mainly packaging and re-exporting). This pattern developed after Indian independence, following a series of barter deals with the USSR in exchange for machinery and fuel with which to prime India's own industrial revolution. Similar deals were later struck with China until interrupted by sharp ideological differences. Trading tea for fuel and equipment was resumed after the collapse of the USSR. But if India embraced new socialist markets for its tea, it carefully refrained from embracing socialist principles with regard to its production. In throwing out an Indian communist proposal to nationalize the tea industry, Nehru and his then Commerce Minister, Morarji Desai, both recognized not only that would there be a serious loss of foreign investment but that future investors might be discouraged. Besides, although it was mainly British companies involved, it was also mainly to Britain that the tea was exported. Today India's tea industry – entirely Indian-managed on the spot and largely Indian-owned – is the largest private labour employer and the second-largest foreign-exchange earner.

Of countries in our third group, Turkey is the most successful and the most unusual in its genesis in that growing tea was a wholly political decision. In 1925 Kemal Ataturk was looking for a drink that could be afforded and drunk by all Turks to replace the expensive, foreign-currency-draining coffee that was favoured by the better-off. With seed from Georgia, then a flourishing tea grower, cultivation was begun along the Black Sea littoral. The State Tea Corporation subsidizes and buys up the tea of small farmers who would not otherwise be prepared to switch from their traditional crops. Producing 165,000 metric tons in 2004, Turkey's tea growers are a significant part of the domestic economy, and Turkey ranks joint fourth among the world's producers.

Among the countries that once exported tea, or at least were self-sufficient, the former Soviet Union has experienced the most spectacular fall. In a commendable recovery from revolution, two world wars and the disasters of collectivization, the USSR had become the world's fourth-largest producer by 1985 with an output of 152,000 metric tons. The heart of its tea production lay in Georgia, with 35 of the USSR's 37 factories, endless rows of robust, if not fine, hedge-planted bushes and a system of mechanical harvesting which was highly efficient. Then came Chernobyl, which laid waste many thousand hectares of tea, and thereafter the break-up of the Soviet Union, disrupting the centrally driven system on which production had depended. Today all the former Soviet territories between them grow only a tenth of what they did in 1985.

The other two most spectacular falls are in Pakistan and Japan. In 2004 Pakistan imported 120,000 metric tons of tea: three times as much tea as it had been *exporting* in 1952. Japan imports 56 million kilos of tea; it used to export both its green and its speciality teas.

From a peak in 1968, when the United Kingdom imported more tea than any other country and was drinking 10.29lb a head, it has dropped to seventh place in terms of total imports, while in consumption per head it lies fourth, behind Ireland, Qatar and Iraq, with Turkey hot on its heels. Were the figures known, I dare say Tibet would be ahead of them all. In value terms, Britain – with its preference for better-quality tea – closes the gap and moves up to third. Although the average British household today spends more on coffee than it does on tea, it still drinks more cups of tea. As in a lasting marriage, the passion of youth has been succeeded by the quiet and loyal affection of middle age. The British love affair with tea endures!

CHAPTER NINETEEN

A Very British Drink

The Court and the coffee house were the marriage brokers to the 350-year love affair between the British people and tea. Perhaps I should say love affairs, for Britannia embraced the Chinaman only to desert him after a couple of centuries for the Indian, though she remained a good friend with the former on an occasional basis. The Court played its part mainly through the influence of two queens. Catherine of Braganza formally introduced the lovers in 1662, but they had caught each other's eye a few years before that, and Anne (reigned 1702–14) presided unobtrusively over their early courtship.

Introductions made, their initial trysts took place in the coffee houses of London and of England's larger towns, where those hussies coffee and chocolate had already flaunted their charms. The first coffee house to be established was that of "Jacob the Jew" in Oxford in 1650. Cambridge entrepreneurs quickly followed suit. So popular did these haunts become among undergraduates as places to gather to read the papers and argue over the latest news that John North, Master of Trinity College, Cambridge, complained that such subjects were "none of their business". In London the first coffee house was established by a Sicilian woman in 1652 and was quickly followed by hundreds more, of which Thomas Garway's in Exchange Alley was one of the more prominent. It was burnt down in the Great Fire of 1666, rebuilt, and later, under the name of Garraway's, lasted another two hundred years.

It is remarkable that the affair began at all, for in the form it first took in England tea was a fairly unappetizing fellow. When Pepys sent out in 1660 for his "cupp of tea, a China drink which I have never drank before", it was brewed by boiling up the leaves in a large cauldron and storing the semi-concentrate liquid cold, or at best luke-warm, in a beer barrel. Then, when a customer called for tea, a small amount would have been tapped from the barrel into a cup and boiling water from the stove added to it. Even if Pepys's office errand boy had been the fleetest of foot in the city, by the time he returned from the Sultan's Head to the Admiralty the tea would almost certainly have been tepid, and quite probably bitter, as sugar also was still an expensive luxury.

However, by the 1670s, if you wished to be seen as a man of taste – if not of sensitive taste buds – you gathered in the coffee house to deal in everything from wine to wool, to gossip and to drink tea. No woman would have frequented such a place but for one purpose. Perhaps respectable women fared better in the Netherlands. The Dutch, whose leisured classes had been drinking tea by now for 50 years, prepared it in a more tasteful way. If you had ordered tea in a Dutch tavern at this time, a tray would have been prepared – or sent out to you in the beer garden on a fine day – with teapot, cups, leaves, water and the means to heat it, for you to brew your drink fresh to your own taste. It was a sign of better things to come.

The coffee house provided an invaluable bridge between the nobility and those who aspired to rise in the world by aping their manners. By 1699 William III's chaplain, John Ovington, could write of tea: "the Drinking of it has of late obtained here so univer-sally, as to be affected both by the Scholar and the Tradesman, to become both a private Regale at Court, and to be made use of in places of public entertainment". By the time Thomas Twining, first of the still-thriving dynasty that created the eponymous teas, opened his own coffee house seven years later, there were over two thousand of them in London alone, but they were still exclusively places of male resort. Twining's genius was in giving impetus to something quite new: the drinking of tea, mainly by women, in the bourgeois home. In 1717, recognizing that no self-respecting woman would enter a coffee house, but equally that no self-respecting woman could long endure not enjoying that which her husband enjoyed, Twining set up a shop next door at the Golden Lion, where dry leaf could be bought and taken home, and much gossip was exchanged by the ladies. It must have irked not a few merchants and men of affairs, on sharing the tea brewed by their wives at home, to find it tasted so much better than the tea at what was in a way the predecessor of the gentleman's club.

Once the process of domestication had begun, it soon developed its own rituals, again mostly in imitation of those reported from court. Queen Anne liked to have a cup of tea on tap at any time of day or night, so kept "a little closet with a tea equipage" nearby, whether upstairs or down. She obviously thought the Emperor of Morocco equally susceptible to the charms of her favourite drink, because she sent him two sets of tea-making utensils and "a little fine tea" in the hope that it would persuade him to release 69 British prisoners that he held. Whether or not she was successful I have been unable to ascertain.

In the middle-class household of England (and the Netherlands) in the eighteenth century, a servant would bring the tea equipage into the drawing room at about three in the afternoon. Hot on its heels would come a kettle of water just boiled. The lady of the house would then unlock the caddy or cabinet containing the tea and sugar, and she, or a designated adult daughter, would infuse the tea straight away and pass it round. Cups, it should be remembered, were smaller and tea was brewed weaker than we are accustomed to today. The kettle would then either be handed back to the servant or placed on the hob, or on a kettle stand by the fire to keep hot. The higher up the social scale the hostess, the more likely that the hot water would be replenished directly from the kitchen as needed.

If the practicalities of tea making were fairly simple, the social niceties that went with it were not. How, for instance, should you indicate to your hostess that you wanted no more tea without the social solecism of actually saying so out loud? The Tibetan custom of placing your hand over your cup was to invite scalded fingers from a gossiping hostess whose mind was not on the bowl but spicier matters. The pragmatic British at first just turned the cup over on the saucer, thus rendering replenishment impossible, but as affectation flourished so this came to be considered vulgarly overt and a more refined signal was devised. If you were unaware of the code your embarrassment could be considerable, as the Prince de Broglie discovered in 1782. "I partook of most excellent tea and I should be even now still drinking it, I believe, if the Ambassador had not charitably notified me at the twelfth cup, that I must put my spoon across it when I wished to finish with this sort of warm water. He said to me: it is almost as ill-bred to refuse a cup of tea when it is offered to you, as it would be for the mistress of the house to propose a fresh one, when the ceremony of the spoon has notified her that we no longer wish to partake of it." It is not clear whether you were more correctly supposed to attempt the difficult task of balancing the teaspoon diagonally across the top of the cup, or the much simpler one of placing it within.

The handling of the teacup while drinking, especially before it had a handle, was also a test of the drinker's social skills and dexterity, though the variety of grips in paintings of the eighteenth and nineteenth centuries suggests that the only rule was to manipulate it elegantly and confidently. As Edward Young knew, the deployment of cup and saucer could also be a prop in the rituals of polite flirtation in the hands of a young woman who could not "take her tea without a stratagem": "*Her two red lips affected Zephyrs blow, | To cool the Bohea, and inflame the Beau; | While one white Finger and a Thumb conspire | To lift the Cup and make the World admire.*"

The advent of the handle presented another opportunity for affectation, which reached its nadir and expired with the crooked little finger of the ladies of Bayswater and the choicer suburbs in the 1920s. Whatever the etiquette, the domestic tea table and the English tea ceremony were considered the proper domain of women until well into the twentieth century. When it was customary for the men to linger at the table after dinner with their port and claret and their risqué tales, the women retired to the drawing room to drink tea and dissect the characters of their friends and no doubt of their husbands too. As one slightly shocked French commentator observed in 1796: "many English women of high standing ... take a particularly exquisite delight in speaking ill of their neighbour". Polite, and more diplomatic, discourse was resumed when the men joined the ladies, but this was woman's territory and the hostess or senior woman was unquestionably in charge.

This was even more the case once afternoon tea became the custom. The habit was the child of the gas lighting invented by William Murdoch (see the author's biography, *The Third Man*, 1994) in 1794 and widespread in many cities and towns well before the middle of the nineteenth century. With working hours no longer limited to daylight, or to what could be performed only with diffi- culty by candles or smoky oil lamps, the gap between dinner at midday and supper in the evening became much longer. Afternoon tea filled that gap in upper- and many middle-class households, although it still remained a mainly female event. Tea, with cake and bread and butter, must first have been served in the first few years of the nineteenth century, for Fanny Kemble came across it for the first time at Belvoir Castle in 1812. If Anne, 7th Duchess of Bedford, really was its instigator, as is usually claimed, she must have had the idea very young, for she was only 22 at that time.

Presumably it would have been considered a social *faux pas* to mispronounce the word "tea" in your spoken invitation, but when the new drink first grew in popularity people were evidently unsure how it should be pronounced. Alexander Pope's lines about Queen Anne in *The Rape of the Lock* (1712) are often quoted as evidence that in the eighteenth century tea was pronounced "tay": "*Where thou, great Anna, whom three realms obey, | Dost sometimes counsel take and sometimes tea.*" But the poet may only have been deliberately aligning this couplet consistently with an earlier one: "*Where the gilt chariot never marks the way | Where none learn ombre, none e're drink bohea.*"

In 1720, however, Matthew Prior's "Young Gentleman in Love": "*Thanked her on his bended knee | Then drank a quart of milk and tea.*" A little later Samuel Johnson, than whom "no person ever enjoyed with more relish the infusion of that fragrant leaf", begged his hostess: "*That thou wilt give to me | With cream and sugar soft- ened well, | Another dish of tea!*" No wonder he was obese! And this couplet inscribed on a teapot made in about 1785 suggest that by that time our present pronunciation was well established: "*When we drink our tea | Let us merry be.*"

If conversation at Anne's Court was dull – Lady Orkney described it as "nothing but ceremony, no manner of conversation ... drank tea, bowed extremely and so returned" – it was much spicier round the tea tables of the upper and middle classes. A brilliant posse of satirists hunted down every pretension and added much piquancy to the early decades of the eighteenth century. Pope and Prior, Swift and Fielding, Congreve and Colley Cibber, Johnson and even Edward Young, when they were not savaging each other, which they often were, savaged the gossip and snobbery that, as Fielding said, seemed "the best sweeteners of tea"; and Cibber thought tea "the universal pretence for bringing the wicked of both sexes together in the morning". Congreve had already noted, on the eve of the century, that the "ladies returned to their tea and scandal, according to their ancient custom".

"Ladies" was not the term used by Swift, the most biting of them all, who thought of them rather as "prudes, coquettes and harridans" whose unkind gossip ensured that *still as their ebbing malice tea supplies | Some victim falls, some reputation dies*". He saved his most withering attack on the grip the tea habit seemed to hold over English society for the year of his death, 1745, when he wrote *Directions to Servants*, a satirical inversion of the instruction manuals of the time which hints at less subservient attitudes to come. His advice to a lady's maid deplores the "execrable Custom got among Ladies ... the Invention of small Chests and Trunks, with Lock and Key, wherein they keep the Tea and Sugar, without which it is impossible for a Waiting-maid to live. For, by this means you are forced to buy brown Sugar, and pour Water upon the Leaves, when they have lost all their Spirit and Taste". Not that locking up the tea was anything new: the Chinese also locked away the best tea from their servants and any caught stealing it, or even serving it with insufficient servility, could get a box on the ear. Even more vengeful was Swift's advice to the butler: "When you are to get Water on for Tea ... to save Firing, and to make more Haste, pour it into the Tea-Pot, from the Pot where Cabbage or Fish have been boyling, which will make it much wholesomer, by curing the acid and corroding Quality of the Tea."

It is hard to escape the conclusion that there was not a little jealousy in these attacks by men who, for the most part, having no, or

singularly unsuccessful, love lives themselves, resented being
excluded from women's "clubbable" activities as absolutely as
women were excluded from theirs. Nor do they seem to have
blushed at their own often greedy enjoyment of tea drinking and
gossip. Johnson, who had met Boswell over a cup of tea in a book-
shop, once implored his hostess to: "*Make the tea so fast | As I can
gulp it down.*" In fact, nearly all the men of letters and learning in
the eighteenth century not only thoroughly enjoyed their tea, but
frequently sang its praises. Attitudes in general mellowed toward
tea drinking as it became just another part of everyday life in many
quite normal households with their typically British preference for
"placid prolixities and slow comforts".

By the end of the century William Cowper (1731–1800) could
urge his readers to relish the prospect of their tea and "*stir the fire,
and close the shutters fast, | Let fall the curtains, wheel the sofa
round*". And when Thomas De Quincey wrote his *Confessions of an
English Opium Eater* (1822) the ritual of tea drinking was not only
being held up as the *sine qua non* of the intelligentsia but also the
epitome of domestic bliss: "Tea, though ridiculed by those who are
naturally coarse in their nervous sensibilities, or are become so from
wine-drinking, and are not susceptible of influence from so refined a
stimulant, will always be the favored beverage of the intellectual ...
Surely every one is aware of the divine pleasures which attend a
wintry fireside: candles at four o'clock, warm hearthrugs, tea, a fair
tea-maker, shutters closed, curtains flowing in ample draperies to the
floor, whilst the wind and rain are raging audibly without." I suspect
De Quincey may have taken something a little stronger than milk in
his cup to have such enchanting visions, in much the same way as
William Hazlitt, struggling no doubt with his essay on coffee houses
(1821–22), half-filled the teapot with leaves before pouring on the
boiling water, in the hope of a bigger "kick". The literature of the
period not only reflected changing attitudes to tea but was also, in a
small way, itself influenced by them.

Women had a degree of freedom in the eighteenth century that
they would not enjoy again until the twentieth. With the opening of
the various public gardens, most notably London's Vauxhall and
Ranelagh, they could safely venture out with perfect propriety to

take tea *alfresco*, alone, with their children or *à deux* with husband or lover. Vauxhall, or Fox Hall, had been opened in the previous century as New Spring Gardens. With its 45-metre-span Rotunda, complete with orchestra stand and surrounding boxes, Ranelagh Gardens opened in 1742 and survived until 1804. It was of the latter that Mozart's father, Leopold, waxed lyrical in 1764 as a place where for his 2s. 6d. he could get "as much bread and butter as he could eat, and as much coffee or tea as he could drink". In view of the state of the Mozart finances he probably preferred paying the shilling entry to Vauxhall "for the pleasure of seeing many thousands of people, and the most beautiful lily garden, and to hear lovely music", though a French visitor found the music "irritating and poor". By the end of the century these public gardens, once so acceptable for respectable dalliance and family outings, had already started to become places of much more dubious resort. Consequently, in a more censorious age, they lost the patronage that made them viable and closed, with the exception of Vauxhall Gardens, which remained until 1859.

In the 1740s, with the price of tea already down from the dizzy heights of 60 shillings a pound it reached in the 1650s and 1660s to a more modest 5s., consumption in England and Wales had risen to almost a pound of tea per head per year. This was largely accounted for by the spread of tea drinking to the middle classes. Whether this was through emulation of their "betters", or was just a natural luxury outlet for the growing disposable income of the bourgeoisie, has been much debated by academics in recent years. I suspect it was a mixture of the two. Whatever the reason, tea drinking became an integral expression of middle-class virtues and vices; a mark of social respectability over which malicious tittle-tattle was exchanged in hushed tones of feigned shock. Such social graces did not come cheap, as the *London Magazine* noted in 1744, reporting that it could "cost more to maintain a fashionable tea table, with its expensive tea and utensils, than to keep two children and a nurse".

Chief among the self-appointed arbiters of fashion and good manners, so apprehensively emulated by the middle class, was Richard "Beau" Nash (1674–1761). In 1705 he established the Assembly Rooms in Bath, to which you were admitted to take tea only if you conformed to his prescribed code of dress and manners. Today you can still get a relaxed cup of tea there and listen to well-played chamber music under less stringent rules. Unfortunately, the fopperies and fads over which Nash presided for the next 40 years came to be confused with good manners, but without having mastered them the aspiring bourgeois could not hope to mix with his social superiors and escape scorn.

Tea crossed not only the gender boundary at this time but increasingly the class boundary, being taken up by Ovington's "scholar and tradesman", the skilled artisan and others beyond. As it did so, so did the defensive disapproval of its consumption among the "better sort" increase. "Tea," complained one Scottish legal luminary in 1743, had "now become so common, that the meanest familys, even of labouring people, particularly in the Burroughs, make their morning's Meal of it, and thereby wholly disuse the ale, which heretofore was their accustomed drink." It was a state of affairs for which the likes of Twinings were largely responsible, as A.P. Herbert's jovial celebration of the firm's two-hundred-and-fiftieth anniversary pointed out: *"Read here as well the fascinating tale | How tea, at breakfast, took the place of ale."*

But it was not just the men who were deserting the brewers at breakfast, for "the same Drug supplies all the labouring women with their afternoons' entertainments ... at present there are very few Coblers in any of the Burroughs of this Country who do not sit down gravely with their Wives and familys to Tea".

La Rochefoucauld commented more dispassionately 40 years later: "The drinking of tea is general throughout England. It is drunk twice a day, and although it is still very expensive, even the humblest peasant will take his tea twice a day, like the proudest: it is a huge consumption. Sugar, even unrefined sugar, which is necessary in large quantities and is very dear, does nothing to prevent this custom from being universal, without any exception."

The further downward spread of the habit of tea drinking to the working class received its greatest impetus from the price crash of 1784–85. And among the labouring classes, too, it had a ritual function. The brewing and collective drinking of tea served three purposes for the working man or woman: stimulus and restoration of energy from its accompanying sugar; a legitimate excuse for a brief respite from otherwise unremitting labour; and a bonding process with fellow workers.

Sir Fredrick Eden, in his influential 1797 survey on *The State of the Poor*, reported: "Exclusive of beer, when he can afford it, and spirits, the quantity of water, which with tea forms a beverage which is seldom qualified with milk or sugar, poured down the throats of a labourer's family is astounding. Any person who will give himself the trouble of stepping into the cottages of Middlesex and Surrey at meal times, will find that in poor families tea is not only the usual beverage, in the morning and evening, but is generally drunk in large quantities even at dinner." Such tut-tutting was slow to dissipate. In 1823 an article in the *Edinburgh Review* scornfully dismisses the working man's indulgence. "When a labourer fancies himself refreshed with a mess of this stuff, sweetened by the coarsest black sugar and with azure blue milk, it is only the warmth of the water that soothes him for the moment." That this attitude persisted until well after mid-century may be inferred from Mrs Gaskell's reproof in 1853 that "expensive tea is a very favourite luxury with well-to-do tradespeople and rich farmer's wives, who turn up their noses at the Congou and Souchong prevalent at many tables of gentility, and will have nothing less than Gunpowder and Pekoe for themselves".

For the middle and upper classes, however, it was generally accepted, in the words of one 1820s politician, that "although Tea may be deemed all artificial necessary, it is become a necessary that few would be willing to relinquish. From a fashionable and expensive luxury, it has been converted into an essential comfort, if not an absolute necessary of life. It may be said with truth to have descended from the palace to the cottage." Some at this time went even further and were "inclined to believe that the man who could willingly forgo the pleasures of the tea-table and the society around it, wants that kind and congenial spirit without which life would be a burden, and the world a dreary waste".

By the time Henry James wrote *Portrait of a Lady* (1881) it was not disputed among the leisured classes that "There are few hours in life more agreeable than the hour dedicated to the ceremony known as afternoon tea"; nor that, as George Gissing put it in *The Private Papers of Henry Ryecroft* (1903), "Nowhere is the English genius for domesticity more notably evidenced than in the festival of afternoon tea." Such by now was the general addiction to tea that its availability, wheresoever and whensoever required, was the yardstick by which the degree of civilization of any place in Britain could be measured.

On the railway journeys that were now inexpensively available to all classes, and to nearly all parts of the country, tea was the staple stimulant of the weary traveller at the station refreshment room. Where would Celia Johnson's and Trevor Howard's *Brief Encounter* have been without it? The other great institution born of the ubiquitous demand for tea was the tea shop. Among the best known of the early ones was the Bishop's Palace Tea Rooms in Glasgow, with décor by Charles Rennie Mackintosh and dubbed, with its ilk, by *The Times* as ideal for "dangling couples".

Since the closure of the last of the public tea gardens, at Vauxhall, there had been a shortage of public places to which respectable women could resort for refreshment and company. The exception was the numerous coffee houses promoted by the Temperance movement, but their rather austere approach would not have appealed to the more exuberant part of the public, which did not share its belief in the evils of strong drink and the benefits of self-denial. The major impetus in meeting the need for more hedonistic places in which to take tea came from the perspicacity of an established tobacconist, Montague Gluckstein, and the business acumen of one of his connections, Joseph Lyons, whose name would become synonymous with the tea shop. Gluckstein recognized the great potential in the major cities of Britain for large-scale catering for the unquenchable thirst for tea, so decided to test his hypothesis by bidding for the catering contract at the Newcastle Exhibition of 1887. As he knew nothing about catering, he called on the experience Lyons had developed from running a tea stall at the earlier Liverpool Exhibition. The pair won the contract and their fulfilment of it must have been something to behold, with its Hungarian band in full fig and, crucially, best-quality tea at just 2d. a cup.

Caution and careful planning must have marked Lyons's approach to turning a trial into a business, for the first Lyons tearoom was not opened until 1894. He may have learned a good deal from the manageress of the ABC (Aerated Bread Company) shop at London Bridge (site today of the Bramah Tea and Coffee Museum), who invited her favoured customers to join her for a pot of tea at the back of the premises. Her employers seized on her suggestion that this activity should be translated into a regular commercial business, and, before long, were running a chain of some 60 tea shops throughout London. Whether she received a bonus for her initiative is not recorded. I suspect that Joseph Lyons did not, however, get his idea for the plush red chairs, chandeliers and waitresses in all-enveloping grey dresses from the baking lady. His entrepreneurial flair led him to own the world's largest chain of tea shops by the 1930s because he recognized that what might attract some customers might equally put others off. While some premises remained luxurious, others of the Lyons Corner Houses and tea shops had attractive but simpler décor, and waitresses, the famous "nippies", who were less formidably dressed. Whether these women took their nickname from their agility or from the traditional "nips", or tongs, with which they offered to put sugar in the customer's tea, I do not know.

An anecdote told by Lincoln Stanhope provides a typical example of the phlegm that characterized the imperial Briton in the second half of the nineteenth century, and the role that tea played in demonstrating that self-confidence. On returning to the Stanhope home, Harrington House, after a prolonged sojourn in India, he found his family in the long gallery having tea, as usual. There were no effusive greetings, no "Thank God you're safe": just his father looking up, unsurprised, and saying, "Hallo, Linky, my dear boy! Delighted to see you. Have a cup of tea?"

Most prominent Britons were fully appreciative of the role that tea had played in their achievements and indeed in their very survival. Looking back many years later to Scot's fateful Antarctic expedition of 1902, Admiral Lord Mount Evans, one of the survivors, recalled: "Those never-to-be-forgotten sledge journeys, in one of which I nearly lost my life after foot-slogging more than seventeen hundred miles, were made possible only by tea-drinking. We had tea for our breakfast in those little green tents, which for months became our homes. Then we struck camp, and after our five-hour forenoon march put up our lunch camp and looked forward more than anything else to the midday brew of tea. We had no milk, of course, but plenty of sugar, and one felt, in those terribly low temperatures, the tea running down, it seemed, right into one's toes."

It was this air of imperturbable confidence that saw Britain victorious, if economically debilitated, through two world wars; an unflappable calm symbolized by the steady drinking of a cup (or mug) of tea whatever the circumstances. One newspaper editor, looking back on the First World War, believed "it was the solvent that was tea [that made] life a little more endurable. [It] accommodated a thousand inter-relationships which threatened friction. The submarine sinkings, the convoy system, the munition question, the War Cabinet itself were suspended regularly every afternoon for a few minutes when the little black teapot made its pre-emptory appearance, flanked with what had once been toast and cake, but what were toast and cake no longer. With it returned a certain Georgian virility." Throughout the First World War the tea ration of Britain's civilian population was 2oz a week. At the end of this slaughterhouse conflict, if any one scene reflected the respective standing of Britain and its principal ally, France, it was the sight of Balfour and Clemenceau sitting down to a drink together – not a glass of wine, but a cup of tea.

But if tea played an important role for Britain in the 1914–18 war, the Second World War proved to be, for tea as for the British, "their finest hour". In 1937, when all but the purblind who led the country could see that war with Germany was inevitable, the tea industry itself devised plans to sustain supplies more stringent than anything actually imposed by government once war was declared. (Churchill had been one of those "ancestral voices prophesying war", and, as First Sea Lord at its outbreak, aptly decreed that the Royal Navy should have unrestricted supplies of tea.) An almost perversely strong sense of individualism, which is so distinctive of the British, was epitomized in a decision by Lord Woolton, Minister for Food, not to follow the precedent of the Great War and pool all tea supplies into a single amorphous blend. He decided, instead, that tea would be made available to the blenders in Britain in three categories: common, medium and fine. These they were free to treat as they wished. Some chose to standardize on a single blend; others, such as Twinings, to distinguish and preserve, in however small a quantity, the fine and specialist brands that had been the connoisseurs' delight before the war. Woolton's reasoning is a British classic: "Not once but thrice when we were in danger did we consider this alternative. It was an extremely hard conclusion to resist, but I decided to take the risk against the weight of evidence – and fortunately the result justified the conclusion. I recall this incident because I think the decision was important. If we had given up during the war the blending of tea, the use of brands, if we had decided on this dull level of equality, we should have lost something in our national life. Taste, individual taste, is worth preserving and cultivating; it adds to the joy of living and flavours existence."

The British sense of individualism was matched by a sense of fair play. With German U-boats already devastating merchant shipping at the rate of more than one ship sunk every day (217 merchant vessels were destroyed between May and October 1940), it was soon evident that tea would have to be rationed. From 9 July 1940, as a temporary measure, tea – along with butter and sugar, meat and bacon – could be obtained only with coupons from a ration book. Like most temporary measures this one remained in force for many years, tea not being freed from rationing until 1952. With Japan in the Axis camp and Indonesia in its hands, the trade from China and Formosa cut off and the Mediterranean closed to Allied shipping, the amount of tea reaching Britain from its main source, India, diminished steadily from 1942–43, when it was 419 million pounds, to 362 million pounds in 1944–45.

As a child I measured progress in the war and its immediate aftermath by the fluctuations in the sweet ration, but for the majority of the adult population it was how much tea a person was allowed that was the barometer. The ration varied according to the level of the tea reserve. It started at 2oz per week; was raised to 4oz on 22 July 1945; reduced to 2oz on 20 July 1947; increased to 4oz on 4 December 1949; and reduced again to 2oz on 16 July 1950. It rose to 4oz on 10 August 1952, and was finally de-rationed in October of that year.

These ups and downs reflected the struggles of the post-war Labour Government to restore a devastated economy and deal with the balance of payments crises caused by the need to repay the loans made by America. As an incidental benefit, the parallel rationing of sugar, which in any case was primarily used for preserving and food sweetening, meant that many Britons experienced the real taste of tea for the first time, rather than of dark-brown, sweet ("two spoonfuls, please") caffeinated water. There has been much backsliding (and consequent obesity) since then. However, tea was considered so central to the war effort that it did not require, as did other rationed groceries, a would-be purchaser to be registered with a particular supplier; tea coupons could be presented to any grocer and honoured. It is a measure of the success of the distribution and rationing scheme that such a request seldom had to be refused.

Because of the way tea was bought wholesale and distributed, it suffered much less from the attentions of the black-marketeers than did home-grown produce. Moreover, quite early in the war the decision was taken that the only way for supplies of tea to be secured and fairly distributed was for the Ministry of Food to buy up all available stocks from India, Ceylon and East Africa on behalf of Britain and its allies and allocate them to wholesalers on the basis of their pre-war share of the market.

But the fairest system man could devise would have been of little use if the tea could not be produced and shipped to Britain, or if it were destroyed by enemy action when it got there. Early on it was decided that tea was too valuable to be kept in its traditional, but now high-risk, warehouses in London. Like the nation's art treasures, it was dispersed about the country for safety. By 1942 there was very little in the capital's 30 warehouses, the bulk being stored in five hundred locations round Britain, and blended for distribution in Cardiff, Bristol, Liverpool, Manchester, Hull, Dundee and Leith – not that any of these places escaped the attentions of the Luftwaffe. It reflects the pull-together spirit of wartime Britain that firms which had been fierce commercial rivals before the war made their warehouses and blending facilities available to others whose own had been put out of action by German bombing. The efficacy of the dispersal is evident in the figures of tea destroyed by enemy action in

1941, the year in which the heaviest loss of tea was suffered. Eight thousand five hundred tons of tea (a small fraction of total imports for the year) was damaged by heat, smoke and rubble. Of this 80 per cent was recovered for use. Only tea that was completely burned (often only the top few inches of a well-lined tea chest) or penetrated by shards of glass was abandoned.

Another British way of dealing with the complexities of life is to make firm, general rules and laws, and then be reasonably flexible when interpreting and applying them. This was the case with tea rationing. It was not just that the armed forces and indeed the home defence services, such as the fire brigades or the Observer Corps, could get all the tea they needed, but so could other categories of civilians. Workers, including now many women, in munitions, and in vehicle and aircraft manufacture, had to make up for an acute shortage of labour – caused by military conscription and the decision not to employ those of foreign origin – by putting in abnormally long hours.

While some of the "office tea clubs" that obtained extra supplies may have been a little specious, there could be no denial that those working in "hot and thirsty" and other essential occupations – from steel-making to hay-making – deserved their extra cups of tea. In the North of England a few "hot" workers still insisted on beer, and a few others on cold tea, but generally the "hot cuppa" was welcomed. The superiority of tea in assisting *sustained* wakefulness and concentration came truly into its own, as did Ernest Bevin's argument that the tea break was the way to achieve "a great increase in production". This wartime precedent was to become a fixture of post-war industrial practice. The majority of industrial enterprises had no experience of simultaneous catering on such a scale, so many factories were largely supplied by the National Canteen Service. This was set up by the tea industry at the beginning of the war from a genuine sense of patriotism, but also with an understandable glance toward the future benefits of inculcating the tea habit. (I also suspect that "morning tea in bed", today part of the reciprocal diplomacy of most households, gathered momentum from all those cups of tea served to so many between 1940 and 1945 in the hour of dawn. Before the Second World War it was a luxury indulged in by fewer than 35 per cent of Britons.)

Workers on scattered sites and, most importantly, the men and women manning searchlight posts and anti-aircraft batteries, fire-watching points and casualty stations, were supplied by an entirely new phenomenon thought up by the International Tea Marketing Expansion Board (ITMEB): the mobile tea canteen, or Tea Car. Securing vehicles for military purposes had first priority, even among those requisitioned second-hand, so obtaining even the truck or van for conversion to a Tea Car was difficult. The first (converted within days of the outbreak of war) was an old piano-removal van, which could dispense as much as 30 gallons – approximately 750 cups – a day for the princely sum of 1d. a cup. Thereafter a gallimaufry of vans of all shapes and sizes was acquired and dozens of these cornucopias – repainted bright red – were soon bringing comfort and encouragement to every corner of Britain. When vans could no longer be obtained, cars were requisitioned to make mini-Tea Cars. Getting vehicles, even equipping them with urns and utensils, tea leaves and snacks, was no use without the people with the time and guts to drive them and dispense the tea. In a stroke of genius the ITMEB approached the anti-alcohol YMCA, which was soon joined by other voluntary organizations from the Red Cross to the WVS, from the Quakers to the Salvation Army, in manning – or rather usually womanning – the Tea Cars.

Gervase Huxley, in his fascinating account of the Tea Cars, tells the story of a tank squadron commander, warily studying the marshy ground before him during a training exercise to see if it was passable for his tanks, being amazed to see a bright-red Tea Car puttering serenely across it. The officer, no doubt blushing to match the Tea Car, ordered his tank squadron to fall in behind it and the column of tanks crossed the boggy ground "like ducklings behind a mother duck".

The Tea Cars' finest hours on the home front were during the Blitz. Often in conditions of great danger, those who operated them calmly and cheerfully doled out tea to rescued and rescuers alike. It was no hyperbole when one American newspaper reporter informed his readers in the USA that "tea in London today is the drink of heroes". Something of that spirit of courageous sangfroid is captured in the recollection of a weary police inspector hurrying to yet another incident:

> Fires were burning fiercely, and the whole sky to the northward, the east and the south was an orange-red glow. The dome of St Paul's stood out, boldly silhouetted against the flame-red skies which, reflected in the river, made old Father Thames look quite beautiful, when the city was in its anguish. There was no sound except that of the bombs falling, the boom of the anti-aircraft guns and the dingle-dangle-dingle-dangle-ding of the firebells as the pumps were rushed to the conflagration ... Just then a mobile canteen came lumbering over the bridge. It stopped abreast my car, and in it were three WVS canteen workers going about their abnormal duty as unconcerned and unafraid as though they were going shopping. One of the women kindly shouted out, "Will you have a cup of tea, police-inspector?"

At another devastated bomb site, "Somehow a mobile canteen had bumped its way past all the chaos, like a small insect stumbling through a tangled skein of knitting wool. Mugs of tea had been handed round. No one spoke, they were too tired for words. Each man sat or lay staring into his mug, almost too exhausted to hold it for long to his lips; staring like crystal gazers into a little world of comfort which was able, for the moment, to blot out the smoke, the heat, the appalling mass of rubble."

The most dramatic appearances of the Tea Cars were inevitably on the front line, from the retreat to Dunkirk and back across the Channel, to the more positive circumstances of the push across North Africa, which inflicted the first land defeat on German forces, and eventually in the wake of the combined Allied forces liberating Europe. Even the Canadians got to like their Tea Car cuppa almost as much as their accustomed coffee. On a smaller scale it was the same story in India after 1941. The ITMEB sent its first Tea Cars to the North-West Frontier and Bombay, and five followed the Fourteenth Army into Burma in 1945. Complete with gramophone programmes of Indian music and divided into two compartments, so that Hindus and Muslims could be served separately, the Indian Tea Cars had served some 21 million cups of free tea by the end of the war.

Given a royal send-off by King George VI and the Queen outside Buckingham Palace, the first 10 Tea Cars sailed for France on 1 February 1940. Proud as they were of the Royal handshake, and the tipping of Secretary for War Anthony Eden's Homburg in their direction, they were no doubt more pleased and impressed to find that Gracie Fields was among those "celebrities", as we should now call them, actually dishing out the char. There were 24 Tea Cars on the beach at Dunkirk and all were destroyed by enemy fire or abandoned. Their crews were lucky to get back whole to England, but no sooner had they done so than they joined their colleagues dispensing tea to the thousands of exhausted troops of the evacuation. In the course of those next few days the Tea Cars served some five thousand gallons of tea.

Richard Dimbleby, whose fruity voice was to become the inescapable accompaniment to all great state occasions in Britain after the war, had no doubt as to the value of the role played by tea: "No story of a day in the life of a man serving in any theatre of war would have been complete, or even accurate, unless the brewing of tea had come into it somewhere. The tougher the circumstances, the more important the tea; and the more difficult it was to prepare, the more sure it was to appear. To many of us, I believe, it became more than just a warming drink. It was the outward mark of security and comfort when these qualities were sadly lacking."

On board ships at sea, tea was just as important. What one writer called "this promiscuous, charlady-like, gossipy supping of tea" afforded "another friendly link between officers and men; things that momentarily seem unendurable in the arduous abnormal life of men in ships at sea take their right place, after a 'cuppa', in the eternal scale of values".

By the end of the war more than five hundred Tea Cars were "on the road" and 96,000 people were fully employed dispensing tea at home and abroad through these and other outlets, such as factory canteens and NAAFIs (Navy, Army and Air Force Institution: clubs for servicemen staffed by civilians, many of them volunteers). However, more than any other manifestation of the benign beverage, it was the Tea Cars that accustomed the British to the idea that tea, like God, was a very present help in time of trouble.

It is possibly an exaggeration to say that, if Hitler had prevented tea from reaching Britain, or the Japanese had cut off the source of supply by taking India, the outcome of the war might have been different, but it would certainly have been a very serious blow to the nation's morale. The first disaster was avoided largely because of the convoy system and the integration of RAF Coastal Command's long-range reconnaissance aircraft with the Royal Navy's other anti-submarine measures, under a unified naval command. And, of course, because of the skill and courage of the men of these services and their – often female – support teams.

That the second calamity did not befall was due to the courage and tenacity of the British and Commonwealth troops, particularly Indians and Gurkhas, who first halted the Japanese advance up Burma toward the heart of the Indian tea industry in Assam, and then drove them back whence they came. The military could not have achieved this without the equal courage, dedication and orga-nizational skills of the tea planters and tea-garden workers who created, almost from nothing, the essential infrastructure for effec-tive movement and logistical support. Until the main Japanese invasion of Burma in January 1942, the role of the tea industry had been to overcome shortages of food, shipping, transport and fuel, and the drain of the younger men to the forces, while still main-taining the supply of tea to the mother country. Now the burden was to be multiplied fourfold.

As the Fourteenth Army made its tenacious fighting retreat all the way from Rangoon to Kohima, it pushed a wave of refugees ahead of it toward India. The first task demanded of the members of the Indian Tea Association was to build and manage camps to receive, eventually, a quarter of a million people, many of whom were sick, all of whom were hungry, destitute and frightened. The second, in parallel, was to build and traffic-manage roads through dense jungle, narrow ravines and mountains rising from 1,700 to 2,700 metres, along which the British Army could be supplied as it fell back and the refugees could flee.

The next challenge was to construct a major network of airfields and aerodromes, not only to provide air cover for ground forces, but to enable the Americans – after Pearl Harbor and their belated entry into the war – to fly massive quantities of war *matériel* over the "hump" of the Himalayas to Chiang Kai-Shek's armies confronting the invading Japanese in China.

Finally, the planters' construction army had to create camps and depots to enable the battered Fourteenth Army to recuperate and regroup after the battle of Imphal at which, with American help, the Japanese were halted. They then had to complete construction of the roads that had carried the retreat and were now to be the "shaft of the arrow", which enabled Allied forces to take the offensive and drive the Japanese out of Burma and Malaya. All these tasks were accomplished by a workforce of almost a hundred thousand men, who had to be equipped, fed, medically cared for, transported and paid. When the tea planters were first asked to help, the Army offered to pay them for their services – an offer they indignantly turned down. Of course, the direct costs of construction were too great to be met by an industry that was also expected to keep tea production at full throttle at the same time, but every man and woman of this navvies' army, managers and labourers alike, was a volunteer. (Those seeking a detailed account of these achievements should read *Forgotten Frontier* by Geoffrey Tyson and *Navvies of the Fourteenth Army* by A.H. Pilcher.)

And what if the Germans had succeeded in invading? Large numbers of men of all ages and occupations were being trained for resistance by guerrilla warfare. But five thousand were being trained in another vital technique – the secret brewing of tea – a weapon considered as essential to effective resistance as guns and explosives! This was, and is, typical both of British blasé-ness, even boldness, and British blindness. No one doubted that the British would continue to drink tea, but no one had thought to ask how tea was to be imported into an occupied Britain. Perhaps the British were relying even then on their long tradition of successful smuggling under the very nose of authority.

More than twelve hundred years ago Lu Yu could justly claim: "Tea is so integral to the Chinese spirit that it matters little how much is produced or drunk in other countries. It will always be

China's drink." And China has certainly reclaimed its heritage in the twenty-first century by keeping two-thirds of its 870,000 metric tons of tea production for it own use. India is the same; the nation that once exported the bulk of the world's tea now drinks 80 per cent of it at home. Japan, too, might well claim tea as its national drink.

But let me try to sum up the stronger claim for the "special relationship" between tea and the British, not in the epigram of a fellow countryman but in the words of two foreigners: an American who truly understood it and described it with wit, elegance and erudition 75 years ago; and a Frenchman who wrote insightfully of tea 160 years ago.

Agnes Repplier put forward the argument that: "the tea-hour in England combines the permanence of an institution with the agreeable formlessness of an incidental occurrence. As an institution it is kindly, as an incident it is stimulating. It conveys at one and the same time a sense of tradition and a sense of intimacy. It cannot make dull people amusing. 'Stupidity is everywhere and invincible.' But it can make them bearable, because they are as a rule peacefully disposed, and the tea-hour is the hour of peace. Sinners and publicans are battling for ever with Scribes and Pharisees; but the noise of their strife is lost in the hissing of the kettle."

The greatest French classical playwright, Racine (1639–99), took tea for breakfast and there is a painting in the Louvre of young Mozart at the keyboard entitled *Le thé à l'anglaise*. France, through many centuries, has been both Britain's ally and her enemy, and the French see with equal clarity our virtues and our vices, so the last word on the British and their *affaire* with tea can safely be left to J.-G. Houssaye: "They have devoted to it an obsession so general and so constant that many of their poets have made it the subject of their song; [their] most famous writers and men of learning have celebrated the virtues of this truly national drink."

Sources

Listed below are sources quoted or otherwise referred to in the text, with the chapters to which they relate in brackets. Owing to shortage of space, precise references are not included, but if serious researchers write to the author c/o the publisher with specific requests and an e-mail address, he will try to supply details.

Books

Alatas, S.H., *The Myth of the Lazy Native*, London 1977 (5)

Anon., *Encyclopaedia Britannica* (9th edn.), article on tea (3)

Anon., *Selection from the Records of the Government of India; Report on Present and Future Prospects of Tea Cultivation in the North West Provinces and in the Punjab*, Calcutta 1857 (2, 6, 8)

Anon., *Tea on Service*, London 1947 (19)

Anon. [A Friend to the Public], *The Tea Purchasers Guide*, London 1785 (17)

Anon. [A Tea Dealer], *Tsiology*, London 1827 (19)

Anon., *Williamson Magor: Stuck to Tea*, Cambridge 1991 (6)

Anon., *Yule Musings*, Lawrie Plantation Services (private pub.) (6)

Antrobus, H.A., *A History of the Assam Tea Company*, Lawrie Plantation Services (private pub.) 1957 (2, 5, 7, 16)

Baildon, Samuel, *Tea in Assam*, Calcutta 1877 (7)

Ball, Samuel, *An Account of the Cultivation and Manufacture of Tea in China*, New York 1980 (1, 2, 10, 12, 13)

Bamber, E.F., *An Account of the Cultivation and Manufacture of Tea in India*, Calcutta 1866 (6, 8)

Barker, G.M., *A Planter's Life in Assam*, Calcutta 1884 (7, 9)

Bentley, C.A., *Report on the Health of the Labour Force at Jitti Tea Estate*, Calcutta 1909 (8)

Berg, Maxine, in *Cambridge Economic History of Modern Britain*, vol. 1, CUP 2004 (14)

Bramah, Edward, *Tea and Coffee*, London 1972 (11)

Breman, Jan, *Taming the Coolie Beast: Plantation Society and the Colonial Order in Southeast Asia*, Delhi 1989 (6, 8)

Bruce, C.A., *The Manufacture of Black Tea etc*, Calcutta 1838 (2, 5)

Chaterjee, Piya, *A Time for Tea*, Durham (NC) 2001 (6, 9)

Cottam, H., *Tea Cultivation in Assam*, Colombo 1877 (7, 8, 11)

Daukes, W.H., *The P&T Lands*, Lawrie Plantation Services (private pub.) 1943 (6, 9)

Daukes, W.H., *P&T Postscript*, Lawrie Plantation Services (private pub.) 1954 (6, 9)

Dozey, E.C., *A Concise History of the Darjeeling District*, Calcutta 1922 (6)

Duncan, Doctor, *The Abuse of Hot Things*, Rotterdam 1705 (3)

Eden, T., *Tea*, London 1958 (2, 10)

Emmerson, R., *British Teapots and Tea Drinking 1700–1850*, London 1992 (14, 19)

Evans, John C., *Tea in China*, New York 1992 (3, 5, 11, 12, 13, 19)

Faulkner, Rupert (ed.), *Tea East and West*, London 2003 (1, 19)

Forrest, D.M., *Tea for the British*, London 1973 (2, 3, 7, 15, 17, 19)

Forrest, D.M., *A Hundred Years of Ceylon Tea*, London 1967 (2, 6, 7, 8)

Fortune, Robert, *A Journey to the Tea Countries of China*, London 1852 (2, 14)

Fukukita, Yasuosuke, *Cha-No-Yu*, Tokyo 1932 (13)

Glendinning, J., *Tale of a Tea Planter*, Felpham (private pub.) 1990 (6)

Graham, P.J., *Tea of the Sages*, Honolulu 1998 (13)

Griffith, W., *Report of the Tea Plant of Upper Assam*, Calcutta 1838 (2)

Griffiths, P.J., *The History of the Indian Tea Industry*, London 1967 (1, 2, 5, 6, 7, 8, 9, 13, 17, 18, 19)

Hall, Nick, *The Tea Industry*, Cambridge 2000 (3, 10)

Hanway, Jonas, *A Journal of Eight Days Journey – to which is added an Essay on Tea*, London 1757 (3, 15)

Harler, C.R., *Tea Growing*, Oxford 1966 (2, 10)

Hetherington, F.A., *The Diary of a Tea Planter*, Lewes 1994 (6, 7, 8)

Hillcoat, C.H., *Notes on Stowage*, London 1894 (11)

Houssaye, J.-G., *Du Thé*, Paris 1843 (1, 5, 19)

Hutchison, J., *Indian Brick Tea for Tibet*, Calcutta 1906 (12)

Hutchison, J., *Report on the Cultivation and Manufacture of Formosa Oolong Tea*, Calcutta 1904 (12)

Huxley, G., *The First Year of the Tea Cars*, London 1940 (Insch Bequest in Linnean Society library) (19)

Jameson, W., *Suggestions for the Importation of Tea Makers, Implements and Seeds into the North West Provinces*, Agra 1852

Jayawardena, K., *The Rise of the Labour Movement in Ceylon*, Durham (NC) 1972 (7, 9)

Larabee, B.W., *The Boston Tea Party*, Boston (MA) 1979 (4)

Lettsom, J.C., *A Natural History of the Tea Tree*, London 1799 (3, 4)

Linschotten, J., *The Voyage of Linschotten to the East Indies*, New York 2001 (1)

Longley, P.R., *Tea Planter Sahib*, London 1967 (6)

Lu Yu, *Cha Ching* (trans. F.R. Carpenter), New York 1974 (3, 5, 12)

McClelland, J., *Report on the Physical Condition of the Assam Tea Plant*, Calcutta 1837 (2)

MacGowan, Alexander, *Tea Planting in the Outer Himalayah*, London 1861 (6, 9)

MacGregor, D.R., *The Tea Clippers*, London 1983 (11)

McPherson, J., *The Neilgherry Tea Planter*, Madras 1870 (Insch Bequest in Linnean Society library) (2)

Moxham, Roy, *Tea Addiction, Exploitation and Empire*, London 2004 (2, 5, 7, 8)

Mui, H., and L. Mui (eds.), *William Melrose in China*, Edinburgh 1973 (1)

Nehlig, Astrid (ed.), *Coffee, Tea, Chocolate and the Brain*, New York 2004 (3)

Perrier-Robert, Annie, *The Book of Tea*, London 2004 (14)

Pinn, F., *The Road to Destiny: Darjeeling Letters*, Calcutta 1986 (7)

Pratt, J.N., *The Tea Lover's Treasury*, Berkeley 1982 (3, 4, 5, 13, 19)

Radford, J., and S.M. Farrington, *Tombs in Tea*, London 2001 (6)

Ramsden, A.R., *Assam Planter*, London 1945 (6, 8, 9)

Reports of the Nowgong Tea Company of Assam Limited, 1866 (bound copy, Insch Bequest in Linnean Society library) (16)

Repplier, Agnes, *To Think of Tea*, London 1933 (15, 19)

Selection from the Records of the Government of India on Tea Cultivation, Calcutta 1857 (2, 6)

Shamas, C., *Consumption and the World of Food*, London 1994 (14)

Short, T., *A Dissertation upon Tea*, 2nd edn., London 1753 (1st edn. 1730) (3, 17)

Stoler, Ann, *Capitalism and Confrontation in Sumatra's Plantation Belt 1870–1979*, New Haven 1985 (6, 8)

Tanna, K .J., *Plantations in the Nilgiris*, Lawrie Plantation Services (private pub.) 1969 (2, 6)

TeaCyclopaedia, Calcutta 1887 (3, 6)

Tyson, G., *Forgotten Frontier*, Calcutta 1945 (6, 19)

Walvin, J., *Fruits of Empire*, London 1997 (14)

Warren, W.K., *Tea Tales of Assam*, Lawrie Plantation Services (private pub.) 1975 (6, 11)

Waugh, Alec, *The Lipton Story*, Cassell 1951 (17)

Yule, Andrew, *Andrew Yule & Co Ltd.*, Calcutta 1984 (6)

Journals

Asiatic Journal, vol. 29 (2)

"A Systematic Review of the Effects of Black Tea", King's College London (3)

Bruce, C.A., "Tea Plantations in Assam", *Journal of the Asiatic Society of Bengal*, vol. 8, 1839 (2, 5)

Bulletin of the Research Institute of the Tea Industry in the USSR, Georgia State Press 1951 (10)

International Camellia Journal 2004, no. 36 (2)

Tea Statistics

Note 1: For very rough equivalent values for £1 in 2005 multiply by:

1660 x 70; 1680 x 77; 1700 x 73; 1720 x 77; 1740 x 80; 1760 x 70; 1780 x 58; 1800 x 30; 1820 x 34; 1840 x 37; 1860 x 43; 1880 x 44; 1900 x 54; 1920 x 19; 1940 x 26; 1960 x 14.

Note 2: To convert kg to lb multiply by 2.2046; lb to kg multiply by 0.45359.

Table 1

Tea statistics for Great Britain

Year	lb (millions)	Tax per lb	Population (millions)	Notes
				Figures rough, specially before 1801 census
1657				Garway sells tea at his coffee house in Exchange Alley
1660–69		8d.–18d. gallon 2s. gallon		
1678	5			
1690		5s. dry leaf		Sugar consumption 4lb per head
1692	41	1s.		
1700	20	2s.	6.1	
1721	1	4s.		Sugar consumption 12lb ph
1723				Walpole replaces import duty by excise
1740–45	0.8			
1745–50	2.4	1s.	7.1	Pelham cut in duty
1750–59	3.2	44% *ad val.* + 1s./lb		Licensing of tea dealers begins 1750
1760–69	5.5	49% *ad val.* + 1s./lb		1767 tea tax debate; 1768 draw-back resumed
1769–83	5.8	50% *ad val.* + 1s./lb		Excise 100–106% *ad val.*
1784	6+	= 119%		Window tax replaces most tea tax

Year	lb (millions)	Tax per lb	Population (millions)	Notes
1785	10.8	= 12½%		plus approx. 5.2 million pounds smuggled
1790				Sugar consumption 24lb ph
1800	10.5			Napoleonic Wars start
1806		90% *ad val.*		
1814		100% *ad val.*		
1815	26			Napoleonic Wars end
1816	36		12.9	
1830	30			
1836	49			All from China until now; first Indian tea 1833
1851			20.8	
1857	69			
1863		1s.	23.0	Gladstone's "hot-water bottle" cuts
1866	6d.	24.6		
1888				Imports from India exceed those from China
1890	194	4d.	38.0	
1900	250*	6d.	37.0	To fund Boer War: only 7% tea non-Empire
1902		8d.		
1904	257	8d.		
1906	270	5d.		
1911			40.8	
1914	317	8d.		
1920	393	1s.		
1929		0		Churchill cut. First zero rate for tea
1932		4d. (Empire 2d.)	44.8	Empire Preference scheme
1936		6d. (Empire 4d.)		
1939	466	8d. (Empire 6d)		
1950	415	2d. (Empire 0)	48.9	
1953				Coffee consumption per head 1.4lb; tea 9.52lb
1960	496			
1964				Tea tax abolished
1970	516			
1980	410		54.3	
1990	313			
2000	293			
2005	278		59.0	

* Rough conversions from metric tons from 1900 onwards.

Table 2

Tea production (top figure) and export (bottom figure) to nearest 000 metric tons

	China	Ceylon	India*	Indonesia*	East Africa+	Rest++
1910	150	82	119	18	–	2
	105	83	116	18	–	1
1930	284	110	198	72	1	2
	50	110	163	72	1	1
1950	73	143	302	35	20	10
	19	135	189	29	16	3
1960	153	197	340	46	46	36
	53	186	195	36	39	12
1970	174	212	450	44	103	111
	61	208	200	37	96	44
1980	328	191	610	99	173	215
	126	184	255	68	163	75
1990	562	234	766	145	288	307
	201	215	236	111	247	
2000	683	307	849	163	358	416
	228	280	204	106	332	178
2005	870	308	928	165	462	697
	290	290	181	101	456	240

*In this and the subsequent table India includes Burma throughout and Bangladesh in place of Pakistan after 1970; Indonesia is used for both modern Indonesia and pre-independence Netherlands East Indies.

+ Of which Kenya 294 (2000) and 329 (2005).

++Turkey 135 (133 home) and Vietnam 112 (88 export). Argentina 74 (66 export) (all 2005)

Table 3

Tea consumption (lb per head)

1956 Top 5		1956 Bottom 5		2005 Top 6		2005 Bottom 5	
UK	10	Iran	1.3	Eire	6.53	Tanzania	0.2
Eire	8.9	Japan	1.3	Qatar	5.53	Italy	0.22
Australia	6.0	Algeria	1.2	Kuwait	5.16	Finland	0.4
New Zealand	5.8	USA	0.7	Iraq	4.96	Austria	0.44
Iraq	5.7	India	0.6	UK	4.85	Belgium	0.44
				Turkey	4.78		

Note: UK coffee consumption: 1965, 1.29kg; 2005, 2.41kg per head.

Picture Credits

The publisher would like to thank the following for their kind permission to reproduce the pictures in this book:

Page 1: *top* The Return to Amsterdam of the Fleet of the Dutch East India Company in 1599 (oil on copper), Andries van Eertvelt (1590–1652), Johnny van Haeften Gallery, London, UK/The Bridgeman Art Library; *bottom left* © the British Library/HIP/Topfoto; *bottom right* Lindley Library/Royal Horticultural Society

Page 2: *top* Time Life Pictures/Getty Images; *bottom* Private collection

Page 3: *top* Tea Culture: Weighing and Purchasing Tea (gouache on paper), Chinese School (19th century) © Peabody Essex Museum, Salem, Massachusetts, USA/The Bridgeman Art Library; *bottom* Hulton Archive/Getty Images

Page 4: *top* Mary Evans Picture Library; *bottom* Image courtesy of The Advertising Archives

Page 5: *top* Victoria & Albert Museum; *bottom* Hulton-Deutsch Collection/Corbis

Page 6: *top* Roger Viollet/Getty Images; *bottom* Mary Evans Picture Library

Page 7: *both* Norwich Castle Museum

Page 8: *top* Fox Photos/Getty Images; *bottom left* China Photos/Getty Images; *bottom right* Quill work tea caddy, English, 18th century, Wynyards Antiques, London, UK/The Bridgeman Art Library

Every effort has been made to contact and to acknowledge correctly the source and/or copyright holder of each picture, and the publisher apologizes for any unintentional errors or omissions, which will be corrected in future editions.

Index